Penguin Education

Critical Sociology

Edited by Paul Connerton

Penguin Modern Sociology Readings

General Editor

Tom Burns

Critical Sociology

Selected Readings

Edited by Paul Connerton

Penguin Books

Penguin Books Ltd,
Harmondsworth, Middlesex, England
Penguin Books,
625 Madison Avenue, New York, New York 10022, U.S.A.
Penguin Books Australia Ltd,
Ringwood, Victoria, Australia
Penguin Books Canada Ltd,
41 Steelcase Road West, Markham, Ontario, Canada
Penguin Books (N.Z.) Ltd,
182–190 Wairau Road, Auckland 10, New Zealand

First published 1976

Made and printed in Great Britain by
Hazell Watson & Viney Ltd, Aylesbury, Bucks
Set in Monotype Times

In memory of John Plamenatz

Contents

Editor's Acknowledgement

I wish to thank Gillian Rose, of St Antony's College, Oxford, for her helpful comments on my efforts to compile this selection of readings.

Introduction

Intellectual life in the English-speaking world has been profoundly enriched by the generation of German scholars who fled from their homeland in the nineteen-thirties; and in the story of this cultural migration the history of the Frankfurt School occupies a major part. First established in Weimar Germany, the Institute for Social Research was transplanted from Frankfurt to New York, and then to California, during the years of exile; the group became dispersed during the late 40s, but the Institute was reconstituted by some of its core members as part of the University of Frankfurt soon after the end of the war.

It was largely owing to the astuteness of Max Horkheimer, who became its Director in 1930, that the School maintained an unbroken institutional continuity throughout its history in Weimar Germany, the United States, and the Federal German Republic. Especially during its early years, he succeeded in drawing around himself a group of many talents. Theodor Adorno combined a primarily musical sensibility with a rigorously philosophical mind; Herbert Marcuse, whose first mentor was Heidegger, achieved in his earliest writings an original fusion of Phenomenology and Marxism; Friedrich Pollock was a political economist; Erich Fromm, a student of psychoanalysis; Karl Wittfogel, a sinologist; Franz Neumann and Otto Kirchheimer were legal scholars; Leo Lowenthal worked in the sociology of literature; and Walter Benjamin, who was for a time more distantly associated with the group, has received belated acknowledgement as one of the most remarkable literary critics of the century.

Much of their work appeared between 1932 and 1941 in the *Zeitschrift für Sozialforschung*. Despite its scope, the *Zeitschrift* retained a degree of cohesion by steering between two extreme positions which at that time typified the relationship between philosophy and the social sciences. One pole, represented by German *Lebensphilosophie* and Phenomenology, was contemptuous of empiricism and pragmatism; the other was represented by the empirical orientation of American social research. Ignoring – or overriding – the seeming disjunction between philosophical speculation and empiricism, the Institute aimed at a fertilizing interpenetration of theoretical and empirical work. It sought to foster by its organizational structure the programme of a 'Critical Theory' which found its paradigm in Marx's *Critique of Political Economy* and its concept of totality in the Hegelian-Marxism of the young Lukács. Common to all three aspects of this programme was the belief that no partial aspect of social life and no isolated phenomenon may be comprehended unless it is related to the historical whole, to the social structure conceived as a global entity.[1]

If Critical Theory was a creation of the early thirties, it was also a discovery of the late sixties. In the intervening period the work of the Institute had become difficult of access. It is true that its critique of mass culture and of the potential for authoritarianism in American society had a substantial impact on intellectual life in the United States. But through an impediment of language the tradition was only partially assimilated in America: in the attempt to retain links with a national culture then threatened with annihilation, the *Zeitschrift* continued to appear in German until the outbreak of the war. But its heritage for long remained elusive even in the German-speaking world. A two-volume edition of Benjamin's writings appeared only in 1955, fifteen years after his death; early work by Marcuse and Horkheimer surfaced again with essay collections like *Negations* and *Kritische Theorie* in 1968; *Dialectic of Enlightenment*, which had provoked little reaction when it first appeared just after the end of the war, was republished in 1969; and the whole of the *Zeitschrift* was republished in 1970. It would probably be wrong to attribute the new clamour for these works solely to the rising temperature of the late sixties, associated among other things with the student movement and the revival of German Marxism. Perhaps in fact the caesura of the Nazi period itself fostered the renaissance of this half-submerged tradition. For the Frankfurt School was the only collective institutionalized representative of the Weimar Repub-

1. For a comprehensive treatment of this first phase of the School see Jay (1973).

lic in the Federal Republic; and it was thus able to offer a point of mediation between past and present, a thread of spiritual continuity.

The tradition has recently been renewed by a second post-war generation. Re-discovery and rejuvenation have run together in tandem. Most prominent, of course, is Jürgen Habermas, whose work ranges over three interlocking areas: the methodology of the social sciences; the connection between the development of the natural sciences and the interest in instrumental control; and the relationship between science, politics and public opinion in advanced capitalist societies. But important work has also been done by Claus Offe in the study of political economy and by Alfred Lorenzer in psychoanalytic theory. One of the most striking features of this renaissance has been a new readiness for public debate with representative figures outside the tradition. Habermas' investigations have spanned out into an arc of controversies: with Popper and Albert in the *Positivismusstreit*; with the Hermeneutics of Gadamer; and with the Systems Theory of Luhmann. At least in the first of these disputes the repercussions of the thirties continue to be felt; the *Methodenstreit* of the sixties documents among other things an intellectual and spiritual crisis brought about by the collapse of German liberalism in 1933 and the still latent fear of a resurgence of totalitarianism in a new guise.

The reception of Critical Theory is a story of impeded assimilation and belated acknowledgement. The problem of accessibility cannot be accounted for solely by a series of accidents; it is not a matter of historical circumstance alone. In part at least the relative inaccessibility of the Frankfurt School is intrinsic to it. The difficulty is inscribed in the language of the texts themselves.

This is particularly so, of course, in the cases of Adorno and Benjamin. Common to both was the aversion to the idea of a 'system'. The literary form best suited to Adorno's sensibility was the essay. His habits of thought had a natural affinity for other small forms: the aphorism, the aperçu, the sketch. His often epigrammatic power drew much of its force from the cherished sense of the unique specificity of things, a sense and a partisanship for the individual, for that which is not or cannot be integrated, whose nature resists systematic form. In spite of his sometimes stilted intensity, his terseness served, and was intended to serve, a polemic end. Recognizing that ideology inhabited not only the substantive propositions of discourse but the very texture and sinew of language itself, he set out to reject – at times by literary shock-tactics – both the existentialist 'jargon of authenticity' and the journalistic habits of comfortingly facile assimilation. Benjamin's writings, too, are of great density; indeed, he sometimes surpasses even Adorno in the brevity of his formulation. But at least one major source of his distinctive discourse lay elsewhere. His chosen mode was the commentary, for whose method and meaning he was indebted to the profound connection in Jewish theology between theological argument and language. From here radiated his characteristic stylistic devices. The 'open form' of his commentaries sought not so much to present something settled or 'contained', but rather to return again and again to a motif, prising open its aspects. The technique of reprise was necessary to a mode of presentation aimed at the filling-out of meanings; and it was by such indirections that he did not so much impart an achieved knowledge but enacted the processes by which insights are earned. Even allowing for their specific differences, both Benjamin and Adorno, with their common rejection of the systematic, belong to a particular historical conjuncture: their work formed part of what has been called the 'exodus from philosophy' which occurred in Germany after the First World War – the turning away from Idealism, from the construction of philosophic systems, towards what, in other hands, issued in the German variants of Existentialism and theology. In Habermas, on the other hand, Critical Theory renews its links with an older tradition. For if Adorno inclined to the aphoristic and Benjamin to the labyrinthine, Habermas' characteristic manner is one of a sustained strenuousness which is more recognizably part of the history and habits of German *Geistesgeschichte*, in which the development of particular arguments and the 'placing' of those arguments in an unfolding history of argument are seen as a single enterprise. Hence the difficulty with Habermas is likely to be found neither in terseness nor in allusiveness but in a consequent tone of high seriousness; and in fact those who have a taste for philosophy seasoned with the sprightly aside, or accompanied by a more mellow urbanity, may perhaps find his style a trifle heavy for congenial digestion.

Yet the modes of presentation characteristic of Critical Theory, although themselves a significant and self-conscious constituent of the tradition, can also be a snare. Two lines of least resistance immediately offer themselves when confronted with the problem of these texts. They may incite either to dismissal or to monumentalization. Perhaps it is only too easy to mock: to hear in the tones of the Frankfurt School a note so high-pitched that it seems addressed only to a small circle of the elect. Alternatively, the language might be found bewitching; in which case the texts may then come to suffer the ironical fate of feeding their own 'culture industry' – of being afforded the historical respect due to museum pieces rather than occasioning the sense that they address any needs of the present. But to treat the texts either as an 'intellectual-family matter', or as historical monuments, is to refuse both the challenge of their serious intent and the task of genuine criticism.

Merely to rehearse these facts is to make one thing clear at the outset: namely, that Critical Theory is best approached not as a 'branch' of sociology but as a phenomenon of German intellectual history. Nowhere is this more transparent than in the meanings clustered around the idea of a critique itself. In a famous programmatic essay Horkheimer cited Marx's *Critique of Political Economy* as the paradigm for a critical theory of society; but the pre-history of Marx's concept of critique remains of central and independent importance for the tradition. The choice of the epithet 'critical' is the token of a multiple allegiance.

The idea of critique is a product of the Enlightenment. The term is older still. It was first used by the Humanists and Reformers to describe the art of informed judgement appropriate to the study of ancient texts, whether the Classics or the Bible. For a time this critical activity was a weapon in the hands of the warring religious parties. But it was a double-edged weapon. Catholics might use philological methods in seeking to demonstrate the necessity of Church tradition, and Protestants might use the same methods in supporting the primacy of Scripture; but the art of critique itself began to claim a status independent of both Church and Scripture. First placed at the service of the one or the other, the appeal to critique gradually displaced the criterion of truth from revelation towards clear and rational, or 'critical', thought.

Thus it was through the thicket of religious disputes focused on textual criticism of the Bible that a new position began to emerge. The warring churches now found themselves confronted by a common enemy. A new line of demarcation had opened up between reason and revelation, and the word 'critique' acquired polemical overtones which it was never subsequently to lose. 'Critique' came to be seen no longer as simply a symptom of the sharpening opposition between reason and revelation. It was viewed as itself the activity which separated the two spheres. It was the essential activity of reason.

For a long time the political competence of the state remained exempt. Just as textual criticism had coexisted with religious allegiance, so now again two positions remained juxtaposed but separate. The process of critique claimed to subject to its judgements all spheres of life which were accessible to reason; but it renounced any attempt to touch on the political sphere. Yet, as before, the peaceful coexistence of competences eventually began to break down. Ostensibly confined to the *République des lettres*, the activity of critique became first indirectly, and then directly, political. In salons, clubs, lodges and coffee-houses a new moral authority, the public, found its earliest institutions.[2] Critique became one of its slogans and an endless stream of books and essays included the words 'critique' or 'critical' in their title. Kant could quite rightly claim in the 1781 Preface to his *Critique of Pure Reason* that his age was the true age of critique and that neither religion nor the legislature was exempt from its test. The process of critique had acquired public force.

The continuing allegiance of Critical Theory to the Enlightenment, which gives rise to a nostalgia manifest in works as different as Horkheimer's *Eclipse of Reason* and Habermas' *Strukturwandel der Öffentlichkeit*, indicates a commitment to this understanding of critique – critique as oppositional thinking, as an activity of

2. See Habermas (1962) and Koselleck (1959).

unveiling, or debunking. But the Frankfurt School are indebted in particular to two new meanings of critique, in which the heritage of the Enlightenment has been assimilated and reformulated. These have their origin in German Idealist philosophy. It is important to distinguish between these two new senses.

In the first, critique denotes reflection on the *conditions* of possible knowledge: on the potential abilities of human beings possessing the faculties of knowing, speaking and acting. Critique in this sense has its root in Kant. In the *Critique of Pure Reason* Kant set out to answer the questions: what are the conditions of our knowledge through which modern natural science is possible, and how far does this knowledge extend? He wished to locate the range of inevitable subjective conditions which both make any theory in natural science possible and place limits upon that theory.

Kant saw that our understanding confronted a difficulty similar to that faced by any producer who seeks to impose a particular form on unyielding matter. The *Critique* begins from the fact that only an incoherent profusion of impressions or sensations are given in perception. Since, on the other hand, we always perceive the world as a world of ordered things, it must be our faculty of perception itself which produces order out of the variety of impressions. This is the decisive work of perception: the production of possible objects of knowledge out of the given material of impressions. The faculty of perception produces, not indeed reality itself, but the mode in which reality appears to us. Things are 'constituted' by us in the sense that we can know them only through certain *a priori* forms or 'categories' which are embedded in the human subject.

In this century an intensified concern with language has led to a reframing of Kant's model. Students of language now attempt to grasp the generative nature of linguistic rules in themselves; here the mastery of the rules – the emergence of a competent human subject who is able to operate the rules – becomes a secondary issue. Wittgenstein's analysis of the notion of 'following a rule'; Chomsky's concepts of 'generative rules' and 'linguistic competence'; Lévi-Strauss' 'Kantianism without a transcendental subject' – all these have contributed to this development: namely, the rational reconstruction of the conditions which make language, cognition and action possible.

But the term 'critique' also contains a second new meaning. Here it denotes reflection on a system of *constraints* which are humanly produced: distorting pressures to which individuals, or a group of individuals, or the human race as a whole, succumb in their process of self-formation. Critique in this sense has its root in Hegel. In the *Phenomenology of Mind* Hegel developed a concept of reflection which presents the idea of a liberation from coercive illusions. This notion was perhaps most vividly expressed in that section of the *Phenomenology* which treats of the relationship between Master and Slave.

Hegel portrays the experience of the Slave as the overcoming of a resistance. The Master–Slave relation is to be understood in terms of their connection with material things. At the outset the Master, having obtained possession of the Slave's labour, tries to reduce him to a mere instrument of his will, a tool which he interposes between himself and nature so that he is protected from direct encounter with the negative side of things, from those qualities in things by virtue of which they are experienced as sources of resistance and constraint. But it is precisely the constraint imposed by the Master on the Slave that opens up for the latter the possibility of a growth beyond the given conditions of his existence. It is true that the life of the Slave remains distorted to the extent that his aims are limited by the commands of the Master; and yet he comes to see the objects on which he works no longer simply as bundles of resistance, for by working on them he has precipitated his human capacities into them, so that, as moulded by him, they come to reflect back to him his own humanity. His labour transforms nature, and therefore himself, for he is now faced by a world which embodies his self-assertion as a subject. Here the way in which the Slave views his situation and the way in which he acts within it belong inextricably together; a change in the Slave's 'theory' about his condition entails a change in his 'practice', in his action within the given context. And the point is a general one, since the Master–Slave relation is for Hegel an example of a universal feature of human life and thought. This feature is what he calls the 'negative'. The negative connotes those historical forces which are incompatible with a certain form of social life and which act upon it destructively: but forces which nonetheless arise inevitably out of the particular social structure which they negate and surpass. Human rationality has a history which consists in the criticism in life and in thought of the constraints imposed by each of its specific historical forms. Hence this understanding of critique implies a particular narrative structure in which the potentialities for development of a given mode of thought or a given social condition are latent within the very structure of the initial terms.

Just as in this century an intensified interest in language has led to a re-formulation of Kant's model, so the concern with constraints on human action has been elaborated by psychoanalysis. Without explicitly invoking the idea of a critique, Freud proposed what was in effect a new procedure of critical reflection. The constraints which this reflection seeks to penetrate are resistant because their weight is anchored within. Freud's 'subject' suffers under the compulsive pressure of restricted patterns of behaviour and perception; he deludes himself about his own actions; he colludes, by internalization, with the constraints that have been imposed upon him. Only by grasping these illusions can the subject, as it were, free himself from himself: he liberates himself from the internalized conflicts which blinded him in his self-awareness and lamed him in his actions. Critique is here grounded in a specific experience, which is set down in Freud's psychoanalysis, in Hegel's *Phenomenology of Mind*, and in Marx's critique of ideology: the experience of an emancipation by means of critical insight into relationships of power, the strength of which lies, at least in part, in the fact that these relationships have not been seen through.

It is perhaps helpful to refer to the first type of critique as 'reconstruction' and to the second type of critique as 'criticism'.[3] There are at least three important differences between *reconstruction* and *criticism*.

Firstly, reconstruction (as proposed for instance by Kant or Chomsky) tries to understand anonymous systems of rules which can be followed by any subject, provided he has the requisite

3. See Habermas (1973).

competences. Criticism (as proposed for instance by Hegel or Freud) is brought to bear on something not anonymous but particular; it examines the shaping of an individual's identity or the identity of a group. Hence it entails the explicit reference to a subject.

Secondly, reconstruction is based on data which are considered to be objective, like sentences, actions, or cognitive insights; these are the conscious operations of the human actor. Criticism, in contrast, is brought to bear on objects of experience whose 'objectivity' is called into question; criticism supposes that there is a degree of inbuilt deformity which masquerades as reality. It seeks to remove this distortion and thereby to make possible the liberation of what has been distorted. Hence it entails a conception of emancipation.

Thirdly, reconstruction explains what is considered to be 'correct' knowledge; for instance, the knowledge we must acquire if we are to operate rules competently. Criticism, however, aims at changing or even removing the conditions of what is considered to be a false or distorted consciousness. Thus reconstruction, by explaining rules which we follow implicitly, may lead to a broadening of the range and a greater sophistication in the possession of our theoretical knowledge. It may do this without necessarily changing our practical conduct. Criticism, on the other hand, renders transparent what had previously been hidden, and in doing so it initiates a process of self-reflection, in individuals or in groups, designed to achieve a liberation from the domination of past constraints. Here a change in practice is therefore a constitutive element of a change in theory.

In addition to assimilating the Enlightenment understanding of critique as oppositional thinking, the Frankfurt School have used the idea of critique in both of these new senses – without perhaps always making the fact of this new double usage sufficiently clear. They have employed the term to denote reflection on the conditions of possible knowledge; and they have also used it to denote the analysis of constraints to which classes of individuals are subject.

This range of meanings coalesced around a particular vision. The vision first crystallized around 1770 when the theology of history was superseded by the German philosophy of history. It was at this point that the role of the 'subject' of history, previously occupied by God, was imputed to Mankind; and the history of Humanity was now read as the result of a single project executed by this single agent.

It might be objected that the idea of Mankind as a collective subject is merely the projection onto a fictive entity of a real subjectivity which is found only in the human individual. The point was made by Marx in his attack on the Young Hegelians. He rejected as mere Idealism their proposition that the combined efforts of individuals in the course of world history could be interpreted as the 'self-production of the species'. Yet he himself frequently spoke of world history as 'the production of mankind through human work' – that is to say, as a process of 'self-production' – and this still seemed to imply that hypostatization of 'man', or of the human species, as the 'subject' of history for which he had castigated the Young Hegelians. However that might be, the idea of a subject of history reappears in a different form with the argument that the emergence of capitalism has produced in the proletariat an agent by whom its own 'negativity' – analysed first as self-alienation and later as surplus-value – can be surpassed.

Horkheimer, Adorno, Marcuse and Habermas all reject important elements in the German philosophy of history. They no longer believe, with Marx, that the truth of their theory will be confirmed primarily in the historical action of the proletariat. And they no longer believe, with Hegel, that progress, however that might be defined, is guaranteed by a logic of history. Yet they are reluctant to abandon their roots in the myth of enlightenment – the view of history as one all-embracing process in which a historical subject attains its essence. Thus the faculties originally ascribed by Kant to the consciousness of his transcendental subject are transferred by the early Horkheimer to the human species.[4] On this interpretation, Kant's *Critique* had sketched out, albeit unknowingly and therefore in a distorted form, the project of a future society which would become truly productive. Located now in a possible future, this rational society, the goal of which is

4. See Horkheimer (1968).

claimed to be 'really invested in every man', would be able to achieve concretely what Kant's transcendental subject could accomplish only formally: to transform chaos into rational order. In Marcuse the Enlightenment heritage assumes the form of what has been aptly called a bifocal vision of history.[5] It is bifocal in the sense that all realms of experience are bounded by two dimensions. The first dimension is the established order, whether political, economic, or sexual. The second dimension represents the aims of men. This second dimension is embodied practically, in attempts to alter that order; intellectually, in concepts which transcend the facts imposed by that order; and passively, in the desires and longings which are frustrated or rendered quiescent by it. Finally, Habermas frequently claims that there is an interest – he sometimes calls it a 'deep-seated anthropological interest' – in emancipation. The subject having this interest is the human species; for Habermas, too, the subject of history, in the last resort, is Mankind. It is true that he has more recently rejected as fictitious the idea of a 'human species which constitutes itself as the subject of world history'.[6] Yet he continues to claim, in a way which re-echoes Horkheimer's interpretation of Kant, that what found distorted expression in that fiction was the intention – to whom precisely that intention is to be imputed becomes obscure – of controlling the development of societies by institutionalized and politically effective public discussion.

Critical Theory is resistant to summary; not least, because almost its only unchanging basic thesis is that it is itself changeable. Through an analysis of the historical conditions which inform its own categories, it seeks to adapt those categories anew to historical reality. Hence the specific positions advanced by the Frankfurt School are best presented negatively, by locating the areas in which they diverge from their chosen paradigm – Marx's *Critique of Political Economy*.

The paradigm was apt for the historical moment at which the idea of a Critical Theory took shape. At the threshold of the 1930s, European society was in the throes of an economic crisis which seemed to demonstrate the self-destructive tendency in-

5. See Cohen (1969). 6. See Habermas, Luhmann (1971).

herent in capitalism and the impotence of liberal democracy. The choice appeared to lie between fascism and communism. The School were thus able to view their work at the outset as part of a revolutionary political struggle; and at the centre of their analysis at the point of its inception they retained Marx's critique of political economy. It is true that they never produced any economic analysis comparable to that produced by more orthodox Marxists. But in the thirties at least their revisionism was limited. They thought in the categories of the young Marx, and they retained some terminological features of the older Marx.

The subsequent divergences were fourfold. From the beginning there is a switch from the infra-structure to the superstructure. Then the critique of political economy is replaced by the critique of instrumental rationality. Next, the system of needs is re-interpreted through an assimilation of Freud. And finally Marx's philosophical anthropology is revised by drawing on the tradition of Hermeneutics. These modifications of Marx's *Critique* do not represent a series of coexistent possibilities; they mark rather the broad lines of a trajectory executed by the Frankfurt School over the period of half a century. There is nonetheless a considerable chronological overlap between the 'stages'.

In its *first* phase, the Frankfurt School recognized that the power of ideology extended beyond the range of discursive propositions. This radically revised the terms of Marx's analysis. Marx had of course geared his interpretation to the conditions of a liberal society: to the mechanics, as well as the content, of its ideology. He viewed the categories employed by the classical economists as inhabiting a timeless realm cut off from the historical movement of the productive forces. But underlying this false independence in theory there was the equally false independence of social practice. Marx saw the distortion in the categories used to interpret the world as the expression in theory of a real distortion in the liberal capitalist economy itself. Because of the discrepancy between individual interest and general interest, the process of material production had acquired an autonomy independent of human needs; the value of the goods circulating on the market was thought to be the qualities of these things in themselves, so that they could no longer be experienced for what they truly were – the systematically distorted expression of social relations. Marx was thus able to re-interpret the categories used by his opponents as a key to the real conditions of which they offered an account; he produced a critique of actual social conditions via a critique of the categories used to justify those conditions. On this view, ideological concepts themselves, labour, commodity, exchange-value and the like, by justifying what existed through recourse to discursive propositions, offered at the same time a point of leverage for ideology-critique: the medium of a possible confrontation between claim and reality.

But the point of critical entry can be more tightly barred. German fascism and organized capitalism together broke down the liberal economy and its attendant ideology. To reiterate the critique of the 'fetishism of commodities' became as inappropriate as to adhere rigidly to the old analysis of the competitive market economy; both missed the new dimensions of domination. It was fascism which first disclosed the decisive political power of the electronic media, their mobilizing power; and it was organized capitalism which, by systematically developing the media, revolutionized the conditions of production in the superstructure.[7] But not in the superstructure alone; for as organized capitalism began to achieve relative stability, the industry that shaped consciousness infiltrated all other sectors of production, and the denial or distortion of human needs tended to move from the economic mechanisms of the labour market to the social-psychological directives of the leisure market – the manipulation of consumption.

For the Frankfurt School the fact of Nazism was a definitive experience. Hence it is hardly surprising that they frequently viewed late capitalism through the lens of German fascism, with the result that the specific differences between totalitarianism and organized capitalism tended to collapse into a one-dimensional vision.[8] But German fascism and organized capitalism did indeed have one thing in common: they both broke down the boundary line between the public and the private spheres which had been characteristic of the liberal epoch. Both political propaganda and

7. See Enzensberger (1970). 8. See Orr (1974).

marketing psychology reached down into private areas of individual life to exploit personal conflicts or to awaken artificial needs in support of a particular system. By blurring the distinction between the private and the institutionalized, they made it more difficult to separate internal desire and external suggestion; the superstructure was more firmly anchored in the individual substructure. It was this which highlighted the capacity of ideologies to dispense with systems of explanatory concepts. It was clearly possible to reduce the 'ideological distance' between concepts and the circumstances to which concepts referred: precisely that ideological distance within which Marx's classical ideology-critique had moved.

The Frankfurt School responded by extending ideology-critique into the domain of social psychology. They sought to view simultaneously the combined effects of 'objective-historical' conditions and 'subjective-natural' conditions. Needs were no longer to be interpreted as natural and constant; they were referred back to specific historical situations. This brought into the foreground the question of how and where social conditions were deposited within the individual. The family was seen as the psychological agent of society; through its process of socialization economic processes were reinforced by conversion into psychic ones. The Frankfurt School located a crucial element in fascism within the psychology of the individual citizen, the so-called 'authoritarian personality', and they sought in investigations like *Studien über Autorität und Familie* to show how authoritarianism was inculcated in the family unit.

They also developed a critical sociology of the arts. Benjamin, Adorno and Marcuse all saw aesthetic imagination as a utopian and therefore liberating faculty. But if art was a legitimate source of critical insight, it could also be infected with ideology. Access to either aspect, it was argued, could be gained only by by-passing twin errors. On the one hand, concern with the art work as such tended to absolutize it and thus to conceal the degree to which it was a historical artefact born of specific social pressures and responding to specific social needs; this reproduced the bourgeois fetishization of the art work which had the effect of turning it into a cultural monument. On the other hand, a sociology of the arts which was concerned mainly with determinants arising from the relations of production and distribution bracketed out the problem of artistic quality; primary emphasis on the relations of production directed attention away from the work's internal dynamics and hence away from the question of how it embodied social information. Adorno's sociology of musical genres and the essays by Benjamin which are only imperfectly classified as literary criticism rejected both biases: the cultural illusion which separated the work of art from its place in the productive process, and the functional illusion which viewed it solely in the perspective of that process.[9]

In its *second* phase the Frankfurt School turned to consider the self-reinforcing qualities in the infra-structure. This entailed a sharper divergence from Marx who had believed the conditions of material production under capitalism to be self-undermining. He argued that the mechanism propelling the movement of history was the contradiction between the forces of production and the relations of production. The forces of production are dependent on the level of scientific knowledge and technical equipment, and on the organization of labour. The relations of production are manifested in property relations. In Marx's view the bourgeoisie could maintain its ascendency only by constantly creating more powerful methods of production. But the relations of production are not transformed at the same rate. Although the capitalist system produces more and more, poverty remains the lot of the majority. And it was this contradiction between the forces and the relations of production, Marx believed, that would eventually lead to a revolutionary crisis.

But the unprecedented increase in the forces of production has had the opposite effect from that anticipated by Marx. It has not been a historically explosive force in the way he had thought it would be. It has become a means of justifying the *status quo*. For now the existing relations of production can be represented as that form of organization which is technically necessary for a rational society; all problems can be made to seem to be questions of technical adjustment. This means that, once they have reached a very

9. See Nupen (1974).

high level of development, the forces of production stand in a new relationship to the relations of production. Previously they offered grounds for a critique of the power structure of society; now they provide a basis for its legitimation.

The change is registered in the *Dialectic of Enlightenment*. But Horkheimer and Adorno want to say more than that technology has become the prop, not the destructive agent, of capitalism. Rather their whole view of the edifice is different. They focus neither on the contradiction between productive forces and productive relations, nor on the conflict between bourgeoisie and proletariat. Their point of departure is the antagonism between two concepts of reason. Practical reason is found in the liberation from externally imposed compulsions and it implies the good life, both private and collective, of individuals as well as of citizens. Instrumental reason is found in the technical control of nature. This appears intellectually in the natural sciences and practically in modern technology. In the course of time the second type of reason has eclipsed the first. What men have learned from nature is how to use it in order wholly to dominate it and other men. The technical domination of nature issues by an inherent process in the domination of men: intellectually, in the rational sciences of man, and practically, in the continually refined administration of human beings by means of social organization. The Enlightenment is said to have changed into Positivism; to serve capital; to become totalitarian; and to culminate in fascism. The success of instrumental reason blocks the possibility of achieving practical reason.

Horkheimer and Adorno have replaced the critique of political economy by the critique of instrumental reason. Elements from Marx's analysis are assimilated but re-situated. Marx connected the principle of commodity exchange with a specific social system of property. Horkheimer and Adorno now view it as the most complete expression of instrumental rationality. The origins of this rationality are seen as reaching back long before the emergence of capitalism; any conceivable end to its sway becomes correspondingly more difficult to localize. Horkheimer suggests that philosophy should provoke a mutual critique of the two types of reason and thus prepare in the intellectual sphere for a possible reconciliation in reality. But neither he nor Adorno believes that this intellectual goal is inevitable; the reconciliation of the two concepts of reason is a utopia whose nature is entirely obscure.

Horkheimer and Adorno had noted, in passing as it were, the disappearance of a potentially revolutionary proletariat. That, too, was an achievement of instrumental reason which blunted the experience of need and scarcity, and hence their political articulation. How then is it still possible to urge the necessity of liberation from a relatively well-functioning and affluent society, where the demand for liberation is without a mass basis and therefore politically impotent? Marcuse's position among the older representatives of the Frankfurt School is distinctive because he seeks to confront this problem. The *third* stage of Critical Theory sees a renewed search for the 'negative'.

A possible way out of the difficulty is to re-define the nature of the conflict which is latent but potentially explosive within the social structure. Since in an affluent society the economic motivation diagnosed by Marx no longer operates as an explosive force, the critique of society might shift its argument from the sphere of political economy to that of metapsychology. A critique which is no longer socially represented by any specific group or institutional sector might choose to shift the level at which it operates. This change of level is a logical result of a critique which, in *One-Dimensional Man* as in *Dialectic of Enlightenment*, sees its object not primarily as late capitalism but as technical rationality. So in *Eros and Civilization* Marcuse offers a revision of Freudian psychoanalysis as a replacement for the now defective economic argument, and the concept of 'instinctual repression' here plays for Marcuse a role similar to that of 'economic exploitation' in Marx. The primary conflict is defined as taking place between technical rationality and latent human needs.

In Freud's view the history of man is the history of his repression. Civilization is based on the permanent subjugation of the instincts and their deflection to socially useful activities. This change is described by Freud as the transformation from the 'pleasure principle' to the 'reality principle'; men learn to give up immediate and uncertain satisfactions for the security of delayed and restrained pleasures. Now Marcuse revises Freud's diagnosis by arguing that the repressions so far characteristic of all human civilizations arise from the special conditions which have until now prevailed in the evolution of culture: the need to master nature in the struggle against scarcity. But if this is so, then the repressive organization of instinctual life is due to factors which do not arise from the inherent nature of the instincts but from specific historical conditions to which the instincts have so far had to adapt. So the 'reality principle' is not universal. It is culturally specific to an economy of scarcity. But in a civilization which tends to remove the obstacle of scarcity, repression is increasingly 'surplus repression': repression in excess of that necessary for maintaining civilization.

On this ground Marcuse suggests that instrumental reason, and hence a society whose guiding principle is technical efficiency, is potentially self-undermining. For technology has now reached a point where it can operate against the repressive use of energy insofar as it minimizes the time spent in the production of the necessities of life, and so makes possible a substantial release of instinctual energy formerly bound up in toil and the domination of nature. There is no longer any inherent necessity, in terms of the struggle for existence, for civilization to be repressive. The possibility of utopia is inherent in the technology of advanced industrial societies. This would involve a psycho-biological, as well as social and political, revolution. It envisages a 'psychic Thermidor'. In this way Marcuse claims to validate his attempt to 'develop the political and sociological substance' of Freud's metapsychology, since psychological categories have become, on this interpretation, 'political categories'.

Whether this is really so is a moot point. In *Eros and Civilization* Marcuse argues that the high level of instrumental rationality is the pre-condition for liberation. But in *One-Dimensional Man* he argues that it is this same development of the productive forces which is the effective basis for stifling potential rebellion or liberation. The swing from hope to despair issues from a blurred vision of the distinctively political. The basic components of Marcuse's vision of technological domination were in fact founded on the over-simple identifications of fascism, monopoly capitalism, totalitarianism and technology, a set of identifications first built up before the Second World War.[10]

The problem is one of topology. It is this: is it possible to define a boundary, and if so what is the nature of that boundary, between technology and the political use of technology? The situation is complicated by the fact that technology has become both an instrument and a competitor of politics. On the one hand, science and technology have become important instruments of political action; on the other hand, they have developed a life of their own and so become a new source of authority and power in society, one with which those directly involved in political action have to reckon. But whether as an instrument or as a competitor they have the effect of devaluing the distinctively political.

The *fourth* stage of Critical Theory, represented by Habermas, re-focuses this issue by enlisting the tradition of Hermeneutics. Habermas distinguishes between instrumental and communicative action. In instrumental action we encounter objects the paradigm for which are moving bodies; in principle, these are capable of manipulation. In communicative action we encounter objects the paradigm for which are speaking and acting subjects; in principle, they can be understood through symbols. The contrast is between instrumental reason which is interested in the domination of nature, and comprehension which is interested in communication without the desire of domination. The distinction has both practical and theoretical consequences.

The practical consequence is the sketch for a theory of politics. Habermas wants to restore a concept of the political which is indebted to the Greek *polis*. In the *polis*, the slaves were subject to the necessity of labour, thus freeing the citizens for political discussion; in contemporary society the place of the slaves could presumably be taken by automation. But Habermas argues that a scientific-technical society could be rational only if the development and application of science and technology were subject to public control; and only if the autonomy and responsibility of workers were secured so that there was a framework of discussion free from domination. He feels the goal must be worked for by establishing a dialogue between men about the ends of life –

10. See Orr, op. cit.

although the institutional mechanics of the dialogue remain unspecific. Thus unlike Horkheimer and Adorno, he believes that practical reason could be a characteristic of society, not only of separate individuals. And unlike Marcuse, he sees the content of utopia as the creation of an ideal situation of public discussion in which communicative distortions are eliminated.

The theoretical consequence is the sketch for a theory of communicative competence. This is reached by first considering forms of distorted communication. Those whose main concern is with the interpretation of texts have for long been accustomed to meet obstacles in the form of distortions and omissions; but these are accidental obstacles. Freud, however, invented a new hermeneutics: the study of texts, of which the dream is the paradigm, in which messages are systematically distorted. In this case, the distortions and omissions are put there by the author of the text intentionally, so that his own product becomes unintelligible to him. Psychoanalysis may thus be viewed as a kind of linguistic analysis which deals with systematically distorted communications – a position which has been elaborated at some length by Habermas' colleague Lorenzer. But to view it in this way is to presuppose a theory of communicative competence. Habermas' theory of this starts from the idea of a smoothly functioning language game which rests on a background consensus. He argues that this consensus is based on the mutual recognition of various kinds of validity claims which are implied in all speech acts – for instance, the claim that the utterance is comprehensible. When one or more such claims become problematic the background consensus is called into question and the claims, previously only implicit, now require discursive justification. Such 'discourses' involve the supposition by the participants that they are in an 'ideal speech situation': the supposition, that is, that they are discussing under conditions which guarantee that the consensus which is arrived at will be the result of the force of the better argument and not of constraints on discussion. Habermas seeks to characterize this absence of constraint formally: the structure of communication can be said to be free from constraint only when for all participants there is an effective equality of chances to take part in the dialogue. Hence the requirements of the ideal speech situation are such that the conditions for ideal discourse are connected with conditions for an ideal form of social life.

This is the link between the theory of communicative competence and the theory of politics. Habermas believes that the anticipation of a form of social life in which autonomy and responsibility are possible are prefigured in the structure of speech itself. Hence he sees the practical and the theoretical consequences of his distinction between instrumental and communicative action as inextricably connected. His claim therefore is that the normative basis of Critical Theory is not arbitrary but that it is inherent in the structure of social action which it analyses. In this way the theory of communicative competence may be seen to take the place of the analysis of the work process, once Marx's philosophical anthropology has been abandoned.

Some of these arguments developed in the course of the *Methodenstreit*, or methodological dispute, which enlivened German intellectual life in the sixties with a mixture of argument and acerbity. Habermas was of course not the only one to have broken a lance or two in that particular skirmish. The public dispute began with a confrontation between Sir Karl Popper and Theodor Adorno at a conference in 1961. Popper formulated his views on the logic of the social sciences in the form of twenty-seven theses. Without replying to these individually, Adorno presented an alternative position. Their disagreement consisted in their scarcely having met. Habermas then entered the lists in 1963 with a postscript to the Popper–Adorno dispute, to which Hans Albert replied in the following year; Habermas answered the reply, and Albert replied again. Any remaining doubts as to the insuperable differences separating the contestants must have been finally dispelled with the appearance of Habermas' *Knowledge and Human Interest* and Albert's *Treatise on Critical Reason*, both in 1968; followed by the essay collection by Adorno *et al.*, *Der Positivismusstreit in der deutschen Soziologie*, whose publication in 1969 provoked from Popper the complaint that his original address of 1961, far from being the focus of a genuine debate, had spawned a loose and baggy monster; although itself the 'unadmitted theme of the whole book', his paper had eventually been 'drowned ...

in an ocean of words'[11]. And it is certainly true that Habermas' running defence of positions *in statu nascendi* had caused the discussion to fan out well beyond the confines of the original dispute; other collective volumes of reciprocal cross-questioning, like *Hermeneutik und Ideologiekritik*, followed hot on the heels of *Der Positivismusstreit*.

But if the upshot of the *Methodenstreit* was unforeseen its origins were far from fortuitous. The Frankfurt School had come into head-on collision with their natural opponents. The critical rationalism of Popper and Albert was the direct descendant of the logical positivism which had flourished in Vienna in the 1920s among the group of philosopher-scientists and mathematicians known as the Vienna Circle, the most prominent of whom were Rudolf Carnap and Karl Popper himself. Like the Critical Theorists, the logical positivists had seen themselves as performing an educative role in the struggle against irrational beliefs which seized hold of collective life. Where they parted company was in their belief that ideological claims could be tested by scientific methods – hence by precisely those criteria of 'instrumental reason' which became the bane of the Frankfurt School.

Critical Rationalism sought to reserve the name of 'knowledge' and 'science' for the results of those operations which were to be found in the evolution of the modern natural sciences. Specifically, it was anchored in Popper's principle of falsifiability, according to which only those statements can be considered as empirically founded about which one could say by what empirical methods they might be disproved. The advance of knowledge was believed to be guaranteed solely by a controlled method of critical testing: the proposition of trial solutions to scientific problems, and their subjection to criticism and the elimination of errors.

Whoever adopted these tenets committed himself not to an abstract principle but to a way of life. Critical rationalism has specific ethical and political consequences. To be effective, the method of controlled critical testing requires institutional guarantees. It is predicated upon and it promotes an 'open' society: a society, that is, where incompatible views can be expressed; where everyone is free to propose solutions and to

11. See Popper (1970).

criticize the proposed solutions of others; and where government policies are changed in the light of criticism. The attitude of the intellectual whose convictions are guided by controlled scientific thinking is to provide the model towards which a well-organized education might lead society as a whole; and it is the duty of intellectuals to work towards this end, in which the eliminative function of violence is replaced by the eliminative function of rational criticism. The politics thus envisaged is a kind of rational social experiment. Hence Popper's *The Open Society and its Enemies* was both a counterpart and a counterblast to the *Dialectic of Enlightenment*. A counterpart, because both sought to understand and to explain the appeal of totalitarian ideas; and a counterblast, because Popper, like Albert, sees the Frankfurt School as the carrier of one of the most dangerous, because potentially totalitarian, traits of German thought: the tendency to irrationality.

In the course of the ensuing dispute, which eventually included others besides Critical Theorists and Critical Rationalists, several distinct areas of disagreement have emerged. Prominent among these are the following:

(1) Popper and Adorno use the terms 'contradiction' and 'critique' in two entirely different senses. For Popper problems arise because a contradiction is observed between our existing knowledge and existing facts. The method of the social sciences, as of the natural sciences, rests on the search for solutions to these problems; it is the control of the tentative search for solutions by the sharpest possible critiques of hypotheses. Thus for Popper critique refers to a formal method for testing scientific propositions. For Adorno, however, a problem is not something basically epistemological, but refers to a problematic condition of the social world. He cites as an example the contradiction between the concepts of a liberal society which implies freedom and equality, and the true content of these categories under liberalism in which inequality of relations between men is determined by social power. This is not a logical contradiction, which could be corrected through more refined hypotheses, but the structural condition of society itself. Thus for Adorno critique does not refer to the critical testing of hypotheses, but rather to the development

of the contradictions in social reality through a knowledge of them.[12]

(2) Habermas then proposed another objection to Popper's idea of a critical test. He argued that no system of basic concepts comparable to that established for the investigation of moving bodies and observable events was in principle possible in the study of society. This is because societies are differently constituted as objects of possible knowledge. They form a network of intentional actions; and statements about intentional action are not reducible to statements about observable events. The investigator must gain access to his data through an understanding of meanings. In place of controlled observation, which guarantees the anonymity of the observing subject and thus of the reproducibility of the observation, there is a participation in a dialogue between investigator and investigated, in which reciprocal interaction occurs. Hence the paradigm is no longer the observation but the dialogue.

(3) Habermas wants to direct attention to the human interests served by natural and human science, and to their respective criteria of success and failure. He claims that in natural science the 'interest' is in technical control, so that the character of natural science as 'value-free' is viewed as a value-characteristic derived from the human decision to develop a form of knowledge which is technically exploitable. This does not mean that the community of scientists are consciously or directly interested in technical control; for although whole branches of theoretical science are in fact supported by industry today, this historical development made its appearance no more than a century ago. What Habermas calls interest cannot be experienced as such; it is an interest in which no one may be interested in any empirically demonstrable way. The claim that natural science is guided by 'interest in possible technical control' can only be understood in the sense that this interest is the condition of the possibility of natural science. That is to say, he is claiming that it is not merely the emergence and continued existence of science, but also its procedure and methodological structure, which must be explained by such an interest. If this claim is to be made good, it must be

12. See Frisby (1972).

demonstrated that there is a systematic relationship between, on the one hand, the logical structure of natural science, and, on the other hand, the pragmatic structure of the possible applications of the information generated within this framework.

Objections have been raised against this by some students of the philosophy of science. When it is said that the sanction of failure in natural science is unsuccessful feedback from prediction and test, and when the scientific community is said to be a 'community of experimenters', an extremely positivistic theory of science is being adopted in which explanation and prediction are viewed as strictly symmetrical. On this view we might indeed see the only function of theoretical scientific statements as that of rendering predictions possible. But it has become clear in the last few years that the deductive covering-law model, as proposed by Hempel, Oppenheim and Popper, fails to do justice to the most important concern of modern natural science – that is, explanation. In discussions of the meaning of models for scientific theories it has been pointed out that models are not merely an instrument of theory construction, but that they are an essential element of theory itself – an element which gives a theory an intelligibility substantially independent of prediction and which contributes to its essential explanatory value.[13]

(4) Habermas takes psychoanalysis as his model in explaining the concept of an emancipatory social science. In psychoanalysis the speech and actions of the patient are understood as a system of symbols whose meaning must be reconstructed; and the problem is to reconstruct the meaning which has become unintelligible to the author himself. This it seeks to accomplish by leading the patient, through a process of self-reflection, to become conscious of needs and motives that were previously repressed, so that he is able to acknowledge that these needs and motives are in fact his own. Habermas argues that this model can be, and should be, applied to society as a whole. The role of the social theorist is to render those to whom he speaks autonomous by enabling them to understand their own situation in the social world. What in the individual is self-reflection is in a society self-education.

Objections have been raised against this transfer of the psycho-

13. See Lobkowicz (1972).

analytic model to large groups. In psychoanalysis, the patient's suffering and his desire to be cured provide the basis for the activity of the doctor who helps the patient to free himself from the compulsions which hold sway over him. This therapeutic relationship presupposes a voluntary subordination of one of the partners to the other; and it also presupposes that both parties are committed to the liberation from psychic constraints. For the analyst, the patient is not an object of manipulation, but a subject who is to be assisted to emancipation. But precisely this common purpose, it has been argued, is absent in social conflicts. What obtains there is a condition of reciprocal resistance. For any ruling class the attempt to gain freedom from a social condition of compulsion must appear as a threat to the rule which it exercises over the other classes. And the oppressed class, for its part, has good reasons for assuming that any attempts it makes to enter into a dialogue with the ruling class may be turned into an opportunity for the latter to strengthen the security of its rule.

Any study of Critical Theory is led back again and again to the consideration of a particular cultural tradition. The methodological disputes in which its adherents were involved during the sixties provoked most passionate engagement within the German academic community; Hegelian-Marxism and Hermeneutics, on which they have drawn extensively, are phenomena of distinctively German intellectual history; and the meaning of critique itself originates in German Idealism. Why then should Critical Theory now claim increasing attention outside Germany?

The first reason is methodological. It relates to the idea of critique as reflection on the conditions of knowledge of the social world. The Critical Theorists argue that no system of basic concepts – comparable to the basic concepts established in natural science for the investigation of moving bodies and observable events – is in principle possible in the study of society, since societies, being systems of communicative action, are differently constituted as objects of possible knowledge. The development of this position connects up with new departures in the social sciences, in particular those coming from Phenomenology, which have tried to think through the fact that the subject in the act of perception is included within the process of cognition as a social act. Likewise, investigations in the theory of communicative competence have brought Critical Theory closer to the work of philosophers like Searle, who tries to arrive at a theory of speech acts based on the ideas of Austin and Strawson; as well as to linguists like Wunderlich, who broaden their investigations to include the general structures of possible speech situations.

The second reason is political. It is related to the idea of critique as an analysis of constraints imposed by the historically variable structures of the social world. Since science and technology are no longer merely elements within the social process of work but have become a primary productive force, a self-reinforcing circle has come into being: society is made increasingly dependent on applied science, and then scientific criteria are appealed to in order to decide whether or not the social world is rationally ordered. Hence the argument of Critical Theorists that modern science has generated mechanisms for justifying the organization of society connects up with the growing awareness in the Western world as a whole that it is necessary to distinguish between the truly liberating effects of natural science, and the use of scientific empiricism, together with the language of pseudo-science, to underwrite particular distributions of social power.

In this selection of Readings I have tried to strike a balance between two options: between, on the one hand, a selection documenting the tradition in terms of its intellectual origins and development, and, on the other hand, a selection tilted in such a way as to reconstruct the thematics of Critical Theory from the perspective of the present stage in its development. But I have also highlighted some less accessible aspects of the Frankfurt School; for this reason I chose to allot much more space to its links with the Hermeneutic tradition than to the considerable impact on it of the Freudian tradition.

The Readings fall into four parts. Part One illustrates the lineage of Critical Theory reaching back to Marx and Hegel. Part Two shows the nature of its links with the Hermeneutic tradition. Part Three indicates the range of problems with which two generations of the School have been occupied. And Part Four is devoted to commentaries: texts which are critical of the School, or which elaborate some of its aspects, or set its work in a distinctive historical context.

References

ADORNO, T. W. *et al.* (1969), *Der Positivismusstreit in der deutschen Soziologie*, Neuwied and Berlin.
COHEN, J. (1969), 'The Philosophy of Marcuse', *New Left Review*, no. 57.
ENZENSBERGER, H. M. (1970), 'Constituents of a Theory of the Media', *New Left Review*, no. 64.
FRISBY, D. (1972), 'The Popper-Adorno Controversy: the Methodological Dispute in German Sociology', *Philosophy of the Social Sciences*, no. 2, pp. 105–19.
HABERMAS, J. (1962), *Strukturwandel der Öffentlichleit*, Neuwied and Berlin.
HABERMAS, J. (1971), *Hermeneutik und Ideologiekritik*, Frankfurt.
HABERMAS, J. (1973), 'A Postscript to *Knowledge and Human Interests*', *Philosophy of the Social Sciences*, no. 3, pp. 157–89.
HABERMAS, J., LUHMANN, N. (1971), *Theorie der Gesellschaft oder Sozialtechnologie*, Frankfurt, p. 179.
HORKHEIMER, M. (1968), *Kritische Theorie* (2nd ed.), Frankfurt, pp. 148–53, 199.
HORKHEIMER, M., ADORNO, T. W. (1969), *Dialektik der Aufklärung*, Frankfurt, pp. 31, 91, 202.
JAY, M. (1973), *The Dialectical Imagination*, Heinemann Educational.
KOSELLEK, R. (1959), *Kritik und Krise*, Freiburg/Munich.
LOBKOWICZ, N. (1972), 'Interest and Objectivity', *Philosophy of the Social Sciences*, no. 2, pp. 193–210.
LORENZER, A. (1970), *Kritik des psychoanalytischen Symbolbegriffs*, Frankfurt.
LORENZER, A. (1970), *Sprachzerstörung und Rekonstruktion*, Frankfurt.
NUPEN, M. (1974), 'The Idea of a Critical Sociology of Music', *Bolt*.
ORR, J. (1974), 'German Social Theory and the Hidden Face of Technology', *Archives européennes de sociologie*, no. 15, pp. 312–36.
POPPER, K. R. (1970), 'Reason or Revolution?', *Archives européennes de sociologie*, no. 11, pp. 252–62.

Part One
The Hegelian–Marxist Tradition

In that section of the *Phenomenology of Mind* which Marx called 'the true birthplace and secret of the Hegelian philosophy', Hegel presented the case for a necessary relationship between the activity of human labour and the growth of self-knowledge: by working on and transforming nature, by imposing his own designs upon matter, man comes to be surrounded by a world which embodies his self-assertion as a 'subject' (Reading 1). The idea of the self-constitution of the human species through work served Marx as the guide for both appropriating and criticizing Hegel's *Phenomenology*. What he attacked in Hegel, and in others, was the attempt to derive historical processes from imaginary subjects; any such attempt, he argued, must itself be historically understood as a result of the estrangement of men from themselves (Reading 2). Later he went on to elaborate the idea of estrangement in terms of the 'fetishism of commodities', by which he meant that form of social life which necessarily appears to those who produce it not as their own product but as if it were a part of nature, obeying its own laws much as the objects of the natural world obey the law of gravity (Reading 3). But Marxism too could become a fetish, forgetful of its historical genesis; and it was only after the First World War that a number of writers like Lukács, Bloch and Korsch, who once more read Marx in the light of Hegel, were responsible for bringing into relief the specific historical situation in which Marxist theory arose. Thus Lukács was applying historical materialism to itself when he argued that its indispensable historical pre-condition was the knitting together of society into a more homogeneous economic unity, a process accomplished for the first time by the spread of the capitalist mode of production (Reading 4).

1 G. W. F. Hegel

Master and Slave

Excerpt from G. W. F. Hegel, *The Phenomenology of Mind*, George Allen and Unwin Ltd, 1966, pp. 229–40. First published in 1807.

Self-consciousness exists in itself and for itself, in that, and by the fact that, it exists for another self-consciousness; that is to say, it *is* only by being acknowledged or 'recognized'. The conception of this its unity in its duplication, of infinitude realizing itself in self-consciousness, has many sides to it and encloses within it elements of varied significance. Thus its moments must on the one hand be strictly kept apart in detailed distinctiveness, and, on the other, in this distinction must, at the same time, also be taken as not distinguished, or must always be accepted and understood in their opposite sense. This double meaning of what is distinguished lies in the nature of self-consciousness – of its being infinite, or directly the opposite of the determinateness in which it is fixed. The detailed exposition of the notion of this spiritual unity in its duplication will bring before us the process of Recognition.

Self-consciousness has before it another self-consciousness; it has come outside itself. This has a double significance. First it has lost its own self, since it finds itself as an *other* being; secondly, it has thereby sublated that other, for it does not regard the other as essentially real, but sees its own self in the other.

It must cancel this its other. To do so is the sublation of that first double meaning, and is therefore a second double meaning. First, it must set itself to sublate the other independent being, in order thereby to become certain of itself as true being; secondly, it thereupon proceeds to sublate its own self, for this other is itself.

This sublation in a double sense of its otherness in a double sense is at the same time a return in a double sense into its self. For, firstly, through sublation, it gets back itself, because it became one with itself again through the cancelling of *its* otherness; but secondly, it likewise gives otherness back again to the other self-consciousness, for it was aware of being in the other, it cancels this its own being in the other and thus lets the other again go free.

This process of self-consciousness in relation to another self-consciousness has in this manner been represented as the action of one alone. But this action on the part of the one has itself the double significance of being at once its own action and the action of that other as well. For the other is likewise independent, shut up within itself, and there is nothing in it which is not there through itself. The first does not have the object before it only in the passive form characteristic primarily of the object of desire, but as an object existing independently for itself, over which therefore it has no power to do anything for its own behoof, if that object does not *per se* do what the first does to it. The process then is absolutely the double process of both self-consciousnesses. Each sees the other do the same as itself; each itself does what it demands on the part of the other, and for that reason does what it does, only so far as the other does the same. Action from one side only would be useless, because what is to happen can only be brought about by means of both.

The action has then a *double entente* not only in the sense that it is an act done to itself as well as to the other, but also in the sense that the act *simpliciter* is the act of the one as well as of the other regardless of their distinction.

In this movement we see the process repeated which came before us as the play of forces; in the present case, however, it is found in consciousness. What in the former had effect only for us [contemplating experience], holds here for the terms themselves. The middle term is self-consciousness which breaks itself up into the extremes; and each extreme is this interchange of its own determinateness, and complete transition into the opposite. While *qua* consciousness, it no doubt comes outside itself, still, in being outside itself it is at the same time restrained within itself, it exists for itself, and its self-externalization is for consciousness. *Consciousness* finds that it immediately is and is not another consciousness, as also that this other is for itself only when it cancels itself as existing for itself, and has self-existence only in the self-existence of the other. Each is the mediating term to the other, through which each mediates and unites itself with itself; and each is to itself and to the other an immediate self-existing reality, which, at the same time, exists thus for itself only through this mediation. They recognize themselves as mutually recognizing one another.

This pure conception of recognition, of duplication of self-consciousness within its unity, we must now consider in the way its process appears for self-consciousness. It will, in the first place, present the aspect of the disparity of the two, or the break-up of the middle term into the extremes, which, *qua* extremes, are opposed to one another, and of which one is merely recognized, while the other only recognizes.

Self-consciousness is primarily simple existence for self, self-identity by exclusion of every other from itself. It takes its essential nature and absolute object to be Ego; and in this immediacy, in this bare fact of its self-existence, it is individual. That which for it is other stands as unessential object, as object with the impress and character of negation. But the other is also a self-consciousness; an individual makes its appearance in antithesis to an individual. Appearing thus in their immediacy, they are for each other in the manner of ordinary objects. They are independent individual forms, modes of consciousness that have not risen above the bare level of life (for the existent object here has been determined as life). They are, moreover, forms of consciousness which have not yet accomplished for one another the process of absolute abstraction, of uprooting all immediate existence, and of being merely the bare, negative fact of self-identical consciousness; or, in other words, have not yet revealed themselves to each other as existing purely for themselves, i.e., as self-consciousness. Each is indeed certain of its own self, but not of the other, and hence its own certainty of itself is still without truth. For its truth would be merely that its own individual existence for itself would be shown to it to be an independent object, or, which is the same thing, that the object would be exhibited as this pure certainty of itself. By the notion of recognition, however, this is not possible, except in the form that as the other is for it, so it is for the other; each in its self through its own action and again through the action of the other achieves this pure abstraction of existence for self.

The presentation of itself, however, as pure abstraction of self-consciousness consists in showing itself as a pure negation of its objective form, or in showing that it is fettered to no determinate existence, that it is not bound at all by the particularity everywhere characteristic of existence as such, and is *not* tied up with life. The process of bringing all this out involves a twofold action – action on the part of the other and action on the part of itself. In so far as it is the other's action, each aims at the destruction and death of the other. But in this there is implicated also the second kind of action, self-activity; for the former implies that it risks its own life. The relation of both self-consciousnesses is in this way so constituted that they prove themselves and each other through a life-and-death struggle. They must enter into this struggle, for they must bring their certainty of themselves, the certainty of being for themselves, to the level of objective truth, and make this a fact both in the case of the other and in their own case as well. And it is solely by risking life that freedom is obtained; only thus is it tried and proved that the essential nature of self-consciousness is not bare existence, is not the merely immediate form in which it at first makes its appearance, is not its mere absorption in the expanse of life. Rather it is thereby guaranteed that there is nothing present but what might be taken as a vanishing moment – that self-consciousness is merely pure self-existence, being-for-self. The individual, who has not staked his life, may, no doubt, be recognized as a Person; but he has not attained the truth of this recognition as an independent self-consciousness. In the same way each must aim at the death of the other, as it risks its own life thereby; for that other is to it of no more worth than itself; the other's reality is presented to the former as an external other, as outside itself; it must cancel that externality. The other is a purely existent consciousness and entangled in manifold ways; it must view its otherness as pure existence for itself or as absolute negation.

This trial by death, however, cancels both the truth which was to result from it, and therewith the certainty of self altogether. For just as life is the natural 'position' of consciousness, independence without absolute negativity, so death is the natural 'negation' of consciousness, negation without independence, which thus remains without the requisite significance of actual recognition. Through death, doubtless, there has arisen the certainty that both did stake their life, and held it lightly both in their own case and in the case of the other; but that is not for those who underwent this struggle. They cancel their consciousness which had its place in this alien element of natural existence; in other words, they cancel themselves and are sublated as terms or extremes seeking to have existence on their own account. But along with this there vanishes from the play of change the essential moment, viz. that of breaking up into extremes with opposite characteristics; and the middle term collapses into a lifeless unity which is broken up into lifeless extremes, merely existent and not opposed. And the two do not mutually give and receive one another back from each other through consciousness; they let one another go quite indifferently, like things. Their act is abstract negation, not the negation characteristic of consciousness, which cancels in such a way that it preserves and maintains what is sublated, and thereby survives its being sublated.

In this experience self-consciousness becomes aware that *life* is as essential to it as pure self-consciousness. In immediate self-consciousness the simple ego is absolute object, which, however, is for us or in itself absolute mediation, and has as its essential moment substantial and solid independence. The dissolution of that simple unity is the result of the first experience; through this there is posited a pure self-consciousness, and a consciousness which is not purely for itself, but for another, i.e. as an existent consciousness, consciousness in the form and shape of thinghood. Both moments are essential, since, in the first instance, they are unlike and opposed, and their reflection into unity has not yet come to light, they stand as two opposed forms or modes of consciousness. The one is independent, and its essential nature is to be for itself; the other is dependent, and its essence is life or existence for another. The former is the Master, or Lord, the latter the Bondsman.

The master is the consciousness that exists *for itself*; but no longer merely the general notion of existence for self. Rather, it is a consciousness existing on its own account which is mediated with itself through an other consciousness, i.e. through an other whose very nature implies that it is bound up with an independent being or with thinghood in general. The master brings himself into relation to both these moments, to a thing as such, the object of desire, and to the consciousness whose essential character is thinghood. And since the master is (*a*) *qua* notion of self-consciousness, an immediate relation of self-existence, but (*b*) is now moreover at the same time mediation, or a being-for-self which is for itself only through an other – he [the master] stands in relation (*a*) immediately to both (*b*) mediately to each through the other. The master relates himself to the bondsman mediately through independent existence, for that is precisely what keeps the bondsman in thrall; it is his chain, from which he could not in the struggle get away, and for that reason he proved himself to be dependent, to have his independence in the shape of thinghood. The master, however, is the power controlling this state of existence, for he has shown in the struggle that he holds it to be merely something negative. Since he is the power dominating existence, while this existence again is the power controlling the other [the bondsman], the master holds, *par consequence*, this other in subordination. In the same way the master relates himself to the thing mediately through the bondsman. The bondsman being a self-consciousness in the broad sense, also takes up a negative attitude to things and cancels them; but the thing is, at the same time, independent for him, and, in consequence, he cannot, with all his negating, get so far as to annihilate it outright and be done with it; that is to say, he merely works on it. To the master, on the other hand, by means of this mediating process, belongs the immediate relation, in the sense of the pure negation of it, in other words he gets the enjoyment. What mere desire did not attain, he now succeeds in attaining, viz. to have done with the thing, and find satisfaction in enjoyment. Desire alone did not get the length of this, because of the independence of the thing. The master, however, who has interposed the bondsman between it and himself, thereby relates himself merely to the dependence of the thing, and enjoys it without qualification and without reserve.

The aspect of its independence he leaves to the bondsman, who labours upon it.

In these two moments, the master gets his recognition through an other consciousness, for in them the latter affirms itself as inessential, both by working upon the thing, and, on the other hand, by the fact of being dependent on a determinate existence; in neither case can this other get the mastery over existence, and succeed in absolutely negating it. We have thus here this moment of recognition, viz. that the other consciousness cancels itself as self-existence, and, *ipso facto*, itself does what the first does to it. In the same way we have the other moment, that this action on the part of the second is the action proper of the first; for what is done by the bondsman is properly an action on the part of the master. The latter exists only for himself, that is his essential nature; he is the negative power without qualification, a power to which the thing is naught. And he is thus the absolutely essential act in this situation, while the bondsman is not so, he is an inessential activity. But for recognition proper there is needed the moment that what the master does to the other he should also do to himself, and what the bondsman does to himself, he should do to the other also. On that account a form of recognition has arisen that is one-sided and unequal.

In all this, the inessential consciousness is, for the master, the object which embodies the truth of his certainty of himself. But it is evident that this object does not correspond to its notion; for just where the master has effectively achieved lordship, he really finds that something has come about quite different from an independent consciousness. It is not an independent, but rather a dependent consciousness that he has achieved. He is thus not assured of self-existence as his truth; he finds that his truth is rather the inessential consciousness, and the fortuitous inessential action of that consciousness.

The truth of the independent consciousness is accordingly the consciousness of the bondsman. This doubtless appears in the first instance outside itself, and not as the truth of self-consciousness. But just as lordship showed its essential nature to be the reverse of what it wants to be, so, too, bondage will, when completed, pass into the opposite of what it immediately is: being a consciousness repressed within itself, it will enter into itself, and change round into real and true independence.

We have seen what bondage is only in relation to lordship. But it is a self-consciousness, and we have now to consider what it is, in this regard, in and for itself. In the first instance, the master is taken to be the essential reality for the state of bondage; hence, for it, the truth is the independent consciousness existing for itself, although this truth is not taken yet as inherent in bondage itself. Still, it does in fact contain within itself this truth of pure negativity and self-existence, because it has experienced this reality within it. For this consciousness was not in peril and fear for this element or that, nor for this or that moment of time, it was afraid for its entire being; it felt the fear of death, the sovereign master. It has been in that experience melted to its inmost soul, has trembled throughout its every fibre, and all that was fixed and steadfast has quaked within it. This complete perturbation of its entire substance, this absolute dissolution of all its stability into fluent continuity, is, however, the simple, ultimate nature of self-consciousness, absolute negativity, pure self-referrent existence, which consequently is involved in this type of consciousness. This moment of pure self-existence is moreover a fact for it; for in the master it finds this as its object. Further, this bondsman's consciousness is not only this total dissolution in a general way; in serving and toiling the bondsman actually carries this out. By serving he cancels in every particular aspect his dependence on and attachment to natural existence, and by his work removes this existence away.

The feeling of absolute power, however, realized both in general and in the particular form of service, is only dissolution implicitly; and albeit the fear of the lord is the beginning of wisdom, consciousness is not therein aware of being self-existent. Through work and labour, however, this consciousness of the bondsman comes to itself. In the moment which corresponds to desire in the case of the master's consciousness, the aspect of the non-essential relation to the thing seemed to fall to the lot of the servant, since the thing there retained its independence. Desire has reserved to itself the pure negating of the object and thereby unalloyed feeling of self. This satisfaction, however, just for that reason is itself only a state of evanescence, for it lacks objectivity or subsistence. Labour, on the other hand, is desire restrained and checked, evanescence delayed and postponed; in other words, labour shapes and fashions the thing. The negative relation to the object passes into the *form* of the object, into something that is permanent and remains; because it is just for the labourer that the object has independence. This negative mediating agency, this activity giving shape and form, is at the same time the individual existence, the pure self-existence of that consciousness, which now in the work it does is externalized and passes into the condition of permanence. The consciousness that toils and serves accordingly attains by this means the direct apprehension of that independent being as its self.

But again, shaping or forming the object has not only the positive significance that the bondsman becomes thereby aware of himself as factually and objectively self-existent; this type of consciousness has also a negative import, in contrast with its first moment, the element of fear. For in shaping the thing it only becomes aware of its own proper negativity, its existence on its own account, as an object, through the fact that it cancels the actual form confronting it. But this objective negative element is precisely the alien, external reality, before which it trembled. Now, however, it destroys this extraneous alien negative, affirms and sets itself up as a negative in the element of permanence, and thereby becomes for itself a self-existent being. In the master, the bondsman feels self-existence to be something external, an objective fact; in fear self-existence is present within himself; in fashioning the thing, self-existence comes to be felt explicitly as his own proper being, and he attains the consciousness that he himself exists in its own right and on its own account (*an und für sich*). By the fact that the form is objectified, it does not become something other than the consciousness moulding the thing through work; for just that form is his pure self-existence, which therein becomes truly realized. Thus precisely in labour where there seemed to be merely some outsider's mind and ideas involved, the bondsman becomes aware, through this re-discovery of himself by himself, of having and being a 'mind of his own'.

For this reflection of self into self the two moments, fear and service in general, as also that of formative activity, are necessary: and at the same time both must exist in a universal manner. Without the discipline of service and obedience, fear remains formal and does not spread over the whole known reality of existence. Without the formative activity shaping the thing, fear remains inward and mute, and consciousness does not become objective for itself. Should consciousness shape and form the thing without the initial state of absolute fear, then it has a merely vain and futile 'mind of its own'; for its form or negativity is not negativity *per se*, and hence its formative activity cannot furnish the consciousness of itself as essentially real. If it has endured not absolute fear, but merely some slight anxiety, the negative reality has remained external to it, its substance has not been through and through infected thereby. Since the entire content of its natural consciousness has not tottered and shaken, it is still inherently a determinate mode of being; having a 'mind of its own' (*der eigene Sinn*) is simply stubbornness (*Eigensinn*), a type of freedom which does not get beyond the attitude of bondage. As little as the pure form can become its essential nature, so little is that form, considered as extending over particulars, a universal formative activity, an absolute notion; it is rather a piece of cleverness which has mastery within a certain range, but not over the universal power nor over the entire objective reality.

2 Karl Marx

The Critique of Hegelian Philosophy

Excerpt from Karl Marx, *Early Writings*, tr. Rodney Livingstone and Gregor Benton, Penguin (in association with *New Left Review*), 1975, pp. 379–83, 384–400.

This is perhaps the place to make a few remarks, by way of explanation and justification, about the Hegelian dialectic, both in general, and in particular as expounded in the *Phenomenology* and *Logic*, as well as about its relation to the modern critical movement.

Modern German criticism was so preoccupied with the old world and so entangled during the course of its development with its subject-matter that it had a completely uncritical attitude to the method of criticism and was completely unaware of the *seemingly formal* but in fact *essential* question of how we now stand in relation to the Hegelian *dialectic*. The lack of awareness about the relation of modern criticism to Hegelian philosophy in general and to the dialectic in particular has been so pronounced that critics like Strauss and Bruno Bauer are still, at least implicitly, imprisoned within Hegelian logic, the first completely so and the second in his *Synoptiker* (where, in opposition to Strauss, he substitutes the 'self-consciousness' of abstract man for the substance of abstract nature) and even in his *Das entdeckte Christentum*. For example, in *Das entdeckte Christentum* we find the following passage:

> As if self-consciousness, in positing the world, that which is different, and in producing itself in that which it produces, since it then does away with the difference between what it has produced and itself and since it is only in the producing and in the movement that it is itself – as if it did not have its purpose in this movement,

etc. Or again: 'They (the French Materialists) could not yet see that the movement of the universe only really comes to exist for itself and enters into unity with itself as the movement of self-consciousness.'

These expressions are not even different in their language from the Hegelian conception. They reproduce it word for word.

How little awareness there was of the relation to Hegel's dialectic while this criticism was under way (Bauer's *Synoptiker*), and how little even the completed criticism of the subject-matter contributed to such an awareness, is clear from Bauer's *Gute Sache der Freiheit*, where he dismisses Herr Gruppe's impertinent question 'and now what will happen to logic?' by referring him to future Critics.

But now that Feuerbach, both in his 'Thesen' in the *Anekdota* and in greater detail in his *Philosophie der Zukunft*, has destroyed the foundations of the old dialectic and philosophy, that very school of Criticism, which was itself incapable of taking such a step but instead watched while it was taken, has proclaimed itself the pure, resolute, absolute Criticism which has achieved self-clarity, and in its spiritual pride has reduced the whole process of history to the relation between the rest of the world, which comes into the category of the 'masses', and itself. It has assimilated all dogmatic antitheses into the *one* dogmatic antithesis between its own sagacity and the stupidity of the world, between the critical Christ and mankind – the '*rabble*'. It has daily and hourly demonstrated its own excellence against the mindlessness of the masses and has finally announced that the critical *Day of Judgement* is drawing near, when the whole of fallen humanity will be arrayed before it and divided into groups, whereupon each group will receive its certificate of poverty. The school of Criticism has made known in print its superiority to human feelings and the world, above which it sits enthroned in sublime solitude, with nothing but an occasional roar of sarcastic laughter from its Olympian lips. After all these delightful capers of idealism (Young Hegelianism) which is expiring in the form of Criticism, it (the critical school) has not once voiced so much as a suspicion of the need for a critical debate with its progenitor, the Hegelian dialectic. It has not even indicated a critical attitude to Feuerbach's dialectic. A completely uncritical attitude towards itself.

Feuerbach is the only person who has a *serious* and a *critical* attitude to the Hegelian dialectic and who has made real discoveries in this field. He is the true conqueror of the old philosophy. The magnitude of his achievement and the quiet simplicity with which he presents it to the world are in marked contrast to the others.

Feuerbach's great achievement is:

(1) To have shown that philosophy is nothing more than religion brought into thought and developed in thought, and that it is equally to be condemned as another form and mode of existence of the estrangement of man's nature.

(2) To have founded *true materialism*, and *real science* by making the social relation of 'man to man' the basic principle of his theory.

(3) To have opposed to the negation of the negation, which claims to be the absolute positive, the positive which is based upon itself and positively grounded in itself.

Feuerbach explains the Hegelian dialectic, and in so doing justifies taking the positive, that is sensuously ascertained, as his starting-point, in the following way:

Hegel starts out from the estrangement of substance (in logical terms: from the infinite, the abstractly universal), from the absolute and fixed abstraction. In ordinary language, he starts out from religion and theology.

Secondly, he supersedes the infinite and posits the actual, the sensuous, the real, the finite, the particular. (Philosophy as supersession of religion and theology.)

Thirdly, he once more supersedes the positive, and restores the abstraction, the infinite. Restoration of religion and theology.

Feuerbach therefore conceives the negation of the negation *only* as a contradiction of philosophy with itself, as philosophy which affirms theology (supersession, etc.) after having superseded it and hence affirms it in opposition to itself.

The positing or self-affirmation and self-confirmation present in the negation of the negation is regarded as a positing which is not yet sure of itself, which is still preoccupied with its opposite, which doubts itself and therefore stands in need of proof, which does not prove itself through its own existence, which is not admitted. It is therefore directly counterposed to that positing which is sensuously ascertained and grounded in itself. (Feuerbach sees negation of the negation, the concrete concept, as thought which surpasses itself in thought and as thought which strives to be direct awareness, nature, reality.)[1]

But since he conceives the negation of the negation from the aspect of the positive relation contained within it as the true and only positive and from the aspect of the negative relation contained within it as the only true act and self-realizing act of all being, Hegel has merely discovered the *abstract*, *logical*, *speculative* expression of the movement of history. This movement of history is not yet the *real* history of man as a given subject, it is simply the *process of his creation*, the *history of his emergence*. We shall explain both the abstract form of this movement and the difference between Hegel's conception of this process and that of modern criticism as formulated in Feuerbach's *Das Wesen des Christentums* or rather, the *critical* form of a movement which in Hegel is still uncritical.

Let us take a look at Hegel's system. We must begin with his *Phenomenology*, which is the true birthplace and secret of the Hegelian philosophy . . .

Hegel commits a double error.

The first appears most clearly in the *Phenomenology*, which is the birthplace of Hegelian philosophy. When, for example, Hegel conceives wealth, the power of the state, etc., as entities estranged from the being of man, he conceives them only in their thought form . . . They are entities of thought, and therefore simply an estrangement of *pure*, i.e. abstract, philosophical thought. Therefore the entire movement ends with absolute knowledge. What these objects are estranged from and what they confront with their claim to reality is none other than abstract thought. The *philosopher*, himself an abstract form of estranged man, sets himself up as the *yardstick* of the estranged world. The entire *history of alienation* and the entire *retraction* of this alienation is therefore nothing more than the *history of the production* of abstract, i.e. absolute, thought, of logical, speculative thought. *Estrangement*, which thus forms the real interest of this alienation and its super-

1. See Feuerbach (1843), paras 29, 30. [All notes except note 6 are editor's notes.]

session, is the opposition of *in itself* and *for itself*, of *consciousness* and *self consciousness*, of *object* and *subject*, i.e. the opposition within thought itself of abstract thought and sensuous reality or real sensuousness. All other oppositions and the movements of these oppositions are only the *appearance*, the *mask*, the *exoteric* form of these two opposites which are alone important and which form the *meaning* of these other, profane oppositions. It is not the fact that the human essence *objectifies* itself in an *inhuman* way, in opposition to itself, but that it *objectifies* itself in *distinction* from and in *opposition* to abstract thought, which constitutes the essence of estrangement as it exists and as it is to be superseded.

The appropriation of man's objectified and estranged essential powers is therefore firstly only an *appropriation* which takes place in *consciousness*, in pure thought, i.e. in *abstraction*. In the *Phenomenology*, therefore, despite its thoroughly negative and critical appearance and despite the fact that its criticism is genuine and often well ahead of its time, the uncritical positivism and equally uncritical idealism of Hegel's later works, the philosophical dissolution and restoration of the empirical world, is already to be found in latent form, in embryo, as a potentiality and a secret. Secondly, the vindication of the objective world for man – e.g. the recognition that *sensuous* consciousness is not *abstractly* sensuous consciousness, but *humanly* sensuous consciousness; that religion, wealth, etc., are only the estranged reality of *human* objectification, of *human* essential powers born into work, and therefore only the *way* to true *human* reality – this appropriation, or the insight into this process, therefore appears in Hegel in such a way that *sense perception*, *religion*, the power of the state, etc., are spiritual entities, for *mind* alone is the *true* essence of man, and the true form of mind is the thinking mind, the logical, speculative mind. The *humanity* of nature and of nature as produced by history, of man's products, is apparent from the fact that they are *products* of abstract mind and therefore factors of the *mind*, *entities of thought*. The *Phenomenology* is therefore concealed and mystifying criticism, criticism which has not attained self-clarity; but in so far as it grasps the *estrangement* of man – even though man appears only in the form of mind – *all* the elements of criticism are concealed within it, and often *prepared* and *worked out* in a way that goes far beyond Hegel's own point of view. The 'unhappy consciousness', the 'honest consciousness', the struggle of the 'noble and base consciousness', etc. etc., these separate sections contain the *critical* elements – but still in estranged form – of entire spheres, such as religion, the state, civil life and so forth. Just as the *entity*, the *object*, appears as a thought-entity, so also the *subject* is always *consciousness* or *self-consciousness*; or rather, the object appears only as *abstract* consciousness and man only as *self-consciousness*. The various forms of estrangement which occur are therefore merely different forms of consciousness and self-consciousness. Since abstract consciousness, which is how the object is conceived, is *in itself* only one moment in the differentiation of self-consciousness, the result of the movement is the identity of self-consciousness and consciousness, absolute knowledge, the movement of abstract thought no longer directed outwards but proceeding only within itself; i.e., the result is the dialectic of pure thought.

The importance of Hegel's *Phenomenology* and its final result – the dialectic of negativity as the moving and producing principle – lies in the fact that Hegel conceives the self-creation of man as a process, objectification as loss of object [*Entgegenständlichung*], as alienation and as supersession of this alienation; that he therefore grasps the nature of *labour* and conceives objective man – true, because real man – as the result of his *own labour*. The *real, active* relation of man to himself as a species-being, or the realization of himself as a real species-being, i.e. as a human being, is only possible if he really employs all his *species-powers* – which again is only possible through the co-operation of mankind and as a result of history – and treats them as objects, which is at first only possible in the form of estrangement.

We shall now demonstrate in detail the one-sidedness and the limitations of Hegel, as observed in the closing chapter of the *Phenomenology*. This chapter ('Absolute Knowledge') contains the concentrated essence of the *Phenomenology*, its relation to the dialectic, and Hegel's *consciousness* of both and their interrelations.

For the present, let us observe that Hegel adopts the standpoint of modern political economy. He sees *labour* as the *essence*, the self-confirming essence, of man; he sees only the positive and not the negative side of labour. Labour is *man's coming to be for himself* within *alienation* or as an *alienated man.* The only labour Hegel knows and recognizes is *abstract mental* labour. So that which above all constitutes the *essence* of philosophy – the *alienation of man who knows himself* or *alienated* science that *thinks* itself – Hegel grasps as its essence, and is therefore able to bring together the separate elements of previous philosophies and present his philosophy as *the* philosophy. What other philosophers did – that they conceived separate moments of nature and of man's life as moments of self-consciousness, indeed, of abstract self-consciousness – this Hegel *knows* by *doing* philosophy. Therefore his science is absolute.

Let us now proceed to our subject.

'*Absolute Knowledge*'. *The last chapter of the* Phenomenology.

The main point is that the *object* of *consciousness* is nothing else but *self-consciousness*, or that the object is only *objectified self-consciousness*, self-consciousness as object. (The positing of man = self-consciousness.)

It is therefore a question of surmounting the *object of consciousness. Objectivity* as such is seen as an *estranged* human relationship which does not correspond to *human nature*, to self-consciousness. The *re-appropriation* of the objective essence of man, produced in the form of estrangement as something alien, therefore means transcending not only *estrangement* but also *objectivity*. That is to say, man is regarded as a *non-objective, spiritual* being.

Hegel describes the process of *surmounting the object of consciousness* in the following way:

The *object* does not only show itself as *returning* into the *self* (according to Hegel that is a *one-sided* conception of the movement, a conception which grasps only one side). Man is equated with self. But the self is only *abstractly* conceived man, man produced by abstraction. Man *is* self [*selbstisch*]. His eyes, his ears, etc., have the *quality of self*; each one of his essential powers has this quality of *self*. But therefore it is quite wrong to say that *self-consciousness* has eyes, ears, essential powers. *Self-consciousness* is rather a quality of human nature, of the human eye, etc.; human nature is not a quality of *self-consciousness*.

The self abstracted and fixed for itself is man as *abstract egoist*, *egoism* raised to its pure abstraction in thought. (We shall come back to this later.)

For Hegel *human nature*, *man*, is equivalent to *self-consciousness*. All estrangement of human nature is therefore *nothing* but *estrangement of self-consciousness*. Hegel regards the estrangement of self-consciousness not as the *expression*, reflected in knowledge and in thought, of the *real* estrangement of human nature. On the contrary, *actual* estrangement, estrangement which appears real, is in its innermost hidden nature – which philosophy first brings to light – nothing more than the *appearance* of the estrangement of real human nature, of *self-consciousness*. The science which comprehends this is therefore called *phenomenology*. All re-appropriation of estranged objective being therefore appears as an incorporation into self-consciousness; the man who takes hold of his being is *only* the self-consciousness which takes hold of objective being. The return of the object into the self is therefore the re-appropriation of the object.

Expressed *comprehensively*, the *surmounting of the object of consciousness* means:

(1) That the object as such presents itself to consciousness as something disappearing.

(2) That it is the alienation of self-consciousness which establishes thingness [*Dingheit*].

(3) That this alienation has not only a *negative* but also a *positive* significance.

(4) That this significance is not only *for us* or in itself, but *for self-consciousness itself*.

(5) *For self-consciousness* the negative of the object, its own supersession of itself, has a *positive* significance – or self-consciousness *knows* the nullity of the object – in that self-consciousness alienates itself, for in this alienation it establishes *itself* as object or establishes the object as itself, for the sake of the indivisible unity of *being-for-itself*.

(6) On the other hand, this other moment is also present in the process, namely, that self-consciousness has superseded and taken back into itself this alienation and objectivity, and is therefore *at home* in *its* other-being *as such*.

(7) This is the movement of *consciousness*, and consciousness is therefore the totality of its moments.

(8) Similarly, consciousness must have related itself to the object in terms of the totality of its determinations, and have grasped it in terms of each of them. This totality of determinations makes the object *intrinsically* [*an sich*] a *spiritual being*, and it becomes that in reality for consciousness through the apprehending of each one of these determinations as determinations of *self* or through what we earlier called the spiritual attitude towards them.[2]

ad (1) That the object as such presents itself to consciousness as something disappearing is the above-mentioned *return of the object into the self*.

ad (2) The *alienation of self-consciousness* establishes *thingness*. Because man is equivalent to self-consciousness, his alienated objective being or *thingness* (that which is an *object for him*, and the only true object for him is that which is an essential object, i.e. his *objective* essence; since it is not *real man*, and therefore not *nature*, for man is *human nature*, who becomes as such the subject, but only the abstraction of man, self-consciousness, thingness can only be alienated self-consciousness) is the equivalent of *alienated self-consciousness*, and *thingness* is established by this alienation. It is entirely to be expected that a living, natural being equipped and endowed with objective, i.e. material essential powers should have *real* natural *objects* for the objects of its being, and that its self-alienation should take the form of the establishment of a *real*, objective world, but as something *external* to it, a world which does not belong to its being and which overpowers it. There is nothing incomprehensible or mysterious about that. It would only be mysterious if the contrary were true. But it is equally clear that a *self-consciousness*, through its alienation, can only establish *thingness*, i.e. an abstract thing, a thing of abstraction and not a *real* thing. It is also clear that thingness is therefore in no way something *independent* or *substantial vis-à-vis* self-consciousness; it is a mere creature, a *postulate* of self-consciousness. And what is postulated, instead of confirming itself, is only a confirmation of

2. These eight points are taken almost word for word from the chapter 'Absolute Knowledge' of Hegel's *Phenomenology of Mind.*

the act of postulating; an act which, for a single moment, concentrates its energy as product and *apparently* confers upon that product – but only for a moment – the role of an independent, real being.

When real, corporeal *man*, his feet firmly planted on the solid earth and breathing all the powers of nature, establishes his real, objective *essential powers* as alien objects by externalization [*Entäusserung*], it is not the *establishing* [*Setzen*] which is subject; it is the subjectivity of *objective* essential powers whose action must therefore be an *objective* one. An objective being acts objectively, and it would not act objectively if objectivity were not an inherent part of its essential nature. It creates and establishes only objects because it is established by objects, because it is fundamentally *nature*. In the act of establishing it therefore does not descend from its 'pure activity' to the *creation* of *objects*; on the contrary, its *objective* product simply confirms its *objective* activity, its activity as the activity of an objective, natural being.

Here we see how consistent naturalism or humanism differs both from idealism and materialism and is at the same time their unifying truth. We also see that only naturalism is capable of comprehending the process of world history.

Man is directly a *natural being*. As a natural being and as a living natural being he is on the one hand equipped with *natural powers*, with *vital powers*, he is an *active* natural being; these powers exist in him as dispositions and capacities, as *drives*. On the other hand, as a natural, corporeal, sensuous, objective being he is a *suffering*, conditioned and limited being, like animals and plants. That is to say, the *objects* of his drives exist outside him as *objects* independent of him; but these objects are objects of his *need*, essential objects, indispensable to the exercise and confirmation of his essential powers. To say that man is a *corporeal*, living, real, sensuous, objective being with natural powers means that he has *real*, *sensuous objects* as the object of his being and of his vital expression, or that he can only *express* his life in real, sensuous objects. To *be* objective, natural and sensuous and to have object, nature and sense outside oneself, or to be oneself object, nature and sense for a third person is one and the same thing. *Hunger* is a natural *need*; it therefore requires a *nature* and an *object* outside itself in order to satisfy and still itself. Hunger is the acknowledged need of my body for an *object* which exists outside itself and which is indispensable to its integration and to the expression of its essential nature. The sun is an *object* for the plant, an indispensable object which confirms its life, just as the plant is an object for the sun, an *expression* of its life-awakening power and its *objective* essential power.

A being which does not have its nature outside itself is not a natural being and plays no part in the system of nature. A being which has no object outside itself is not an objective being. A being which is not itself an object for a third being has no being for its *object*, i.e. it has no objective relationships and its existence is not objective.

A non-objective being is a *non-being*.

Imagine a being which is neither an object itself nor has an object. In the first place, such a being would be the *only* being; no other being would exist outside it, it would exist in a condition of solitude. For as soon as there are objects outside me, as soon as I am not *alone*, I am *another*, a reality *other* than the object outside me. For this third object I am therefore a *reality* other than it, i.e. *its* object. A being which is not the object of another being therefore presupposes that *no* objective being exists. As soon as I have an object, this object has me for its object. But a non-objective being is an unreal, non-sensuous, merely thought, i.e. merely conceived being, a being of abstraction. To be *sensuous*, i.e. to be real, is to be an object of sense, a *sensuous* object, and thus to have sensuous objects outside oneself, objects of one's sense perception. To be sensuous is to *suffer* (to be subjected to the actions of another).

Man as an objective sensuous being is therefore a *suffering* being, and because he feels his suffering [*Leiden*], he is a *passionate* [*leidenschaftliches*] being. Passion is man's essential power vigorously striving to attain its object.

But man is not only a natural being; he is a *human* natural being; i.e. he is a being for himself and hence a *species-being*, as which he must confirm and realize himself both in his being and in his knowing. Consequently, *human* objects are not natural objects as they immediately present themselves, nor is *human sense*, in its immediate and objective existence, *human* sensibility and human objectivity. Neither objective nor subjective nature is immediately present in a form adequate to the *human* being. And as everything natural must *come into being*, so man also has his process of origin in *history*. But for him history is a conscious process, and hence one which consciously supersedes itself. History is the true natural history of man. (We shall return to this later.)

Thirdly, since this establishing of thingness is itself only an appearance, an act which contradicts the nature of pure activity, it must be superseded once again and thingness must be denied.

ad 3, 4, 5, 6.

(3) This alienation of consciousness has not only a *negative* but also a *positive* significance, and (4) it has this positive significance not only *for us* or in itself, but for consciousness itself.

(5) *For self-consciousness* the negative of the object or its own supersession of itself has a *positive* significance – or self-consciousness *knows* the nullity of the object – in that self-consciousness alienates *itself*, for in this alienation it *knows* itself as object or, for the sake of the indivisible unity of *being-for-itself*, the object as itself. (6) On the other hand the other moment is also present in the process, namely, that self-consciousness has superseded and taken back into itself this alienation and objectivity, and is therefore *at home* in its *other-being as such*.

To recapitulate. The appropriation of estranged objective being or the supersession of objectivity in the form of *estrangement* – which must proceed from indifferent otherness to real, hostile estrangement – principally means for Hegel the supersession of *objectivity*, since it is not the *particular* character of the object but its *objective* character which constitutes the offence and the estrangement as far as self-consciousness is concerned. The object is therefore negative, self-superseding, a *nullity*. This nullity of the object has not only a negative but also a *positive* significance for consciousness, for it is precisely the *self-confirmation* of its non-objectivity and *abstraction*. For *consciousness itself* the nullity of the object therefore has a positive significance because it *knows* this nullity, the objective being, as its *self-alienation*; because it knows that this nullity exists only as a result of its own self-alienation . . .

The way in which consciousness is, and in which something is for it, is *knowing*. Knowing is its only act. Hence something comes to exist for consciousness in so far as it *knows* that *something*. Knowing is its only objective relationship. It knows the nullity of the object, i.e. that the object is not distinct from it, the non-existence of the object for it, in that it knows the object as its own *self-alienation*; that is, it knows itself – i.e. it knows knowing, considered as an object – in that the object is only the *appearance* of an object, an illusion, which in essence is nothing more than knowing itself which has confronted itself with itself and hence with a *nullity*, a something which has *no* objectivity outside knowing. Knowing knows that when it relates itself to an object it is only *outside* itself, alienates itself; that it only *appears* to itself as an object, or rather, that what appears to it as an object is only itself.

On the other hand, says Hegel, this other moment is also present in the process, namely, that self-consciousness has superseded and taken back into itself this alienation and objectivity, and is therefore *at home* in its *other-being as such*.

This discussion is a compendium of all the illusions of speculation.

Firstly, consciousness – self-consciousness – is *at home* in its *other-being as such*. It is therefore, if we here abstract from Hegel's abstraction and talk instead of self-consciousness, of the self-consciousness of man, *at home in its other-being as such*. This implies, for one thing, that consciousness – knowing as knowing, thinking as thinking – claims to be the direct *opposite* of itself, claims to be the sensuous world, reality, life – thought over-reaching itself in thought (Feuerbach).[3] This aspect is present in so far as consciousness as mere consciousness is offended not by estranged objectivity but by *objectivity as such*.

Secondly it implies that self-conscious man, insofar as he has acknowledged and superseded the spiritual world, or the general spiritual existence of his world, as self-alienation, goes on to re-affirm it in this alienated form and presents it as his true existence, restores it and claims to be *at home in his other-being as such*.

3. In his *Grundsätze der Philosophie der Zukunft* (§30) Feuerbach writes: 'Hegel is a thinker who *over-reaches* himself in thought'.

Thus, for example, having superseded religion and recognized it as a product of self-alienation, he still finds himself confirmed in *religion* as *religion.* Here *is* the root of Hegel's *false* positivism or of his merely *apparent* criticism: it is what Feuerbach calls the positing, negating and re-establishing of religion or theology, but it needs to be conceived in a more general way. So reason is at home in unreason as unreason. Man, who has realized that in law, politics, etc., he leads an alienated life, leads his true human life in this alienated life as such. Self-affirmation, self-confirmation in *contradiction* with itself and with the knowledge and the nature of the object is therefore true *knowledge* and true *life.*

Therefore there can no longer be any question about a compromise on Hegel's part with religion, the state, etc., since this untruth is the untruth of his principle.

If I *know* religion as *alienated* human self-consciousness, then what I know in it as religion is not my self-consciousness but my alienated self-consciousness confirmed in it. Thus I know that the self-consciousness which belongs to the essence of my own self is confirmed not in *religion* but in the *destruction* and *supersession* of religion.

In Hegel, therefore, the negation of the negation is not the confirmation of true being through the negation of apparent being. It is the confirmation of apparent being or self-estranged being in its negation, or the negation of this apparent being as an objective being residing outside man and independent of him, and its transformation into the subject.

The act of superseding therefore plays a special role in which negation and preservation (affirmation) are brought together.

Thus, for example, in Hegel's *Philosophy of Right*, *private right* superseded equals *morality*, morality superseded equals *family*, family superseded equals *civil society*, civil society superseded equals *state* and state superseded equals *world history.* In *reality* private right, morality, family, civil society, state, etc., continue to exist, but have become *moments* and modes of human existence which are meaningless in isolation but which mutually dissolve and engender one another. They are *moments of movement.*

In their real existence this character of *mobility* is hidden. It first appears, is first revealed, in thought and in philosophy.

Hence my true religious existence is my existence in the *philosophy of religion*, my true political existence is my existence in the *philosophy of right*, my true natural existence is my existence in the *philosophy of nature*, my true artistic existence is my existence in the *philosophy of art* and my true *human* existence is my *existence in philosophy*. Similarly, the true existence of religion, state, nature and art is the *philosophy* of religion, nature, the state and art. But if the philosophy of religion, etc., is for me the true existence of religion, then I am truly religious only as a *philosopher of religion*, and I therefore deny *real* religiosity and the really *religious* man. But at the same time I *confirm* them, partly in my own existence or in the alien existence which I oppose to them – for this *is* merely their *philosophical* expression – and partly in their particular and original form, for I regard them as merely *apparent* other-being, as allegories, forms of their own true existence concealed under sensuous mantles, i.e. forms of my *philosophical* existence.

Similarly, *quality* superseded equals *quantity*, quantity superseded equals *measure*, measure superseded equals *essence*, essence superseded equals *appearance*, appearance superseded equals *reality*, reality superseded equals the *concept*, the concept superseded equals *objectivity*, objectivity superseded equals the *absolute idea*, the absolute idea superseded equals *nature*, nature superseded equals *subjective* spirit, subjective spirit superseded equals *ethical* objective spirit, ethical spirit superseded equals *art*, art superseded equals *religion*, religion superseded equals *absolute knowledge*.

On the one hand this act of superseding is the act of superseding an entity of thought; thus, private property as *thought* is superseded in the *thought* of morality. And because thought imagines itself to be the direct opposite of itself, i.e. *sensuous reality*, and therefore regards its own activity as *sensuous*, *real* activity, this supersession in thought, which leaves its object in existence in reality, thinks it has actually overcome it. On the other hand, since the object has now become a moment of thought for the thought which is doing the superseding, it is regarded in its real existence as a confirmation of thought, of self-consciousness, of abstraction.

From one aspect the existence which Hegel *supersedes* in

philosophy is therefore not *real* religion, state, nature, but religion already in the form of an object of knowledge, i.e. *dogmatics*; hence also *jurisprudence*, *political science* and *natural science*. From this aspect he therefore stands in opposition both to the *actual* being and to the immediate non-philosophical *science* or non-philosophical *concepts* of this being. He therefore contradicts their current conceptions.

From the other aspect the man who is religious, etc., can find his final confirmation in Hegel.

We should now examine the *positive* moments of the Hegelian dialectic, within the determining limits of estrangement.

(a) *The act of superseding* as an objective movement which *re-absorbs* alienation into itself. This is the insight, expressed within estrangement, into the *appropriation* of objective being through the supersession of its alienation; it is the estranged insight into the *real objectification* of man, into the real appropriation of his objective being through the destruction of the *estranged* character of the objective world, through the supersession of its estranged mode of existence, just as atheism as the supersession of God is the emergence of theoretical humanism, and communism as the supersession of private property the vindication of real human life as man's property, the emergence of practical humanism. Atheism is humanism mediated with itself through the supersession of religion; communism is humanism mediated with itself through the supersession of private property. Only when we have superseded this mediation – which is, however, a necessary pre-condition – will *positive* humanism, positively originating in itself, come into being.

But atheism and communism are no flight, no abstraction, no loss of the objective world created by man or of his essential powers projected into objectivity, no impoverished regression to unnatural, primitive simplicity. They are rather the first real emergence, the realization become real for man, of his essence as something real.

Therefore, in grasping the *positive* significance of the negation which has reference to itself, even if once again in estranged form, Hegel grasps man's self-estrangement, alienation of being, loss of objectivity and loss of reality as self-discovery, expression of being, objectification and realization. In short, he sees labour – within abstraction – as man's *act of self-creation* and man's relation to himself as an alien being and the manifestation of himself as an alien being as the emergence of *species-consciousness* and *species-life*.

(b) But in Hegel, apart from or rather as a consequence of the inversion we have already described, this act appears, firstly, to be *merely formal* because it is abstract and because human nature itself is seen only as *abstract thinking being*, as self-consciousness.

And secondly, because the conception is *formal* and *abstract*, the supersession of alienation becomes a confirmation of alienation. In other words, Hegel sees this movement of *self-creation* and *self-objectification* in the form of *self-alienation* and *self-estrangement* as the *absolute* and hence the final *expression of human life* which has itself as its aim, is at rest in itself and has attained its own essential nature.

This movement in its abstract form as dialectic is therefore regarded as *truly human life*. And since it is still an abstraction, an estrangement of human life, it is regarded as a *divine process*, but as the divine process of man. It is man's abstract, pure, absolute being (as distinct from himself), which itself passes through this process.

Thirdly, this process must have a bearer, a subject; but the subject comes into being only as the result; this result, the subject knowing itself as absolute self-consciousness, is therefore *God, absolute spirit, the self-knowing and self-manifesting idea.* Real man and real nature become mere predicates, symbols of this hidden, unreal man and this unreal nature. Subject and predicate therefore stand in a relation of absolute inversion to one another; a *mystical subject–object* or *subjectivity encroaching upon the object*, the *absolute subject* as a *process*, as a *subject* which *alienates* itself and returns to itself from alienation, while at the same time re-absorbing this alienation, and the subject as this process; pure, *ceaseless* revolving within itself.

First, the formal and abstract conception of man's act of self-creation or self-objectification.

Because Hegel equates man with self-consciousness, the estranged object, the estranged essential reality of man is nothing but consciousness, nothing but the thought of estrangement, its *abstract* and hence hollow and unreal expression, *negation*. The supersession of alienation is therefore likewise nothing but an abstract, hollow supersession of that hollow abstraction, the *negation of the negation*. The inexhaustible, vital, sensuous, concrete activity of self-objectification is therefore reduced to its mere abstraction, *absolute negativity*, an abstraction which is then given permanent form as such and conceived as independent activity, as activity itself. Since this so-called negativity is nothing more than the *abstract*, *empty* form of that real living act, its content can only be a *formal* content, created by abstraction from all content. Consequently there are general, abstract *forms of abstraction* which fit every content and are therefore indifferent to all content; forms of thought and logical categories torn away from *real* mind and *real* nature. (We shall expound the *logical* content of absolute negativity later.)

Hegel's positive achievement in his speculative logic is to present *determinate concepts*, the universal *fixed thought-forms* in their independence of nature and mind, as a necessary result of the universal estrangement of human existence, and thus also of human thought, and to comprehend them as moments in the process of abstraction. For example, *being* superseded is essence, essence superseded is the concept, the concept superseded is . . . the absolute idea. But what is the absolute idea? It is compelled to supersede its own self again, if it does not wish to go through the whole act of abstraction once more from the beginning and to reconcile itself to being a totality of abstractions or a self-comprehending abstraction. But the abstraction which comprehends itself as abstraction knows itself to be nothing; it must relinquish itself, the abstraction, and so arrives at something which is its exact opposite, *nature*. Hence the whole of the *Logic* is proof of the fact that abstract thought is nothing for itself, that the absolute idea is nothing for itself and that only *nature* is something.

The absolute idea, the abstract idea which '*considered* from the aspect of its unity with itself is *intuition* [*Anschauen*]',[4] and which 'in its own absolute truth *resolves* to let the moment of its

4. See Hegel (1830), p. 222.

particularity or of initial determination and other-being, the *immediate idea*, as its reflection, *issue freely from itself as nature*',[5] this whole idea, which conducts itself in such a strange and baroque fashion, and which has caused the Hegelians such terrible headaches, is purely and simply *abstraction*, i.e. the abstract thinker; abstraction which, taught by experience and enlightened as to its own truth, resolves under various conditions – themselves false and still abstract – to *relinquish itself* and to establish its other-being, the particular, the determinate, in place of its self-pervasion [*Beisichsein*], non-being, universality and indeterminateness; to let *nature*, which it concealed within itself as a mere abstraction, as a thing of thought, *issue freely from itself*, i.e. to abandon abstraction and to take a look at nature, which exists *free* from abstraction. The abstract idea, which directly becomes *intuition*, is quite simply nothing more than abstract thought which relinquishes itself and decides to engage in *intuiting*. This entire transition from logic to philosophy of nature is nothing more than the transition – so difficult for the abstract thinker to effect, and hence described by him in such a bizarre manner – from *abstracting* to *intuiting*. The *mystical* feeling which drives the philosopher from abstract thinking to intuition is *boredom*, the longing for a content.

The man estranged from himself is also the thinker estranged from his *essence*, i.e. from his natural and human essence. His thoughts are therefore fixed phantoms existing outside nature and man. In his *Logic* Hegel has locked up all these phantoms, conceiving each of them firstly as negation, i.e. as *alienation* of *human* thought, and secondly as negation of the negation, i.e. as supersession of this alienation, as a *real* expression of human thought. But since this negation of the negation is itself still trapped in estrangement, what this amounts to is in part the restoration of these fixed phantoms in their estrangement and in part a failure to move beyond the final stage, the stage of self-reference in alienation, which is the true existence of these phantoms.[6] Insofar

5. ibid.

6. That is, Hegel substitutes the act of abstraction revolving within itself for these fixed abstractions; in so doing he has the merit, first of all, of having revealed the source of all these inappropriate concepts which originally

as this abstraction apprehends itself and experiences an infinite boredom with itself, we find in Hegel an abandonment of abstract thought which moves solely within thought, which has no eyes, teeth, ears, anything, and a resolve to recognize *nature* as being and to go over to intuition.

But *nature* too, taken abstractly, for itself, and fixed in its separation from man, is *nothing* for man. It goes without saying that the abstract thinker who decides on intuition, intuits nature abstractly. Just as nature lay enclosed in the thinker in a shape which even to him was shrouded and mysterious, as an absolute idea, a thing of thought, so what he allowed to come forth from himself was simply this *abstract nature*, nature as a thing of thought – but with the significance now of being the other-being of thought, real, intuited nature as distinct from abstract thought. Or, to put it in human terms, the abstract thinker discovers from intuiting nature that the entities which he imagined he was creating out of nothing, out of pure abstraction, in a divine dialectic, as the pure products of the labour of thought living and moving within itself and never looking out into reality, are nothing more than *abstractions* from *natural forms*. The whole of nature only repeats to him in a sensuous, external form the abstractions of logic. He *analyses* nature and these abstractions again. His intuiting of nature is therefore only the act of confirmation of his abstraction from the intuition of nature, a conscious re-enactment of the process by which he produced his abstraction. Thus, for example, Time is equated with Negativity referred to itself.[7] In the natural form, superseded Movement as Matter corresponds to superseded Becoming as Being. Light is the *natural* form of *Reflection-in-itself*. Body as *Moon* and *Comet* is the *natural* form of the *antithesis*

---

belonged to separate philosophers, of having combined them and of having created as the object of criticism the exhaustive range of abstraction rather than one particular abstraction. We shall later see why Hegel separates thought from the *subject*; but it is already clear that if man is not human, then the expression of his essential nature cannot be human, and therefore that thought itself could not be conceived as an expression of man's being, of man as a human and natural subject, with eyes, ears, etc., living in society, in the world and in nature. [*Marx's note.*]

7. See Hegel, op. cit., p. 225.

which, according to the *Logic*, is the *positive grounded upon itself* and the *negative* grounded upon itself. The Earth is the *natural* form of the logical *ground*, as the negative unity of the antithesis, etc.

Nature as nature, i.e. insofar as it is sensuously distinct from the secret sense hidden within it, nature separated and distinct from these abstractions is *nothing*, a *nothing proving itself to be nothing*, it is *devoid of sense*, or only has the sense of an externality to be superseded.

'In the finite-*teleological* view is to be found the correct premise that nature does not contain the absolute end within itself.'[8]

Its end is the confirmation of abstraction.

'Nature has revealed itself as the idea in the *form* of *other-being*. Since the *idea* in this form is the negative of itself or *external to itself*, nature is not only external relative to this idea, but *externality* constitutes the form in which it exists as nature.'[9]

Externality here should not be understood as *self-externalizing sensuousness* accessible to light and to sensuous man. It is to be taken in the sense of alienation, a flaw, a weakness, something which ought not to be. For that which is true is still the idea. Nature is only the *form* of its *other-being*. And since abstract thought is the *essence*, that which is external to it is in essence something merely *external*. The abstract thinker recognizes at the same time that *sensuousness*, *externality* in contrast to thought which moves and lives *within itself*, is the essence of nature. But at the same time he expresses this antithesis in such a way that this *externality of nature*, its *antithesis* to thought, is its *defect* and that insofar as it is distinct from abstraction it is a defective being. A being which is defective not only for me, not only in my eyes, but in itself, has something outside itself which it lacks. That is to say, its essence is something other than itself. For the abstract thinker nature must therefore supersede itself, since it is already posited by him as a potentially *superseded* being.

For us, mind has *nature* as its *premise*, since it is nature's *truth* and therefore its *absolute primus*. In this truth nature has *disappeared*, and mind has yielded as the idea which has attained being-for-itself, whose

8. ibid. 9. ibid., p. 227.

object as well as *subject* is *the concept*. This identity is *absolute negativity*, for whereas in nature the concept has its perfect external objectivity, in this its alienation has been superseded and the concept has become identical with itself. It is this identity only in that it is a return from nature.[10]

Revelation, as the *abstract idea*, is unmediated transition to, the *coming-to-be* of, nature; as the revelation of the mind which is free it is the *establishing* of nature as *its own* world; an establishing which, as reflection, is at the same time a *presupposing* of the world as independently existing nature. Revelation in its concept is the creation of nature as the mind's being, in which it procures the affirmation and truth of its freedom.

'The *absolute* is *mind*: this is the highest definition of the absolute.'[11]

References

BAUER, B. (1841–2), *Kritik der Evangelischen Geschichte der Synoptiker*, vols. 1–2, Leipzig; vol. 3, Brunswick.

BAUER, B. (1842), *Die gute Sache der Freiheit und meine eigene Angelegenheit*, Zürich and Winterthur, pp. 193 ff.

BAUER, B. (1843), *Das entdeckte Christentum: Eine Erinnerung an das achtzehnte Jahrhundert und ein Beitrag zur Krisis des neunzehnten*, Zürich and Winterthur.

FEUERBACH, L. (1843), *Grundsätze der Philosophie der Zukunft*, Zürich and Winterthur.

HEGEL, G. W. F. (1830) *Encyclopädie der philosophischen Wissenschaften in brundarise* (3rd ed.), Heidelberg, p. 222.

RUGE, A. (ed.) (1843), *Anekdota zur neuesten deutschen Philosophie und Publizistik*, Zürich and Winterthur, vol. 2, p. 62.

10. ibid., p. 392. 11. ibid., p. 393.

3 Karl Marx

The Fetishism of Commodities

Excerpt from Karl Marx, *Capital*, vol. 1, first published in 1867, tr. Ben Fowkes, Penguin Books (in association with *New Left Review*), 1976, pp. 163–77.

A commodity appears at first sight an extremely obvious, trivial thing. But its analysis brings out that it is a very strange thing, abounding in metaphysical subtleties and theological niceties. So far as it is a use-value, there is nothing mysterious about it, whether we consider it from the point of view that by its properties it satisfies human needs, or that it first takes on these properties as the product of human labour. It is absolutely clear that, by his activity, man changes the forms of the materials of nature in such a way as to make them useful to him. The form of wood, for instance, is altered if a table is made out of it. Nevertheless the table continues to be wood, an ordinary, sensuous thing. But as soon as it emerges as a commodity, it is transformed into a thing which transcends sensuousness. It not only stands with its feet on the ground, but, in relation to all other commodities, it stands on its head, and evolves out of its wooden brain grotesque ideas, far more wonderful than if it were to begin dancing of its own free will.[1]

The mystical character of the commodity does not therefore arise from its use-value. Just as little does it proceed from the nature of the determinants of value. For in the first place, however varied the useful kinds of labour, or productive activities, it is a physiological fact that they are functions of the human organism,

1. One may recall that China and the tables began to dance when the rest of the world appeared to be standing still – *pour encourager les autres*.*

* To encourage the others. A reference to the simultaneouse mergence, in the 1850s, of the Taiping revolt in China and the craze for spiritualism which swept over upper-class German society. The rest of the world was 'standing still' in the period of reaction immediately after the defeat of the 1848 Revolutions.

and that each such function, whatever may be its nature or its form, is essentially the expenditure of human brain, nerves, muscles and sense organs. Secondly, with regard to the foundation of the quantitative determination of value, namely the duration of that expenditure or the quantity of labour, this is quite palpably different from its quality. In all situations, the labour-time it costs to produce the means of subsistence must necessarily concern mankind, although not to the same degree at different stages of development.[2] And finally, as soon as men start to work for each other in any way, their labour also assumes a social form.

Whence, then, arises the enigmatic character of the product of labour, as soon as it assumes the form of a commodity? Clearly, it arises from this form itself. The quality of the kinds of human labour takes on a physical form in the equal objectivity of the products of labour as values; the measure of the expenditure of human labour-power by its duration takes on the form of the magnitude of the value of the products of labour; and finally the relationships between the producers, within which the social characteristics of their labours are manifested, take on the form of a social relation between the products of labour.

The mysterious character of the commodity form consists therefore simply in the fact that the commodity reflects back the social characteristics of men's own labour as objective characteristics of the products of labour themselves, as the socio-natural properties of these things. Hence it also reflects back the social relation of the producers to the sum total of labour as a social relation between objects, a relation which leads an existence outside the producers. Through this substitution, the products of labour become commodities, sensuous things which are at the same time supra-sensible or social. In the same way, the impression made by a thing on the optic nerve is perceived not as a subjective excitation of that nerve but as the objective form of a thing outside the eye. In the act of seeing, of course, light is really transmitted from one thing, the external object, to another thing,

2. Among the ancient Germans the size of a piece of land was measured according to the labour of a day; hence the acre was called *Tagwerk*, *Tagwanne* (*jurnale*, or *terra jurnalis*, or *diornalis*), *Mannwerk*, *Mannskraft*, *Mannsmaad*, *Mannshauet*, etc. See von Maurer (1854), p. 129 ff.

the eye. It is a physical relation between physical things. As against this, the commodity-form, and the value-reaction of the products of labour within which it appears, have absolutely no connection with the physical nature of the commodity and the material [*dinglich*] relations arising out of this. It is nothing but the definite social relation between men themselves which assumes here, for them, the fantastic form of a relation between things. In order, therefore, to find an analogy we must take flight into the misty realm of religion. There the products of the human brain appear as autonomous figures endowed with a life of their own, which enter into relations both with each other and with the human race. So it is in the world of commodities with the products of men's hands. I call this the fetishism which attaches itself to the products of labour as soon as they are produced as commodities, and is therefore inseparable from the production of commodities.

As the foregoing analysis has already demonstrated, this fetishism of the world of commodities arises from the peculiar social character of the labour which produces them.

Objects of utility become commodities only because they are the products of the labour of private individuals who work independently of each other. The sum total of the labour of all these private individuals forms the aggregate labour of society. Since the producers do not come into social contact until they exchange the products of their labour, the specific social characteristics of their private labours appear only within this exchange. In other words, the labour of the private individual manifests itself as an element of the total labour of society only through the relations which the act of exchange establishes between the products, and, through their mediation, between the producers. To the producers, therefore, the social relations between their private labours appear as what they are, i.e. they do not appear as direct social relations between persons in their work, but rather as material [*dinglich*] relations between persons and social relations between things.

It is only by being exchanged that the products of labour acquire a socially uniform objectivity as values, which is distinct from their sensuously varied objectivity as articles of utility. This division of the product of labour into a useful thing and a thing possessing value appears in practice only when exchange has already acquired an extension and an importance great enough to allow useful things to be produced for the purpose of being exchanged, so that their character as values has already to be taken into consideration during production. From this moment on, the labour of the individual producer acquires a twofold social character. On the one hand, it must, as a definite useful kind of labour, satisfy a definite social need, and thus maintain its position as an element of the total labour, as a branch of the social division of labour, which originally sprang up spontaneously. On the other hand, it can satisfy the manifold needs of the individual producer himself only insofar as every particular kind of useful private labour can be exchanged with, i.e. counts as the equal of every other kind of useful private labour. Equality in the full sense between different kinds of labour can be arrived at only if we abstract from their real inequality, if we reduce them to the characteristic they have in common, that of being the expenditure of human labour power, of human labour in the abstract. The private producer's brain reflects this twofold social character of his labour only in the forms which appear in practical intercourse, in the exchange of products. Hence the socially useful character of his private labour is reflected in the form that the product of labour has to be useful, and the social character of the equality of the various kinds of labour is reflected in the form of the common character, as values, possessed by these materially different things, the products of labour.

Men do not therefore bring the products of their labour into relation with each other as values because they see these objects merely as the material integuments of homogeneous human labour. The reverse is true: by equating their different products to each other in exchange as values, they equate their different kinds of labour as human labour. They do this without being aware of it.[3] Value, therefore, does not have its description

3. Therefore, when Galiani said: Value is a relation between persons ('*La Ricchezza è una ragione tra due persone*') he ought to have added: a relation concealed beneath a material shell. (Galiani, *Della Moneta*, p. 221, Vol. 3 of Custodi's collection, 1803).

branded on its forehead; it rather transforms every product of labour into a social hieroglyphic. Later on, men try to decipher the hieroglyphic, to get behind the secret of their own social product: for the characteristic which objects of utility have of being values is as much men's social product as is their language. The belated scientific discovery that the products of labour, insofar as they are values, are merely the material expressions of the human labour expended to produce them, marks an epoch in the history of mankind's development, but by no means banishes the semblance of objectivity possessed by the social characteristics of labour. Something which is only valid for this particular form of production, the production of commodities, namely the fact that the specific social character of private labours carried on independently of each other consists in their equality as human labour, and, in the product, assumes the form of the existence of value, appears to those caught up in the relations of commodity production (and this is true both before and after the above-mentioned scientific discovery) to be just as ultimately valid as the fact that the scientific dissection of the air into its component parts left the atmosphere itself unaltered in its physical configuration.

What initially concerns producers in practice when they make an exchange is how much of some other product they get for their own; in what proportions can the products be exchanged? As soon as these proportions have attained a certain customary stability, they appear to result from the nature of the products, so that, for instance, one ton of iron and two ounces of gold appear to be equal in value, in the same way as a pound of gold and a pound of iron are equal in weight, despite their different physical and chemical properties. The value character of the products of labour becomes firmly established only when they act as magnitudes of value. These magnitudes vary continually, independently of the will, foreknowledge and actions of the exchangers. Their own movement within society has for them the form of a movement by things, and these things, far from being under their control, in fact control them. The production of commodities must be fully developed before the scientific conviction emerges, from experience itself, that all the different kinds of private labour (which are carried on independently of each other, and yet, as spontaneously developed branches of the social division of labour, are in a situation of all-round dependence on each other) are continually being reduced to the quantitative proportions in which society requires them. The reason for this reduction is that in the midst of the accidental and ever-fluctuating exchange relations between the products, the labour-time socially necessary to produce them asserts itself as a regulative law of nature. In the same way, the law of gravity asserts itself when a person's house collapses on top of him.[4] The determination of the magnitude of value by labour-time is therefore a secret hidden under the apparent movements in the relative values of commodities. Its discovery destroys the semblance of the merely accidental determination of the magnitude of the value of the products of labour, but by no means abolishes its material form.

Reflection on the forms of human life, hence also scientific analysis of those forms, takes a course directly opposite to their real development. Reflection begins *post festum*,* and therefore with the results of the process of developments ready to hand. The forms which stamp products as commodities and which are therefore the preliminary requirements for the circulation of commodities, already possess the fixed quality of natural forms of social life before man seeks to give an account, not of their historical character, for in his eyes they are immutable, but of their content and meaning. Consequently, it was solely the analysis of the prices of commodities which led to the determination of the magnitude of value, and solely the common expression of all commodities in money which led to the establishment of their character as values. It is however precisely this finished form of the world of commodities – the money form – which conceals the social character of private labour and the social relations between the individual workers, by making those relations appear as relations between material objects, instead of revealing them plainly. If I state that coats or boots stand in a relation to linen because the latter is the universal incarnation of abstract human labour, the absurdity of

4. 'What are we to think of a law which can only assert itself through periodic crises? It is just a natural law based on the unconsciousness of the participants' (Engels, 1844).

* After the feast, i.e. after the events reflected on have taken place.

the statement is self-evident. Nevertheless, when the producers of coats and boots bring these commodities into a relation with linen, or with gold or silver (and this makes no difference here), as the universal equivalent, the relation between their own private labour and the collective labour of society appears to them in exactly this absurd form.

The categories of bourgeois economics consist precisely of forms of this kind. They are forms of thought which are socially valid, and therefore objective, for the relations of production belonging to this historically determined mode of social production, i.e. commodity production. The whole mystery of commodities, all the magic and necromancy that surrounds the products of labour on the basis of commodity production, vanishes therefore as soon as we come to other forms of production.

As political economists are fond of Robinson Crusoe stories,[5] let us first look at Robinson on his island. Undemanding though he is by nature, he still has needs to satisfy, and must therefore perform useful labours of various kinds: he must make tools, knock together furniture, tame llamas, fish, hunt and so on. Of his prayers and the like, we take no account here, since our friend takes pleasure in them and sees them as recreation. Despite the diversity of his productive functions, he knows that they are only different forms of activity of one and the same Robinson, hence only different modes of human labour. Necessity itself compels him to divide his time with precision between his different func-

5. Even Ricardo has his Robinson Crusoe stories. 'Ricardo's primitive fisherman and primitive hunter are from the outset owners of commodities who exchange their fish and game in proportion to the labour-time which is materialized in these exchange-values. On this occasion he slips into the anachronism of allowing the primitive fisherman and hunter to calculate the value of their implements in accordance with the annuity tables used on the London Stock Exchange in 1817. Apart from bourgeois society, the only social system with which Ricardo was acquainted seems to have been the "parallelograms of Mr Owen".'* (Karl Marx [1859], pp. 38, 39 [English translation, p. 60].)

* The 'parallelograms' were the utopian socialist Robert Owen's suggestion for the most appropriate layout for a workers' settlement, made in *A New View of Society* (1813) and immediately seized on by his critics. Ricardo's reference to them is from his *On Protection of Agriculture*, London, 1822, p. 21.

tions. Whether one function occupies a greater space in his total activity than another depends on the magnitude of the difficulties to be overcome in attaining the useful effect aimed at. Our friend Robinson Crusoe learns this by experience, and having saved a watch, ledger, ink and pen from the shipwreck, he soon begins, like a good Englishman, to keep a set of books. His stock-book contains a catalogue of the useful objects he possesses, of the various operations necessary for their production, and finally of the labour-time that specific quantities of these products have on average cost him. All the relations between Robinson and these objects that form his self-created wealth are here so simple and transparent that even Mr Sedley Taylor* could understand them. And yet those relations contain all the essential determinants of value.

Let us now transport ourselves from Robinson's island, bathed in light, to medieval Europe, shrouded in darkness. Here, instead of the independent man, we find everyone dependent – serfs and lords, vassals and suzerains, laymen and clerics. Personal dependence characterizes the social relations of material production as much as it does the other spheres of life based on that production. But precisely because relations of personal dependence form the given social foundation, there is no need for labour and its products to assume a fantastic form different from their reality. They take the shape, in the transactions of society, of services in kind and payments in kind. The natural form of labour, its particularity – and not, as in a society based on commodity production, its universality – is here its immediate social form. The *corvée* can be measured by time just as well as the labour which produces commodities, but every serf knows that what he expends in the service of his lord is a specific quantity of his own personal labour-power. The tithe owed to the priest is more clearly apparent than his blessing. Whatever we may think, then, of the different roles in which men confront each other in such a society, the social relations between individuals in the performance of their labour

* The original German has here 'Herr M. Wirth', chosen by Marx as a run-of-the-mill vulgar economist and propagandist familiar to German readers. Engels introduced 'Mr Sedley Taylor', a Cambridge don against whom he polemicized in his preface to the fourth German edition.

appear at all events as their own personal relations, and are not disguised as social relations between things, between the products of labour.

For an example of labour in common, i.e. directly associated labour, we do not need to go back to the spontaneously developed form which we find at the threshold of the history of all civilized peoples.[6] We have one nearer to hand in the patriarchal rural industry of a peasant family which produces corn, cattle, yarn, linen and clothing for its own use. These things confront the family as so many products of its collective labour, but they do not confront each other as commodities. The different kinds of labour which create these products – such as tilling the fields, tending the cattle, spinning, weaving and making clothes – are already in their natural form social functions; for they are functions of the family, which, just as much as a society based on commodity production, possesses its own spontaneously developed division of labour. The distribution of labour within the family and the labour-time expended by the individual members of the family, are regulated by differences of sex and age as well as by seasonal variations in the natural conditions of labour. The fact that the expenditure of the individual labour-powers is measured by duration appears here, by its very nature, as a social characteristic of labour itself, because the individual labour-powers, by their very nature, act only as instruments of the joint labour-power of the family.

Let us finally imagine, for a change, an association of free men, working with the means of production held in common, and expending their many different forms of labour-power in full self-

6. 'A ridiculous notion has spread abroad recently that communal property in its natural, spontaneous form is specifically Slav, indeed exclusively Russian. In fact, it is the primitive form that we can prove to have existed among Romans, Teutons and Celts, and which indeed still exists to this day in India, in a whole range of diverse patterns, albeit sometimes only as remnants. A more exact study of the Asiatic, and specifically of the Indian form of communal property would indicate the way in which different forms of spontaneous, primitive communal property give rise to different forms of its dissolution. Thus the different original types of Roman and Germanic private property can be deduced from the different forms of Indian communal property.' (Karl Marx [1859], p. 10 [English translation, p. 33].)

awareness as one single social labour force. All the characteristics of Robinson's labour are repeated here, but with the difference that they are social instead of individual. All Robinson's products were exclusively the result of his own personal labour and they were therefore directly objects of utility for him personally. The total product of our imagined association is a social product. One part of this product serves as fresh means of production and remains social. But another part is consumed by the members of the association as means of subsistence. This part must therefore be divided amongst them. The way this division is made will vary with the particular kind of social organization of production and the corresponding level of social development attained by the producers. We shall assume, but only for the sake of a parallel with the production of commodities, that the share of each individual producer in the means of subsistence is determined by his labour-time. Labour-time would in that case play a double part. Its apportionment in accordance with a definite social plan maintains the correct proportion between the different functions of labour and the various needs of the associations. On the other hand, labour-time also serves as a measure of the part taken by each individual in the common labour, and of his share in the part of the total product destined for individual consumption. The social relations of the individual producers, both towards their labour and the products of their labour, are here transparent in their simplicity, in production as well as in distribution.

For a society of commodity producers, whose general social relation of production consists in the fact that they treat their products as commodities, hence as values, and in this material [*sachlich*] form bring their individual, private labours into relation with each other as homogeneous human labour, Christianity with its religious cult of man in the abstract, more particularly in its bourgeois development, i.e. in Protestantism, Deism, etc., is the most fitting form of religion. In the ancient Asiatic, Classical-antique, and other such modes of production, the transformation of the product into a commodity, and therefore men's existence as producers of commodities, plays a subordinate role, which however increases in importance as these communities approach nearer and nearer to the stage of their dissolution. Trading nations, properly so called, exist only in the interstices of the ancient world, like the gods of Epicurus in the *intermundia*,* or Jews in the pores of Polish Society. Those ancient social organisms of production are much more simple and transparent than those of bourgeois society. But they are founded either on the immaturity of man as an individual, when he has not yet torn himself loose from the umbilical cord of his natural species-connection with other men, or on direct relations of dominance and servitude. They are conditioned by a low stage of development of the productive powers of labour and correspondingly limited relations between men within the process of creating and reproducing their material life, hence also limited relations between man and nature. These real limitations are reflected in the ancient worship of nature, and in other elements of tribal religions. The religious reflections of the real world can, in any case, vanish only when the practical relations of everyday life between man and man, and man and nature, generally present themselves to him in a transparent and rational form. The veil is not removed from the countenance of the social life-process, i.e. the process of material production, until it becomes production by freely associated men, and stands under their conscious and planned control. This, however, requires that society possess a material foundation, or a series of material conditions of existence, which in their turn are the natural and spontaneous product of a long and tormented historical development.

Political economy has indeed analysed, however incompletely,[7]

* According to the Greek philosopher Epicurus (*c.* 341–*c.* 270 B.C.), the gods existed only in the *intermundia*, or spaces between different worlds, and had no influence on the course of human affairs. Very few of the writings of Epicurus have been preserved in the original Greek, and this particular idea survived only by being included in Cicero, *De natura deorum*, Book I, Section 18.

7. The insufficiency of Ricardo's analysis of the magnitude of value – and his analysis is by far the best – will appear from the third and fourth books of this work.* As regards value in general, classical political economy in fact nowhere distinguishes explicitly and with a clear awareness between labour as it appears in the value of a product, and the same labour as it appears in

* These are the books that appeared, respectively, as Volume 3 of *Capital*, and *Theories of Surplus Value* (3 volumes).

value and its magnitude, and has uncovered the content concealed within these forms. But it has never once asked the question why this content has assumed that particular form, that is to say, why labour is expressed in value, and why the measurement of labour by its duration is expressed in the magnitude of value of the product.[8] These formulas, which bear the unmistakable stamp of

---

the product's use-value. Of course the distinction is made in practice, since labour is treated sometimes from its quantitative aspect, and at other times qualitatively. But it does not occur to the economists that a purely quantitative distinction between the kinds of labour presupposes their qualitative unity or equality, and therefore their reduction to abstract human labour. For instance, Ricardo declares that he agrees with Destutt de Tracy when the latter says: 'As it is certain that our physical and moral faculties are alone our original riches, the employment of those faculties, labour of some kind, is our original treasure, and it is always from this employment – that all those things are created which we call riches . . . It is certain too, that all those things only represent the labour which has created them, and if they have a value, or even two distinct values, they can only derive them from that' (the value) 'of the labour from which they emanate' (Ricardo [1821], p. 334).† We would here only point out that Ricardo imposes his own more profound interpretation on the words of Destutt. Admittedly Destutt does say that all things which constitute wealth 'represent the labour which has created them', but, on the other hand, he also says that they acquire their 'two different values' (use-value and exchange-value) from 'the value of labour'. He thus falls into the commonplace error of the vulgar economists, who assume the value of one commodity (here labour) in order in turn to use it to determine the values of other commodities. But Ricardo reads him as if he had said that labour (not the value of labour) is represented both in use-value and in exchange-value. Nevertheless, Ricardo himself makes so little of the dual character of the labour represented in this twofold way that he is forced to spend the whole of his chapter 'Value and Riches, their Distinctive Properties' on a laborious examination of the trivialities of a J. B. Say. And at the end he is therefore quite astonished to find that while Destutt agrees with him that labour is the source of value, he nevertheless also agrees with Say about the concept of value.‡

†Destutt de Tracy (1826), pp. 35, 36.

‡'I am sorry to be obliged to add that M. de Tracy supports, by his authority, the definitions which M. Say has given of the words "value", "riches", and "utility"' (Ricardo [1821], p. 334).

8. It is one of the chief failings of classical political economy that it has never succeeded, by means of its analysis of commodities, and in particular of their value, in discovering the form of value which in fact turns value into exchange-value. Even its best representatives, Adam Smith and Ricardo, treat the form of value as something of indifference, something external to

belonging to a social formation in which the process of production has mastery over man, instead of the opposite, appear to the political economists' bourgeois consciousness to be as much a self-evident and nature-imposed necessity as productive labour itself. Hence the pre-bourgeois forms of the social organization of production are treated by political economy in much the same way as the Fathers of the Church treated pre-Christian religions.[9]

---

the nature of the commodity itself. The explanation for this is not simply that their attention is entirely absorbed by the analysis of the magnitude of value. It lies deeper. The value form of the product of labour is the most abstract, but also the most universal form of the bourgeois mode of production; by that fact it stamps the bourgeois mode of production as a particular kind of social production of a historical and transitory character. If then we make the mistake of treating it as the eternal natural form of social production, we necessarily overlook the specificity of the value form, and consequently of the commodity form together with its further developments, the money form, the capital form, etc. We therefore find that economists who are entirely agreed that labour-time is the measure of the magnitude of value, have the strangest and most contradictory ideas about money, that is, about the universal equivalent in its finished form. This emerges sharply when they deal with banking, where the commonplace definitions of money will no longer hold water. Hence there has arisen in opposition to the classical economists a restored Mercantilist System (Ganilh, etc.), which sees in value only the social form, or rather its insubstantial semblance. Let me point out once and for all that by classical political economy I mean all the economists who, since the time of W. Petty, have investigated the real internal framework [*Zusammenhang*] of bourgeois relations of production, as opposed to the vulgar economists who only flounder around within the apparent framework [*Zusammenhang*] of those relations, ceaselessly ruminate on the materials long since provided by scientific political economy, and seek there plausible explanations of the crudest phenomena for the domestic purposes of the bourgeoisie. Apart from this, the vulgar economists confine themselves to systematizing in a pedantic way, and proclaiming for everlasting truths, the banal and complacent notions held by the bourgeois agents of production about their own world, which is to them the best possible one.

9. 'The economists have a singular way of proceeding. For them, there are only two kinds of institutions, artificial and natural. The institutions of feudalism are artificial institutions, those of the bourgeoisie are natural institutions. In this they resemble the theologians, who likewise establish two kinds of religion. Every religion which is not theirs is an invention of men, while their own is an emanation of God . . . Thus there has been history, but there is no longer any' (Karl Marx [1847], p. 113). Truly comical is

The degree to which some economists are misled by the fetishism attached to the world of commodities or by the objective appearance of the social characteristics of labour is shown, among other things, by the dull and tedious dispute over the part played by nature in the formation of exchange-value. Since exchange-value is a definite social manner of expressing the labour bestowed

---

M. Bastiat, who imagines that the ancient Greeks and Romans lived by plunder alone. For if people live by plunder for centuries there must, after all, always be something there to plunder; in other words, the objects of plunder must be continually reproduced. It seems, therefore, that even the Greeks and the Romans had a process of production, hence an economy, which constituted the material basis of their world as much as the bourgeois economy constitutes that of the present-day world. Or perhaps Bastiat means that a mode of production based on the labour of slaves is based on a system of plunder? In that case he is on dangerous ground. If a giant thinker like Aristotle could err in his evaluation of slave labour, why should a dwarf economist like Bastiat be right in his evaluation of wage-labour? I seize this opportunity of briefly refuting an objection made by a German-American publication to my work *Zur Kritik der Politischen Ökonomie*, 1859. My view is that each particular mode of production, and the relations of production corresponding to it at each given moment, in short 'the economic structure of society', is 'the real foundation, on which arises a legal and political superstructure and to which correspond definite forms of social consciousness', and that 'the mode of production of material life conditions the general process of social, political and intellectual life'.* In the opinion of the German-American publication this is all very true for our own times, in which material interests are preponderant, but not for the Middle Ages, dominated by Catholicism, nor for Athens and Rome, dominated by politics. In the first place, it strikes us as odd that anyone should suppose that these well-worn phrases about the Middle Ages and ancient world were unknown to anyone else. One thing is clear: the Middle Ages could not live on Catholicism, nor could the ancient world on politics. On the contrary, it is the manner in which they gained their livelihood which explains why in one case politics, in the other case Catholicism, played the chief part. For the rest, one needs no more than a slight acquaintance with, for example, the history of the Roman Republic, to be aware that its secret history is the history of landed property. And then there is Don Quixote, who long ago paid the penalty for wrongly imagining that knight errantry was compatible with all economic forms of society.

* These passages are taken from the Preface to *A Contribution to the Critique of Political Economy*, written in January 1859 (English translation, pp. 20–21).

on a thing, it can have no more natural content than has, for example, the rate of exchange.

Since the commodity-form is the most general and the most undeveloped form of bourgeois production, it makes its appearance at an early date, though not in the same predominant, and therefore characteristic, manner as nowadays. Hence its fetish character is still relatively easy to penetrate. But when we come to more concrete forms, even this appearance of simplicity vanishes. Where did the illusions of the Monetary System come from? The adherent of the Monetary System did not see gold and silver as representing money as a social relation of production, but in the form of natural objects with peculiar social properties. And what of modern political economy, which looks down so disdainfully on the Monetary System? Does not its fetishism become quite palpable when it deals with capital? How long is it since the disappearance of the Physiocratic illusion that ground rent grows out of the soil, not out of society?

But, to avoid anticipating, we will content ourselves here with one more example relating to the commodity-form itself. If commodities could speak, they would say this: our use-value may interest men, but it does not belong to us as objects. What does belong to us as objects, however, is our value. Our own intercourse as commodities proves it. We relate to each other merely as exchange values. Now listen how those commodities speak through the mouth of the economist:

'Value (i.e. exchange-value) is a property of things, riches (i.e. use-value) of man. Value, in this sense, necessarily implies exchanges, riches do not.'[10]

'Riches (use-value) are the attribute of man, value is the attribute of commodities. A man or a community is rich, a pearl or a diamond is valuable . . . A pearl or a diamond is valuable as a pearl or diamond.'[11]

So far no chemist has ever discovered exchange-value either in a pearl or a diamond. The economists who have discovered this chemical substance, and who lay special claim to critical acumen, nevertheless find that the use-value of material objects belongs to

10. Anon. (1821), p. 16. 11. S. Bailey (1837), p. 165.

them independently of their material properties, while their value, on the other hand, forms a part of them as objects. What confirms them in this view is the peculiar circumstance that the use-value of a thing is realized without exchange, i.e. in the direct relations between the thing and man, while, inversely, its value is realized only in exchange, i.e. in a social process. Who would not call to mind at this point the advice given by the good Dogberry to the night-watchman Seacoal?*

'To be a well-favoured man is the gift of fortune; but reading and writing comes by nature.'[12]

References

ANON (1821), *Observations on Some Verbal Disputes in Political Economy, Particularly Relating to Value, and to Supply and Demand*, London, p. 16.

BAILEY, S. (1837), *Money and Its Vicissitudes*, London.

CICERO, *De Natura Deorum*, Book 1, Section 18.

CUSTODI (1803), *Scritori Classici Italiana di Economia Politica, Parte Moderna*, Milan, vol. 3, p. 221.

DESTUTT DE TRACY, A. (1826), *Eléments d'Idéologie*, vols. 4 and 5, Paris.

ENGELS, F. (1844), 'Umrisse zu einer Kritik der Nationalökonomie', in the *Deutsche-Französische Jahrbüche*, Karl Marx and Arnold Ruge (ed.). Translated as 'Outlines of a Critique of Political Economy', and published as an appendix to *Economic and Philosophic Manuscripts*, tr. M. Milligan, London, 1959, pp. 175–209.

MARX, K. (1847), *Misère de la Philosophie. Réponse à la Philosophie de la Misère par M. Proudhon*, p. 113. Translated as *The Poverty of Philosophy*, Lawrence & Wishart, 1956, p. 105.

MARX, K. (1859), *Zur Kritik der Politischen Ökonomie*, Munich, pp. 10, 38, 39. Translated as *Critique of Political Economy*, Lawrence & Wishart, 1971, pp. 33, 60.

MAURER, G. L. VON (1854), *Einleitung zur Geschichte der Mark-, Hof-, usw. Verfassung*, Munich, p. 129 ff.

* In Shakespeare's comedy *Much Ado About Nothing*, Act 3, Scene 3.

12. Both the author of *Observations etc.*, and S. Bailey accuse Ricardo of converting exchange-value from something relative into something absolute. The reverse is true. He has reduced the apparent relativity which these things (diamonds, pearls, etc.) possess to the true relation hidden behind the appearance, namely their relativity as mere expressions of human labour. If the followers of Ricardo answer Bailey somewhat rudely, but by no means convincingly, this is because they are unable to find in Ricardo's own works any elucidation of the inner connection between value and the form of value, or exchange-value.

RICARDO, D. (1821), *The Principles of Political Economy*, 3rd ed., London, p. 334.
RICARDO, D. (1822), *On Protection of Agriculture*, London, p. 21.

4 Georg Lukács

The Changing Function of Historical Materialism

Excerpt from Georg Lukács, *History and Class Consciousness*, Merlin Press, 1971, pp. 223, 224–32, 237–9. First published in 1923.

The victory gained by the proletariat evidently confronts it with the task of perfecting as far as possible the intellectual weapons which have hitherto enabled it to hold its own in the class struggle. Among these weapons historical materialism is, of course, pre-eminent . . .

The most important function of historical materialism is to deliver a precise judgement on the capitalist social system, to unmask capitalist society. Throughout the class struggle of the proletariat, therefore, historical materialism has constantly been used at every point, where, by means of all sorts of ideological frills, the bourgeoisie had concealed the true situation, the state of the class struggle; it has been used to focus the cold rays of science upon these veils and to show how false and misleading they were and how far they were in conflict with the truth. For this reason the chief function of historical materialism did not lie in the elucidation of pure scientific knowledge, but in the field of action. Historical materialism did not exist for its own sake, it existed so that the proletariat could understand a situation and so that, armed with this knowledge, it could act accordingly.

In the capitalist era, then, historical materialism was an instrument of war. In consequence, the resistance offered to historical materialism by bourgeois thought was by no means simply a matter of narrow-mindedness. It was the expression of the bourgeoisie's correct class instinct as embodied in bourgeois historiography. It would be suicidal for the bourgeoisie to grant recognition to historical materialism. Any member of the bourgeoisie who admitted the scientific truth of historical materialism would thereby abandon his own class consciousness and with it the strength needed to defend the interests of his own class effectively. On the other hand, it would be no less suicidal for the proletariat to remain satisfied with the scientific value of historical materialism and to see in it nothing more than an instrument of knowledge. The essence of the class struggle of the proletariat can in fact be defined by its union of theory and practice so that knowledge leads to action without transition.

The survival of the bourgeoisie rests on the assumption that it never obtains a clear insight into the social pre-conditions of its own existence. A glance at the history of the nineteenth century reveals a profound and continuous parallel between the gradual growth of this self-knowledge and the decline of the bourgeoisie. At the end of the eighteenth century the bourgeoisie was ideologically strong and unbroken. The same thing was still true at the beginning of the nineteenth century when its ideology, the idea of bourgeois freedom and democracy had not yet been undermined from within by the natural workings of economics, and when the bourgeoisie could still hope, and moreover hope in good faith, that this democratic, bourgeois freedom and the supremacy of economics would one day lead to the salvation of all mankind.

The glory and the pathos of this faith does more than fill the history of the first bourgeois revolutions – above all the Great French Revolution. It is this, too, which confers upon the great scientific pronouncements of the bourgeois class (e.g. the economics of Adam Smith and Ricardo) their forthrightness and the strength to strive for the truth and to reveal what they have discovered without cloaking it.

The history of bourgeois ideology is the history of the destruction of this faith in its mission to save the world by making the whole of society bourgeois. From the time of Sismondi's theory of crisis and Carlyle's social criticism the process by which bourgeois ideology has undermined itself develops with constantly increasing intensity. What began as the reactionary feudal criticism of emergent capitalism develops increasingly, with the criticism between mutually hostile ruling classes into the self-criticism of the bourgeoisie and finally turns into its bad conscience when criticism is progressively concealed and kept secret. As Marx observes:

The bourgeoisie had a true insight into the fact that all the weapons which it had forged against feudalism turned their points against itself, that all the means of education which it had produced rebelled against its own civilisation, that all the gods which it had created had fallen away from it.[1]

For this reason the idea of class struggle is openly expressed twice in the history of bourgeois ideology. It is one of the determining factors in its 'heroic' period, in its vigorous struggle for social hegemony (above all in France where political and ideological conflicts were most acute), and it recurs in its last period of crisis and dissolution. The social theory of the great employers' associations, for example, is often the frank and even cynical expression of a class point of view. The final, imperialist, phase of capitalism is generally given to modes of self-expression that ideologically tear down veils and that produce in the ruling circles of the bourgeoisie an ever more explicit description of 'what is the case'. (Consider, for example, the ideology of the power-state in imperialist Germany and also the fact that the economy of the war and the post-war periods has forced the theoreticians of the bourgeoisie to see economic forms as consisting of something more than purely fetishistic relations and to concede that there is a connection between economics and the gratification of human wants.)

This is not to say that the limitations imposed on the bourgeoisie by its place in the process of production could be overcome, or that, like the proletariat, the bourgeoisie could henceforth start from a position of a true knowledge of the real driving forces of history. On the contrary, this lucidity with regard to individual problems or phases only makes the blindness *vis-à-vis* the totality stand out more clearly. For this 'lucidity' is on the one hand for 'internal use only'; the same progressive group of the bourgeoisie which saw through the economic ramifications of imperialism more clearly than many 'socialists' knows very well that this knowledge would be highly dangerous for sections of its own class, to say nothing of society as a whole. (Consider in this context the metaphysics of history that tends to accompany im-

1. Marx (1852 [English translation, p. 260]).

perialist theories of power.) But if this does in part point to a conscious deception it does, on the other hand, indicate something rather more than a simple deception. That is to say, the amalgam of 'clear insight' in the case of individual economic problems, with a fantastic and chaotic metaphysical view of the state, of society and of the historical process as a whole is the inevitable consequence of the class situation of the bourgeoisie and from this not even the most conscious strata are exempted. But whereas at the period of its ascendency the extreme limits of its understanding of society were still obscure and unconscious, today the objective disintegration of capitalist society is reflected in the total incoherence and irreconcilability of opinions joined together in one ideology.

In this we find expressed a – mostly unconscious and certainly unacknowledged – ideological capitulation to historical materialism. For the economic theories now being developed no longer have a purely bourgeois base, as they did in the age of classical economics. Precisely in countries like Russia where the growth of capitalism came relatively late and where, in consequence, there was a direct need for theoretical backing it turned out that the theory that did emerge bore a strongly 'Marxist' character. (Struve, Tugan-Baranovski, etc.) But the same phenomenon was observable at the same time in Germany (e.g. Sombart) and in other countries. And the theories of war-economy and planned economies show that this tendency is becoming stronger.

There is no contradiction in the fact that simultaneously – say, from Bernstein onwards – a section of socialist theory came more and more strongly under bourgeois influence. For even at the time clear-sighted Marxists realized that there was no question here of a conflict of aims within the workers' movement. With increasing frequency leading 'comrades' have crossed over openly into the bourgeois camp (the cases of Briand and Millerand, Parvus and Lensch are only the most notorious instances) and however this is to be judged from the standpoint of the proletariat, its meaning for the bourgeoisie is unmistakable: namely that it is incapable of defending its own position ideologically and with its own resources. It not only needs these renegades from the camp of the proletariat but also – and this is the main point at issue – it is unable to dispense with the scientific method of the proletariat, admittedly in a distorted form. The existence of the theoretical renegades from Bernstein to Parvus is doubtless the symptom of an ideological crisis within the proletariat; but at the same time it signifies the capitulation of the bourgeoisie before historical materialism.

For the proletariat fought capitalism by forcing bourgeois society into a self-knowledge which would inevitably make that society appear problematic to itself. *Parallel with the economic struggle a battle was fought for the consciousness of society. Now, to become conscious is synonymous with the possibility of taking over the leadership of society.* The proletariat is the victor in the class struggle not only on the level of power but, at the same time, in the battle for social consciousness, for in the last 50–60 years it has had increasing success in eroding bourgeois ideology and in evolving its own consciousness to the point where it becomes decisive for the whole of society.

Historical materialism is the most formidable weapon in this struggle. It is consequently just as much a function of the growth and disintegration of capitalist society as are other ideologies. This point has often been made with regard to historical materialism by bourgeois thinkers. A common argument against the validity of historical materialism and one regarded by bourgeois thought as decisive, is that the methods of historical materialism must be applied to itself. For it to be a valid system of thought it must be the case that every so-called ideological formation is a function of economic realities: and (as the ideology of the embattled proletariat) it, too, is *a fortiori* just such an ideology, and just such a function of capitalist society.

I believe that this objection can be upheld in part, but to concede it is not to the detriment of the scientific status of historical materialism. Historical materialism both can and must be applied to itself. But this must not be allowed to lead to total relativism, let alone to the conclusion that historical materialism is not the correct historical method. The substantive truths of historical materialism are of the same type as were the truths of classical economics in Marx's view: they are truths within a particular social order and system of production. As such, but only as such, their claim to validity is absolute. But this does not preclude the emergence of societies in which by virtue of their different social structures other categories and other systems of truth prevail. To what conclusion should we then come? Above all we must investigate the social premises of the substance of historical materialism just as Marx himself scrutinized the social and economic preconditions of the truths of classical economics.

The answer to this question can likewise be found in Marx. Historical materialism in its classical form (which has unfortunately only penetrated the general consciousness in a vulgarized form) means the *self-knowledge of capitalist society*. And this not only in the ideological sense outlined above. Rather is it the case that this ideological problem is itself nothing other than the intellectual expression of the objective economic situation. In this sense the decisive result of historical materialism is that the totality and the driving forces of capitalism cannot be grasped or conceptualized by the crude, abstract, unhistorical and external categories of the science of the bourgeoisie. Thus historical materialism is, in the first instance, a theory of bourgeois society and its economic structure. 'But in theory,' Marx observes,

> it is assumed that the laws of capitalist production operate in their pure form. In reality there exists only approximation; but this approximation is the greater, the more developed the capitalist mode of production and the less it is adulterated and amalgamated with survivals of former economic conditions.[2]

This correspondence of theory with reality can be seen in the fact that, on the one hand, the laws of economics inform the whole of society, but, on the other hand, they are able to function as pure 'laws of nature' by virtue of their purely economic power, i.e. without the aid of non-economic factors. Marx frequently emphasizes the distinction between capitalist and pre-capitalist societies as being the difference between a capitalism which is only just emerging and is therefore locked in struggle for the control of society and a capitalism which is already dominant. He says:

2. Marx (1887 [English translation, p. 172]).

the law of supply and demand of labour ... the dull compulsion of economic relations completes the subjection of the labourer to the capitalist. Direct, *extra-economic* force is of course still used, but *only exceptionally*. In the ordinary run of things, the labourer can be left to the 'natural laws of production' ... *It is otherwise during the historical genesis of capitalist production.*[3]

From this economic structure (which is found, of course, only as a tendency, but as a tendency which decisively conditions every theory), it follows that the different aspects of the social structure can and must become independent of each other and, thereby, conscious of themselves. The great upsurge of the theoretical sciences at the end of the eighteenth and the beginning of the nineteenth centuries, classical economics in England and classical philosophy in Germany show that these partial systems, these aspects of the structure and evolution of bourgeois society, have gained a consciousness of their autonomy. Economics, law and the state appear here as *closed* systems which control the whole of society by virtue of the perfection of their own power and by their own built-in laws. So that when individual scholars, such as Andler, attempt to prove that all the particular truths attributed to historical materialism were in fact discovered before Marx and Engels they miss the essential point and would be mistaken even if their demonstration were valid on all points; and this is, of course, far from being the case. For, as far as *method* is concerned, historical materialism was an epoch-making achievement precisely because it was able to see that these apparently quite independent, hermetic and autonomous systems were really aspects of a comprehensive whole and that their apparent independence could be transcended.

This semblance of independence, however, is no mere 'error' simply to be 'corrected' by historical materialism. It is rather the intellectual and conceptual expression of the objective social structure of capitalist society. To annul it and to transcend it means, therefore, to transcend capitalist society – in thought. It means anticipating its annulment by the accelerating power of thought. For this very reason, however, the annulled independence of the special systems is preserved within the rightly under-

3. Marx (1867 [English translation, p. 737]). My italics.

stood totality. That is to say, the right understanding of their lack of autonomy, their dependence on the economic structure of the whole of society entails the knowledge that this 'semblance' of independence, of cohesion and autonomy is a necessary part of the way in which they manifest themselves in capitalist society.

In pre-capitalist society the particular aspects of the economic process (as, for instance, interest-bearing capital and the production of commodities itself) remain separate from each other in a completely abstract way which permits neither an immediate interaction nor one that can be raised to the level of social-consciousness. On the other hand, some of these aspects join with each other or with non-economic factors in the economic process to form – within such social structures – an indissoluble unity (for example, handicraft and agriculture on the feudal manor, or tax and rent in Indian serfdom).

In capitalism, however, all the elements of the structure of society interact dialectically. Their apparent independence of each other, their way of concentrating themselves into self-regulating systems, the fetishistic semblance of autonomy, all this is – as an essential aspect of capitalism as understood by the bourgeoisie – the necessary transition to a proper and complete understanding of them. Only by taking these tendencies towards independence to their logical conclusion (a thing which bourgeois science, of course, never managed to do even during its best periods) can they be understood as being mutually interdependent and as belonging to and fitting into the totality of the economic structure of society.

The Marxist point of view which regards, e.g. the economic problems of capitalism no longer from the standpoint of the individual capitalist but from that of the classes, could be reached subjectively, in the context of the history of dogma, only as the continuation and the dialectic reversal of the purely capitalist outlook. On the other hand, the 'obedience of the phenomena to natural laws', which is claimed here, i.e. their complete independence of human will, knowledge and purpose, forms the objective pre-condition for their re-shaping at the hands of materialist dialectics. Problems like accumulation or average profit-rates, but also the relation of the state and the law to the total economy, show quite clearly how appearances which are constantly unmasking themselves are the historical and methodical pre-condition of the construction and application of historical materialism.

It is therefore no accident – as indeed it could hardly be otherwise when we are concerned with real truths about society – that historical materialism evolved into a scientific method around the middle of the nineteenth century. It is not the result of chance that social truths are always found when the soul of an age is revealed in them; the age in which the reality corresponding to the method becomes incarnate. For, as we have already explained, historical materialism is simply the self-knowledge of capitalist society.

Nor is it an accident that economics became an independent discipline under capitalism. Thanks to its commodity and communications arrangements capitalist society has given the whole of economic life an identity notable for its autonomy, its cohesion and its exclusive reliance on immanent laws. This was something quite unknown in earlier forms of society. For this reason, classical economics with its system of laws is closer to the natural sciences than to any other. The economic system whose essence and laws it investigates does in fact show marked similarities with the objective structure of that Nature which is the object of study of physics and the other natural sciences. It is concerned with relations that are completely unconnected with man's humanity and indeed with any anthropomorphisms – be they religious, ethical, aesthetic or anything else. Man appears in it only as an abstract number, as something which can be reduced to number or to numerical relations. Its concern, as Engels put it, is with laws that are only understood, not controlled, with a situation in which – to quote Engels again – the producers have lost control of the conditions of life of their own society. As a result of the objectification, the reification of society, their economic relations have achieved complete autonomy, they lead an independent life, forming a closed, self-validating system. Hence it is no accident that capitalist society became the classical terrain for the application of historical materialism . . .

To the degree to which capitalism carried out the socialization of all relations it became possible to achieve self-knowledge, the true, concrete self-knowledge of man as a *social being*. And this not merely in the sense that earlier, undeveloped thought had been unable to grasp this fact (which existed then also), just as it is clear that Copernican astronomy was true before Copernicus but had not been recognized as such. But the absence of such self-knowledge on the part of society is itself only the intellectual reflex of the fact that objective, economic socialization in this sense had not yet been established. The umbilical cord between man and nature had not yet been cut by the process of civilization. For every piece of historical knowledge is an act of self-knowledge. The past only becomes transparent when the present can practise self-criticism in an appropriate manner; 'as soon as it is ready for self-criticism to a certain extent, *dynamei* so to speak'.[4] Until that time the past must either be naïvely identified with the structure of the present or else it is held to be wholly alien, barbaric and senseless, beyond all understanding. Thus we see that the road to an understanding of pre-capitalist societies with a non-reified structure could not be opened up until historical materialism had perceived that the reification of all man's social relations is both a product of capitalism and hence also an ephemeral, historical phenomenon. (The connection between the scientific exploration of primitive society and Marxism is no mere accident.) For only now, with the prospect opening up of re-establishing non-reified relations between man and man and between man and nature, could those factors in primitive, pre-capitalist formations be discovered in which these (non-reified) forms were present – albeit in the service of quite different functions. And only now could the essential nature of these forms be understood without their being distorted by the mechanical application of the categories of capitalist society.

It was, therefore, no error to apply historical materialism in its classical form rigorously and unconditionally to the history of the nineteenth century. For in that century all the forces which impinged upon society functioned in fact purely as the forms of the 'objective spirit' become manifest. In pre-capitalist societies this was not really the situation. In such societies economic life did not yet possess that independence, that cohesion and imman-

4. Marx (1859 [English translation, pp. 301 et seq.]).

ence, nor did it have the sense of setting its own goals and being its own master that we associate with capitalist society.

It follows from this that historical materialism cannot be applied in quite the same manner to pre-capitalist social formations as to capitalism. Here we need much more complex and subtle analyses in order to show, on the one hand, what role was played from among all the forces controlling society by the *purely* economic forces in so far as they can be said to have existed in a 'pure' state in the strict sense of the word. And on the other hand to show the impact of these economic forces upon the other institutions of society. For this reason much greater caution is required when applying historical materialism to earlier societies than to changes in society in the nineteenth century. Connected with this is the fact that while the nineteenth century could only achieve self-knowledge by means of historical materialism, research into the structure of older societies conducted on historical materialist principles, e.g. into early Christianity or the early history of the Orient such as Kautsky has undertaken, has shown itself to be insufficiently subtle when compared with more recent scientific studies, and their analyses have generally not been able to do justice to their subject. Historical materialism has had its greatest successes in the analysis of social formations, of law and of related phenomena, e.g. strategy. For this reason studies such as those of Mehring's – one thinks here of the *Lessing Legend* – are profound and subtle when they are dealing with Napoleon's or Frederick the Great's organization of the army and the state. But they become much less definitive and exhaustive when he turns to the literary, scientific and religious institutions of the same epoch.

Vulgar Marxism has wholly neglected this distinction. Its application of historical materialism has succumbed to the same error that Marx castigated in the case of vulgar economics: it mistook purely historical categories, moreover categories relevant only to capitalist society, for eternally valid ones.

References

MARX, K. (1852), *The Eighteenth Brumaire of Louis Bonaparte*. In *Selected Writings*, vol. 1, T. B. Bottomore and M. Rubel (eds), C. A. Watts, 1956, p. 260.

MARX, K. (1859), *A Contribution to the Critique of Political Economy*. This edition published by Lawrence & Wishart, 1971, pp. 301 et seq.

MARX, K. (1867), *Capital*, vol. 1. This edition published by Lawrence & Wishart, 1970, p. 737. (My italics.)

MARX, K. (1887), *Capital*, vol. 3. This edition published by Lawrence & Wishart, 1972, p. 172.

Part Two
The Hermeneutic Tradition

Hermeneutics is the art of interpretation which aims to disclose an underlying coherence or sense in a text, or a text-analogue, whose meaning is in one way or another unclear. Whether beyond this it is possible to speak of a single science of hermeneutics is a matter of debate. Indeed, Ricoeur has suggested that there are two basically different hermeneutic styles, one of which views hermeneutics as the manifestation or restoration of a meaning addressed to the interpreter in the manner of a message or proclamation, while the other views it as a procedure of demystification, a reduction of illusion or lies (Reading 9).

Dilthey was the first to develop the view that in the sciences of man interpretation is essential to explanation. In attempting to demonstrate how reliable knowledge of historical experience is possible, he saw the decisive step as being that of showing how it was possible to make the transition from the life-experience of the individual to a historical experience which in principle could no longer be directly experienced by any individual (Reading 5). Gadamer, like Dilthey, wishes to show how meanings can be reconstituted in the act of interpretation, but he argues that Dilthey understood interpretation too much as a procedure or method. We cannot, in Gadamer's view, relate to historical tradition as to an object existing in apartness from us; the community which binds us to tradition is in constant process of being constituted by our own interpretative activity (Reading 6).

More recently a number of writers, within and outside the Critical Theory tradition, have brought once again to the fore the sense in which interpretation is essential to explanation in the sciences of man. Both Taylor and Lorenzer see the object of these sciences as the interpretation of inter-subjective meanings. Taylor argues that since human practices cannot be identified in abstraction from the language we use to describe, or to invoke, or to carry out those practices, the distinction between 'social reality' and 'the language of description of that social reality' is artificial; and that these inter-subjective meanings cannot be adequately grasped by mainstream political science, since what the latter lacks is the notion of a meaning as existing not simply for an individual (Reading 8). Likewise, Lorenzer stresses the transactional element inherent in all symbolizations: the symbols of language – both conscious and unconscious – always structure and imply certain types of inter-personal relationships which have a historical dimension. From this he arrives at the thesis that the neurotic individual is subject to a double alienation: he is caught in a private language which he does not perceive as private; and he is caught in repetitive patterns of action which he can neither understand nor correct because his language – that is, his capacity to operate symbols – has become corrupted (Reading 7).

5 Wilhelm Dilthey

The Rise of Hermeneutics

Excerpt from Wilhelm Dilthey, 'Die Entstehung der Hermeneutik', 1900; *Gesammelte Schriften*, Bd. V, B. G. Teubner, Leipzig and Berlin, 1923, pp. 317–20, 323–31. Translated by Thomas Hall.

In an earlier essay I discussed the representation of individuation in the human world, how it is produced by art, especially poetry. Now we are confronted by the question of the *scientific* knowledge of individuals, in fact of the great forms of singular human existence generally. Is such a knowledge possible and what means do we have to achieve it?

A question of the utmost importance. Our actions always presuppose the understanding of other people; a large part of human happiness arises from sympathy with other frames of mind; the whole of philological and historical science is based on the supposition that this sympathy with the individual can be raised to the level of objectivity. The historical awareness built on this supposition enables modern man to have humanity's entire past within him: he looks beyond all the confines of his own age to past cultures; he absorbs the power of these cultures and then enjoys their magic: from this his happiness is greatly increased. And if the systematic humanities (*Geisteswissenschaften*) derive general statutory relationships and all-embracing connections from this objective conception of the individual, then the processes of comprehension and interpretation still remain the basis for them too. Therefore in their security these sciences are as dependent as history on whether the comprehension of the individual can be raised to the state of *universality*. Thus a problem confronts us at the gateway to the Humanities which is peculiar to them as opposed to all knowledge of nature.

Certainly the Humanities have an advantage over all knowledge of nature in that their subject-matter is not a phenomenon given in the senses, a mere reflex of a real thing in a consciousness, but is itself immediate inner reality, and moreover a coherence experienced from within. Yet even from the way in which this reality is given in *inner experience* there arise great difficulties for its objective interpretation. These will not be discussed here. Furthermore, the inner experience whereby I become aware of my own circumstances can never bring my own individuality for itself to my consciousness. It is only in comparing myself with others that I experience the individual in me; only now do I become conscious of that in my own existence which differs from other people; and Goethe was only too right when he said that this, the most important of all our experiences, is very hard and that our insight into the extent, nature and limits of our powers will always be very imperfect. Existence outside ourselves, however, is given to us in the first instance only in sense data, in gestures, sounds and actions from outside. Only by a process of reproduction (*Nachbilden*) of that which comes into the senses in single signals do we complete this inner picture. We must transfer everything – material, structure, the most individual characteristics of this completion – from our own state of being. How then can an individually formed consciousness bring a strange and quite differently constituted individuality to objective cognition through such reproduction?

The process by which we come to know an inner picture (*ein Inneres*) through signs which are given from outside through the senses we call *understanding* (*Verstehen*). This is the everyday term; and a specific psychological terminology, which is so much needed, can arise only when every firmly established expression that is clear and usably defined is adhered to uniformly by all writers. The understanding of nature – *interpretatio naturae* – is a figurative expression. But the interpretation of one's own circumstances is also described by us improperly as understanding. I can easily say: I do not understand how I could behave in this way, indeed I do not understand myself any more. But in saying this I wish to say that an expression of my being which has appeared in the outside world seems to me like that of a stranger and that, as such, I cannot interpret it; or in the other case, that I have fallen into a state at which I must stare as if it were a strange one. Accordingly, we refer to understanding as the process by which, from signals given as sense-data, we perceive a psychic structure whose expression they are.

This understanding extends from the interpretation of childish babbling up to that of *Hamlet* or of the *Critique of Reason.* In stones, marble, musically formed sounds, in gestures, words and writing, in actions, economic systems and constitutions, it is the same human spirit which speaks to us and requires interpretation. And indeed the process of understanding must have common features everywhere, so far as it is determined by the common conditions and means of this mode of cognition. In these basic elements it is the same. If, for example, I wish to understand Leonardo, then the interpretation of actions, paintings, pictures and written works combines together in a homogeneous uniform process.

Understanding shows different levels. These are determined primarily by interest. If the interest is restricted, then so is the understanding. How impatiently we listen to many an argument; we only notice one point which is of practical importance for ourselves without having any interest in the inner life of the speaker. Whereas in other cases we strive, by every expression, every word, to penetrate into the inner life of the speaker. But even the most strenuous attention can only become a skilled process in which a controllable level of objectivity is reached, if the expression of life is fixed and we can return to it again and again. Such *skilled understanding of permanently fixed expressions of life is called exegesis or interpretation.* In this sense there is also an exegetic art which has as its subject-matter sculptures or paintings, and Friedrich August Wolf long ago called for archaeological hermeneutics and criticism. Welcker has advocated it and Preller sought to develop it. Yet Preller himself stresses that such interpretation of mute works is driven to seek clarification from literature.

Here lies the immeasurable significance of literature for our understanding of spiritual life and of history; in language alone the inner life of man finds its complete, exhaustive and objectively intelligible expression. Hence the art of understanding focuses on exegesis or *interpretation of those remnants of human existence which are contained in written works.*

The exegesis and the critical treatment, inseparably connected with this, of these remnants was accordingly the point of departure for philology. The essence of philology is *the personal art and virtuosity in such treatment of surviving written monuments*, and only in conjunction with this skill and its results can any other interpretation of monuments or historically-recorded actions develop. We can be mistaken with regard to the motives of people's actions in history, and these people themselves can spread a deceptive light over them. But the work of a great poet or discoverer, of a religious genius or a true philosopher, can only ever be the true expression of his soul. In this human society, filled with lies, such a work is always true and it is capable of a complete and objective interpretation, in contrast to every other utterance in fixed signs; indeed it immediately casts light on the other artistic monuments of an age and on the historical actions of contemporaries.

This art of interpretation has developed as gradually, regularly and slowly as has the experimental investigation of nature. It arose and survives in the individual virtuosity of the philologist. Thus it is naturally transferred to others, predominantly through personal contact with the great virtuoso of interpretation or with his work. But at the same time every art proceeds according to *rules*. These teach one how to overcome difficulties. They pass on the proceeds of personal skill. Therefore there arose early from the art of exegesis the *statement of its rules*. And out of the clash of these rules, out of the battle between different views about the interpretation of key works and the resulting need to establish these rules, there arose the science of hermeneutics. This *theory teaches the art of the exegesis of literary monuments.*

While this determines the possibility of universally-valid exegesis from the analysis of understanding, it finally advances to the *very general* problem with which this discussion began. Next to the analysis of inner experience appears the analysis of understanding, and both together demonstrate the *possibility* and *limits* of universally valid cognition for the human sciences (*Geisteswissenschaften*), insofar as the latter are determined by the way in which psychic facts are originally given to us.

I should like now to demonstrate this regular movement in the history of hermeneutics: how out of the demand for deep and universally valid understanding there arose philological virtuosity, from this the determination of rules, the classification of rules according to an aim, which was more closely determined by the position of science in a given era, until eventually, in the analysis of understanding, the certain point of departure was found for the prescribing of rules . . .

After the Renaissance, interpretation and the prescription of rules for interpretation entered a new phase. Men were separated from Classical and Christian Antiquity by language, conditions of life, and nationality. Henceforth, interpretation became – in contrast to the former practice in Rome – a transposition into an alien spiritual life by means of grammatical, factual and historical studies. And this new philology, polymaths and criticism frequently had to work only with second-hand information and fragments. Thus it had to be creative and constructive in a new way. And so philology, hermeneutics and criticism were raised to a higher level. An extensive hermeneutic literature has grown up in the last four centuries. It forms two main streams: for the classical and the biblical texts were the two great forces which men were striving to assimilate. The classical-philological method of prescribing rules termed itself '*ars critica*'. Such works, among which those of Scioppius, Clericus and the unfinished work of Valesius stand out, contained a theory of the hermeneutic art in their opening sections. Countless essays and prefaces dealt with *de interpretatione*. But we owe the final establishment of hermeneutics to biblical interpretation. The Canonic text was the *Clavis* of Flacius (1567).

In this work, the substance of the rules of interpretation hitherto discovered was, for the first time, connected with a theoretical structure by means of the *postulate* that a universal understanding must be attainable by proceeding according to these rules. Flacius was made conscious of this basic point of view, which in fact governs hermeneutics, by the battles of the sixteenth century. Flacius had to fight on two fronts. Both the Anabaptists and restored Catholicism proclaimed the obscurity of the scriptures. In opposing this, Flacius learned especially from Calvin's exegesis which had gone back frequently from actual interpretation to its basic principles. The most urgent task for a contemporary Lutheran was the refutation of the Catholic doctrine of tradition which had just then been newly formulated. In the argument against the Protestant scriptural principle, the right of tradition to determine the interpretation of scripture could be based only on the assertion that no adequate and universally acceptable interpretation could be derived from the scriptures themselves. The Council of Trent which sat from 1545 to 1563 dealt with these questions from its fourth session onwards, and in 1564 the first authentic issue of the Decretals appeared. Some time after the work of Flacius, Bellarmine, the representative of Tridentine Catholicism, attacked the intelligibility of the Bible very shrewdly in a polemical tract of 1581 and thereby sought to prove the necessity of tradition to supplement the Bible. In the context of these struggles, Flacius undertook the task of demonstrating hermeneutically the possibility of a universally valid interpretation. And in wrestling with this task he became aware of methods and rules for solving the problem which no earlier hermeneutics had produced.

If the interpreter comes across difficulties in his text then there is a sublime form of aid available to resolve them: the context of scripture found in thriving Christian practice. If we translate this from the dogmatic mode of thought into our own, then this hermeneutic value of religious experience is only a single instance of the principle according to which the exegesis on the basis of the factual context is contained as a factor in every process of interpretation. By the side of this religious principle of interpretation, however, there is also that of understanding. The most obvious of these is grammatical interpretation. But Flacius was the first to grasp the significance of the psychological or technical principle of exegesis, according to which a single section of the work must be interpreted from the intention and composition of the whole. And for this technical interpretation he was the first to make methodical use of the findings of rhetoric about the inner connectedness of a literary product, its composition and its affective elements. The reconstruction of Aristotelian rhetoric by Melancthon had paved the way for him in this respect. Flacius himself was conscious of having been the first to utilize this tool for the clear analysis of texts, an aid which is contained in the context, the aim, the proportion and congruence of individual parts or sections. He brings the hermeneutic value of these under a general aspect of the methodological theory. 'Everywhere else the individual parts of a whole receive their meaning from their relationship to this whole and its other parts.' He follows this inner form of a work right into its style and the individual affective elements and sketches subtle character portraits of the Pauline and Johannine styles. This was a great step forward, admittedly within the confines of the rhetorical conception. For every piece of writing for Melancthon and Flacius is constructed according to rules just as it must be understood according to rules. Every piece of writing is like a logical automaton which is clothed in style, imagery and figures of speech.

The formal defects of Flacius' work were overcome in Baumgarten's hermeneutics. Here, however, a second great theological-hermeneutic movement established itself. In Baumgarten's reports from a library in Halle the English Freethinkers and commentators on the Old Testament began, along with Dutch interpreters, to step out of ethnology into the German scene. Semler and Michaelis joined him and took part in his work. Michaelis was the first to apply a unified historical view of language, history, nature and law to the interpretation of the Old Testament. Semler, the predecessor of the great Christian Bauer, shattered the unity of the New Testament canon, set himself the proper task of comprehending each individual scriptural text according to its own local character, and then connected these writings in a new unity which is contained in the vivid historical conception of the struggles within primitive Christianity between the Jewish Christians and the Christians of a freer order. In his *Preparations for a Theological Hermeneutics* he traced the whole science with firm resolution back to two factors: interpretation from linguistic usage and from historical circumstances. With this the liberation of exegesis from dogma was completed and the grammatical-historical school was founded. The sensitive and cautious spirit of Ernesti then created the classical text for this new type of hermeneutics in the *Interpretes*. Schleiermacher too developed his own hermeneutics from his reading of this work. Nevertheless, even these steps forward were made within strict limits. In the hands of these exegetes the composition and thought-patterns of every text of an era were dissolved into the same threads: the range of ideas conditioned by the particular time and place. According to this pragmatic view of history, a religiously and morally identical human nature is restricted only by extraneous elements of time and place. It is unhistorical.

Hitherto, classical and biblical hermeneutics had followed a parallel course. Did not both have to be conceived of as applications of hermeneutics in general? Meier, the pupil of Wolf, took this step in his *Essay on a General Art of Interpretation* of 1757. He expressed the idea of his science in the most general of terms possible: it should lay down the rules which are to be observed in every interpretation of signs. But his book shows once again that one cannot invent new sciences according to views on architectonics and symmetry. Only blind windows arise in this way, through which no one can see. A truly effective hermeneutics could develop only when the virtuosity of philological interpretation is combined with genuine philosophical ability. Such a man was Schleiermacher.

The conditions under which he worked were as follows. Winckelmann's interpretation of works of art; Herder's brilliant empathy into the soul of eras and peoples; and that philology which tended towards the new aesthetic viewpoint pursued by Heyne, Friedrich August Wolf and his pupils, among whom Heindorf worked in the closest contact with Schleiermacher in the field of Platonic studies. All these elements were united in Schleiermacher with the procedure of German transcendental philosophy of going back beyond what is given in consciousness to a creative potential which, working uniformly and unconscious of itself, produces the entire form of the world in us. From precisely this combination of these two impulses there arose his particular art of interpretation and the definitive foundation of scientific hermeneutics.

Until then hermeneutics had been at best a framework of rules whose parts, the individual rules, were held together by the purpose of a universally valid interpretation. Hermeneutics had distinguished the functions which work together in this process of interpretation as the grammatical, historical, aesthetic-rhetorical, and factual exegesis. And, from the philological virtuosity of many centuries, it had brought to light the rules according to which these functions must work. Beyond these rules Schleiermacher now worked backwards to the analysis of understanding; that is, to the perception of this purposeful action itself; and from this perception he deduced the possibility of a universally valid interpretation, its aids, limits and rules. But he could analyse understanding as a reproduction (*Nachbilden*), as reconstruction, only in its living connection to the process of literary production itself. In the living view of the creative process in which a vital literary work arises, he recognized the condition for the perception of the other process which understands from written signs the whole of a work and from this the intention and mentality of its creator.

But a new psychological-historical conception was needed to solve the problem thus posed. We have traced the relationship which is involved here from the connection which existed between Greek interpretation and rhetoric as the artistic theory of a definite kind of literary production. But the conception of both processes had always remained a logical-rhetorical one. The categories according to which it was carried out were always those of making, logical connection, logical order, and then the dressing of this logical product with style and figures of speech and imagery. Now, however, totally new concepts are used to understand a literary product. Now there exists a homogeneous and creatively effective potential which, unconscious of its own effect and formation, takes up and develops the initial impetus behind a work. Receptivity and spontaneous formation are inseparable in it. Individuality is at work here, right down to the fingertips and in the individual words. Its supreme manifestation is the external and internal form of the literary work. And now confronting this work is the insatiable demand to complement its own individuality through the views of others. Understanding and interpretation are always thus active in life itself; and they achieve their perfection in the skilled exegesis of vital works and of the context of those works in the mind of their creator. This was the new view in the particular form which it assumed in Schleiermacher's mind.

Therein lay, however, a further condition for this great project of a universal hermeneutics: namely, that the new psychological-historical views were fully developed by Schleiermacher's contemporaries and by him personally to the philological art of interpretation. Just at that time the German spirit in Schiller, Wilhelm von Humboldt and the Schlegel brothers, had turned from poetic production to the interpretative understanding of the historical world. It was a powerful movement; Böckh, Dissen, Welcker, Hegel, Ranke, Savigny were influenced by it. Friedrich Schlegel became Schleiermacher's guide towards the art of philology. The concepts which guided Schlegel in his brilliant works on Greek poetry, Goethe and Boccaccio, were those of the inner form of the work, the history of the writer's development, and the whole of literature articulated in itself. And beyond such single achievements of a reconstructive philological art there lay for him the plan of a science of criticism, an '*ars critica*', which should be based on a theory of productive literary potential. This plan came very close to Schleiermacher's hermeneutics and criticism.

And from Schlegel there now also came the plan of the Plato translation. In the course of this the technique of the new interpretation was formed which Böckh and Dissen then applied to Pindar. Plato must be understood as a philosophical artist. The aim of interpretation is to establish the unity between the character of Plato's philosophizing and the artistic form of his works. Philosophy is still living, intimately bound up with conversation; its written representation is but a fixation for the aid of memory. Thus it must be dialogue and, what is more, of such an artistic form that it makes necessary a personal reconstruction of the living train of thought. At the same time, however, according to the strict unity of this Platonic thought, each dialogue must continue what has gone earlier, prepare what will come later, and continue to spin the threads of the various parts of the philosophy. If one pursues these relationships between the dialogues there arises a connection between the major works which supplies the key to Plato's basic intention. Only when this artistically formed connection has been grasped does true comprehension of Plato come about, according to Schleiermacher; compared with this the identification of the chronology of his works is less significant, although this itself will coincide to a large extent with the connection. Böckh was able to say in his famous review that this masterpiece was the first to make Plato accessible to philological science.

Now for the first time a masterly philosophical power was combined, in Schleiermacher's mind, with this kind of philological virtuosity. He was trained in transcendental philosophy, which was the first system to present adequate means for the general formulation and solution of the hermeneutic problem: thus arose the general science and theory of exegesis.

In the autumn of 1804, after reading Ernesti's *Interpretes*, Schleiermacher developed the first outline of his theory, as he wanted to open his course of lectures on exegesis in Halle with it. We possess the hermeneutics which arose in this way only in a very unsatisfactory version. It gained impact above all from a pupil of Schleiermacher's, Böckh.

From Schleiermacher's hermeneutics I shall extract the propositions on which the further development seems to me to depend.

All exegesis of written works is only the artistic development of the process of understanding which extends over the whole of life and applies to every kind of writing and speech. The analysis of understanding is consequently the foundation for the procedural rules laid down for exegesis. But this can be completed only in connection with the analysis of the production of written works. The combination of rules which determine the means and limits of exegesis can be based only on the relationship between understanding and production.

The possibility of universally valid interpretation can be deduced from the nature of understanding. In this process the individuality of the interpreter and that of his author do not face each other as two incomparable facts. Both have been formed on the basis of a common human nature, and this makes possible the common ground which all men share and which is necessary for speech and comprehension. Here Schleiermacher's formulaic expressions can be further clarified psychologically. All individual differences are, in the final analysis, not determined by qualitative diversities between people but only by differences of degree in their mental processes. But when the interpreter tentatively projects his own vitality, as it were, into a historical milieu, he is able from this standpoint momentarily to stress and to reinforce certain mental processes, to let others take a less prominent place, and thus to bring about a reconstruction of an alien life within himself.

If one now considers the logical side of this process, then a connection is recognized only from relatively precise individual signs, assisted constantly by the grammatical, logical and historical knowledge available. Expressed in our logical terminology, this logical aspect of understanding thus consists in the combined action of induction, the application of more general truths to the particular case, and procedures of comparison. The more immediate task would be to establish the particular forms which this list of logical operations and their combinations here assume.

We see here the central difficulty of all interpretative skill. The whole of a work must be understood from the individual words and their combinations, and yet the full comprehension of the details presupposes the understanding of the whole. This circle is repeated in the relationship of the individual work to the disposition and development of its author, and once again in the relationship of the individual work to its literary genre. Schleiermacher solved this problem most neatly in his Introduction to Plato's *Republic*, and I find other instances of the same procedure in postscripts to his lectures on exegesis . . . Theoretically one comes up against the limits of all exegesis here; it always completes its task only up to a certain point. Thus all understanding remains only relative and can never be completed. *Individuum est ineffabile.*

The dissection of the exegetic procedure into grammatical, historical, aesthetic and factual interpretation, as Schleiermacher found it, was rejected by him. These distinctions show only that grammatical, historical, factual and aesthetic knowledge must be present when the exegesis begins and can have an effect on every act of that exegesis. But the process of exegesis itself can only be dissected into two aspects which are contained in the recognition of a spiritual creation from linguistic signs. Grammatical exegesis proceeds in the text from connection to connection until it reaches the highest concurrences within the work as a whole. Psychological exegesis sets out from projection into the creative inner process; it proceeds to the outer and inner form of the work, and then from there to the consideration of the unity of the work in the psychological make-up and development of its author.

With this the point is reached from which Schleiermacher masterfully develops the rules of the art of exegesis. The basic element is the doctrine of outer and inner form, and the opening moves towards a general theory of literary production, in which the Organon of literary history would lie, are especially profound.

The final aim of the hermeneutic procedure is to understand the author better than he has understood himself: a proposition which is the necessary consequence of the doctrine of unconscious creation.

6 Hans-Georg Gadamer

The Historicity of Understanding

Excerpt from Hans-Georg Gadamer, *Wahrheit und Methode*, J. C. B. Mohr, Tübingen, 1965. English copyright © Sheed and Ward Ltd, London, 1975, pp. 258–74.

Let us consider first how hermeneutics sets about its work. What follows for understanding from the hermeneutic condition of belonging to a tradition? We remember here the hermeneutical rule that we must understand the whole in terms of the detail and the detail in terms of the whole. This principle stems from ancient rhetoric, and modern hermeneutics has taken it and applied it to the art of understanding. It is a circular relationship in both cases. The anticipation of meaning in which the whole is envisaged becomes explicit understanding in that the parts, that are determined by the whole, themselves also determine this whole.

We know this from the learning of ancient languages. We learn that we must 'construe' a sentence before we attempt to understand the individual parts of the sentence in their linguistic meaning. But this process of construing is itself already governed by an expectation of meaning that follows from the context of what has gone before. It is also necessary for this expected meaning to be adjusted if the text calls for it. This means, then, that the expectation changes and that the text acquires the unity of a meaning from another expected meaning. Thus the movement of understanding is constantly from the whole to the part and back to the whole. Our task is to extend in concentric circles the unity of the understood meaning. The harmony of all the details with the whole is the criterion of correct understanding. The failure to achieve this harmony means that understanding has failed.

Schleiermacher differentiated this hermeneutic circle of part and whole in both its objective and its subjective aspect. As the single word belongs within the total context of the sentence, so the single text belongs within the total context of a writer's work, and the latter within the whole of the particular literary genre or of literature. At the same time, however, the same text, as a manifestation of a creative moment, belongs to the whole of its author's inner life. Full understanding can take place only within this objective and subjective whole. Following this theory, Dilthey speaks then of 'structure' and of the 'centring in a mid-point', from out of which there follows the understanding of the whole. In this he is applying to the historical world what has always been a principle of all textual interpretation: namely, that a text must be understood in terms of itself.

The question is, however, whether this is an adequate account of the circular movement of understanding. Here we must go back to the result of our analysis of Schleiermacher's hermeneutics. We may set aside Schleiermacher's ideas on subjective interpretation. When we try to understand a text, we do not try to recapture the author's attitude of mind but, if this is the terminology we are to use, we try to recapture the perspective within which he has formed his views. But this means simply that we try to accept the objective validity of what he is saying. If we want to understand, we shall try to make his arguments even more cogent. This happens even in conversation, so how much truer is it of the understanding of what is written down that we are moving in a dimension of meaning that is intelligible in itself and as such offers no reason for going back to the subjectivity of the author. It is the task of hermeneutics to clarify this miracle of understanding, which is not a mysterious communion of souls, but a sharing of a common meaning.

But even the objective side of this circle, as Schleiermacher describes it, does not reach the heart of the matter. We have seen that the goal of all communication and understanding is agreement concerning the object. Hence the task of hermeneutics has always been to establish agreement where it had failed to come about or been disturbed in some way. The history of hermeneutics can offer a confirmation of this if, for example, we think of Augustine, who sought to relate the Christian gospel to the Old Testament, or of early Protestantism, which faced the same problem, or finally, the age of the Enlightenment, when it is almost like a renunciation of agreement to seek to acquire 'full understanding' of a text only by means of historical interpretation. It is something qualitatively new when romanticism and Schleiermacher base a universal historical consciousness by no longer seeing the binding form of tradition, from which they come and in which they stand, as the firm foundation of all hermeneutical endeavour.

One of the immediate predecessors of Schleiermacher, Friedrich Ast, still had a view of hermeneutical work that was markedly concerned with content, in that, for him, its purpose was to establish harmony between the world of classical antiquity and Christianity, between a newly discovered genuine antiquity and the Christian tradition. This is something new, in comparison with the Enlightenment, in that this hermeneutics no longer accepts or rejects tradition in accord with the criterion of natural reason. But in its attempt to bring about a meaningful agreement between the two traditions to which it sees itself as belonging, this kind of hermeneutics is still pursuing the task of all preceding hermeneutics, namely to achieve in understanding agreement in content.

In going beyond the 'particularity' of this reconciliation of the ancient classical world and Christianity, Schleiermacher and, following him, nineteenth-century science, conceive the task of hermeneutics in a way that is formally universal. They were able to harmonize it with the natural sciences' ideal of objectivity, but only by ignoring the concretion of historical consciousness in hermeneutical theory.

Heidegger's description and existential account of the hermeneutic circle constitutes in contrast a decisive turning-point. The hermeneutic theory of the nineteenth century often spoke of the circular structure of understanding, but always within the framework of a formal relation of the part and the whole or its subjective reflex, the intuitive anticipation of the whole and its subsequent articulation in the parts. According to this theory, the circular movement of understanding runs backwards and forwards along the text and disappears when it is perfectly understood. This view of understanding culminated logically in Schleiermacher's theory of the divinatory act, by means of which one places oneself entirely within the writer's mind and from there resolves all that is strange and unusual about the text. As against this approach, Heidegger describes the circle in such a way that the understanding of the text remains permanently determined by the anticipatory movement of fore-understanding. The circle of the whole and the part is not dissolved in perfect understanding but, on the contrary, is most fully realized.

The circle, then, is not formal in nature, it is neither subjective nor objective, but describes understanding as the interplay of the movement of tradition and the movement of the interpreter. The anticipation of meaning that governs our understanding of a text is not an act of subjectivity, but proceeds from the communality that binds us to the tradition. But this is contained in our relation to tradition, in the constant process of education. Tradition is not simply a pre-condition into which we come, but we produce it ourselves, in as much as we understand, participate in the evolution of tradition and hence further determine it ourselves. Thus the circle of understanding is not a 'methodological' circle, but describes an ontological structural element in understanding . . .

Thus the meaning of the connection with tıadition, i.e. the element of tradition in our historical, hermeneutical attitude, is fulfilled in the fact that we share fundamental prejudices with tradition. Hermeneutics must start from the position that a person seeking to understand something has a relation to the object that comes into language in the transmitted text and has, or acquires, a connection with the tradition out of which the text speaks. On the other hand, hermeneutical consciousness is aware that it cannot be connected with this object in some self-evident, unquestioned way, as is the case with the unbroken stream of a tradition. There is a polarity of familiarity and strangeness on which hermeneutic work is based: only that this polarity is not to be seen, psychologically, with Schleiermacher, as the tension that conceals the mystery of individuality, but truly hermeneutically, i.e. in regard to what has been said: the language in which the text addresses us, the story that it tells us. Here, too, there is a tension. The place between strangeness and familiarity that a transmitted text has for us is that intermediate place between being an historically intended separate object and being part of a tradition. The true home of hermeneutics is in this intermediate area.

It follows from this intermediate position in which hermeneutics operates that its work is not to develop a procedure of understanding, but to clarify the conditions in which understanding takes place. But these conditions are not of the nature of a 'procedure' or a method, which the interpreter must of himself bring to bear on the text, but rather they must be given. The prejudices and fore-meanings in the mind of the interpreter are not at his free disposal. He is not able to separate in advance the productive prejudices that make understanding possible from the prejudices that hinder understanding and lead to misunderstandings.

This separation, rather, must take place in the understanding itself, and hence hermeneutics must ask how it happens. But this means it must place in the foreground what has remained entirely peripheral in previous hermeneutics: temporal distance and its significance for understanding.

This point can be clarified by comparing it with the hermeneutic theory of romanticism. We shall recall that the latter conceived understanding as the reproduction of an original production. Hence it was possible to say that one should be able to understand an author better than he understood himself. We examined the origin of this statement and its connection with the aesthetics of genius, but must now come back to it, as our present inquiry lends it a new importance.

That subsequent understanding is superior to the original production and hence can be described as superior understanding does not depend so much on the conscious realization that places him on the same level as the author (as Schleiermacher said), but denotes rather an inevitable difference between the interpreter and the author that is created by the historical distance between them. Every age has to understand a transmitted text in its own way, for the text is part of the whole of the tradition in which the age takes an objective interest and in which it seeks to understand itself. The real meaning of a text, as it speaks to the interpreter, does not depend on the contingencies of the author and whom he originally wrote for. It certainly is not identical with them, for it is always partly determined also by the historical situation of the interpreter and hence by the totality of the objective course of history. A writer like Chladenius, who does not yet see understanding in terms of history, is saying the same thing in a naïve, ingenuous way when he says that an author does not need to know the real meaning of what he has written, and hence the interpreter can, and must, often understand more than he. But this is of fundamental importance. Not occasionally only, but always, the meaning of a text goes beyond its author. That is why understanding is not merely a reproductive, but always a productive attitude as well. Perhaps it is not correct to refer to this productive element in understanding as 'superior understanding'. For this phrase is, as we have shown, the application of a principle of criticism from the age of the Enlightenment on the basis of the aesthetics of genius. Understanding is not, in fact, superior understanding, neither in the sense of superior knowledge of the subject because of clearer ideas, nor in the sense of fundamental superiority that the conscious has over the unconscious nature of creation. It is enough to say that we understand in a different way, if we understand at all.

This concept of understanding undoubtedly breaks right out of the circle drawn by romantic hermeneutics. Because what we are now concerned with is not individuality and what it thinks, but the objective truth of what is said, a text is not understood as a mere expression of life, but taken seriously in its claim to truth. That this is what is meant by 'understanding' was once self-evident (we need only recall Chladenius).

But this dimension of the hermeneutical problem was discredited by historical consciousness and the psychological turn that Schleiermacher gave to hermeneutics, and could only be regained when the impasses of historicism appeared and led finally to the new development inspired chiefly, in my opinion, by Heidegger. For the hermeneutic importance of temporal distance could be understood only as a result of the ontological direction that Heidegger gave to understanding as an 'existential' and of his temporal interpretation of the mode of being of there-being.

Time is no longer primarily a gulf to be bridged, because it separates, but it is actually the supportive ground of process in which the present is rooted. Hence temporal distance is not something that must be overcome. This was, rather, the naïve assumption of historicism, namely that we must set ourselves within the spirit of the age, and think with its ideas and its thoughts, not with our own, and thus advance towards historical objectivity. In fact the important thing is to recognize the distance in time as a positive and productive possibility of understanding. It is not a yawning abyss, but is filled with the continuity of custom and tradition, in the light of which all that is handed down presents itself to us. Here it is not too much to speak of a genuine productivity of process. Everyone knows that curious impotence of our judgement where the distance in time has not given us sure criteria. Thus the judgement of contemporary works of art is desperately uncertain for the scientific consciousness. Obviously we approach such creations with the prejudices we are not in control of, presuppositions that have too great an influence over us for us to know about them; these can give to contemporary creations an extra resonance that does not correspond to their true content and their true significance. Only when all their relations to the present time have faded away can their real nature appear, so that the understanding of what is said in them can claim to be authoritative and universal.

It is this experience that has led to the idea in historical studies that objective knowledge can be arrived at only when there has been a certain historical distance. It is true that what a thing has to say, its intrinsic content, first appears only after it is divorced from the fleeting circumstances of its actuality. The positive conditions of historical understanding include the self-contained quality of an historical event, which allows it to appear as a whole, and its distance from the opinions concerning its import with which the present is filled. The implicit prerequisite of the historical method, then, is that the permanent significance of something can first be known objectively only when it belongs within a self-contained context. In other words, when it is dead enough to have only historical interest. Only then does it seem possible to exclude the subjective involvement of the observer. This is, in fact, a paradox, the epistemological counterpart to the old moral problem of whether anyone can be called happy before his death. Just as Aristotle (Eth Nic 1, 7) showed what a sharpening of the powers of human judgement this kind of problem can bring about, so hermeneutical reflection cannot fail to find here a sharpening of the methodological self-consciousness of science. It is true that certain hermeneutic requirements are automatically fulfilled when a historical context has become of no more than historical interest. Certain sources of error are automatically excluded. But it is questionable whether this is the end of the hermeneutical problem. Temporal distance has obviously another meaning than that of the quenching of our interest in the object. It lets the true meaning of the object emerge fully. But the discovery of the true meaning of a text or a work of art is never finished; it is in fact an infinite process. Not only are fresh sources of error constantly excluded, so that the true meaning has filtered out of it all kinds of things that obscure it, but there emerge continually new sources of understanding, which reveal unsuspected elements of meaning. The temporal distance which performs the filtering process is not a closed dimension, but is itself undergoing constant movement and extension. And with the negative side of the filtering process brought about by temporal distance there is also the positive side, namely the value it has for understanding. It not only lets those prejudices that are of a particular and limited nature die away, but causes those that bring about genuine understanding to emerge clearly as such.

It is only this temporal distance that can solve the really critical question of hermeneutics, namely of distinguishing the true prejudices, by which we understand, from the false ones by which we misunderstand. Hence the hermeneutically trained mind will also include historical consciousness. It will make conscious the prejudices governing our own understanding, so that the text, as another's meaning, can be isolated and valued on its own. The isolation of a prejudice clearly requires the suspension of its validity for us. For so long as our mind is influenced by a prejudice, we do not know and consider it as a judgement. How then are we able to isolate it? It is impossible to make ourselves aware of it while it is constantly operating unnoticed, but only when it is, so to speak, stimulated. The encounter with a text from the past can provide this stimulus. For what leads to understanding must be something that has already asserted itself in its own separate validity. Understanding begins, as we have already said above [pp. 117, 120], when something addresses us. This is the primary hermeneutical condition. We now know what this requires, namely the fundamental suspension of our own prejudices. But all suspension of judgements and hence, *a fortiori*, of prejudices, has logically the structure of a question.

The essence of the question is the opening up, and keeping open, of possibilities. If a prejudice becomes questionable, in view of what another or a text says to us, this does not mean that it is simply set aside and the other writing or the other person accepted as valid in its place. It shows, rather, the naïvety of historical objectivism to accept this disregarding of ourselves as what actually happens. In fact our own prejudice is properly brought into play through its being at risk. Only through its being given full play is it able to experience the other's claim to truth and make it possible for he himself to have full play. (In this passage the author plays on the German expressions *ins Spiel bringen*, *auf dem Spiele stehen* and *sich ausspielen*.)

The naïvety of so-called historicism consists in the fact that it does not undertake this reflection, and in trusting to its own methodological approach forgets its own historicality. We must here appeal from a badly understood historical thinking to one that can better perform the task of understanding. True historical thinking must take account of its own historicality. Only then will it not chase the phantom of an historical object which is the object of progressive research, but learn to see in the object the counterpart of itself and hence understand both. The true historical object is not an object at all, but the unity of the one and the other, a relationship in which exist both the reality of history and the reality of historical understanding. A proper hermeneutics would have to demonstrate the effectiveness of history within understanding itself. I shall refer to this as 'effective-history'. Understanding is, essentially, an effective-historical relation.

The principle of effective-history

The fact that the interest of the historian is directed not only towards the historical phenomenon and the work that has been handed down but also, secondarily, towards their effect in history (which also includes the history of research) is regarded in general as a mere supplement to the historical problematic that, from Hermann Grimm's *Raffael* to Gundolf and beyond, has given rise to many valuable insights. To this extent, effective-history is not new. But that this kind of effective-historical approach be required every time that a work of art or an element of the tradition is led from the twilight region between tradition and history to be seen clearly and openly in terms of its own meaning – this is a new demand (addressed not to research, but to methodological consciousness itself) that proceeds inevitably from the analysis of historical consciousness.

It is not, of course, a hermeneutical requirement in the sense of the traditional concept of hermeneutics. I am not saying that historical inquiry should develop this effective-historical problematic that would be something separate from that which is concerned directly with the understanding of the work. The requirement is of a more theoretical kind. Historical consciousness must become aware that in the apparent immediacy with which it approaches a work of art or a tradition, there is also contained, albeit unrecognized and hence not allowed for, this other element. If we are trying to understand a historical phenomenon from the historical distance that is characteristic of our hermeneutical situation, we are always subject to the effects of effective-history. It determines in advance both what seems to us worth inquiring about and what will appear as an object of investigation, and we more or less forget half of what is really there – in fact, we miss the whole truth of the phenomenon when we take its immediate appearance as the whole truth.

In our understanding, which we imagine is so straightforward, we find that, by following the criterion of intelligibility, the other presents himself so much in terms of our own selves that there is no longer a question of self and other. Historical objectivism, in appealing to its critical method, conceals the involvement of the historical consciousness itself in effective-history. By the method of its foundational criticism it does away with the arbitrariness of cosy re-creations of the past, but it preserves its good conscience by failing to recognize those presuppositions – certainly not arbitrary, but still fundamental – that govern its own approach to understanding, and hence falls short of reaching that truth which, despite the finite nature of our understanding, could be reached. In this historical objectivism resembles statistics, which are such an excellent means of propaganda because they let facts speak and hence simulate an objectivity that in reality depends on the legitimacy of the questions asked.

We are not saying, then, that effective-history must be developed as a new independent discipline ancillary to the human sciences, but that we should learn to understand ourselves better and recognize that in all understanding, whether we are expressly aware of it or not, the power of this effective-history is at work. When a naïve faith in scientific method ignores its existence, there can be an actual deformation of knowledge. We know it from the history of science as the irrefutable proof of something that is obviously false. But looking at the whole situation, we see that the power of effective-history does not depend on its being recognized. This, precisely, is the power of history over finite human consciousness, namely that it prevails even where faith in method leads one to deny one's own historicality. The demand that we should become conscious of this effective-history is pressing because it is necessary for scientific consciousness. But this does not mean that it can be fulfilled in an absolute way. That we should become completely aware of effective-history is just as hybrid a statement as when Hegel speaks of absolute knowledge, in which history would become completely transparent to itself and hence be raised to the level of a concept. Rather, effective historical consciousness is an element in the act of understanding itself and, as we shall see, is already operative in the choice of the right question to ask.

Effective-historical consciousness is primarily consciousness of the hermeneutical situation. To acquire an awareness of a situation is, however, always a task of particular difficulty. The very idea of a situation means that we are not standing outside it and hence are unable to have any objective knowledge of it.[1] We are always within the situation, and to throw light on it is a task that

1. The structure of the concept of situation has been illuminated chiefly by K. Jaspers *(Die geistige Situation der Zeit)* and Erich Rothacker.

is never entirely completed. This is true also of the hermeneutic situation, i.e. the situation in which we find ourselves with regard to the tradition that we are trying to understand. The illumination of this situation – effective-historical reflection – can never be completely achieved, but this is not due to a lack in the reflection but lies in the essence of the historical being which is ours. To exist historically means that knowledge of oneself can never be complete. All self-knowledge proceeds from what is historically pre-given, what we call, with Hegel, 'substance', because it is the basis of all subjective meaning and attitude and hence both prescribes and limits every possibility of understanding any tradition whatsoever in terms of its unique historical quality. This almost defines the aim of philosophical hermeneutics: its task is to move back along the path of Hegel's *Phenomenology of Mind* until we discover in all that is subjective the substantiality that determines it.

Every finite present has its limitations. We define the concept of 'situation' by saying that it represents a standpoint that limits the possibility of vision. Hence an essential part of the concept of situation is the concept of 'horizon'. The horizon is the range of vision that includes everything that can be seen from a particular vantage point. Applying this to the thinking mind, we speak of narrowness of horizon, of the possible expansion of horizon, of the opening up of new horizons, etc. The word has been used in philosophy since Nietzsche and Husserl to characterize the way in which thought is tied to its finite determination, and the nature of the law of the expansion of the range of vision. A person who has no horizon is a man who does not see far enough and hence overvalues what is nearest to him. Contrariwise, to have an horizon means not to be limited to what is nearest, but to be able to see beyond it. A person who has an horizon knows the relative significance of everything within this horizon, as near or far, great or small. Similarly, the working out of the hermeneutical situation means the achievement of the right horizon of inquiry for the questions evoked by the encounter with tradition.

In the sphere of historical understanding we also like to speak of horizons, especially when referring to the claim of historical consciousness to see the past in terms of its own being, not in terms of our contemporary criteria and prejudices, but within its own historical horizon. The task of historical understanding also involves acquiring the particular historical horizon, so that what we are seeking to understand can be seen in its true dimensions. If we fail to place ourselves in this way within the historical horizon out of which tradition speaks, we shall misunderstand the significance of what it has to say to us. To this extent it seems a legitimate hermeneutical requirement to place ourselves in the other situation in order to understand it. We may ask, however, whether this does not mean that we are failing in the understanding that is asked of us. The same is true of a conversation that we have with someone simply in order to get to know him, i.e. to discover his standpoint and his horizon. This is not a true conversation, in the sense that we are not seeking agreement concerning an object, but the specific contents of the conversation are only a means to get to know the horizon of the other person. Examples are oral examinations, or some kinds of conversation between doctor and patient. The historical consciousness is clearly doing something similar when it places itself within the situation of the past and hence is able to acquire the right historical horizon. Just as in a conversation, when we have discovered the standpoint and horizon of the other person, his ideas become intelligible, without our necessarily having to agree with him, the person who thinks historically comes to understand the meaning of what has been handed down, without necessarily agreeing with it, or seeing himself in it.

In both cases, in our understanding we have, as it were, withdrawn from the situation of trying to reach agreement. He himself cannot be reached. By including from the beginning the other person's standpoint in what he is saying to us, we are making our own standpoint safely unattainable. We have seen, in considering the origin of historical thinking, that in fact it makes this ambiguous transition from means to ends, i.e. it makes an end of what is only a means. The text that is understood historically is forced to abandon its claim that it is uttering something true. We think we understand when we see the past from a historical standpoint, i.e. place ourselves in the historical situation and seek to reconstruct the historical horizon. In fact, however, we have given up the claim to find, in the past, any truth valid and intelligible for ourselves. Thus this acknowledgement of the otherness of the other, which makes him the object of objective knowledge, involves the fundamental suspension of his claim to truth.

The question is, however, whether this description really corresponds to the hermeneutical phenomenon. Are there, then, two different horizons here, the horizon in which the person seeking to understand lives, and the particular historical horizon within which he places himself? Is it a correct description of the art of historical understanding to say that we are learning to place ourselves within alien horizons? Are there such things as closed horizons, in this sense? We recall Nietzsche's complaint (*Unzeitgemässe Betrachtungen* 11, at the beginning) against historicism that it destroyed the horizon bounded by myth in which alone a culture is able to live. Is the horizon of one's own present time ever closed in this way, and can a historical situation be imagined that has this kind of closed horizon?

Or is this a romantic reflection, a kind of Robinson Crusoe dream of the historical enlightenment, the fiction of an unattainable island, as artificial as Crusoe himself for the alleged primary phenomenon of the *solus ipse*? Just as the individual is never simply an individual, because he is always involved with others, so too the closed horizon that is supposed to enclose a culture is an abstraction. The historical movement of human life consists in the fact that it is never utterly bound to any one standpoint, and hence can never have a truly closed horizon. The horizon is, rather, something into which we move and that moves with us. Horizons change for a person who is moving. Thus the horizon of the past, out of which all human life lives and which exists in the form of tradition, is always in motion. It is not historical consciousness that first sets the surrounding horizon in motion. But in it this motion becomes aware of itself.

When our historical consciousness places itself within historical horizons, this does not entail passing into alien worlds unconnected in any way with our own, but together they constitute the one great horizon that moves from within and, beyond the frontiers of the present, embraces the historical depths of our self-consciousness. It is, in fact, a single horizon that embraces everything contained in historical consciousness. Our own past, and that other past towards which our historical consciousness is directed, help to shape this moving horizon out of which human life always lives, and which determines it as tradition.

Understanding of the past, then, undoubtedly requires an historical horizon. But it is not the case that we acquire this horizon by placing ourselves within a historical situation. Rather, we must always already have a horizon in order to be able to place ourselves within a situation. For what do we mean by 'placing ourselves' in a situation? Certainly not just disregarding ourselves. This is necessary, of course, in that we must imagine the other situation. But into this other situation we must also bring ourselves. Only this fulfils the meaning of 'placing ourselves'. If we place ourselves in the situation of someone else, for example, then we shall understand him, i.e. become aware of the otherness, the indissoluble individuality of the other person, by placing ourselves in his position.

This placing of ourselves is not the empathy of one individual for another, nor is it the application to another person of our own criteria, but it always involves the attainment of a higher universality that overcomes, not only our own particularity, but also that of the other. The concept of the 'horizon' suggests itself because it expresses the wide, superior vision that the person who is seeking to understand must have. To acquire a horizon means that one learns to look beyond what is close at hand – not in order to look away from it, but to see it better within a larger whole and in truer proportion. It is not a correct description of historical consciousness to speak, with Nietzsche, of the many changing horizons into which it teaches us to place ourselves. If we disregard ourselves in this way, we have no historical horizon. Nietzsche's view that historical study is deleterious to life is not directed, in fact, against historical consciousness as such, but against the self-alienation that it undergoes when it regards the method of modern historical science as its own true nature. We have already pointed out that a truly historical consciousness always sees its own present in such a way that it sees itself, as it sees the historically other, within the right circumstances. It requires a special effort to acquire an historical horizon. We are always affected, in hope and fear, by what is nearest to us, and hence approach, under its influence, the testimony of the past. Hence it is constantly necessary to inhibit the over-hasty assimilation of the past to our own expectations of meaning. Only then will we be able to listen to the past in a way that enables it to make its own meaning heard.

We have shown above that this is a process of making distinctions. Let us consider what this idea of making distinctions involves. It is always reciprocal. Whatever is being distinguished must be distinguished from something which, in turn, must be distinguished from it. Thus all distinguishing also makes visible that from which something is distinguished. We have described this above as the operation of prejudices. We started by saying that a hermeneutical situation is determined by the prejudices that we bring with us. They constitute, then, the horizon of a particular present, for they represent that beyond which it is impossible to see. But now it is important to avoid the error of thinking that it is a fixed set of opinions and evaluations that determine and limit the horizon of the present, and that the otherness of the past can be distinguished from it as from a fixed ground.

In fact the horizon of the present is being continually formed, in that we have continually to test all our prejudices. An important part of this testing is the encounter with the past and the understanding of the tradition from which we come. Hence the horizon of the present cannot be formed without the past. There is no more an isolated horizon of the present than there are historical horizons. Understanding, rather, is always the fusion of these horizons which we imagine to exist by themselves. We know the power of this kind of fusion chiefly from earlier times and their naïve attitude to themselves and their origin. In a tradition this process of fusion is continually going on, for there old and new continually grow together to make something of living value, without either being explicitly distinguished from the other.

If, however, there is no such thing as these horizons that are distinguished from one another, why do we speak of the fusion of horizons and not simply of the formation of the one horizon, whose bounds are set in the depths of tradition? To ask the question means that we are recognizing the special nature of the situation in which understanding becomes a scientific task, and that it is necessary to work out this situation as a hermeneutical situation. Every encounter with tradition that takes place within historical consciousness involves the experience of the tension between the text and the present. The hermeneutic task consists in not covering up this tension by attempting a naïve assimilation but consciously bringing it out. This is why it is part of the hermeneutic approach to project an historical horizon that is different from the horizon of the present. Historical consciousness is aware of its own otherness and hence distinguishes the horizon of tradition from its own. On the other hand, it is itself, as we are trying to show, only something laid over a continuing tradition, and hence it immediately re-combines what it has distinguished in order, in the unity of the historical horizon that it thus acquires, to become again one with itself.

The projecting of the historical horizon, then, is only a phase in the process of understanding, and does not become solidified into the self-alienation of a past consciousness, but is overtaken by our own present horizon of understanding. In the process of understanding there takes place a real fusing of horizons, which means that as the historical horizon is projected, it is simultaneously removed. We described the conscious act of this fusion as the task of the effective-historical consciousness. Although this task had been obscured by aesthetic historical positivism in the train of romantic hermeneutics, it is, in fact, the central problem of hermeneutics. It is the problem of application that exists in all understanding.

References

ARISTOTLE, *The Nichomachean Ethics*, tr. H. Rackham, London, 1926, 1, 7.
JASPERS, K. (1953), *Die geistige Situation der Zeit*, Berlin.
NIETZSCHE, F. *Unzeitgemässe Betrachtungen*, 11, in *Werke*, de Gruyter, Berlin, 1972.

7 Alfred Lorenzer

Symbols and Stereotypes

Excerpt from Alfred Lorenzer, *Sprachzerstörung und Rekonstruktion*, Suhrkamp, Frankfurt, 1970, pp. 72–92. Translated by Thomas Hall.

The history of the psychoanalytical concept of the symbol goes back to the early stages of Freudian theory. Conceived of at first as a sign, as a 'symptom of memory', on the basis of a 'physiological' psychology, the notion gained the dimension of 'meaning' from its employment in cases of hysterical illness. The phenomena termed 'symbolization' were understood as expressions of a particular association of meanings. The interpretation of dreams, however, led soon after to a third nuance of the concept, that of the 'dream symbol'. These dream symbols (and with them the whole of symbolism) came to be regarded finally as fixed signs belonging to a vocabulary of unconscious contents – contents which were constant and 'independent of particular circumstances'.

In turning from the first to the second view of the concept – that is to say, in taking up the idea of meaning – psychoanalysis had undergone a fundamental change: the transformation from a 'psychology on a physiological basis' to a science which inquires into the 'meaning' of what it examines. The transition from the second to the third nuance of the concept led to another no less thoroughgoing change, although in a different respect. Subjectivity seemed to be surmounted, to be replaced by the objectivity of a vocabulary of the 'language of the unconscious', independent of both the idiosyncrasies of the individual and the particular characteristics of a culture. This objectivity was, indeed, to be revealed in the course of discussion as a 'false objectivity'; but it proved hard to cast off, because the task of integrating the concept of the symbol into psychoanalytic theory created major difficulties. On the one hand, for reasons which we do not intend to discuss in detail here, it was essential to return to a view of the symbol as a 'subjective' creation; but, on the other hand, the boundary between unconscious and conscious processes was not to be obscured. After protracted discussions a solution presented itself in the form of the expedient of accepting the strict coexistence of two distinct psychic organizations. The lower plane was regarded as a creation of the primary process, to which belongs the formation of symbols. The higher plane of mature psychic activity, on the other hand, is occupied by the secondary, rational processes. Ernest Jones brought the debate on symbol-formation to an end in 1916–18 with the various drafts of a well-known work, the key proposition of which was to be: 'Only that which is repressed is in need of symbolic representation. This conclusion is the touchstone of the psychoanalytic theory of symbolism.'[1]

This definition of the concept of the symbol guided psychoanalytic thought for the following four or five decades. It appeared to provide an excellent, firm basis for the psychoanalytic theory of symbols. Isolated voices were, indeed, raised again and again in objection to it, but in the last decade and a half Jones's formulation has become the target of concentrated critical attack.

This criticism has generally taken as its starting-point the knowledge of the process of concept formation which has developed in the last half-century outside the field of psychoanalysis, in the most diverse fields of knowledge: in mathematical logic, in linguistic and developmental psychology, and not least in philosophy in the context of discussions on linguistic problems, a new understanding of the symbol has grown up. What is noteworthy for our purposes is the fact that all these hypotheses tend in one direction, which is directly opposed to that of Jones's conception. Whereas for Jones the symbol was the expression of the unconscious, in other words of processes excluded from the ego, in mathematical logic, for instance, the symbol was regarded as the clearest form of rational operation. This difference in itself counted for little, for it was possible to see in it nothing more than a mere difference of terminology resulting from a variation

1. Jones (1918).

in conventional usage. There seemed to be no problem, thanks to the possibility of registering two distinct groups of symbols alongside one another.

However, the difference became irreconcilable at the moment when, just as a conception of the symbol diverging from that of psychoanalysis was being set up, the question of symbol formation was raised, and was answered with the assumption of a unified process of symbolization reaching from the lower to the higher levels of creation.

Developmental psychology, for instance, has advanced good reasons for assuming a universal capacity for symbolization: in other words, a universal process by which symbols are formed. But this unified process of symbol formation is seen as centred on that level of skill which is designated in psychoanalysis as a secondary process, whereas psychoanalysis had rooted the activity of symbol formation in primary processes. This problem comes into focus when we consider the work of Cassirer. His famous dictum 'Instead of thinking of man as animal rationale, we should define him as animal symbolicum'[2] makes the opposition evident. In Cassirer's work, too, it becomes clear how untenable is the parallel of two conceptions of the symbol – 'a symbol formation in the primary process' rooted in the unconscious, and a creation of 'rational symbols' by the secondary process. Cassirer has described mythical thought as an archaic stage of symbol formation and in so doing he has sketched illustrations which correspond exactly with Freud's description of operations under the influence of the primary process.

In elaborating further Cassirer's line of thought Susanne K. Langer has made the situation still clearer, sharpening the opposition by distinguishing between 'discursive' and 'presentative' modes of symbol formation. To discursive symbolism, in her view, belongs the articulated symbolism of language; whereas presentative symbolism covers an area which shows exactly those structural rules which according to Freud are to be found in the primary processes, such as condensation, displacement, etc. Presentative symbolism, according to Langer, also possesses greater proximity to the emotions and shows projective mechanisms.

2. Cassirer (1944).

Moreover, to dispel any doubt about the homogeneity of discursive and presentative symbolism on the basis of a unified symbol formation, Langer states that presentative symbolism is no less important a skill of the human mind; symbols always grow from a unified creative process. They form a chain:

Ideas first adumbrated in fantastic form become real intellectual property only when discursive language rises to their expression. That is why myth is the indispensable forerunner of metaphysics; and metaphysics is the literal formulation of basic abstractions, on which our comprehension of sober facts is based.[3]

There is no need of further examples to demonstrate that all these different new lines of thought and experiences call into question the psychoanalytic theory of symbols as modified by Jones. Since the 1930s psychoanalysts also have increasingly felt the inevitability of a conflict of views – in particular Kubie in his work on creativity,[4] but others too have made isolated comments on the subject.

Finally, at the Annual General Meeting of the American Psychoanalytic Association in 1960,[5] the revision of Jones's concept of the symbol was called for by a whole series of speakers. Definitions such as 'Symbolism is an act essential to thought and prior to it' and 'Symbolization is the essential act of the mind' made it clear that the long era of the psychoanalytic view of the symbol was coming to an end. Of course, any new concept of the symbol would be confronted once again with those questions which had appeared to be already settled. How are dream symbols related to the unconscious? In what way is neurotic symbolism generally determined by unconscious happenings?

If one turns these questions round, then they can be put thus: How does the new view of the symbol fit into the whole of psychoanalytic theory? How is the connection of symbol and regression, symbol and unconscious processes, symbol and repression, to be visualized? If we regard dream symbols as exemplary instances of symbol formation from unconscious material, then the real question is: how, on the one hand, can we assume the

3. Langer (1960). 4. Kubie (1958). 5. Segel (1961).

existence of a unified centre of symbol formation while, on the other hand, accounting for the opposition between unconscious contents and contents which are capable of being conscious?

There can be only one answer. The two positions can be reconciled meaningfully only if one distinguishes *the centre of symbol formation* from the *stimuli* out of which symbols arise. The 'centre' must be sought in the 'ego'; whereas the 'stimuli' may be located anywhere, including the unconscious with its great store of repressed contents. Accordingly, the formation of symbols proceeds as follows: unconscious materials are in certain circumstances 'released' by the unconscious to be absorbed and assimilated by the perceiving ego. The dream symbol, for example, is the product of an 'inner' perception which assimilates this almost inaccessible material.

Thus in place of *the old duplication of the loci of formation* with their different contents and mechanisms there appears *a single centre of symbol formation by the ego*; and the unconscious or id must be understood as a stimulus of a particular kind and intensity in interplay with the ego. Certainly not the sole source of stimuli. In dreams, for instance, there are four distinct sources of stimuli – not taking into account the distinction between id and superego. That is to say, there are stimuli from the external world and bodily functions; there are recent impressions, i.e. remnants of the day (including subliminal influences); then there are the forms stored in the memory which become especially effective in secondary dream-work; and finally there is the reservoir of the 'unconscious'. This last source has a particular significance.

The thesis of a bipolar structure in the formation of perceptions – *in which the ego is the centre of organization and the unconscious is the centre of stimuli* – preserves the stress on the distinction between unconscious and conscious but at the same time purifies psychoanalytic theory from the ontologization of the unconscious.

The ego alone can be considered as a shaping, symbol-forming mechanism; whereas on the other hand the function of the unconscious must be seen as a reservoir of material stimuli which is *not yet* or *no longer* potentially conscious.

But how does the new view of the symbol fit into psychoanalytic theory if we consider the problem of the symbol from a quite different angle – from the point of view of the psychoanalytic theory of instincts? Beres ventured a firm conclusion on this. He draws attention to 'the unique capacity to awake an image, concept or thought without direct or immediate external stimulus whereas the animal responds only to an immediate stimulus'.[6] He gives a still more precise emphasis to the special position of man by a formulation which at the same time assigns a precise significance to the symbol:

> This unique human capacity is designated as the capacity to form mental representations in contrast to the capacity which man shares with animals to experience mental registrations . . . Mental registration is the basis of memory but for the evocation of imagery additional – what is postulated as a mental representation.

This identification of symbols and representations is more than a scholastic exercise. The newly acquired definition of the concept of representation is placed by Beres, after careful consideration, in the context of the concept of psychic energy. Symbols have an economic function. On this Beres says: 'I have described the theory that to make possible the delay of response there are mental representations which are cathected by the bound energies of the instinctual drives and which can be evoked to consciousness as images, fantasies or thoughts.'

In other words, the processes of cathexis play themselves out in symbols. This view follows inevitably, once the revised theory of symbols is connected with the theory of representations, taking into account all those insights which have been achieved in the last decade in the theory of representations (Hartmann, Jacobson, Sandler, etc.). The results of the revision of the theory of symbols and representations can be placed side by side and issue in the following conclusions:

(1) Representations are symbols, i.e. products of a process of symbol formation.

(2) Representations are the elements of processes of cathexis.

(3) It is an obvious move to unite the two conclusions and state that instinctual drives play themselves out in symbols.

6. Beres (1965).

However, as soon as this conclusion is accepted, it leads to an unfortunate dilemma. Must we deduce that there are no unconscious representations? Is the sphere of the unconscious empty, an area of mere dispositions, without objects to which a cathexis could attach itself? It is unnecessary to elaborate such possibilities any further in order to recognize that this would undermine a central point of psychoanalytic theory.

From the impossibility of integrating unconscious representations into the model of the symbol, it is certainly not permissible to deny them the character of objects of cathexis. It is impossible to reduce them to mere dispositions.

In fact this conclusion would be premature. It would pass over a number of experiences which demand that we recognize the existence of unconscious representations. The old reasoning is still valid, as much in the case of unconscious representations as anywhere else: unconscious images rise to the surface in therapy; unconscious representations may be transformed into symbols which prove the derivation of these images from life-experience, i.e. from the formative processes of the individual. And, moreover, even before any re-symbolization takes place, the arsenal of neurotic symptoms offers compelling evidence of the presence of an attachment of instinctual energy to a representation which was excluded from the realm of symbolic representations. The genetic connection between representations, which appear as images in the conscious, and unconscious representations, gives us a clear insight into the peculiarity of unconscious images in contrast with conscious ones. Both are structures, but we may distinguish them by saying that there can be two kinds of structured representation, conscious and unconscious. Conscious representations have the character of symbols, whereas unconscious representations are not symbolic structures. I have proposed, on the basis of a formula of Freud's, that they should be termed 'stereotypes'.

It must be emphasized that stereotypes as representations have a genetic connection with symbols. Stereotypes – that is to say, unconscious representations – stem from symbolic representations which have been formed in the process of socialization and have been 'excommunicated' in the process of repression: that is, they have been excluded from communication in language and action. The fact that they have not thereby lost their capacity to influence behaviour, their dynamic-energetic relevance, has been demonstrated by psychoanalytic experience.

The multiplicity of this genetic connection becomes strikingly clear when one considers a peculiarity of the psychoanalytic theory of representations: representations of objects or of the self by no means consist of a single, simple symbol, but are always compound, a collection of symbols. That constitutes their 'historicity'. The object-representation 'mother', for instance, even if we take into account only the conscious elements – the 'symbols' – proves to be a many-layered complex of verbally comprehensible 'discursive' symbols, as well as non-verbal 'presentative' symbols. This applies to unconscious representations in a special way; here the mother-image divides up into a series of constituent images, each with a different specific aspect, e.g. the tender mother, the punishing mother, etc. At different moments of psychoanalytic therapy such facets come to the surface as historically exact pictures of specific moments: the mother in such-and-such a situation on a particular day. This is often a matter of screen memories, i.e. of memories which represent, in the manner of a typical portrait, specific decisive characteristics of the circumstances of a relationship. In the end, however, the images may be traced back to *original occurrences*, to those 'scenes' into which the process of repression has broken up the whole of the situation, so as to desymbolize the tabooed parts of the situation.

From all this it may be deduced that a cathexis of the images as object representations can never be viewed as a simple process. It is not a question of an attachment of energy to a 'point', but always of a multi-layered attachment to individual facets of the object-representation. This formal peculiarity is observable in the work of mourning. Freud has given a precise description of this in the following passage:

In the first place, normal mourning, too, overcomes the loss of the object, and it, too, while it lasts, absorbs all the energies of the ego . . . Each single one of the memories and situations of expectancy which demonstrate the libido's attachment to the lost object is met by the verdict of reality that the object no longer exists; and the ego, confronted as it were with the question whether it shall share this fate, is persuaded by the sum of the narcissistic satisfactions that it derives from being alive to sever its attachment to the object that has been abolished. We may perhaps suppose that this work of severance is so slow and gradual that by the time it has been finished the expenditure of energy necessary for it is also dissipated.[7]

Let us sum up the characteristics of the stereotype:

(1) They fulfil the same dynamic function as symbols.

(2) They may be transformed into symbols and have been transformed out of symbols.

(3) Whereas symbols can be evoked independently of the real situation, stereotypes require a scene to be set up in which they can be released. If this is present, a discharge takes place which is strikingly illustrated in the enactment of hysteria. The reverse side of this dependence on scenic arrangement is the absence of evocation if it is possible to avoid the situational stimulus with sufficient care. Scenic arrangement may in any case not be thought of as being restricted to real events. Fantasy situations may also have a precipitating function when they join together.

(4) Whereas symbols are characterized by the distinction of 'object' and 'symbol', there is no such autonomy in the case of the stereotype. As Beres established, the 'retardation function' in mature action is based on the autonomy of the symbols: which means, in the context of the present discussion, on the representations which have a symbol-character. With the possibility of picturing to oneself the symbol independently of any scenic context, the symbol acquires its value in the emotional economy as an instrument of communication. Because the symbol is identical with the real external love-object, and at the same time can be distinguished from it, instinctual dynamics can be separated from the scenic presence of the object. The most important consequences of this situation are:

(a) Action may be replaced by a trial-action with slight expenditure of energy. Everything can be played through 'in the mind' first, before the action is undertaken.

(b) The employment of symbols brings into play a retarding factor, that very retarding factor which is typical of the

7. Freud (1914).

higher, i.e. the secondary processes. This retarding factor, which loosens the automatic character of events – instinctual release, for instance – is connected with yet another circumstance, namely the fact that symbols form a multi-layered system, bound together by a rich network of cross-connections. The fabric of language may make this clearer. Every operation with a symbol is complicated by the whole system of symbols. Stereotyped impulses, on the other hand, operate without being retarded and independently of symbolic structures behind the back of the individual – a process which finds expression sometimes in motor actions, sometimes in dreams or daydreams. In every case, however, the 'scene' runs its course due to an inner automatism which is inaccessible to reflection. This leads to the next feature.

(5) This feature is the instinctual-economic reverse-side of the dependence of scenic arrangement mentioned under (3). Stereotyped instinctual discharges are strictly determined. They are so inseparably bound to the precipitating scenic impulse that we speak of the *repetition-compulsion.* This total determination (and lack of capacity for reflection) sets neurotic processes apart from those which are mediated by symbols. In the case of the latter the *cause* cannot be put in the same way; the search for a *motive* cannot here take the form of the investigation of a cause. A further common feature of all stereotyped processes is their irreversibility. Against all expectation neurotic stereotypes, or 'scenic patterns', prove to be inexhaustible and irreversible. On the contrary, we are familiar with the process of imprinting (to borrow this term from reflex theory) which becomes more and more effortless. This irreversibility, this repetitiveness of stereotyped behaviour, set in at a specific historical point: at the *original occurrence.* At this moment of development any capacity for flexible adaptability also came to an end. Versatility is replaced by an invariable rigidity.

This catalogue of characteristics compels us to consider a parallel, one which is strange at first sight but nevertheless impossible to reject on closer examination, with the behaviour of animal organisms. In the brief outline we give here we must forgo a list of the ethological parallels. It must suffice to establish summarily that stereotyped behaviour corresponds in decisive structural elements with the behaviour of 'drive training limitation' worked out by Lorenz. In the release schemata of animals we encounter an arrangement of characteristics which is comparable to the neurotic behaviour stereotype, as soon as the transformation of behaviour through symbolically mediated action is abstracted from the whole text of neurotic reactions. What then remains is the pattern of an arrangement which we would characterize as stereotyped behaviour.

The features of this stereotyped behaviour may be summarized as follows: lack of capacity to recognize; determinism; unhindered discharge; irreversibility; autonomy and a tendency to imprinting; attachment to the environment, i.e. attachment to a 'scene' and 'scenic reproduction' or repetition-compulsion; genesis in the history of an individual's development. All these features are shared by stereotyped behaviour as it results from repression, and the behaviour patterns of animal organisms which acquire a release-scheme.

This allusion to the parallels between neurotically stereotyped behaviour and animal instinct training limitation should not, however, be understood as an equation of the two. In human behaviour *stereotyped behaviour is always mixed with symbolically mediated action.* The ego plays a part at least in the form of rationalizations or secondary revisions (such as secondary dream-work). The very fact of remembering a dream should warn us against undervaluing the achievement of the ego. These revisions and interventions are only particular instances of an unceasing combination of stereotypes with symbols in the formation of secondary centres of motivation. Stereotyped behaviour is always bound up with symbolically mediated action.

The difference between stereotyped and symbolically mediated behaviour becomes particularly clear in the contrast between 'reaction' and 'action', especially with regard to the characteristics which Winch has laid down for 'rule-governed behaviour'[8]– which I would identify with symbolically mediated behaviour.

A further point in which human and animal behaviour clearly

8. Winch (1958).

differs is that of genetic origin. The formation of the release mechanisms in animals must be understood as a progressive fulfilment of a set pattern of events; whereas the formation of stereotyped behaviour in neurosis occurs where a previously achieved differentiation – that is to say, operation with symbols – has been abandoned. This abandonment of an already-developed ability and the reversion to a pre-symbolic level follows a course quite opposed to the gradual development in animals, and is in fact a mechanism of decay. The development of a release mechanism in animals and repression are two different things, even though in one limited respect both produce the same result – stereotyped behaviour.

The transformation of symbols into stereotypes, i.e. of symbolic into desymbolized representations, results from repression.

Let us describe this process in a typical course of infantile development: the relationship of a boy in the oedipal phase to his mother. This relationship changes during the oedipal conflict in such a way that the symbol comes into opposition with the whole system of symbols, and finally only the choice between a removal of the cathexis or a disavowal of the conflict-laden process remains. Since the love-object and the relevant object representation cannot be dispensed with, the representation has to lose its character as a 'symbol'. The instinctual cathexis is retained while being desymbolized, a process in which the attachment of the drive to the object must be seen as the cause of the desymbolization. One could also express this process by saying: because the object representation can neither be dispensed with, nor consciously tolerated 'with cathexis', it is 'denied'. In a reversal of Freud's observation we can thus understand repression as an 'inner denial'.

One peculiarity of object representations – their fundamentally relational character – should have become clear in the description of these processes. If we say that a love-object must be desymbolized on account of the forbidden instinctual cathexis, this is meaningful only if we take into account the fact that the object representation includes a collection of images each of which has different 'behavioural aspects'. As an example let us once again cite the 'tender mother', that is to say the 'mother who behaves, has behaved, or should behave in such-and-such a way to the experiencing subject'. Behaviour here becomes meaningful in a 'context', i.e. as behaviour 'in-relation-to'. Corresponding to the object representation 'in-relation-to' there is a self-representation which completes the behaviour in a relationship situation. Thus a mother-image is never desymbolized in itself – the notion of the setting-aside of the 'symbol of an object' is meaningless. Only a concept which works on the assumption that the representations are 'objects of relationships in an act', which sees them in a quite definite *scenic arrangement* corresponding to a precise point in some life-history, throws light on the circumstances. If we accept this idea we must accept a further consequence. Since according to our hypothesis repression as an 'inner denial' is identical with desymbolization, and that means 'the transformation of a symbolic representation into a stereotype while preserving its relational character', then we must ascribe the same relational character to the stereotype as the symbolic object representations already possessed – and on account of which they were desymbolized. The stereotype too must be regarded as a representation of behaviour 'in-relation-to'. From this it follows further that if the representation of the love-object is desymbolized, then the same fate befalls the corresponding position of the self-representation which is the part of the scene corresponding to the object.

So much for the transformation of symbols into stereotypes. But there is another kind of change in the sphere of the symbols themselves. Representations can increasingly transform their character as 'symbols' into that of 'signs'. There is an increasing emptying of meaning which must be understood as a decrease of 'emotional significance for the subject'. Loss of resonance in this context always means a loss in the subject's capacity to be affected by the objects, which gives rise to a tendency to loss of relationship at corresponding points in both self-representations and object-representations. Likewise, the transformation of symbols into signs means an increasing objectification. Signs differ from symbols in having a one-to-one relationship; that is, a perfection of denotation with a lessening in the range of connotation. In this transformation what is signified is isolated and delimited as an object. When we transfer this observation to the representations of relational objects we are forced to the conclusion that object-representations more and more lose their relational character. In a formal analysis of signs the psychological experience of lack of warmth and of affective vitality in the process of intellectualization and isolation appears as an increasing dissolution of their relational character. This means a dissolution of their 'gestural character' with an increasing separation of self and object.

The following opposition may be noted. Repression issues in desymbolization, a formal regression of the process of symbol formation in the direction of the formation of stereotypes, in which instead of symbolically-mediated behaviour (with reflection on the motive) a stereotyped blind acting and reacting sets in. On the other hand, in the compulsive neurotic pattern of isolation and intellectualization, symbolization runs on ahead in a further transformation of symbols into signs.

Corresponding to this, there is a line of increasing gestural content from signs to symbols. This line leads on from symbols to stereotypes to the point where self and object fuse into one. If one connects the experiences afforded by the observation of dreams with insights into infantile development, it becomes clear how at the level of stereotypes the most far-reaching accentuation of the 'standing-in-relation-to-the-object' ends in a 'primary confusion' of object and subject.

To sum up:

(1) With the conversion from symbols to stereotypes the 'gestural functional aspect' is strengthened.

(2) On the other hand, with increasing 'objectification' in the area of signs, the 'scenic' or 'situational' aspect of object-representations largely (or altogether) disappears. The more symbols turn into 'signs', the greater the decrease in scenic character. Situated midway between stereotypes and signs, symbols (in the narrower sense) possess a well-balanced relationship: such that in a certain situation of balance it is possible to refer with equal justification to 'object-representations in a certain scenic order' and to 'situations which become concrete when attached to certain objects'. This scenic-situational aspect is reinforced in the passage into the field of stereotypes, in crossing the borderline of

the unconscious – that is, in repression. When the threshold of repression is crossed in the direction of stereotypes two things occur:

(a) the scenic-situational aspect prevails, absorbing the object, as it were;

(b) the scenic-situational aspect loses its 'symbolic organization'. The 'situation' can no more be visualized, now, than can the 'object' – 'situations', like object-representations, are desymbolized. They can no longer be grasped. The situation grasped by an act of reflection is replaced by the uncomprehended scene – the internal psychic pattern of a relationship to the outside world stimulated by instinctual responses and directed schematically. Thus repression means two things. On the one hand it is a process which must be understood as a desymbolization, as a qualitative leap. But on the other hand repression also signifies the domination of the 'situational', or more correctly the 'scenic', character of the object-representations and self-representations: the appearance of a compulsive scenic interplay of instinctual representations and schema (as the inner representations of a release mechanism bound to the external world). In addition to the process of symbolization, the suspension of what is objective into what is functional is a process which occupies another, no less important, stage in transformation. This has notable theoretical consequences: desymbolization plus total acting-out must be viewed as a process of functionalization. For the psychology of stereotyped behaviour has the status of a functionalistic system. To be sure, it has this status only with regard to stereotyped behaviour, and it must be added that psychoanalysis cannot maintain this view without interruption.

The re-formulation of the concept of the symbol, and the introduction of the concept of the stereotype in the sense of a 'desymbolized representation', would remain incomplete if the problem of the significant gesture, as developed by G. H. Mead,[9] were left out of the discussion.

Mead developed his understanding of the 'gesture' from the work of Wundt. In the course of the phylogenetic development of language, gesture becomes a symbol which in its early stages may

9. Mead (1967).

be regarded as part of a social action. Already in this starting-point the correspondence with the line of development which we have here presented is striking. As may easily be seen, the line of desymbolization takes the reverse direction under the pressure of repression. We have examined how in repression symbols (the symbol of the comprehended situation, of the symbolic self, and of the object-representation) are dissolved into a scenic interplay. 'Scene' can be identified here with what was characterized above as 'social action'. A pure 'scene' means in this instance pre-linguistic communication. Mead discusses it as an exchange of non-significant gestures.

These gestures must not be interpreted as the expression of feelings but as

> parts of complex acts in which different forms were involved. They became the tools through which the other forms responded. When they did give rise to a certain response, they were themselves changed in response to the change which took place in the other form. They are part of the organization of the social act, and highly important elements in that organization.[10]

Thus gestures are *parts of scenes*; and the passage from gestures to significant gestures is a passage from pre-linguistic to linguistic communication. The gesture gains its significance through the fact that a commonly-accepted meaning is attached to it:

> Only in terms of gestures as significant symbols is the existence of mind or intelligence possible; for only in terms of gestures which are significant symbols can thinking – which is simply an internalized or implicit conversation of the individual with himself by means of such gestures – take place. The internalization in our experience of the external conversations of gestures which we carry on with other individuals in the social process is the essence of thinking; and the gestures thus internalized are significant symbols because they have the same meanings for all individual members of the given society or social group.[11]

We shall confine our discussion to the relationships within an inherited linguistic community. Within such a linguistic community the gesture can receive the character of a significant symbol only if it is absorbed into the linguistic context. Thus the differ-

10. ibid., p. 44. 11. ibid., p. 47.

ence between stereotyped and symbolically-mediated behaviour may be demonstrated again. Stereotyped behaviour may be characterized as participation in a sequence of actions, i.e. a 'scene' in which the game follows its own course behind the back of individuals. Symbolically-mediated action, on the other hand, is behaviour in which individuals can reflect on a representation which provides a basis for communication. Here there is an unbroken ability to keep in view the rules acquired in the socialization process. Symbolically-mediated action presupposes the possession of a system of significant gestures – i.e. a *language*.

We may now complete these remarks with a more precise statement: stereotyped behaviour may be characterized as '*exclusion from linguistic communication*'. On this level of behaviour the scene must be 'acted out'. It can neither be grasped as a 'situation', nor can behaviour (of oneself or of others) be *understood* as 'behaviour-in-relation-to', i.e. as a significant gesture. Above all object-representation and self-representation cannot even be perceived, let alone distinguished. Both object-representations and self-representations are 'unconscious': they are 'present' but they are not recognizable and – it must be added – they are structures which can be cathected in an indivisible scenic interplay.

The scene is tied to the external world: that is to say, it can only be provoked by a stimulus, but given that stimulus it is automatically precipitated. We described repression as desymbolization, as a decline into scenic acting-out – repression is exclusion from linguistic communication.

With this formulation some interesting questions arise: if we describe repression as exclusion from linguistic communication, should we identify 'neurotic behaviour' as behaviour resulting from unconscious motivation, i.e. as speechless? This assumption appears to be an obvious one, but it is untenable. Behaviour which results from unconscious motivation never occurs in an unbroken manner. In every case, no matter whether it concerns acting-out, parapraxis, dream-work, verbal communications or whatever, we find the phenomena of secondary processing. The process that we saw at work in symbol formation and then found described as a multiple function by Waelder, inevitably comes into play – even in the severely handicapped psychotic patient with a minimal ego-function. It can be said with just as much justice that the secondary processing removes the loss of speech, as that it intensifies it. For through the incessant transformation of all behaviour the subject's self-control – which a decline into stereotyped behaviour must be regarded as – is compensated for just as much as it is concealed. Because stereotyped is regularly combined with symbolically-mediated behaviour and because the latter transforms the former, stereotyped behaviour is inaccessible to observation, and above all to self-observation. Therein consists the 'living lie' of the neurotic.

But the process of falsification extends deeper still. We may illustrate this with an example: a patient quarrels with an employer because he 'transfers the protest against his father to the employer'. In a precise analysis of his behaviour we find a mixture of things: behaviour which is appropriate in terms of the real situation (e.g. the patient treats his employer politely, as his role requires); the fulfilment of instinctual needs (he has outbursts of fury, which are a reproduction of his early infantile behaviour); reactions (the employer plays the game by letting the authoritarian father be evoked); rationalization (the employer himself is thoroughly despotic); defensive procedures, psychosomatic mechanisms, etc. All this may be summed up in the formula: a 'scene' is being reproduced. But the true situation is unrecognizable, it is misunderstood. In other words, the 'scene' which is acted out is in fact symbolized, it is understood as a 'situation' – but wrongly, for it is not perceived as the situation which it really is. Let us concentrate on the perception of 'objects'. The employer is
(1) treated in the scene as a 'father'.
(2) in the falsified situation looked on as an 'employer'.
Correspondingly the patient experiences his role
(1) in the scene as a 'son'.
(2) who understands himself in the – falsified – situation as a 'subordinate'.
The same event is simultaneously 'not understood' and falsely understood.

We can view the same behaviour as a simultaneous exchange of 'non-significant' and 'significant' gestures.

This is a matter not of speechlessness, but of a peculiar confusion of language. This confusion becomes very apparent in the mixing-up of object-representations. 'Employer' here corresponds to the formula:

'Employer' = employer (+ father).

The part in brackets is dynamically dominant, the other is dominant in the conscious part of the mind. But both are effective together.

'Employer' ≐ employer + father.

Obviously the concept in quotation marks, 'employer', has

(1) a range of meaning valid only for this patient – it is part of a 'private language'.

(2) at the same time it is part of an everyday language, which seems to pose no problems of common understanding for the self-understanding of the person concerned. But this is not the case. Clearly it would be misleading to speak here of a mere exclusion from the linguistic community. The concept is re-integrated, becoming part of a *pseudo-communicative private language*.

References

BERES, D. (1965), *Bulletin of the Menninger Clinic*, p. 1.

CASSIRER, E. (1944), *An Essay on Man*, Yale University Press.

FREUD, S. (1914), Standard Edition, vol. 14, Hogarth Press, 1957.

JONES, E. (1918), *Papers on Psychoanalysis*, Baillière Tyndall, 2nd ed.

KUBIE, L. S. (1958), *Neurotic Distortion of the Creative Process*, University of Kansas Press.

LANGER, S. (1960), *Philosophy in a New Key*, Harvard University Press, pp. 201–2.

MEAD, G. H. (1967), *Mind, Self and Society*, University of Chicago Press, pp. 44, 47.

SEGEL, N. P. (1961), in *Journal of the American Psychoanalytic Association*, vol. 9, p. 146.

WINCH, P. (1958), *The Idea of a Social Science*, Routledge & Kegan Paul.

8 Charles Taylor

Hermeneutics and Politics

Excerpt from Charles Taylor, 'Interpretation and the Science of Man', *Review of Metaphysics*, vol. 25, no. 3, 1971, pp. 1–32, 35–45.

Is there a sense in which interpretation is essential to explanation in the sciences of man? The view that it is, that there is an unavoidably 'hermeneutical' component in the sciences of man, goes back to Dilthey. But recently the question has come again to the fore, for instance, in the work of Gadamer, in Ricoeur's interpretation of Freud, and in the writings of Habermas.

Interpretation, in the sense relevant to hermeneutics, is an attempt to make clear, to make sense of an object of study. This object must, therefore, be a text, or a text-analogue, which in some way is confused, incomplete, cloudy, seemingly contradictory – in one way or another, unclear. The interpretation aims to bring to light an underlying coherence or sense.

This means that any science which can be called 'hermeneutical', even in an extended sense, must be dealing with one or another of the confusingly interrelated forms of meaning. Let us try to see a little more clearly what this involves.

(1) We need, first, an object or field of objects, about which we can speak in terms of coherence or its absence, of making sense or nonsense.

(2) Second, we need to be able to make a distinction, even if only a relative one, between the sense or coherence made, and its embodiment in a particular field of carriers or signifiers. For otherwise, the task of making clear what is fragmentary or confused would be radically impossible. No sense could be given to this idea. We have to be able to make for our interpretations claims of the order: the meaning confusedly present in this text or text-analogue is clearly expressed here. The meaning, in other words, is one which admits of more than one expression, and, in

this sense, a distinction must be possible between meaning and expression.

The point of the above qualification, that this distinction may be only relative, is that there are cases where no clear, unambiguous non-arbitrary line can be drawn between what is said and its expression. It can be plausibly argued (I think convincingly, although there isn't space to go into it here) that this is the normal and fundamental condition of meaningful expression, that exact synonymy, or equivalence of meaning, is a rare and localized achievement of specialized languages or uses of civilization. But this, if true (and I think it is), doesn't do away with the distinction between meaning and expression. Even if there is an important sense in which a meaning re-expressed in a new medium cannot be declared identical, this by no means entails that we can give no sense to the project of expressing a meaning in a new way. It does, of course, raise an interesting and difficult question about what can be meant by expressing it in a clearer way: what is the 'it' which is clarified if equivalence is denied? I hope to return to this in examining interpretation in the sciences of man.

Hence the object of a science of interpretation must be describable in terms of sense and nonsense, coherence and its absence; and must admit of a distinction between meaning and its expression.

(3) There is also a third condition it must meet. We can speak of sense or coherence, and of their different embodiments, in connection with such phenomena as gestalts, or patterns in rock formations, or snow crystals, where the notion of expression has no real warrant. What is lacking here is the notion of a subject for whom these meanings are. Without such a subject, the choice of criteria of sameness and difference, the choice among the different forms of coherence which can be identified in a given pattern, among the different conceptual fields in which it can be seen, is arbitrary.

In a text or text-analogue, on the other hand, we are trying to make explicit the meaning expressed, and this means expressed by or for a subject or subjects. The notion of expression refers us to that of a subject. The identification of the subject is by no means necessarily unproblematical, as we shall see further on; it may be one of the most difficult problems, an area in which prevailing epistemological prejudice may blind us to the nature of our object of study. I think this has been the case, as I will show below. And moreover, the identification of a subject does not assure us of a clear and absolute distinction between meaning and expression as we saw above. But any such distinction, even a relative one, is without any anchor at all, is totally arbitrary, without appeal to a subject.

The object of a science of interpretation must thus have: sense, distinguishable from its expression, which is for or by a subject.

Before going on to see in what way, if any, these conditions are realized in the sciences of man, I think it would be useful to set out more clearly what rides on this question, why it matters whether or not we think of the sciences of man as hermeneutical, what the issue is at stake here.

The issue here is at root an epistemological one. But it is inextricable from an ontological one, and, hence, cannot but be relevant to our notions of science and of the proper conduct of inquiry. We might say that it is an ontological issue which has been argued ever since the seventeenth century in terms of epistemological considerations which have appeared to some to be unanswerable.

The case could be put in these terms: what are the criteria of udgement in a hermeneutical science? A successful interpretation is one which makes clear the meaning originally present in a confused, fragmentary, cloudy form. But how does one know that this interpretation is correct? Presumably because it makes sense of the original text: what is strange, mystifying, puzzling, contradictory is no longer so, is accounted for. The interpretation appeals throughout to our understanding of the 'language' of expression, which understanding allows us to see that this expression is puzzling, that it is in contradiction to that other, etc., and that these difficulties are cleared up when the meaning is expressed in a new way.

But this appeal to our understanding seems to be crucially inadequate. What if someone does not 'see' the adequacy of our interpretation, does not accept our reading? We try to show him how it makes sense of the original non- or partial sense. But for him to follow us he must read the original language as we do, he must recognize these expressions as puzzling in a certain way, and hence be looking for a solution to our problem. If he does not, what can we do? The answer, it would seem, can only be more of the same. We have to show him through the reading of other expressions why this expression must be read in the way we propose. But success here requires that he follow us in these other readings, and so on, it would seem, potentially forever. We cannot escape an ultimate appeal to a common understanding of the expressions, of the 'language' involved. This is one way of trying to express what has been called the 'hermeneutical circle'. What we are trying to establish is a certain reading of text or expressions, and what we appeal to as our grounds for this reading can only be other readings. The circle can also be put in terms of part-whole relations: we are trying to establish a reading for the whole text, and for this we appeal to readings of its partial expressions; and yet because we are dealing with meaning, with making sense, where expressions only make sense or not in relation to others, the readings of partial expressions depend on those of others, and ultimately of the whole.

Put in forensic terms, as we started to do above, we can only convince an interlocutor if at some point he shares our understanding of the language concerned. If he does not, there is no further step to take in rational argument; we can try to awaken these intuitions in him, or we can simply give up; argument will advance us no further. But of course, the forensic predicament can be transferred into my own judging: if I am this ill-equipped to convince a stubborn interlocutor, how can I convince myself? How can I be sure? Maybe my intuitions are wrong or distorted, maybe I am locked into a circle of illusion.

Now one, and perhaps the only, sane response to this would be to say that such uncertainty is an ineradicable part of our epistemological predicament. That even to characterize it as 'uncertainty' is to adopt an absurdly severe criterion of 'certainty', which deprives the concept of any sensible use. But this has not been the only or even the main response of our philosophical tradition. And it is another response which has had an important and far-reaching effect on the sciences of man. The demand has been for a level of certainty which can only be attained by breaking beyond the circle.

There are two ways in which this break-out has been envisaged. The first might be called the 'rationalist' one and could be thought to reach a culmination in Hegel. It does not involve a negation of intuition, or of our understanding of meaning, but rather aspires to attainment of an understanding of such clarity that it would carry with it the certainty of the undeniable. In Hegel's case, for instance, our full understanding of the whole in 'thought' carries with it a grasp of its inner necessity, such that we see how it could not be otherwise. No higher grade of certainty is conceivable. For this aspiration the word 'break-out' is badly chosen; the aim is rather to bring understanding to an inner clarity which is absolute.

The other way, which we can call 'empiricist', is a genuine attempt to go beyond the circle of our own interpretations, to get beyond subjectivity. The attempt is to reconstruct knowledge in such a way that there is no need to make final appeal to readings or judgements which cannot be checked further. That is why the basic building block of knowledge on this view is the impression, or sense-datum, a unit of information which is not the deliverance of a judgement, which has by definition no element in it of reading or interpretation, which is a brute datum. The highest ambition would be to build our knowledge from such building blocks by judgements which could be anchored in a certainty beyond subjective intuition. This is what underlies the attraction of the notion of the association of ideas, or if the same procedure is viewed as a method, induction. If the original acquisition of the units of information is not the fruit of judgement or interpretation, then the verification that two such elements occur together need not either be the fruit of interpretation, of a reading or intuition which cannot be checked. For if the occurrence of a single element is a brute datum, then so is the co-occurrence of two such elements. The path to true knowledge would then repose crucially on the correct recording of such co-occurrences.

This is what lies behind an ideal of verification which is central to an important tradition in the philosophy of science, whose main contemporary protagonists are the logical empiricists. Verification must be grounded ultimately in the acquisition of brute data. By 'brute data', I mean here and throughout data whose validity cannot be questioned by offering another interpretation or reading, data whose credibility cannot be founded or undermined by further reasoning.[1] If such a difference of interpretation can arise over given data, then it must be possible to structure the argument so as to distinguish the basic, brute data from the inferences made on the basis of them.

The inferences themselves, of course, to be valid must similarly be beyond the challenge of a rival interpretation. Here the logical empiricists added to the armoury of traditional empiricism which set great store by the method of induction, the whole domain of logical and mathematical inference which has been central to the rationalist position (with Leibniz at least, although not with Hegel), and which offered another brand of unquestionable certainty.

Of course, mathematical inference and empirical verification were combined in such a way that two theories or more could be verified of the same domain of facts. But this was a consequence to which logical empiricism was willing to accommodate itself. As for the surplus meaning in a theory which could not be rigorously co-ordinated with brute data, it was considered to be quite outside the logic of verification.

As a theory of perception, this epistemology gave rise to all sorts of problems, not least of which was the perpetual threat of scepticism and solipsism inseparable from a conception of the basic data of knowledge as brute data, beyond investigation. As

1. The notion of brute data here has some relation to, but is not at all the same as the 'brute facts' discussed by Elizabeth Anscombe, 'On Brute Facts', *Analysis*, v. 18, 1957–8, pp. 69–72, and John Searle, *Speech Acts*, Cambridge, 1969, pp. 50–53. For Anscombe and Searle, brute facts are contrasted to what may be called 'institutional facts', to use Searle's term, i.e., facts which presuppose the existence of certain institutions. Voting would be an example. But, as we shall see below in part II, some institutional facts, such as X's having voted Liberal, can be verified as brute data in the sense used here, and thus find a place in the category of political behaviour. What cannot as easily be described in terms of brute data are the institutions themselves.

a theory of perception, however, it seems largely a thing of the past, in spite of a surprising recrudescence in the Anglo-Saxon world in the thirties and forties. But there is no doubt that it goes marching on, among other places, as a theory of how the human mind and human knowledge actually function.

In a sense, the contemporary period has seen a better, more rigorous statement of what this epistemology is about in the form of computer-influenced theories of intelligence. These try to model intelligence as consisting of operations on machine-recognizable input which could themselves be matched by programmes which could be run on machines. The machine criterion provides us with our assurance against an appeal to intuition or interpretations which cannot be understood by fully explicit procedures operating on brute data – the input.[2]

The progress of natural science has lent great credibility to this epistemology, since it can be plausibly reconstructed on this model, as for instance has been done by the logical empiricists. And, of course, the temptation has been overwhelming to reconstruct the sciences of man on the same model; or rather to launch them in lines of inquiry that fit this paradigm, since they are constantly said to be in their 'infancy'. Psychology, where an earlier vogue of behaviourism is being replaced by a boom of computer-based models, is far from the only case.

The form this epistemological bias – one might say obsession – takes is different for different sciences. Later I would like to look at a particular case, the study of politics, where the issue can be followed out. But in general, the empiricist orientation must be hostile to a conduct of inquiry which is based on interpretation, and which encounters the hermeneutical circle as this was characterized above. This cannot meet the requirements of inter-subjective, non-arbitrary verification which it considers essential to science. And along with the epistemological stance goes the ontological belief that reality must be susceptible to understanding and explanation by science so understood. From this follows

2. Cf. discussion in M. Minsky, *Computation*, Englewood Cliffs, N. J., 1967, pp. 104–7, where Minsky explicitly argues that an effective procedure, which no longer requires intuition or interpretation, is one which can be realized by a machine.

a certain set of notions of what the sciences of man must be.

On the other hand, many, including myself, would like to argue that these notions about the sciences of man are sterile, that we cannot come to understand important dimensions of human life within the bounds set by this epistemological orientation. This dispute is, of course, familiar to all in at least some of its ramifications. What I want to claim is that the issue can be fruitfully posed in terms of the notion of interpretation as I began to outline it above.

I think this way of putting the question is useful because it allows us at once to bring to the surface the powerful epistemological beliefs which underlie the orthodox view of the sciences of man in our academy, and to make explicit the notion of our epistemological predicament implicit in the opposing thesis. This is in fact rather more way-out and shocking to the tradition of scientific thought than is often admitted or realized by the opponents of narrow scientism. It may not strengthen the case of the opposition to bring out fully what is involved in a hermeneutical science as far as convincing waverers is concerned, but a gain in clarity is surely worth a thinning of the ranks – at least in philosophy.

Before going on to look at the case of political science, it might be worth asking another question: why should we even pose the question whether the sciences of man are hermeneutical? What gives us the idea in the first place that men and their actions constitute an object or a series of objects which meet the conditions outlined above?

The answer is that on the phenomenological level or that of ordinary speech (and the two converge for the purposes of this argument) a certain notion of meaning has an essential place in the characterization of human behaviour. This is the sense in which we speak of a situation, an action, a demand, a prospect having a certain meaning for a person.

Now it is frequently thought that 'meaning' is used here in a sense which is a kind of illegitimate extension from the notion of linguistic meaning. Whether it can be considered an extension or not is another matter; it certainly differs from linguistic meaning.

But it would be very hard to argue that it is an illegitimate use of the term.

When we speak of the 'meaning' of a given predicament, we are using a concept which has the following articulation. (a) Meaning is for a subject: it is not the meaning of the situation *in vacuo*, but its meaning for a subject, a specific subject, a group of subjects, or perhaps what its meaning is for the human subject as such (even though particular humans might be reproached with not admitting or realizing this). (b) Meaning is of something; that is, we can distinguish between a given element – situation, action or whatever – and its meaning. But this is not to say that they are physically separable. Rather we are dealing with two descriptions of the element, in one of which it is characterized in terms of its meaning for the subject. But the relations between the two descriptions are not symmetrical. For, on the one hand, the description in terms of meaning cannot be unless descriptions of the other kind apply as well; or put differently, there can be no meaning without a substrate. But on the other hand, it may be that the same meaning may be borne by another substrate – e.g. a situation with the same meaning may be realized in different physical conditions. There is a necessary role for a potentially substitutable substrate; or all meanings are of something.

And thirdly, (c) things only have meaning in a field, that is, in relation to the meanings of other things. This means that there is no such thing as a single, unrelated meaningful element; and it means that changes in the other meanings in the field can involve changes in the given element. Meanings can't be identified except in relation to others, and in this way resemble words. The meaning of a word depends, for instance, on those words with which it contrasts, on those which define its place in the language (e.g. those defining 'determinable' dimensions, like colour, shape), on those which define the activity or 'language game' it figures in (describing, invoking, establishing communion), and so on. The relations between meanings in this sense are like those between concepts in a semantic field.

Just as our colour concepts are given their meaning by the field of contrast they set up together, so that the introduction of new concepts will alter the boundaries of others, so the various meanings that a subordinate's demeanour can have for us, as deferential, respectful, cringing, mildly mocking, ironical, insolent, provoking, downright rude, are established by a field of contrast; and, as with finer discrimination on our part, or a more sophisticated culture, new possibilities are born, so other terms of this range are altered. And as the meaning of our terms 'red', 'blue', 'green' is fixed by the definition of a field of contrast through the determinable term 'colour', so all these alternative demeanours are only available in a society which has, among other types, hierarchical relations of power and command. And corresponding to the underlying language game of designating coloured objects is the set of social practices which sustain these hierarchical structures and are fulfilled in them.

Meaning in this sense – let us call it experiential meaning – thus is for a subject, of something, in a field. This distinguishes it from linguistic meaning which has a four- and not three-dimensional structure. Linguistic meaning is for subjects and in a field, but it is the meaning of signifiers and it is about a world of referents. Once we are clear about the likenesses and differences, there should be little doubt that the term 'meaning' is not a misnomer, the product of an illegitimate extension into this context of experience and behaviour.

There is thus a quite legitimate notion of meaning which we use when we speak of the meaning of a situation for an agent. And that this concept has a place is integral to our ordinary consciousness and hence speech about our actions. Our actions are ordinarily characterized by the purpose sought and explained by desires, feelings, emotions. But the language by which we describe our goals, feelings, desires is also a definition of the meaning things have for us. The vocabulary defining meaning – words like 'terrifying', 'attractive' – is linked with that describing feeling – 'fear', 'desire' – and that describing goals – 'safety', 'possession'.

Moreover, our understanding of these terms moves inescapably in a hermeneutical circle. An emotion term like 'shame', for instance, essentially refers us to a certain kind of situation, the 'shameful', or 'humiliating', and a certain mode of response, that of hiding oneself, of covering up, or else 'wiping out' the blot. That is, it is essential to this feeling's being identified as shame that it be related to this situation and give rise to this type of disposition. But this situation in its turn can only be identified in relation to the feelings which it provokes; and the disposition is to a goal which can similarly not be understood without reference to the feelings experienced: the 'hiding' in question is one which will cover up my shame; it is not the same as hiding from an armed pursuer; we can only understand what is meant by 'hiding' here if we understand what kind of feeling and situation is being talked about. We have to be within the circle.

An emotion term like 'shame' can only be explained by reference to other concepts which in turn cannot be understood without reference to shame. To understand these concepts we have to be in on a certain experience, we have to understand a certain language, not just of words, but also a certain language of mutual action and communication, by which we blame, exhort, admire, esteem each other. In the end we are in on this because we grow up in the ambit of certain common meanings. But we can often experience what it is like to be on the outside when we encounter the feeling, action, and experiential meaning language of another civilization. Here there is no translation, no way of explaining in other, more accessible concepts. We can only catch on by getting somehow into their way of life, if only in imagination. Thus if we look at human behaviour as action done out of a background of desire, feeling, emotion, then we are looking at a reality which must be characterized in terms of meaning. But does this mean that it can be the object of a hermeneutical science as this was outlined above?

There are, to remind ourselves, three characteristics that the object of a science of interpretation has: it must have sense or coherence; this must be distinguishable from its expression, and this sense must be for a subject.

Now insofar as we are talking about behaviour as action, hence in terms of meaning, the category of sense or coherence must apply to it. This is not to say that all behaviour must 'make sense', if we mean by this be rational, avoid contradiction, confusion of purpose, and the like. Plainly a great deal of our action falls short of this goal. But in another sense, even contradictory, irrational action is 'made sense of', when we understand why it was engaged in. We make sense of action when there is a coherence between the actions of the agent and the meaning of his situation for him. We find his action puzzling until we find such a coherence. It may not be bad to repeat that this coherence in no way implies that the action is rational; the meaning of a situation for an agent may be full of confusion and contradiction; but the adequate depiction of this contradiction makes sense of it.

Making sense in this way through coherence of meaning and action, the meanings of action and situation, cannot but move in a hermeneutical circle. Our conviction that the account makes sense is contingent on our reading of action and situation. But these readings cannot be explained or justified except by reference to other such readings, and their relation to the whole. If an interlocutor does not understand this kind of reading, or will not accept it as valid, there is nowhere else the argument can go. Ultimately, a good explanation is one which makes sense of the behaviour; but then to appreciate a good explanation, one has to agree on what makes good sense; what makes good sense is a function of one's readings; and these in turn are based on the kind of sense one understands.

But how about the second characteristic, that sense should be distinguishable from its embodiment? This is necessary for a science of interpretation because interpretation lays a claim to make a confused meaning clearer; hence there must be some sense in which the 'same' meaning is expressed, but differently.

This immediately raises a difficulty. In talking of experiential meaning above, I mentioned that we can distinguish between a given element and its meaning, between meaning and substrate. This carried the claim that a given meaning *may* be realized in another substrate. But does this mean that we can *always* embody the same meaning in another situation? Perhaps there are some situations, standing before death, for instance, which have a meaning which can't be embodied otherwise.

But fortunately this difficult question is irrelevant for our purposes. For here we have a case in which the analogy between text and behaviour implicit in the notion of a hermeneutical science of man only applies with important modifications. The text is replaced in the interpretation by another text, one which is clearer. The text-analogue of behaviour is not replaced by another such text-analogue. When this happens we have revolutionary theatre, or terroristic acts designed to make propaganda of the deed, in which the hidden relations of a society are supposedly shown up in a dramatic confrontation. But this is not scientific understanding, even though it may perhaps be based on such understanding, or claim to be.

But in science the text-analogue is replaced by a text, an account. Which might prompt the question, how we can even begin to talk of interpretation here, of expressing the same meaning more clearly, when we have two such utterly different terms of comparison, a text and a tract of behaviour? Is the whole thing not just a bad pun?

This question leads us to open up another aspect of experiential meaning which we abstracted from earlier. Experiential meanings are defined in fields of contrast, as words are in semantic fields.

But what was not mentioned above is that these two kinds of definition aren't independent of each other. The range of human desires, feelings, emotions, and hence meanings is bound up with the level and type of culture, which in turn is inseparable from the distinctions and categories marked by the language people speak. The field of meanings in which a given situation can find its place is bound up with the semantic field of the terms characterizing these meanings and the related feelings, desires, predicaments.

But the relationship involved here is not a simple one. There are two simple types of models of relation which could be offered here, but both are inadequate. We could think of the feeling vocabulary as simply describing pre-existing feelings, as marking distinctions which would be there without them. But this is not adequate because we often experience in ourselves or others how achieving, say, a more sophisticated vocabulary of the emotions makes our emotional life more sophisticated and not just our descriptions of it. Reading a good, powerful novel may give me the picture of an emotion which I had not previously been aware of. But we can't draw a neat line between an increased ability to identify and an altered ability to feel emotions which this enables.

The other simple inadequate model of the relationship is to

jump from the above to the conclusion that thinking makes it so. But this clearly won't do either, since not just any new definition can be forced on us, nor can we force it on ourselves; and some which we do gladly take up can be judged inauthentic, or in bad faith, or just wrong-headed by others. These judgements may be wrong, but they are not in principle illicit. Rather we make an effort to be lucid about ourselves and our feelings, and admire a man who achieves this.

Thus, neither the simple correspondence view is correct, nor the view that thinking makes it so. But both have *prima facie* warrant. There is such a thing as self-lucidity, which points us to a correspondence view; but the achievement of such lucidity means moral change, that is, it changes the object known. At the same time, error about oneself is not just an absence of correspondence; it is also in some form inauthenticity, bad faith, self-delusion, repression of one's human feelings, or something of the kind; it is a matter of the quality of what is felt just as much as what is known about this, just as self-knowledge is.

If this is so, then we have to think of man as a self-interpreting animal. He is necessarily so, for there is no such thing as the structure of meanings for him independently of his interpretation of them; for one is woven into the other. But then the text of our interpretation is not that heterogeneous from what is interpreted; for what is interpreted is itself an interpretation; a self-interpretation which is embedded in a stream of action. It is an interpretation of experiential meaning which contributes to the constitution of this meaning. Or to put it in another way: that of which we are trying to find the coherence is itself partly constituted by self-interpretation.

Our aim is to replace this confused, incomplete, partly erroneous self-interpretation by a correct one. And in doing this we look not only to the self-interpretation but to the stream of behaviour in which it is set; just as in interpreting a historical document we have to place it in the stream of events which it relates to. But, of course, the analogy is not exact, for here we are interpreting the interpretation and the stream of behaviour in which it is set together, and not just one or the other.

There is thus no utter heterogeneity of interpretation to what it is about; rather there is a slide in the notion of interpretation. Already to be a living agent is to experience one's situation in terms of certain meanings; and this in a sense can be thought of as a sort of proto-'interpretation'. This is in turn interpreted and shaped by the language in which the agent lives these meanings. This whole is then at a third level interpreted by the explanation we proffer of his actions.

In this way the second condition of a hermeneutical science is met. But this account poses in a new light the question mentioned at the beginning whether the interpretation can ever express the same meaning as the interpreted. And in this case, there is clearly a way in which the two will not be congruent. For if the explanation is really clearer than the lived interpretation then it will be such that it would alter in some way the behaviour if it came to be internalized by the agent as his self-interpretation. In this way a hermeneutical science which achieves its goal, that is, attains greater clarity than the immediate understanding of agent or observer, must offer us an interpretation which is in this way crucially out of phase with the explicandum.

Thus, human behaviour seen as action of agents who desire and are moved, who have goals and aspirations, necessarily offers a purchase for descriptions in terms of meaning – what I have called 'experiential meaning'. The norm of explanation which it posits is one which 'makes sense' of the behaviour, which shows a coherence of meaning. This 'making sense of' is the proffering of an interpretation; and we have seen that what is interpreted meets the conditions of a science of interpretation: first, that we can speak of its sense or coherence; and second, that this sense can be expressed in another form, so that we can speak of the interpretation as giving clearer expression to what is only implicit in the explicandum. The third condition, that this sense be for a subject, is obviously met in this case, although who this subject is is by no means an unproblematical question as we shall see later on.

This should be enough to show that there is a good *prima facie* case to the effect that men and their actions are amenable to explanation of a hermeneutical kind. There is, therefore, some reason to raise the issue and challenge the epistemological orientation which would rule interpretation out of the sciences of man. A great deal more must be said to bring out what is involved in the hermeneutical sciences of man. But before getting on to this, it might help to clarify the issue with a couple of examples drawn from a specific field, that of politics.

In politics, too, the goal of a verifiable science has led to the concentration on features which can supposedly be identified in abstraction from our understanding or not understanding experiential meaning. These – let us call them brute data identifications – are what supposedly enable us to break out from the hermeneutical circle and found our science four square on a verification procedure which meets the requirements of the empiricist tradition.

But in politics the search for such brute data has not gone to the lengths which it has in psychology, where the object of science has been thought of by many as behaviour qua 'colourless movement', or as machine-recognizable properties. The tendency in politics has been to stop with something less basic, but – so it is thought – the identification of which cannot be challenged by the offering of another interpretation or reading of the data concerned. This is what is referred to as 'behaviour' in the rhetoric of political scientists, but it has not the rock-bottom quality of its psychological homonym.

Political behaviour includes what we would ordinarily call actions, but ones that are supposedly brute data identifiable. How can this be so? Well, actions are usually described by the purpose or end-state realized. But the purposes of some actions can be specified in what might be thought to be brute data terms; some actions, for instance, have physical end-states, like getting the car in the garage or climbing the mountain. Others have end-states which are closely tied by institutional rules to some unmistakable physical movement; thus, when I raise my hand in the meeting at the appropriate time, I am voting for the motion. The only questions we can raise about the corresponding actions, given such movements or the realization of such end-states, are whether the agent was aware of what he was doing, was acting as against simply emitting reflex behaviour, knew the institutional significance of his movement, etc. Any worries on this score generally turn out to be pretty artificial in the contexts political scientists are concerned with; and where they do arise they can be checked by relatively simple devices, e.g. asking the subject: did you mean to vote for the motion?

Hence, it would appear that there are actions which can be identified beyond fear of interpretative dispute; and this is what gives the foundation for the category of 'political behaviour'. Thus, there are some acts of obvious political relevance which can be specified thus in physical terms, such as killing, sending tanks into the streets, seizing people and confining them to cells; and there is an immense range of others which can be specified from physical acts by institutional rules, such as voting for instance. These can be the object of a science of politics which can hope to meet the stringent requirements of verification. The latter class particularly has provided matter for study in recent decades – most notably in the case of voting studies.

But of course a science of politics confined to such acts would be much too narrow. For on another level these actions also have meaning for the agents which is not exhausted in the brute data descriptions, and which is often crucial to understanding why they were done. Thus, in voting for the motion I am also saving the honour of my party, or defending the value of free speech, or vindicating public morality, or saving civilization from breakdown. It is in such terms that the agents talk about the motivation of much of their political action, and it is difficult to conceive a science of politics which doesn't come to grips with it.

Behavioural political science comes to grips with it by taking the meanings involved in action as facts about the agent, his beliefs, his affective reactions, his 'values', as the term is frequently used. For it can be thought verifiable in the brute data sense that men will agree to subscribe or not to a certain form of words (expressing a belief, say); or express a positive or negative reaction to certain events, or symbols; or agree or not with the proposition that some act is right or wrong. We can thus get at meanings as just another form of brute data by the techniques of the opinion survey and content analysis.

An immediate objection springs to mind. If we are trying to deal with the meanings which inform political action, then surely interpretative acumen is unavoidable. Let us say we are trying to understand the goals and values of a certain group, or grasp their vision of the polity; we might try to probe this by a questionnaire asking them whether they assent or not to a number of propositions, which are meant to express different goals, evaluations, beliefs. But how did we design the questionnaire? How did we pick these propositions? Here we relied on our understanding of the goals, values, vision involved. But then this understanding can be challenged, and hence the significance of our results questioned. Perhaps the finding of our study, the compiling of proportions of assent and dissent to these propositions is irrelevant, is without significance for understanding the agents or the polity concerned. This kind of attack is frequently made by critics of mainstream political science, or for that matter social science in general.

To this the proponents of this mainstream reply with a standard move of logical empiricism: distinguishing the process of discovery from the logic of verification. Of course, it is our understanding of these meanings which enables us to draw up the questionnaire which will test people's attitudes in respect to them. And, of course, interpretative dispute about these meanings is potentially endless; there are no brute data at this level, every affirmation can be challenged by a rival interpretation. But this has nothing to do with verifiable science. What is firmly verified is the set of correlations between, say, the assent to certain propositions and certain behaviour. We discover, for instance, that people who are active politically (defined by participation in a certain set of institutions) are more likely to consent to certain sets of propositions supposedly expressing the values underlying the system.[3] This finding is a firmly verified correlation no matter what one thinks of the reasoning, or simple hunches, that went into designing the research which established it. Political science as a body of knowledge is made up of such correlations; it does not give a truth value to the background reasoning or hunch. A good interpretative nose may be useful in hitting on the right correlations to test, but science is never called on to arbitrate the disputes between interpretations.

Thus, in addition to those overt acts which can be defined

3. Cf. H. McClosky (1964).

physically or institutionally, the category of political behaviour can include assent or dissent to verbal formulae, or the occurrence or not of verbal formulae in speech, or expressions of approval or rejection of certain events or measures as observed in institutionally defined behaviour (for instance, turning out for a demonstration).

Now there are a number of objections which can be made to this notion of political behaviour; one might question in all sorts of ways how interpretation-free it is in fact. But I would like to question it from another angle. One of the basic characteristics of this kind of social science is that it reconstructs reality in line with certain categorial principles. These allow for an intersubjective social reality which is made up of brute data, identifiable acts and structures, certain institutions, procedures, actions. It allows for beliefs, affective reactions, evaluations as the psychological properties of individuals. And it allows for correlations between these two orders or reality: e.g., that certain beliefs go along with certain acts, certain values with certain institutions, etc.

To put it another way, what is objectively (inter-subjectively) real is brute data identifiable. This is what social reality *is*. Social reality described in terms of its meaning for the actors, such that disputes could arise about interpretation which couldn't be settled by brute data (e.g., are people rioting to get a hearing, or are they rioting to redress humiliation, out of blind anger, because they recover a sense of dignity in insurrection?), this is given subjective reality, that is, there are certain beliefs, affective reactions, evaluations which individuals make or have about or in relation to social reality. These beliefs or reactions can have an effect on this reality; and the fact that such a belief is held is a fact of objective social reality. But the social reality which is the object of these attitudes, beliefs, reactions can only be made up of brute data. Thus any description of reality in terms of meanings which is open to interpretative question is only allowed into this scientific discourse if it is placed, as it were, in quotes and attributed to individuals as their opinion, belief, attitude. That this opinion, belief, etc., is held is thought of as a brute datum, since it is redefined as the respondent's giving a certain answer to the questionnaire.

This aspect of social reality which concerns its meanings for the agents has been taken up in a number of ways, but recently it has been spoken of in terms of political culture. Now the way this is defined and studied illustrates clearly the categorial principles above. For instance, political culture is referred to by Almond and Powell as the 'psychological dimension of the political system' (p. 23).[4] Further on they state: 'Political culture is the pattern of individual attitudes and orientations towards politics among the members of a political system. It is the subjective realm which underlies and gives meaning to political actions' (p. 50).[5] The authors then go on to distinguish three different kinds of orientations, cognitive (knowledge and beliefs), affective (feelings), and evaluative (judgements and opinions).

From the point of view of empiricist epistemology, this set of categorial principles leaves nothing out. Both reality and the meanings it has for actors are coped with. But what it in fact cannot allow for are inter-subjective meanings, that is, it cannot allow for the validity of descriptions of social reality in terms of meanings, hence not as brute data, which are not in quotation marks and attributed as opinion, attitude, etc. to individual(s). Now it is this exclusion that I would like to challenge in the name of another set of categorial principles, inspired by a quite other epistemology.

We spoke earlier about the brute data identification of acts by means of institutional rules. Thus, putting a cross beside someone's name on a slip of paper and putting this in a box counts in the right context as voting for that person; leaving the room, saying or writing a certain form of words, counts as breaking off the negotiations; writing one's name on a piece of paper counts as signing the petition, etc. But what is worth looking at is what underlies this set of identifications. These identifications are the application of a language of social life, a language which marks distinctions among different possible social acts, relations, structures. But what underlies this language?

Let us take the example of breaking off negotiations above.

4. See Almond and Powell (1966).
5. ibid.

The language of our society recognizes states or actions like the following: entering into negotiation, breaking off negotiations, offering to negotiate, negotiating in good (bad) faith, concluding negotiations, making a new offer, etc. In other more jargon infested language, the semantic 'space' of this range of social activity is carved up in a certain way, by a certain set of distinctions which our vocabulary marks; and the shape and nature of these distinctions is the nature of our language in this area. These distinctions are applied in our society with more or less formalism in different contexts.

But of course this is not true of every society. Our whole notion of negotiation is bound up for instance with the distinct identity and autonomy of the parties, with the willed nature of their relations; it is a very contractual notion. But other societies have no such conception. It is reported about the traditional Japanese village that the foundation of its social life was a powerful form of consensus, which put a high premium on unanimous decision.[6] Such a consensus would be considered shattered if two clearly articulated parties were to separate out, pursuing opposed aims and attempting either to vote down the opposition or push it into a settlement on the most favourable possible terms for themselves. Discussion there must be, and some kind of adjustment of differences. But our idea of bargaining, with the assumption of distinct autonomous parties in willed relationship, has no place there; nor does a series of distinctions, like entering into and leaving negotiation, or bargaining in good faith (e.g. with the genuine intention of seeking agreement).

Now the difference between our society and one of the kind just described could not be well expressed if we said we have a vocabulary to describe negotiation which they lack. We might say, for instance, that we have a vocabulary to describe the heavens that they lack, viz., that of Newtonian mechanics; for here we assume that they live under the same heavens as we do, only understand it differently. But it is not true that they have the same kind of bargaining as we do. The word, or whatever

6. Cf. Thomas C. Smith (1959), ch. 5. This type of consensus is also found in other traditional societies. Cf., for instance, the *desa* system of the Indonesian village.

word of their language we translate as 'bargaining', must have an entirely different gloss, which is marked by the distinctions their vocabulary allows in contrast to those marked by ours. But this different gloss is not just a difference of vocabulary, but also one of social reality.

But this still may be misleading as a way of putting the difference. For it might imply that there is a social reality which can be discovered in each society and which might exist quite independently of the vocabulary of that society, or indeed of any vocabulary, as the heavens would exist whether men theorized about them or not. And this is not the case; the realities here are practices; and these cannot be identified in abstraction from the language we use to describe them, or invoke them, or carry them out. That the practice of negotiation allows us to distinguish bargaining in good or bad faith, or entering into or breaking off negotiations, presupposes that our acts and situation have a certain description for us, e.g., that we are distinct parties entering into willed relations. But they cannot have these descriptions for us unless this is somehow expressed in our vocabulary of this practice; if not in our descriptions of the practices (for we may as yet be unconscious of some of the important distinctions) in the appropriate language for carrying them on. (Thus, the language marking a distinction between public and private acts or contexts may exist even where these terms or their equivalents are not part of this language; for the distinction will be marked by the different language which is appropriate in one context and the other, be it perhaps a difference of style, or dialect, even though the distinction is not designated by specific descriptive expressions.)

The situation we have here is one in which the vocabulary of a given social dimension is grounded in the shape of social practice in this dimension; that is, the vocabulary wouldn't make sense, couldn't be applied sensibly, where this range of practices didn't prevail. And yet this range of practices couldn't exist without the prevalence of this or some related vocabulary. There is no simple one-way dependence here. We can speak of mutual dependence if we like, but really what this points up is the artificiality of the distinction between social reality and the language of description of that social reality. The language is constitutive of the reality, is essential to its being the kind of reality it is. To separate the two and distinguish them as we quite rightly distinguish the heavens from our theories about them is forever to miss the point.

This type of relation has been recently explored, e.g., by John Searle, with his concept of a constitutive rule. As Searle points out, we are normally induced to think of rules as applying to behaviour which could be available to us whether or not the rule existed. Some rules are like this, they are regulative like commandments: don't take the goods of another. But there are other rules, e.g., that governing the Queen's move in chess, which are not so separable. If one suspends these rules, or imagines a state in which they have not yet been introduced, then the whole range of behaviour in question, in this case, chess playing, would not be. There would still, of course, be the activity of pushing a wood piece around on a board made of squares 8 by 8; but this is not chess any longer. Rules of this kind are constitutive rules. By contrast again, there are other rules of chess, such as that one say 'j'adoube' when one touches a piece without intending to play it, which are clearly regulative.[7]

I am suggesting that this notion of the constitutive be extended beyond the domain of rule-governed behaviour. That is why I suggest the vaguer word 'practice'. Even in an area where there are no clearly defined rules, there are distinctions between different sorts of behaviour such that one sort is considered the appropriate form for one action or context, the other for another action or context; e.g., doing or saying certain things amounts to breaking off negotiations, doing or saying other things amounts to making a new offer. But just as there are constitutive rules, i.e., rules such that the behaviour they govern could not exist without them, and which are in this sense inseparable from that behaviour, so I am suggesting that there are constitutive distinctions, constitutive ranges of language which are similarly inseparable, in that certain practices are not without them.

We can reverse this relationship and say that all the institutions and practices by which we live are constituted by certain distinctions and hence a certain language which is thus essential to them. We can take voting, a practice which is central to large

7. Cf. the discussion in Stanley Cavell (1969), pp. 21–31.

numbers of institutions in a democratic society. What is essential to the practice of voting is that some decision or verdict be delivered (a man elected, a measure passed), through some criterion of preponderance (simple majority, two-thirds majority or whatever) out of a set of micro-choices (the votes of the citizens, M.P.s, delegates). If there is not some such significance attached to our behaviour, no amount of marking and counting pieces of paper, raising hands, walking out into lobbies amounts to voting. From this it follows that the institution of voting must be such that certain distinctions have application: e.g., that between someone being elected, or a measure passed, and their failing of election, or passage; that between a valid vote and an invalid one which in turn requires a distinction between a real choice and one which is forced or counterfeited. For no matter how far we move from the Rousseauian notion that each man decide in full autonomy, the very institution of the vote requires that in some sense the enfranchised choose. For there to be voting in a sense recognizably like ours, there must be a distinction in men's self-interpretations between autonomy and forced choice.

This is to say that an activity of marking and counting papers has to bear intentional descriptions which fall within a certain range before we can agree to call it voting, just as the intercourse of two men or teams has to bear descriptions of a certain range before we will call it negotiation. Or in other words, that some practice is voting or negotiation has to do in part with the vocabulary established in a society as appropriate for engaging in it or describing it.

Hence implicit in these practices is a certain vision of the agent and his relation to others and to society. We saw in connection with negotiation in our society that it requires a picture of the parties as in some sense autonomous, and as entering into willed relations. And this picture carries with it certain implicit norms, such as that of good faith mentioned above, or a norm of rationality, that agreement correspond to one's goals as far as attainable, or the norm of continued freedom of action as far as attainable. These practices require that one's actions and relations be seen in the light of this picture and the accompanying norms, good faith, autonomy, and rationality. But men do not see themselves in this way in all societies, nor do they understand these norms in all societies. The experience of autonomy as we know it, the sense of rational action and the satisfactions thereof, are unavailable to them. The meaning of these terms is opaque to them because they have a different structure of experiential meaning open to them.

We can think of the difference between our society and the simplified version of the traditional Japanese village as consisting in this, that the range of meaning open to the members of the two societies is very different. But what we are dealing with here is not subjective meaning which can fit into the categorial grid of behavioural political science, but rather inter-subjective meanings. It is not just that the people in our society all or mostly have a given set of ideas in their heads and subscribe to a given set of goals. The meanings and norms implicit in these practices are not just in the minds of the actors but are out there in the practices themselves, practices which cannot be conceived as a set of individual actions, but which are essentially modes of social relation, of mutual action.

The actors may have all sorts of beliefs and attitudes which may be rightly thought of as their individual beliefs and attitudes, even if others share them; they may subscribe to certain policy goals or certain forms of theory about the polity, or feel resentment at certain things, and so on. They bring these with them into their negotiations, and strive to satisfy them. But what they do not bring into the negotiations is the set of ideas and norms constitutive of negotiation themselves. These must be the common property of the society before there can be any question of anyone entering into negotiation or not. Hence they are not subjective meanings, the property of one or some individuals, but rather inter-subjective meanings, which are constitutive of the social matrix in which individuals find themselves and act.

The inter-subjective meanings which are the background to social action are often treated by political scientists under the heading 'consensus'. By this is meant convergence of beliefs on certain basic matters, or of attitude. But the two are not the same. Whether there is consensus or not, the condition of there being either one or the other is a certain set of common terms of reference. A society in which this was lacking would not be a society in the normal sense of the term, but several. Perhaps some multi-racial or multi-tribal states approach this limit. Some multi-national states are bedevilled by consistent cross-purposes, e.g., my own country. But consensus as a convergence of beliefs or values is not the opposite of this kind of fundamental diversity. Rather the opposite of diversity is a high degree of inter-subjective meanings. And this can go along with profound cleavage. Indeed, inter-subjective meanings are a condition of a certain kind of very profound cleavage, such as was visible in the Reformation, or the American Civil War, or splits in Left-wing parties, where the dispute is at fever pitch just because both sides can fully understand the other.

In other words, convergence of belief or attitude or its absence presupposes a common language in which these beliefs can be formulated, and in which these formulations can be opposed. Much of this common language in any society is rooted in its institutions and practices; it is constitutive of these institutions and practices. It is part of the inter-subjective meanings. To put the point another way, apart from the question of how much people's beliefs converge is the question of how much they have a common language of social and political reality in which these beliefs are expressed. This second question cannot be reduced to the first; inter-subjective meaning is not a matter of converging beliefs or values. When we speak of consensus we speak of beliefs and values which could be the property of a single person, or many, or all; but inter-subjective meanings could not be the property of a single person because they are rooted in social practice.

We can perhaps see this if we envisage the situation in which the ideas and norms underlying a practice are the property of single individuals. This is what happens when single individuals from one society interiorize the notions and values of another, e.g., children in missionary schools. Here we have a totally different situation. We *are* really talking now about subjective beliefs and attitudes. The ideas are abstract, they are mere social 'ideals'. Whereas in the original society, these ideas and norms are rooted in their social relations, and are that on the basis of which they can formulate opinions and ideals.

We can see this in connection with the example we have been using all along, that of negotiations. The vision of a society based on negotiation is coming in for heavy attack by a growing segment of modern youth, as are the attendant norms of rationality and the definition of autonomy. This is a dramatic failure of 'consensus'. But this cleavage takes place in the ambit of this inter-subjective meaning, the social practice of negotiation as it is lived in our society. The rejection wouldn't have the bitter quality it has if what is rejected were not understood in common, because it is part of a social practice which we find it hard to avoid, so pervasive is it in our society. At the same time there is a reaching out for other forms which have still the 'abstract' quality of ideals which are subjective in this sense, that is, not rooted in practice; which is what makes the rebellion look so 'unreal' to outsiders, and so irrational.

Inter-subjective meanings, ways of experiencing action in society which are expressed in the language and descriptions constitutive of institutions and practices, do not fit into the categorial grid of mainstream political science. This allows only for an inter-subjective reality which is brute data identifiable. But social practices and institutions which are partly constituted by certain ways of talking about them are not so identifiable. We have to understand the language, the underlying meanings, which constitute them.

We can allow, once we accept a certain set of institutions or practices as our starting point and not as objects of further questioning, that we can easily take as brute data that certain acts are judged to take place or certain states judged to hold within the semantic field of these practices. For instance, that someone has voted Liberal, or signed the petition. We can then go on to correlate certain subjective meanings – beliefs, attitudes, etc. – with this behaviour or its lack. But this means that we give up trying to define further just what these practices and institutions are, what the meanings are which they require and hence sustain. For these meanings do not fit into the grid; they are not subjective beliefs or values, but are constitutive of social reality. In order to get at them we have to drop the basic premise that social reality is made up of brute data alone. For any characterization of the meaning underlying these practices is open to question by someone offering an alternative interpretation. The negation of this is what was meant as brute data. We have to admit that intersubjective social reality has to be partly defined in terms of meanings; that meanings as subjective are not just in causal interaction with a social reality made up of brute data, but that as intersubjective they are constitutive of this reality.

We have been talking here of inter-subjective meanings. And earlier I was contrasting the question of inter-subjective meaning with that of consensus as convergence of opinions. But there is another kind of non-subjective meaning which is also often inadequately discussed under the head of 'consensus'. In a society with a strong web of inter-subjective meanings, there can be a more or less powerful set of common meanings. By these I mean notions of what is significant which are not just shared in the sense that everyone has them, but are also common in the sense of being in the common reference world. Thus, almost everyone in our society may share a susceptibility to a certain kind of feminine beauty, but this may not be a common meaning. It may be known to no one, except perhaps market researchers, who play on it in their advertisements. But the survival of a national identity as francophones is a common meaning of *Québecois*; for it is not just shared, and not just known to be shared, but its being a common aspiration is one of the common reference points of all debate, communication, and all public life in the society.

We can speak of a shared belief, aspiration, etc. when there is convergence between the subjective beliefs, aspirations, of many individuals. But it is part of the meaning of a common aspiration, belief, celebration, etc. that it be not just shared but part of the common reference world. Or to put it another way, its being shared is a collective act, it is a consciousness which is communally sustained, whereas sharing is something we do each on his own, as it were, even if each of us is influenced by the others.

Common meanings are the basis of community. Inter-subjective meaning gives a people a common language to talk about social reality and a common understanding of certain norms, but only with common meanings does this common reference world contain significant common actions, celebrations, and feelings. These are objects in the world that everybody shares. This is what makes community.

Once again, we cannot really understand this phenomenon through the usual definition of consensus as convergence of opinion and value. For what is meant here is something more than convergence. Convergence is what happens when our values are shared. But what is required for common meanings is that this shared value be part of the common world, that this sharing be shared. But we could also say that common meanings are quite other than consensus, for they can subsist with a high degree of cleavage; this is what happens when a common meaning comes to be lived and understood differently by different groups in a society. It remains a common meaning, because there is the reference point which is the common purpose, aspiration, celebration. Such is for example the American Way, or freedom as understood in the U.S.A. But this common meaning is differently articulated by different groups. This is the basis of the bitterest fights in a society, and this we are also seeing in the U.S. today. Perhaps one might say that a common meaning is very often the cause of the most bitter lack of consensus. It thus must not be confused with convergence of opinion, value, attitude.

Of course, common meanings and inter-subjective meanings are closely interwoven. There must be a powerful net of inter-subjective meanings for there to be common meanings; and the result of powerful common meanings is the development of a greater web of inter-subjective meanings as people live in community.

On the other hand, when common meanings wither, which they can do through the kind of deep dissensus we described earlier, the groups tend to grow apart and develop different languages of social reality, hence to share less inter-subjective meanings.

Hence, to take our above example again, there has been a powerful common meaning in our civilization around a certain vision of the free society in which bargaining has a central place. This has helped to entrench the social practice of negotiation which makes us participate in this inter-subjective meaning. But there is a severe challenge to this common meaning today, as we have seen. Should those who object to it really succeed in building up an alternative society, there would develop a gap between those who remain in the present type of society and those who had founded the new one.

Common meanings, as well as inter-subjective ones, fall through the net of mainstream social science. They can find no place in its categories. For they are not simply a converging set of subjective reactions, but part of the common world. What the ontology of mainstream social science lacks is the notion of meaning as not simply for an individual subject; of a subject who can be a 'we' as well as an 'I'. The exclusion of this possibility, of the communal, comes once again from the baleful influence of the epistemological tradition for which all knowledge has to be reconstructed from the impressions imprinted on the individual subject. But if we free ourselves from the hold of these prejudices, this seems a wildly implausible view about the development of human consciousness: we are aware of the world through a 'we' before we are through an 'I'. Hence we need the distinction between what is just shared in the sense that each of us has it in our individual worlds, and that which is in the common world. But the very idea of something which is in the common world in contradistinction to what is in all the individual worlds is totally opaque to empiricist epistemology. Hence it finds no place in mainstream social science. What this results in must now be seen ...

It is an obvious fact, with which politics has been concerned since at least Plato, that some societies enjoy an easier, more spontaneous cohesion which relies less on the use of force than others. It has been an important question of political theory to understand what underlies this difference. Among others, Aristotle, Machiavelli, Montesquieu, de Tocqueville have dealt with it.

Contemporary mainstream political scientists approach this question with the concept 'legitimacy'. The use of the word here can be easily understood. Those societies which are more spontaneously cohesive can be thought to enjoy a greater sense of legitimacy among their members. But the application of the term has been shifted. 'Legitimacy' is a term in which we discuss the authority of the state or polity, its right to our allegiance. However we conceive of this legitimacy, it can only be attributed to a polity in the light of a number of surrounding conceptions – e.g., that it provides men freedom, that it emanates from their will, that it secures them order, the rule of law, or that it is founded on tradition, or commands obedience by its superior qualities. These conceptions are all such that they rely on definitions of what is significant for men in general or in some particular society or circumstances, definitions of paradigmatic meaning which cannot be identifiable as brute data. Even where some of these terms might be given an 'operational definition' in terms of brute data – a term like 'freedom' for instance, can be defined in terms of the absence of legal restriction, à la Hobbes – this definition would not carry the full force of the term, and in particular that whereby it could be considered significant for men.

According to the empiricist paradigm, this latter aspect of the meaning of such a term is labelled 'evaluative' and is thought to be utterly heterogeneous from the 'descriptive' aspect. But this analysis is far from firmly established; no more so in fact than the empiricist paradigm of knowledge itself with which it is closely bound up. A challenge to this paradigm in the name of a hermeneutical science is also a challenge to the distinction between 'descriptive' and 'evaluative' and the entire conception of '*Wertfreiheit*' which goes with it.

In any case, whether because it is 'evaluative' or can only be applied in connection with definitions of meaning, 'legitimate' is not a word which can be used in the description of social reality according to the conceptions of mainstream social science. It can only be used as a description of subjective meaning. What enters into scientific consideration is thus not the legitimacy of a polity but the opinions or feelings of its member individuals concerning its legitimacy. The differences between different societies in their manner of spontaneous cohesion and sense of community are to be understood by correlations between the beliefs and feelings of their members towards them on the one hand and the prevalence of certain brute data identifiable indices of stability in them on the other.

Thus Robert Dahl in *Modern Political Analysis* (pp. 31–2)[8] speaks of the different ways in which leaders gain 'compliance' for their policies. The more citizens comply because of 'internal rewards and deprivations', the less leaders need to use 'external rewards and deprivations'. But if citizens believe a government is legitimate, then their conscience will bind them to obey it; they will be internally punished if they disobey; hence government will have to use less external resources, including force.

Less crude is the discussion of Seymour Lipset in *Political Man* (Chapter 3).[9] But it is founded on the same basic ideas, viz. that legitimacy defined as subjective meaning is correlated with stability. 'Legitimacy involves the capacity of the system to engender and maintain the belief that the existing political institutions are the most appropriate ones for the society.' (p. 64.)

Lipset is engaged in a discussion of the determinants of stability in modern politics. He singles out two important ones in this chapter, effectiveness and legitimacy. 'Effectiveness means actual performance, the extent to which the system satisfies the basic functions of government as most of the population and such powerful groups within it as big business or the armed forces see them.' (op. cit.) Thus we have one factor which has to do with objective reality, what the government has actually done; and the other which has to do with subjective beliefs and 'values'. 'While effectiveness is primarily instrumental, legitimacy is evaluative.' (op. cit.) Hence from the beginning the stage is set by a distinction between social reality and what men think and feel about it.

Lipset sees two types of crisis of legitimacy that modern societies have confronted more or less well. One concerns the status of major Conservative institutions which may be under threat from the development of modern industrial democracies. The second concerns the degree to which all political groups have access to the political process. Thus, under the first head, some traditional groups, such as landed aristocracy or clericals, have been roughly handled in a society like France, and have remained alienated from the democratic system for decades afterwards; whereas in England the traditional classes were more gently handled, them-

8. See Dahl (1963). 9. See Lipset (1963).

selves were willing to compromise and have been slowly integrated and transformed into the new order. Under the second head, some societies managed to integrate the working class or bourgeoisie into the political process at an early stage, whereas in others they have been kept out till quite recently, and consequently, have developed a deep sense of alienation from the system, have tended to adopt extremist ideologies, and have generally contributed to instability. One of the determinants of a society's performance on these two heads is whether or not it is forced to confront the different conflicts of democratic development all at once or one at a time. Another important determinant of legitimacy is effectiveness.

This approach which sees stability as partly the result of legitimacy beliefs, and these in turn as resulting partly from the way the status, welfare, access to political life of different groups fare, seems at first blush eminently sensible and well designed to help us understand the history of the last century or two. But this approach has no place for a study of the inter-subjective and common meanings which are constitutive of modern civilization. And we may doubt whether we can understand the cohesion of modern societies or their present crisis if we leave these out of account.

Let us take the winning of the allegiance of the working class to the new industrial régimes in the nineteenth and early twentieth century. This is far from being a matter simply or even perhaps most significantly of the speed with which this class was integrated into the political process and the effectiveness of the régime. Rather the consideration of the granting of access to the political process as an independent variable may be misleading.

It is not just that we often find ourselves invited by historians to account for class cohesion in particular countries in terms of other factors, such as the impact of Methodism in early nineteenth century England (Elie Halévy) or the draw of Germany's newly successful nationalism. These factors could be assimilated to the social scientist's grid by being classed as 'ideologies' or widely-held 'value-systems' or some other such concatenations of subjective meaning.

But perhaps the most important such 'ideology' in accounting for the cohesion of industrial democratic societies has been that of the society of work, the vision of society as a large-scale enterprise of production in which widely different functions are integrated into interdependence; a vision of society in which economic relations are considered as primary, as it is not only in Marxism (and in a sense not really with Marxism) but above all with the tradition of Classical Utilitarianism. In line with this vision there is a fundamental solidarity between all members of society that labour (to use Arendt's language),[10] for they are all engaged in producing what is indispensable to life and happiness in far-reaching interdependence.

This is the 'ideology' which has frequently presided over the integration of the working class into industrial democracies, at first directed polemically against the 'unproductive' classes, e.g., in England with the anti-Corn Law League, and later with the campaigns of Joseph Chamberlain ('when Adam delved and Eve span/who was then the gentleman'), but later as a support for social cohesion and solidarity.

But, of course, the reason for putting 'ideology' in quotes above is that this definition of things, which has been well integrated with the conception of social life as based on negotiation, cannot be understood in the terms of mainstream social science, as beliefs and 'values' held by a large number of individuals. For the great interdependent matrix of labour is not just a set of ideas in people's heads but is an important aspect of the reality which we live in modern society. And at the same time, these ideas are embedded in this matrix in that they are constitutive of it; that is, we wouldn't be able to live in this type of society unless we were imbued with these ideas or some others which could call forth the discipline and voluntary co-ordination needed to operate this kind of economy. All industrial civilizations have required a huge wrench from the traditional peasant populations on which they have been imposed; for they require an entirely unprecedented level of disciplined, sustained, monotonous effort, long hours unpunctuated by any meaningful rhythm, such as that of seasons or festivals. In the end this way of life can only be

10. See Arendt (1959).

accepted when the idea of making a living is endowed with more significance than that of just avoiding starvation: and this it is in the civilization of labour.

Now this civilization of work is only one aspect of modern societies, along with the society based on negotiation and willed relations (in Anglo-Saxon countries), and other common and inter-subjective meanings which have different importance in different countries. My point is that it is certainly not implausible to say that it has some importance in explaining the integration of the working class in modern industrial democratic society. But it can only be called a cluster of inter-subjective meaning. As such it cannot come into the purview of mainstream political science; and an author like Lipset cannot take it into consideration when discussing this very problem.

But, of course, such a massive fact doesn't escape notice. What happens rather is that it is re-interpreted. And what has generally happened is that the interdependent productive and negotiating society has been recognized by political science, but not as one structure of inter-subjective meaning among others, rather as the inescapable background of social action as such. In this guise it no longer need be an object of study. Rather it retreats to the middle distance, where its general outline takes the role of universal framework, within which (it is hoped) actions and structures will be brute data identifiable, and this for any society at any time. The view is then that the political actions of men in all societies can be understood as variants of the processing of 'demands' which is an important part of our political life. The inability to recognize the specificity of our inter-subjective meanings is thus inseparably linked with the belief in the universality of North Atlantic behaviour types or 'functions' which vitiates so much of contemporary comparative politics.

The notion is that what politics is about perennially is the adjustment of differences, or the production of symbolic and effective 'outputs' on the basis of demand and support 'inputs'. The rise of the inter-subjective meaning of the civilization of work is seen as the increase of correct perception of the political process at the expense of 'ideology'. Thus Almond and Powell introduce the concept of 'political secularization' to describe 'the emergence of a pragmatic, empirical orientation' to politics (p. 58).[11] A secular political culture is opposed not only to a traditional one, but also to an 'ideological' culture, which is characterized by 'an inflexible image of political life, closed to conflicting information' and 'fails to develop the open, bargaining attitudes associated with full secularization'. (p. 61.) The clear understanding here is that a secularized culture is one which essentially depends less on illusion, which sees things as they are, which is not infected with the 'false consciousness' of traditional or ideological culture (to use a term which is not in the mainstream vocabulary). This way of looking at the civilization of work, as resulting from the retreat of illusion before the correct perception of what politics perennially and really is, is thus closely bound up with the epistemological premises of mainstream political science and its resultant inability to recognize the historical specificity of this civilization's inter-subjective meanings. But the weakness of this approach, already visible in the attempts to explain the rise of this civilization and its relation to others, becomes even more painful when we try to account for its present malaise, even crisis.

The strains in contemporary society, the breakdown of civility, the rise of deep alienation, which is translated into even more destructive action, tend to shake the basic categories of our social science. It is not just that such a development was quite unpredicted by this science, which saw in the rise of affluence the cause rather of a further entrenching of the bargaining culture, a reduction of irrational cleavage, an increase of tolerance, in short 'the end of ideology'. For prediction, as we shall see below, cannot be a goal of social science as it is of natural science. It is rather that this mainstream science hasn't the categories to explain this breakdown. It is forced to look on extremism either as a bargaining gambit of the desperate, deliberately raising the ante in order to force a hearing. Or, alternatively, it can recognize the novelty of the rebellion by accepting the hypothesis that heightened demands are being made on the system owing to a revolution of 'expectations', or else to the eruption of new desires or aspirations which hitherto had no place in the bargain-

11. See Almond and Powell (1966).

ing process. But these new desires or aspirations must be in the domain of individual psychology, that is, they must be such that their arousal and satisfaction is to be understood in terms of states of individuals rather than in terms of the inter-subjective meanings in which they live. For these latter have no place in the categories of the mainstream, which thus cannot accommodate a genuine historical psychology.

But some of the more extreme protests and acts of rebellion in our society cannot be interpreted as bargaining gambits in the name of any demands, old or new. These can only be interpreted within the accepted framework of our social science as a return to ideology, and hence as irrational. Now in the case of some of the more bizarre and bloody forms of protest, there will be little disagreement: they will be judged irrational by all but their protagonists. But within the accepted categories this irrationality can only be understood in terms of individual psychology; it is the public eruption of private pathology: it cannot be understood as a malady of society itself, a malaise which afflicts its constitutive meanings.[12]

No one can claim to begin to have an adequate explanation for these major changes which our civilization is undergoing. But in contrast to the incapacity of a science which remains within the accepted categories, a hermeneutical science of man which has a place for a study of inter-subjective meaning can at least begin to explore fruitful avenues. Plainly the discipline which was integral to the civilization of work and bargaining is beginning to fail. The structures of this civilization, interdependent work, bargaining, mutual adjustment of individual ends, are beginning to

12. Thus Lewis Feuer in *The Conflict of Generations*, New York, 1969, attempts to account for the 'misperception of social reality' in the Berkeley student uprising in terms of a generational conflict (pp. 166–70), which in turn is rooted in the psychology of adolescence and attaining adulthood. Yet Feuer himself in his first chapter notes the comparative recency of self-defining political generations, a phenomenon which dates from the post-Napoleonic era (p. 33). But an adequate attempt to explain this historical shift, which after all underlies the Berkeley rising and many others, would I believe have to take us beyond the ambit of individual psychology to psycho-history, to a study of the intrication of psychological conflict and inter-subjective meanings. A variant of this form of study has been adumbrated in the work of Erik Erikson.

change their meaning for many, and are beginning to be felt not as normal and best suited to man, but as hateful or empty. And yet we are all caught in these inter-subjective meanings insofar as we live in this society, and in a sense more and more all-pervasively as it progresses. Hence the virulence and tension of the critique of our society which is always in some real sense a self-rejection (in a way that the old socialist opposition never was).

Why has this set of meanings gone sour? Plainly, we have to accept that they are not to be understood at their face value. The free, productive, bargaining culture claimed to be sufficient for man. If it was not, then we have to assume that while it did hold our allegiance, it also had other meanings for us which commanded this allegiance and which have now gone.

This is the starting point of a set of hypotheses which attempt to re-define our past in order to make our present and future intelligible. We might think that the productive, bargaining culture offered in the past common meanings (even though there was no place for them in its philosophy), and hence a basis for community, which were essentially linked with its being in the process of building. It linked men who could see themselves as breaking with the past to build a new happiness in America, for instance. But in all essentials that future is built; the notion of a horizon to be attained by future greater production (as against social transformation) verges on the absurd in contemporary America. Suddenly the horizon which was essential to the sense of meaningful purpose has collapsed, which would show that like so many other Enlightenment-based dreams the free, productive, bargaining society can only sustain man as a goal, not as a reality.

Or we can look at this development in terms of identity. A sense of building their future through the civilization of work can sustain men as long as they see themselves as having broken with a millenial past of injustice and hardship in order to create qualitatively different conditions for their children. All the requirements of a humanly acceptable identity can be met by this predicament, a relation to the past (one soars above it but preserves it in folkloric memory), to the social world (the interdependent world of free, productive men), to the earth (the raw material which awaits shaping), to the future and one's own death (the everlasting monument in the lives of prosperous children), to the absolute (the absolute values of freedom, integrity, dignity).

But at some point the children will be unable to sustain this forward thrust into the future. This effort has placed them in a private haven of security, within which they are unable to reach and recover touch with the great realities: their parents have only a negated past, lives which have been oriented wholly to the future; the social world is distant and without shape; rather one can only insert oneself into it by taking one's place in the future-oriented productive juggernaut. But this now seems without any sense; the relation to the earth as raw material is therefore experienced as empty and alienating, but the recovery of a valid relation to the earth is the hardest thing once lost; and there is no relation to the absolute where we are caught in the web of meanings which have gone dead for us. Hence past, future, earth, world, and absolute are in some way or another occluded; and what must arise is an identity crisis of frightening proportions.

These two hypotheses are mainly focused on the crisis in U.S. civilization, and they would perhaps help account for the fact that the U.S. is in some sense going first through this crisis of all Atlantic nations; not, that is, only because it is the most affluent, but more because it has been more fully based on the civilization of work than European countries who retained something of more traditional common meanings.

But they might also help us to understand why alienation is most severe among groups which have been but marginal in affluent bargaining societies. These have had the greatest strain in living in this civilization while their identity was in some ways antithetical to it. Such are blacks in the U.S., and the community of French-speaking Canadians, each in different ways. For many immigrant groups the strain was also great, but they forced themselves to surmount the obstacles, and the new identity is sealed in the blood of the old, as it were.

But for those who would not or could not succeed in thus transforming themselves, but always lived a life of strain on the defensive, the breakdown of the central, powerful identity is the trigger to a deep turn-over. It can be thought of as a liberation but at the same time it is deeply unsettling, because the basic parameters of former life are being changed, and there are not yet the new images and definitions to live a new fully acceptable identity. In a sense we are in a condition where a new social compact (rather the first social compact) has to be made between these groups and those they live with, and no one knows where to start.

In the last pages, I have presented some hypotheses which may appear very speculative; and they may indeed turn out to be without foundation, even without much interest. But their aim was mainly illustrative. My principal claim is that we can only come to grips with this phenomenon of breakdown by trying to understand more clearly and profoundly the common and inter-subjective meanings of the society in which we have been living. For it is these which no longer hold us, and to understand this change we have to have an adequate grasp of these meanings. But this we cannot do as long as we remain within the ambit of mainstream social science, for it will not recognize inter-subjective meaning, and is forced to look at the central ones of our society as though they were the inescapable background of all political action. Breakdown is thus inexplicable in political terms; it is an outbreak of irrationality which must ultimately be explained by some form of psychological illness.

Mainstream science may thus venture into the area explored by the above hypotheses, but after its own fashion, by forcing the psycho-historical facts of identity into the grid of an individual psychology, in short, by re-interpreting all meanings as subjective. The result might be a psychological theory of emotional maladjustment, perhaps traced to certain features of family background, analogous to the theories of the authoritarian personality and the California F-scale. But this would no longer be a political or social theory. We would be giving up the attempt to understand the change in social reality at the level of its constitutive inter-subjective meanings.

References

ALMOND, G. A., and POWELL, G. B. (1966), *Comparative Politics in a Developmental Approach*, Boston and Toronto.

ANSCOMBE, E. (1957–8), 'On Brute Acts', *Analysis*, vol. 18, pp. 50–53.

ARENDT, H. (1959), *The Human Condition*, New York.
CAVELL, S. (1969), *Must We Mean What We Say?*, New York, pp. 21–31.
DAHL, R. (1963), *Modern Political Analysis*, Foundation of Modern Political Science Series, Englewood Cliffs, New Jersey, U.S.A.
FEUER, L. (1969), *The Conflict of Generations*, New York.
GADAMER, H. G. (1960), *Wahrheit und Methode*, Tübingen.
HABERMAS, J. (1968), *Erkenntnis und Interesse*, Suhrkamp Verlag, Frankfurt. Translated as *Knowledge and Human Interests*, Heinemann Educational 1972.
HALÉVY, E. (1913), *Histoire du Peuple anglais au XIXe siècle*, Paris.
LIPSET, S. (1963), *Political Man*, New York.
MCCLOSKY, H. (1964), 'Consensus and Ideology in American Politics', *American Political Science Review*, vol. 58, pp. 361–82.
MINSKY, M. (1967), *Computation*, Englewood Cliffs, New Jersey, U.S.A., pp. 104–7.
RICOEUR, P. (1965), *De l'Interprétation*, Paris.
SEARLE, J. R. (1969), *Speech Acts: an Essay in the Philosophy of Language*, Cambridge University Press, pp. 33–42.
SMITH, T. C. (1959), *The Agrarian Origins of Modern Japan*, Stanford University Press, U.S.A., ch. 5.

9 Paul Ricoeur

Hermeneutics: Restoration of Meaning or Reduction of Illusion?

Excerpt from Paul Ricoeur, *Freud and Philosophy. An Essay on Interpretation*, Yale University Press, New Haven and London, 1970, pp. 26–36. First published in 1965.

The difficulty – it initiated my research in the first place – is this: there is no general hermeneutics, no universal canon for exegesis, but only disparate and opposed theories concerning the rules of interpretation. The hermeneutic field, whose outer contours we have traced, is internally at variance with itself.

I have neither the intention nor the means to attempt a complete enumeration of hermeneutic styles. The more enlightening course, it seems to me, is to start with the polarized opposition that creates the greatest tension at the outset of our investigation. According to the one pole, hermeneutics is understood as the manifestation and restoration of a meaning addressed to me in the manner of a message, a proclamation, or as is sometimes said, a kerygma; according to the other pole, it is understood as a demystification, as a reduction of illusion. Psychoanalysis, at least on a first reading, aligns itself with the second understanding of hermeneutics.

From the beginning we must consider this double possibility: this tension, this extreme polarity, is the truest expression of our 'modernity'. The situation in which language today finds itself comprises this double possibility, this double solicitation and urgency: on the one hand, purify discourse of its excrescences, liquidate the idols, go from drunkenness to sobriety, realize our state of poverty once and for all; on the other hand, use the most 'nihilistic', destructive, iconoclastic movement so as to *let speak* what once, what each time, was *said*, when meaning appeared anew, when meaning was at its fullest. Hermeneutics seems to me to be animated by this double motivation: willingness to suspect, willingness to listen; vow of rigour, vow of obedience. In our time we have not finished doing away with *idols* and we have barely begun to listen to *symbols*. It may be that this situation, in its apparent distress, is instructive: it may be that extreme iconoclasm belongs to the restoration of meaning.

The underlying reason for initially posing the problem in the above way is to bring into the open the crisis of language that today makes us oscillate between demystification and restoration of meaning. To my mind, an introduction to the psychoanalysis of culture has had to proceed in this roundabout way. In the next chapter we will try to probe deeper into this prolegomena and relate the crisis of language to an ascesis of reflection whose first movement is to let itself be dispossessed of the origin of meaning.

To finish locating psychoanalysis within the general discussion of language, the terms of the conflict need to be sketched.

Interpretation as recollection of meaning

This section is concerned with hermeneutics as the restoration of meaning. The point at issue in the psychoanalysis of culture and the school of suspicion is better understood if we first contrast what is radically opposed to them.

The contrary of suspicion, I will say bluntly, is faith. What faith? No longer, to be sure, the first faith of the simple soul, but rather the second faith of one who has engaged in hermeneutics, faith that has undergone criticism, post-critical faith. Let us look for it in the series of philosophic decisions that secretly animate a phenomenology of religion and lie hidden even within its apparent neutrality. It is a rational faith, for it interprets; but it is a faith because it seeks, through interpretation, a second naïveté. Phenomenology is its instrument of hearing, of recollection, of restoration of meaning. 'Believe in order to understand, understand in order to believe' – such is its maxim; and its maxim is the 'hermeneutic circle' itself of believing and understanding.

We will take our examples from the phenomenology of religion in the wide sense, embracing here the work of Leenhardt, Van der Leeuw, and Eliade, to which I add my own research in *The Symbolism of Evil*.

It will be our task to disengage and display the rational faith that runs through the purely intentional analysis of religious symbolism and 'converts' this listening analysis from within.

The first imprint of this faith in a revelation through the word is to be seen in the care or concern for the *object*, a characteristic of all phenomenological analysis. That concern, as we know, presents itself as a 'neutral' wish to describe and not to reduce. One reduces by explaining through causes (psychological, social, etc.), through genesis (individual, historical, etc.), through function (affective, ideological, etc.). One describes by disengaging the (noetic) intention and its (noematic) correlate – the *something* intended, the implicit object in ritual, myth, and belief. Thus, in the case of the symbolism of the pure and the impure, the task is to understand what is signified, what quality of the sacred is intended, what shade of threat is implied in the analogy between spot and stain, between physical contamination and the loss of existential integrity. In my own research, concern for the object consisted in surrender to the movement of meaning which, starting from the literal sense – the spot or contamination – points to something grasped in the region of the sacred. To generalize from this, we shall say that the theme of the phenomenology of religion is the *something* intended in ritual actions, in mythical speech, in belief or mystical feeling; its task is to dis-implicate that object from the various intentions of behaviour, discourse, and emotion. Let us call this intended object the 'sacred', without determining its nature, whether it be the *tremendum numinosum*, according to Rudolf Otto; 'the powerful', according to Van der Leeuw; or 'fundamental Time', according to Eliade. In this general sense, and with a view to underlining the concern for the intentional object, we may say that every phenomenology of religion is a phenomenology of the sacred. However, is it possible for a phenomenology of the sacred to stay within the limits of a neutral attitude governed by the *epochê*, by the bracketing of absolute reality and of every question concerning the absolute? The *epochê* requires that I participate in the belief in the reality of the religious object, but in a neutralized mode; that I believe with the believer, but without positing absolutely the object of his belief.

But while the scientist as such can and must practise this

method of bracketing, the philosopher as such cannot and must not avoid the question of the absolute validity of his object. For would I be interested in the object, could I stress concern for the object, through the consideration of cause, genesis, or function, if I did not expect, from within understanding, this something to 'address' itself to me? Is not the expectation of being spoken to what motivates the concern for the object? Implied in this expectation is a confidence in language: the belief that language, which bears symbols, is not so much spoken by men as spoken to men, that men are born into language, into the light of the logos 'who enlightens every man who comes into the world'. It is this expectation, this confidence, this belief, that confers on the study of symbols its particular seriousness. To be truthful, I must say it is what animates all my research. But it is also what today is contested by the whole stream of hermeneutics that we shall soon place under the heading of 'suspicion'. This latter theory of interpretation begins by doubting whether there is such an object and whether this objeet could be the place of the transformation of intentionality into kerygma, manifestation, proclamation. This hermeneutics is not an explication of the object, but a tearing off of masks, an interpretation that reduces disguises.

Second, according to the phenomenology of religion, there is a 'truth' of symbols; this truth, in the neutral attitude of the Husserlian *epochê* means merely the fulfilment – *die Erfüllung* – of the signifying intention. For a phenomenology of religion to be possible, it is necessary and sufficient that there be not only one but several ways of fulfilling various intentions of meaning according to various regions of objects. Verification, in the sense of logical positivism, is one type of fulfilment among others and not the canonical mode of fulfilment; it is a type required by the corresponding type of object, namely, the physical object and, in another sense, the historical object – but not by the concept of truth as such, or, in other words, by the requirement of fulfilment in general. It is in virtue of this multiplicity of types of fulfilment that phenomenology, in a reduced, neutralized mode, speaks of religious experience, not by analogy, but according to the specific type of object and the specific mode of fulfilment in that field.

We encountered this problem of fulfilment in the order of symbolic meanings in our investigation of the analogical bond between the primary or literal 'signifier' and the secondary 'signified' – for example, the bond between spot and stain, between deviation (or wandering) and sin, between weight (or burden) and fault. Here we run up against a primordial, unfailing relationship, which never has the conventional and arbitrary character of 'technical' signs that mean only what is posited in them.

In this relationship of meaning to meaning resides what I have called the *fullness* of language. The fullness consists in the fact that the second meaning somehow dwells in the first meaning. In his *Traité d'histoire générale des religions*, Mircea Eliade clearly shows that the force of the cosmic symbolism resides in the non-arbitrary bond between the visible heavens and the order they manifest: thanks to the analogical power that binds meaning to meaning, the heavens *speak* of the wise and the just, the immense and the ordered. Symbols are bound in a double sense: bound *to* and bound *by*. On the one hand, the sacred is *bound to* its primary, literal, sensible meanings; this is what constitutes the opacity of symbols. On the other hand, the literal meaning is *bound by* the symbolic meaning that resides in it; this is what I have called the revealing power of symbols, which gives them their force in spite of their opacity. The revealing power of symbols opposes symbols to technical signs, which merely signify what is posited in them and which, therefore, can be emptied, formalized, and reduced to mere objects of a calculus. Symbols alone *give* what they say.

But in saying this have we not already broken the phenomenological neutrality? I admit it. I admit that what deeply motivates the interest in full language, in bound language, is this inversion of the movement of thought which now addresses itself to me and makes me a subject that is spoken to. And this inversion is produced in analogy. How? How does that which binds meaning to meaning bind me? The movement that draws me toward the second meaning assimilates me to what is said, makes me participate in what is announced to me. The similitude in which the force of symbols resides and from which they draw their revealing power is not an objective likeness, which I may look upon like a relation laid out before me; it is an existential assimilation, according to the movement of analogy, of my being to being.

This allusion to the ancient theme of participation helps us make a third step along the path of explication, which is also the path of intellectual honesty: the fully declared philosophical decision animating the intentional analysis would be a modern version of the ancient theme of reminiscence. After the silence and forgetfulness made widespread by the manipulation of empty signs and the construction of formalized languages, the modern concern for symbols expresses a new desire to be addressed.

This expectancy of a new Word, of a new tidings of the Word, is the implicit intention of every phenomenology of symbols, which first puts the accent on the object, then underscores the fullness of symbol, to finally greet the revealing power of the primal word.

Interpretation as exercise of suspicion

We shall complete our assigning of a place to Freud by giving him not just one interlocutor but a whole company. Over against interpretation as restoration of meaning we shall oppose interpretation according to what I collectively call the school of suspicion.

A general theory of interpretation would thus have to account not only for the opposition between two interpretations of interpretation, the one as recollection of meaning, the other as reduction of the illusions and lies of consciousness; but also for the division and scattering of each of these two great 'schools' of interpretation into 'theories' that differ from one another and are even foreign to one another. This is no doubt truer of the school of suspicion than of the school of reminiscence. Three masters, seemingly mutually exclusive, dominate the school of suspicion: Marx, Nietzsche and Freud. It is easier to show their common opposition to a phenomenology of the sacred, understood as a propaedeutic to the 'revelation' of meaning, than their interrelationship within a single method of demystification. It is relatively easy to note that these three figures all contest the primacy of the object in our representation of the sacred, as well as the fulfilling of the intention of the sacred by a type of analogy of being that would engraft us on to being through the power of an assimilating intention. It is also easy to recognize that this contesting is an exercise of suspicion in three different ways; 'truth as lying' would be the negative heading under which one might place these three exercises of suspicion. But we are still far from having assimilated the positive meaning of the enterprises of these three thinkers. We are still too attentive to their differences and to the limitations that the prejudices of their times impose upon their successors even more than upon themselves. Thus Marx is relegated to economics and the absurd theory of the reflex consciousness; Nietzsche is drawn toward biologism and a perspectivism incapable of expressing itself without contradiction; Freud is restricted to psychiatry and decked out with a simplistic pan-sexualism.

If we go back to the intention they had in common, we find in it the decision to look upon the whole of consciousness primarily as 'false' consciousness. They thereby take up again, each in a different manner, the problem of the Cartesian doubt, to carry it to the very heart of the Cartesian stronghold. The philosopher trained in the school of Descartes knows that things are doubtful, that they are not such as they appear; but he does not doubt that consciousness is such as it appears to itself; in consciousness, meaning and consciousness of meaning coincide. Since Marx, Nietzsche and Freud, this, too, has become doubtful. After the doubt about things, we have started to doubt consciousness.

These three masters of suspicion are not to be misunderstood, however, as three masters of scepticism. They are, assuredly, three great 'destroyers'. But that of itself should not mislead us; destruction, Heidegger says in *Sein und Zeit*, is a moment of every new foundation, including the destruction of religion, insofar as religion is, in Nietzsche's phrase, a 'Platonism for the people'. It is beyond destruction that the question is posed as to what thought, reason, and even faith still signify.

All three clear the horizon for a more authentic word, for a new reign of Truth, not only by means of a 'destructive' critique, but by the invention of an art of *interpreting*. Descartes triumphed over the doubt as to things by the evidence of consciousness; they triumph over the doubt as to consciousness by an exegesis of meaning. Beginning with them, understanding is hermeneutics:

henceforward, to seek meaning is no longer to spell out the consciousness of meaning, but to *decipher its expressions*. What must be faced, therefore, is not only a threefold suspicion, but a threefold guile. If consciousness is not what it thinks it is, a new relation must be instituted between the patent and the latent; this new relation would correspond to the one that consciousness had instituted between appearances and the reality of things. For Marx, Nietzsche and Freud, the fundamental category of consciousness is the relation hidden-shown or, if you prefer, simulated-manifested. That the Marxists are stubbornly insistent on the 'reflex' theory, that Nietzsche contradicts himself in dogmatizing about the 'perspectivism' of the will to power, that Freud mythologizes with his 'censorship', 'watchman', and 'disguises' – still, what is essential does not lie in these encumbrances and impasses. What is essential is that all three create with the means at hand, with and against the prejudices of their times, a mediate *science* of meaning, irreducible to the immediate *consciousness* of meaning. What all three attempted, in different ways, was to make their 'conscious' methods of deciphering coincide with the 'unconscious' *work* of ciphering which they attributed to the will to power, to social being, to the unconscious psychism. *Guile will be met by double guile.*

Thus the distinguishing characteristic of Marx, Freud and Nietzsche is the general hypothesis concerning both the process of false consciousness and the method of deciphering. The two go together, since the man of suspicion carries out in reverse the work of falsification of the man of guile. Freud entered the problem of false consciousness via the double road of dreams and neurotic symptoms; his working hypothesis has the same limits as his angle of attack, which was, as we shall state fully in the sequel, an economics of instincts. Marx attacks the problem of ideologies from within the limits of economic alienation, now in the sense of political economy. Nietzsche, focusing on the problem of 'value' – of evaluation and transvaluation – looks for the key to lying and masks on the side of the 'force' and 'weakness' of the will to power.

Fundamentally, the *Genealogy of Morals* in Nietzsche's sense, the theory of ideologies in the Marxist sense, and the theory of ideals and illusions in Freud's sense represent three convergent procedures of demystification.

Yet there is perhaps something they have even more in common, an underlying relationship that goes even deeper. All three begin with suspicion concerning the illusions of consciousness, and then proceed to employ the stratagem of deciphering; all three, however, far from being detractors of 'consciousness', aim at extending it. What Marx wants is to liberate *praxis* by the understanding of necessity; but this liberation is inseparable from a 'conscious insight' which victoriously counter-attacks the mystification of false consciousness. What Nietzsche wants is the increase of man's power, the restoration of his force; but the meaning of the will to power must be recaptured by meditating on the ciphers 'superman', 'eternal return', and 'Dionysus', without which the power in question would be but worldly violence. What Freud desires is that the one who is analysed, by making his own the meaning that was foreign to him, enlarge his field of consciousness, live better, and finally be a little freer and, if possible, a little happier. One of the earliest homages paid to psychoanalysis speaks of 'healing through consciousness'. The phrase is exact – if one means thereby that analysis wishes to substitute for an immediate and dissimulating consciousness a mediate consciousness taught by the reality principle. Thus the same doubter who depicts the ego as a 'poor creature' in subjection to three masters, the id, the superego, and reality or necessity, is also the exegete who rediscovers the logic of the illogical kingdom and who dares, with unparalleled modesty and discretion, to terminate his essay on *The Future of an Illusion* by invoking the god Logos, soft of voice but indefatigable, in no wise omnipotent, but efficacious in the long run.

This last reference to Freud's 'reality principle' and to its equivalents in Nietzsche and Marx – eternal return in the former, understood necessity in the latter – brings out the positive benefit of the ascesis required by a reductive and destructive interpretation: confrontation with bare reality, the discipline of Ananke, of necessity.

While finding their positive convergence, our three masters of suspicion also present the most radically contrary stance to the phenomenology of the sacred and to any hermeneutics understood as the recollection of meaning and as the reminiscence of being.

At issue in this controversy is the fate of what I shall call, for the sake of brevity, the mytho-poetic core of imagination. Over against illusion and the fable-making function, demystifying hermeneutics sets up the rude discipline of necessity. It is the lesson of Spinoza: one first finds himself a slave, he understands his slavery, he rediscovers himself free within understood necessity. The *Ethics* is the first model of the ascesis that must be undergone by the libido, the will to power, the imperialism of the dominant class. But, in return, does not this discipline of the real, this ascesis of the necessary lack the grace of imagination, the upsurge of the possible? And does not this grace of imagination have something to do with the Word as Revelation?

This is what is at issue in the debate.

Part Three
Critical Theory: The Frankfurt School

Horkheimer produced a programmatic statement for the Institute of Social Research, of which he was Director, in 1937 when he sketched out the idea of a 'Critical Theory' of society which took its bearings from Marx's critique of political economy, while setting Marx's work in the perspective of German Idealist philosophy (Reading 10). During the following decade the work of the Institute was significantly modified by its period of exile in the United States; and when the Institute returned to Germany after the war it carried with it what it had learned of American sociological techniques and began a series of monographs which, unlike the studies of the pre-Nazi period, were based more on field work, interviews, sample surveys and so on. Nonetheless, Pollock's critique of public opinion research (Reading 11), like Adorno's critique of empirical sociology (Reading 12), still display a characteristic distance from the mainstream social science they encountered in the United States. Apart from the impact of the Freudian tradition, which was significant in building up their social-psychological studies of Fascism, two other important threads run through the work of Critical Theorists in this period, both of which are indicative of the distinctively German provenance of the tradition. One was the attempt to develop a more sophisticated study of ideologies than that provided by Marx, particularly in the direction of the sociology of literature and the arts, which would establish detailed interconnections between different literary and artistic forms and different modes of productive activity. Benjamin's essay on the short story (Reading 14) illustrates this preoccupation; and Adorno's paper on cultural criticism (Reading 13) is at one and the same time another instance of the genre and an argument for its *raison d'être*. The other thread was the continuing concern with the role of the natural sciences in the forces of production and as a potential source of legitimation in society (Readings 10, 16).

More recently, as was noted in the Introduction, Critical Theory has been characterized by a growing concern with linguistic and hermeneutic problems. Thus Habermas' paper on systematically distorted communication (Reading 17), part of the aim of which is to argue that a hermeneutic interpretation can also be a causal explanation, draws substantially on the work of Lorenzer which views neurosis as a corruption of the process of symbolization and hence of language (Reading 7). Nevertheless, the growing critical distance from Marx's analysis of political economy has also stimulated a new attack on the problem of developing a more adequate set of categories for dealing with the distinctive features of advanced capitalist societies. Habermas has explored some ways in which the expanding functions required of the state apparatus increase the need for legitimation and bring about crises in motivation (Reading 18); while Offe attempts to chart the concrete mechanisms mediating between economics and politics – mechanisms which have 'politicized' commodity exchange but have in no sense neutralized the politicized economy as the ultimate regulator in the functioning of political institutions (Reading 19).

10 Max Horkheimer

Traditional and Critical Theory

Excerpt from Max Horkheimer, *Critical Theory*; *Selected Essays*, tr. M. J. O. O'Connell and others, Herder & Herder, New York, 1972, pp. 188–94, 197, 199–204, 206–11, 244–6. First published in 1937.

What is 'theory'? The question seems a rather easy one for contemporary science. Theory for most researchers is the sum-total of propositions about a subject, the propositions being so linked with each other that a few are basic and the rest derive from these. The smaller the number of primary principles in comparison with the derivations, the more perfect the theory. The real validity of the theory depends on the derived propositions being consonant with the actual facts. If experience and theory contradict each other, one of the two must be re-examined. Either the scientist has failed to observe correctly or something is wrong with the principles of the theory. In relation to facts, therefore, a theory always remains a hypothesis. One must be ready to change it if its weaknesses begin to show as one works through the material. Theory is stored-up knowledge, put in a form that makes it useful for the closest possible description of facts. Poincaré compares science to a library that must ceaselessly expand. Experimental physics is the librarian who takes care of acquisitions, that is, enriches knowledge by supplying new material. Mathematical physics – the theory of natural science in the strictest sense – keeps the catalogue; without the catalogue one would have no access to the library's rich contents. 'That is the role of mathematical physics. It must direct generalization, so as to increase what I have called just now the output of science.'[1] The general goal of all theory is a universal systematic science, not limited to any particular subject matter but embracing all possible objects. The division of sciences is being broken down by deriving the principles for special areas from the same basic premises. The

1. Poincaré (1905), p. 145.

same conceptual apparatus which was elaborated for the analysis of inanimate nature is serving to classify animate nature as well, and anyone who has once mastered the use of it, that is, the rules for derivation, the symbols, the process of comparing derived propositions with observable fact, can use it at any time. But we are still rather far from such an ideal situation.

Such, in its broad lines, is the widely accepted idea of what theory is. Its origins supposedly coincide with the beginnings of modern philosophy. The third maxim in Descartes' scientific method is the decision

> to carry on my reflections in due order, commencing with objects that were the most simple and easy to understand, in order to rise little by little, or by degrees, to knowledge of the most complex, assuming an order, even if a fictitious one, among those which do not follow a natural sequence relative to one another.[2]

The derivation as usually practised in mathematics is to be applied to all science. The order in the world is captured by a deductive chain of thought.

> Those long chains of deductive reasoning, simple and easy as they are, of which geometricians make use in order to arrive at the most difficult demonstrations, had caused me to imagine that all those things which fall under the cognizance of men might very likely be mutually related in the same fashion; and that, provided only that we abstain from receiving anything as true which is not so, and always retain the order which is necessary in order to deduce the one conclusion from the other, there can be nothing so remote that we cannot reach to it, nor so recondite that we cannot discover it.

Depending on the logician's own general philosophical outlook, the most universal propositions from which the deduction begins are themselves regarded as experiential judgements, as inductions (as with John Stuart Mill), as evident insights (as in rationalist and phenomenological schools), or as arbitrary postulates (as in the modern axiomatic approach). In the most advanced logic of the present time, as represented by Husserl's *Logische Untersuchungen*, theory is defined 'as an enclosed system of pro-

2. Descartes (1637), p. 92.

positions for a science as a whole'.[3] Theory in the fullest sense is 'a systematically linked set of propositions, taking the form of a systematically unified deduction'.[4] Science is 'a certain totality of propositions . . ., emerging in one or other manner from theoretical work, in the systematic order of which propositions a certain totality of objects acquires definition'.[5] The basic requirement which any theoretical system must satisfy is that all the parts should intermesh thoroughly and without friction. Harmony, which includes lack of contradictions, and the absence of superfluous, purely dogmatic elements which have no influence on the observable phenomena, are necessary conditions, according to Weyl.[6]

Insofar as this traditional conception of theory shows a tendency, it is towards a purely mathematical system of symbols. As elements of the theory, as components of the propositions and conclusions, there are ever fewer names of experiential objects and ever more numerous mathematical symbols. Even the logical operations themselves have already been so rationalized that, in large areas of natural science at least, theory formation has become a matter of mathematical construction.

The sciences of man and society have attempted to follow the lead of the natural sciences with their great successes. The difference between those schools of social science which are more oriented to the investigation of facts and those which concentrate more on principles has nothing directly to do with the concept of theory as such. The assiduous collecting of facts in all the disciplines dealing with social life, the gathering of great masses of detail in connection with problems, the empirical inquiries, through careful questionnaires and other means, which are a major part of scholarly activity, especially in the Anglo-Saxon universities since Spencer's time – all this adds up to a pattern which is, outwardly, much like the rest of life in a society dominated by industrial production techniques. Such an approach seems quite different from the formulation of abstract principles and the analysis of basic concepts by an armchair scholar, which are

3. Husserl (1929), p. 89. 4. ibid., p. 79. 5. ibid., p. 91.
6. Weyl (1927), pp. 118 ff.

typical, for example, of one sector of German sociology. Yet these divergences do not signify a structural difference in ways of thinking. In recent periods of contemporary society the so-called human studies (*Geisteswissenschaften*) have had but a fluctuating market value and must try to imitate the more prosperous natural sciences whose practical value is beyond question.

There can be no doubt, in fact, that the various schools of sociology have an identical conception of theory and that it is the same as theory in the natural sciences. Empirically oriented sociologists have the same idea of what a fully elaborated theory should be as their theoretically oriented brethren. The former, indeed, are persuaded that in view of the complexity of social problems and the present state of science any concern with general principles must be regarded as indolent and idle. If theoretical work is to be done, it must be done with an eye unwaveringly on the facts; there can be no thought in the foreseeable future of comprehensive theoretical statements. These scholars are much enamoured of the methods of exact formulation and, in particular, of mathematical procedures, which are especially congenial to the conception of theory described above. What they object to is not so much theory as such but theories spun out of their heads by men who have no personal experience of the problems of an experimental science. Distinctions like those between community and society (Tönnies), mechanical and organic solidarity (Durkheim), or culture and civilization (A. Weber) as basic forms of human sociality prove to be of questionable value as soon as one attempts to apply them to concrete problems. The way that sociology must take in the present state of research is (it is argued) the laborious ascent from the description of social phenomena to detailed comparisons and only then to the formation of general concepts.

The empiricist, true to his traditions, is thus led to say that only complete inductions can supply the primary propositions for a theory and that we are still far from having made such inductions. His opponent claims the right to use other methods, less dependent on progress in data-collection, for the formation of primary categories and insights. Durkheim, for example, agrees with many basic views of the empirical school but, in dealing with principles, he opts for an abridgement of the inductive process. It is impossible, he claims, to classify social happenings on the basis of purely empirical inventories, nor can research make classification easier in the way in which it is expected to do so.

Its [induction's] role is to put into our hands points of reference to which we can refer other observations than those which have furnished us with these very points of reference. But for this purpose it must be made not from a complete inventory of all the individual characteristics but from a small number of them, carefully chosen . . . It will spare the observer many steps because it will guide him . . . We must, then, choose the most essential characteristics for our classification.[7]

Whether the primary principles are obtained by selection, intuition or pure stipulation makes no difference, however, to their function in the ideal theoretical system. For the scientist must certainly apply his more or less general propositions, as hypotheses, to ever new facts. The phenomenologically-oriented sociologist will indeed claim that once an essential law has been ascertained every particular instance will, beyond any doubt, exemplify the law. But the really hypothetical character of the essential law is manifested as soon as the question arises whether in a particular case we are dealing with an instance of the essence in question or of a related essence, whether we are faced with a poor example of one type or a good example of another type. There is always, on the one hand, the conceptually formulated knowledge and, on the other, the facts to be subsumed under it. Such a subsumption or establishing of a relation between the simple perception or verification of a fact and the conceptual structure of our knowing is called its theoretical explanation.

We need not enter here into the details of the various kinds of classification. It will be enough to indicate briefly how the traditional concept of theory handles the explanation of historical events. The answer emerged clearly in the controversy between Eduard Meyer and Max Weber. Meyer regarded as idle and unanswerable the question of whether, even if certain historical personages had not reached certain decisions, the wars they

7. Durkheim (1895), p. 80.

caused would nonetheless sooner or later have occurred. Weber tried to show that if the question were indeed idle and unanswerable, all historical explanation would become impossible. He developed a 'theory of objective possibility', based on the theories of the physiologist, von Kries, and of writers in jurisprudence and national economy such as Merkel, Liefmann and Radbruch. For Weber, the historian's explanations, like those of the expert in criminal law, rest not on the fullest possible enumeration of all pertinent circumstances but on the establishment of a connection between those elements of an event which are significant for historical continuity, and particular, determinative happenings. This connection, for example the judgement that a war resulted from the policies of a statesman who knew what he was about, logically supposes that, if such a policy had not existed, some other effect would have followed. If one maintains a particular causal nexus between historical events, one is necessarily implying that if the nexus had not existed, then in accordance with the rules that govern our experience another effect would have followed in given circumstances. The rules of experience here are nothing but the formulations of our knowledge concerning economic, social, and psychological interconnections. With the help of these we reconstruct the probable course of events, going beyond the event itself to what will serve as explanation.[8] We are thus working with conditional propositions as applied to a given situation. If circumstances *a*, *b*, *c*, and *d* are given, then event *q* must be expected; if *d* is lacking, event *r*; if *g* is added, event *s*, and so on. This kind of calculation is a logical tool of history as it is of science. It is in this fashion that theory in the traditional sense is actually elaborated.

What scientists in various fields regard as the essence of theory thus corresponds, in fact, to the immediate tasks they set for themselves. The manipulation of physical nature and of specific economic and social mechanisms demand alike the amassing of a body of knowledge such as is supplied in an ordered set of hypotheses. The technological advances of the bourgeois period are inseparably linked to this function of the pursuit of science. On the one hand, it made the facts fruitful for the kind of scientific

8. Weber (1949).

knowledge that would have practical application in the circumstances, and, on the other, it made possible the application of knowledge already possessed. Beyond doubt, such work is a moment in the continuous transformation and development of the material foundations of that society. But the conception of theory was absolutized, as though it were grounded in the inner nature of knowledge as such or justified in some other ahistorical way, and thus it became a reified, ideological category . . .

The traditional idea of theory is based on scientific activity as carried on within the division of labour at a particular stage in the latter's development. It corresponds to the activity of the scholar which takes place alongside all the other activities of a society but in no immediately clear connection with them. In this view of theory, therefore, the real social function of science is not made manifest; it speaks not of what theory means in human life, but only of what it means in the isolated sphere in which for historical reasons it comes into existence. Yet as a matter of fact the life of society is the result of all the work done in the various sectors of production. Even if therefore the division of labour in the capitalist system functions but poorly, its branches, including science, do not become for that reason self-sufficient and independent. They are particular instances of the way in which society comes to grips with nature and maintains its own inherited form. They are moments in the social process of production, even if they be almost or entirely unproductive in the narrower sense. Neither the structures of industrial and agrarian production nor the separation of the so-called guiding and executory functions, services, and works, or of intellectual and manual operations are eternal or natural states of affairs. They emerge rather from the mode of production practised in particular forms of society. The seeming self-sufficiency enjoyed by work processes whose course is supposedly determined by the very nature of the object corresponds to the seeming freedom of the economic subject in bourgeois society. The latter believe they are acting according to personal determinations, whereas in fact even in their most complicated calculations they but exemplify the working of an incalculable social mechanism . . .

The whole perceptible world as present to a member of

bourgeois society and as interpreted within a traditional world-view which is in continuous interaction with that given world, is seen by the perceiver as a sum-total of facts; it is there and must be accepted. The classificatory thinking of each individual is one of those social reactions by which men try to adapt to reality in a way that best meets their needs. But there is at this point an essential difference between the individual and society. The world which is given to the individual and which he must accept and take into account is, in its present and continuing form, a product of the activity of society as a whole. The objects we perceive in our surroundings – cities, villages, fields, and woods – bear the mark of having been worked on by man. It is not only in clothing and appearance, in outward form and emotional make-up that men are the product of history. Even the way they see and hear is inseparable from the social life-process as it has evolved over the millennia. The facts which our senses present to us are socially preformed in two ways: through the historical character of the object perceived and through the historical character of the perceiving organ. Both are not simply natural; they are shaped by human activity, and yet the individual perceives himself as receptive and passive in the act of perception. The opposition of passivity and activity, which appears in knowledge theory as a dualism of sense-perception and understanding, does not hold for society, however, in the same measure as for the individual. The individual sees himself as passive and dependent, but society, though made up of individuals, is an active subject, even if a non-conscious one and, to that extent, a subject only in an improper sense. This difference in the existence of man and society is an expression of the cleavage which has up to now affected the historical forms of social life. The existence of society has either been founded directly on oppression or been the blind outcome of conflicting forces, but in any event not the result of conscious spontaneity on the part of free individuals. Therefore the meaning of 'activity' and 'passivity' changes according as these concepts are applied to society or to individuals. In the bourgeois economic mode the activity of society is blind and concrete, that of individuals abstract and conscious.

Human production also always has an element of planning to

it. To the extent then that the facts which the individual and his theory encounter are socially produced, there must be rationality in them, even if in a restricted sense. But social action always involves, in addition, available knowledge and its application. The perceived fact is therefore co-determined by human ideas and concepts, even before its conscious theoretical elaboration by the knowing individual. Nor are we to think here only of experiments in natural science. The so-called purity of objective event to be achieved by the experimental procedure is, of course, obviously connected with technological conditions, and the connection of these in turn with the material process of production is evident. But it is easy here to confuse two questions: the question of the mediation of the factual through the activity of society as a whole, and the question of the influence of the measuring instrument, that is, of a particular action, upon the object being observed. The latter problem, which continually plagues physics, is no more closely connected with the problem that concerns us here than is the problem of perception generally, including perception in everyday life. Man's physiological apparatus for sensation itself largely anticipates the order followed in physical experiment. As man reflectively records reality, he separates and rejoins pieces of it, and concentrates on some particulars while failing to notice others. This process is just as much a result of the modern mode of production, as the perception of a man in a tribe of primitive hunters and fishers is the result of the conditions of his existence (as well, of course, as of the object of perception).

In this context the proposition that tools are prolongations of human organs can be inverted to state that the organs are also prolongations of the tools. In the higher stages of civilization conscious human action unconsciously determines not only the subjective side of perception but in larger degree the object as well. The sensible world which a member of industrial society sees about him every day bears the marks of deliberate work: tenement houses, factories, cotton, cattle for slaughter, men, and, in addition, not only objects such as subway trains, delivery trucks, autos, and airplanes, but the movements in the course of which they are perceived. The distinction within this complex totality between what belongs to unconscious nature and what to the action of man in society cannot be drawn in concrete detail. Even where there is question of experiencing natural objects as such, their very naturalness is determined by contrast with the social world and, to that extent, depends upon the latter.

The individual, however, receives sensible reality, as a simple sequence of facts, into his world of ordered concepts. The latter too, though their context changes, have developed along with the life process of society. Thus, though the ordering of reality by understanding and the passing of judgement on objects usually take place as a foregone conclusion and with surprising unanimity among members of a given society, yet the harmony between perception and traditional thought and among the monads or individual subjects of knowledge is not a metaphysical accident. The power of healthy human understanding, or common sense, for which there are no mysteries, as well as the general acceptance of identical views in areas not directly connected with class conflicts, as for example in the natural sciences, are conditioned by the fact that the world of objects to be judged is in large measure produced by an activity that is itself determined by the very ideas which help the individual to recognize that world and to grasp it conceptually.

In Kant's philosophy this state of affairs is expressed in idealist form. The doctrine of purely passive sensation and active understanding suggests to him the question of whence the understanding derives its assured expectation that the manifold given in sensation will always obey the rules of the understanding. He explicitly rejects the thesis of a pre-established harmony, 'a kind of preformation-system of pure reason', in which reason has innate and sure rules with which objects are in accord.[9] His own explanation is that sensible appearances are already formed by the transcendental subject, that is, through the activity of reason, when they are received by perception and consciously judged.[10] In the most important chapters of the *Critique of Pure Reason* Kant tried to give a more detailed explanation of the 'transcendental affinity' or subjective determination of sensible material, a process of which the individual is unaware.

The difficulty and obscurity which, by Kant's own admission,

9. Kant (1781), p. 175.   10. ibid., A 110, pp. 137–8.

mark the sections on the deduction and schematism of the pure concepts of understanding may be connected with the fact that Kant imagines the supra-individual activity, of which the individual is unaware, only in the idealist form of a consciousness-in-itself, that is a purely intellectual source. In accordance with the theoretical vision available in his day, he does not see reality as product of a society's work, work which taken as a whole is chaotic, but at the individual level is purposeful. Where Hegel glimpses the cunning of a reason that is nonetheless world-historical and objective, Kant sees 'an art concealed in the depths of the human soul, whose real modes of activity nature is hardly likely ever to allow us to discover, and to have open to our gaze'.[11]

At least Kant understood that behind the discrepancy between fact and theory which the scholar experiences in his professional work, there lies a deeper unity, namely, the general subjectivity upon which individual knowledge depends. The activity of society thus appears to be a transcendental power, that is, the sum-total of spiritual factors. However, Kant's claim that its reality is sunk in obscurity, that is, that it is irrational despite all its rationality, is not without its kernel of truth. The bourgeois type of economy, despite all the ingenuity of the competing individuals within it, is not governed by any plan; it is not consciously directed to a general goal; the life of society as a whole proceeds from this economy only at the cost of excessive friction, in a stunted form, and almost, as it were, accidentally. The internal difficulties in the supreme concepts of Kantian philosophy, especially the ego of transcendental subjectivity, pure or original apperception, and consciousness-in-itself, show the depth and honesty of his thinking. The two-sidedness of these Kantian concepts, that is, their supreme unity and purposefulness, on the one hand, and their obscurity, unknownness, and impenetrability, on the other, reflects exactly the contradiction-filled form of human activity in the modern period. The collaboration of men in society is the mode of existence which reason urges upon them, and so they do apply their powers and thus confirm their own rationality. But at the same time their work and its results are alienated from them,

11. ibid., B 181, p. 183.

and the whole process with all its waste of work-power and human life, and with its wars and all its senseless wretchedness, seems to be an unchangeable force of nature, a fate beyond man's control.

In Kant's theoretical philosophy, in his analysis of knowledge, this contradiction is preserved. The unresolved problem of the relation between activity and passivity, *a priori* and sense data, philosophy and psychology, is therefore not due to purely subjective insufficiency but is objectively necessary. Hegel discovered and developed these contradictions, but finally resolved them in a higher intellectual realm. Kant claimed that there existed a universal subject which, however, he could not quite describe. Hegel escaped this embarrassment by postulating the absolute spirit as the most real thing of all. According to him, the universal has already adequately evolved itself and is identical with all that happens. Reason need no longer stand over against itself in purely critical fashion; in Hegel reason has become affirmative, even before reality itself is affirmed as rational. But, confronted with the persisting contradictions in human existence and with the impotence of individuals in face of situations they have themselves brought about, the Hegelian solution seems a purely private assertion, a personal peace treaty between the philosopher and an inhuman world . . .

We must go on now to add that there is a human activity which has society itself for its object.[12] The aim of this activity is not simply to eliminate one or other abuse, for it regards such abuses as necessarily connected with the way in which the social structure is organized. Although it itself emerges from the social structure, its purpose is not, either in its conscious intention or in its objective significance, the better functioning of any element in the structure. On the contrary, it is suspicious of the very categories of better, useful, appropriate, productive, and valuable, as these are understood in the present order, and refuses to take them as non-scientific presuppositions about which one can do nothing. The individual as a rule must simply accept the basic

12. In the following pages this activity is called 'critical' activity. The term is used here less in the sense it has in the idealist critique of pure reason than in the sense it has in the dialectical critique of political economy. It points to an essential aspect of the dialectical theory of society.

conditions of his existence as given and strive to fulfil them; he finds his satisfaction and praise in accomplishing as well as he can the tasks connected with his place in society and in courageously doing his duty despite all the sharp criticism he may choose to exercise in particular matters. But the critical attitude of which we are speaking is wholly distrustful of the rules of conduct with which society as presently constituted provides each of its members. The separation between individual and society in virtue of which the individual accepts as natural the limits prescribed for his activity is relativized in critical theory. The latter considers the overall framework which is conditioned by the blind interaction of individual activities (that is, the existent division of labour and the class distinctions) to be a function which originates in human action and therefore is a possible object of planful decision and rational determination of goals.

The two-sided character of the social totality in its present form becomes, for men who adopt the critical attitude, a conscious opposition. In recognizing the present form of economy and the whole culture which it generates to be the product of human work as well as the organization which mankind was capable of and has provided for itself in the present era, these men identify themselves with this totality and conceive it as will and reason. It is their own world. At the same time, however, they experience the fact that society is comparable to non-human natural processes, to pure mechanisms, because cultural forms which are supported by war and oppression are not the creations of a unified, self-conscious will. That world is not their own but the world of capital.

Previous history thus cannot really be understood; only the individuals and specific groups in it are intelligible, and even these not totally, since their internal dependence on an inhuman society means that even in their conscious action such individuals and groups are still in good measure mechanical functions. The identification, then, of men of critical mind with their society is marked by tension, and the tension characterizes all the concepts of the critical way of thinking. Thus, such thinkers interpret the economic categories of work, value, and productivity exactly as they are interpreted in the existing order, and they regard any other interpretation as pure idealism. But at the same time they consider it rank dishonesty simply to accept the interpretation; the critical acceptance of the categories which rule social life contains simultaneously their condemnation. This dialectical character of the self-interpretation of contemporary man is what, in the last analysis, also causes the obscurity of the Kantian critique of reason. Reason cannot become transparent to itself as long as men act as members of an organism which lacks reason. Organism as a naturally developing and declining unity cannot be a sort of model for society, but only a form of deadened existence from which society must emancipate itself. An attitude which aims at such an emancipation and at an alteration of society as a whole might well be of service in theoretical work carried on within reality as presently ordered. But it lacks the pragmatic character which attaches to traditional thought as a socially useful professional activity.

In traditional theoretical thinking, the genesis of particular objective facts, the practical application of the conceptual systems by which it grasps the facts, and the role of such systems in action, are all taken to be external to the theoretical thinking itself. This alienation, which finds expression in philosophical terminology as the separation of value and research, knowledge and action, and other polarities, protects the savant from the tensions we have indicated and provides an assured framework for his activity. Yet a kind of thinking which does not accept this framework seems to have the ground taken out from under it. If a theoretical procedure does not take the form of determining objective facts with the help of the simplest and most differentiated conceptual systems available, what can it be but an aimless intellectual game, half conceptual poetry, half impotent expression of states of mind? The investigation into the social conditioning of facts and theories may indeed be a research problem, perhaps even a whole field for theoretical work, but how can such studies be radically different from other specialized efforts? Research into ideologies, or sociology of knowledge, which has been taken over from the critical theory of society and established as a special discipline, is not opposed either in its aim or in its other ambitions to the usual activities that go on within classificatory science.

In this reaction to critical theory, the self-awareness of thought as such is reduced to the discovery of the relationship that exists between intellectual positions and their social location. Yet the structure of the critical attitude, inasmuch as its intentions go beyond prevailing social ways of acting, is no more closely related to social disciplines thus conceived than it is to natural science. Its opposition to the traditional concept of theory springs in general from a difference not so much of objects as of subjects. For men of the critical mind, the facts, as they emerge from the work of society, are not extrinsic in the same degree as they are for the savant or for members of other professions who all think like little savants. The latter look towards a new kind of organization of work. But insofar as the objective realities given in perception are conceived as products which in principle should be under human control and, in the future at least, will in fact come under it, these realities lose the character of pure factuality.

The scholarly specialist 'as' scientist regards social reality and its products as extrinsic to him, and 'as' citizen exercises his interest in them through political articles, membership in political parties or social service organizations, and participation in elections. But he does not unify these two activities, and his other activities as well, except, at best, by psychological interpretation. Critical thinking, on the contrary, is motivated today by the effort really to transcend the tension and to abolish the opposition between the individual's purposefulness, spontaneity, and rationality, and those work-process relationships on which society is built. Critical thought has a concept of man as in conflict with himself until this opposition is removed. If activity governed by reason is proper to man, then existent social practice, which forms the individual's life down to its least details, is inhuman, and this inhumanity affects everything that goes on in the society. There will always be something that is extrinsic to man's intellectual and material activity, namely nature as the totality of as yet unmastered elements with which society must deal. But when situations which really depend on man alone, the relationships of men in their work, and the course of man's own history are also accounted part of 'nature', the resultant extrinsicality is not only not a supra-historical eternal category (even pure nature in the sense described is not that), but it is a sign of contemptible weakness. To surrender to such weakness is non-human and irrational.

Bourgeois thought is so constituted that in reflection on the subject which exercises such thought a logical necessity forces it to recognize an ego which imagines itself to be autonomous. Bourgeois thought is essentially abstract, and its principle is an individuality which inflatedly believes itself to be the ground of the world or even to be the world without qualification, an individuality separated off from events. The direct contrary of such an outlook is the attitude which holds the individual to be the unproblematic expression of an already constituted society; an example would be a nationalist ideology. Here the rhetorical 'we' is taken seriously; speech is accepted as the organ of the community. In the internally rent society of our day, such thinking, except in social questions, sees non-existent unanimities and is illusory.

Critical thought and its theory are opposed to both the types of thinking just described. Critical thinking is the function neither of the isolated individual nor of a sum-total of individuals. Its subject is rather a definite individual in his real relation to other individuals and groups, in his conflict with a particular class, and, finally, in the resultant web of relationships with the social totality and with nature. The subject is no mathematical point like the ego of bourgeois philosophy; his activity is the construction of the social present. Furthermore, the thinking subject is not the place where knowledge and object coincide, nor consequently the starting-point for attaining absolute knowledge. Such an illusion about the thinking subject, under which idealism has lived since Descartes, is ideology in the strict sense, for in it the limited freedom of the bourgeois individual puts on the illusory form of perfect freedom and autonomy. As a matter of fact, however, in a society which is untransparent and without self-awareness the ego, whether active simply as thinker or active in other ways as well, is unsure of itself too. In reflection on man, subject and object are sundered; their identity lies in the future, not in the present. The method leading to such an identification may be called explanation in Cartesian language, but in genuinely critical thought explanation signifies not only a logical process but a concrete historical one as well. In the course of it both the social structure as a whole and the relation of the theoretician to society are altered, that is both the subject and the role of thought are changed. The acceptance of an essential unchangeableness between subject, theory, and object thus distinguishes the Cartesian conception from every kind of dialectical logic.

Postscript[13]

In the preceding essay I pointed out two ways of knowing: one is based on the *Discourse on Method*, the other on Marx's critique of political economy. Theory in the traditional sense established by Descartes and everywhere practised in the pursuit of the specialized sciences organizes experience in the light of questions which arise out of life in present-day society. The resultant network of disciplines contains information in a form which makes it useful in any particular circumstances for the greatest possible number of purposes. The social genesis of problems, the real situations in which science is put to use, and the purposes which it is made to serve are all regarded by science as external to itself.

The critical theory of society, on the other hand, has for its object men as producers of their own historical way of life in its totality. The real situations which are the starting-point of science are not regarded simply as data to be verified and to be predicted according to the laws of probability. Every datum depends not on nature alone but also on the power man has over it. Objects, the kind of perception, the questions asked, and the meaning of the answers all bear witness to human activity and the degree of man's power.

13. The 'Postscript' appeared in the *Zeitschrift für Sozialforschung*, vol. 6, no. 3, along with an essay by Herbert Marcuse entitled 'Philosophie und kritische Theorie'. Marcuse's essay has since been reprinted in his *Kultur und Gesellschaft*, vol. 1, Frankfurt am Main, 1965, pp. 102 ff. English translation: 'Philosophy and critical theory', in: *Negations. Essays in Critical Theory*, with translations from the German by Jeremy J. Shapiro, Allen Lane, 1968.

In thus relating matter – that is, the apparently irreducible facts which the scientific specialist must respect – to human production, the critical theory of society agrees with German idealism. Ever since Kant, idealism has insisted on the dynamic moment in the relationship and has protested against the adoration of facts and the social conformism this brings with it. 'As in mathematics,' says Fichte, 'so in one's whole view of the world; the only difference is that in interpreting the world one is unconscious that he is interpreting, for the interpretation takes place necessarily, not freely.'[14] This thought was a commonplace in German idealism. But the activity exercised on the matter presented to man was regarded as intellectual; it was the activity of a meta-empirical consciousness-in-itself, an absolute ego, the spirit, and consequently the victory over the dumb, unconscious, irrational side of this activity took place in principle in the person's interior, in the realm of thought.

In the materialist conception, on the contrary, the basic activity involved is work in society, and the class-related form of this work puts its mark on all human patterns of reaction, including theory. The intervention of reason in the processes whereby knowledge and its object are constituted, or the subordination of these processes to conscious control, does not take place therefore in a purely intellectual world, but coincides with the struggle for certain real ways of life.

The elaboration of theories in the traditional sense is regarded in our society as an activity set off from other scientific and non-scientific activities, needing to know nothing of the historical goals and tendencies of which such activity is a part. But the critical theory in its concept formation and in all phases of its development very consciously makes its own that concern for the rational organization of human activity which it is its task to illumine and legitimate. For this theory is not concerned only with goals already imposed by existent ways of life, but with men and all their potentialities.

To that extent the critical theory is the heir not only of German idealism but of philosophy as such. It is not just a research hypothesis which shows its value in the ongoing business of men;

14. Fichte (1805).

it is an essential element in the historical effort to create a world which satisfies the needs and powers of men. However extensive the interaction between the critical theory and the special sciences whose progress the theory must respect and on which it has for decades exercised a liberating and stimulating influence, the theory never aims simply at an increase of knowledge as such. Its goal is man's emancipation from slavery. In this it resembles Greek philosophy, not so much in the Hellenistic age of resignation as in the golden age of Plato and Aristotle. After the fruitless political projects of both these men the Stoics and Epicureans confined themselves to developing a doctrine of individualistic practices. The new dialectical philosophy, however, has held on to the realization that the free development of individuals depends on the rational constitution of society. In radically analysing present social conditions it became a critique of the economy.

References

DESCARTES, R. (1637), 'Discourse on Method', in *The Philosophical Works of Descartes*, tr. Elizabeth S. Haldane and G. R. T. Ross, Cambridge University Press, 1931, vol. 1, p. 92.

DURKHEIM, E. (1895), *The Rules of Sociological Method*, tr. from the 8th edition by Sarah A. Solovay and John H. Mueller, University of Chicago Press, 1938, p. 80.

FICHTE, J. G. (1805), 'Logik und Metaphysik', in *Nachgelassene Schriften*, vol. 2, Berlin, 1937, p. 47.

HUSSERL, E. (1929), *Formale und transzendentale Logik*, Halle, Berlin, pp. 79, 89, 91.

KANT, I. (1781), *Critique of Pure Reason*, A110, B167, B181, tr. Norman Kemp Smith, Macmillan, 1933, pp. 137–8, 175, 183.

MARCUSE, H. (1965), 'Philosophie und Kritische Theorie', *Kultur und Gesellschaft*, vol. 1, Frankfurt am Main. Translated as 'Philosophy and critical theory' in *Negations. Essays in Critical Theory*, tr. Jeremy J. Shapiro, Allen Lane, 1968.

POINCARÉ, H. (1905), *Science and Hypothesis*, tr. W. J. Greenstreet, Walter Scott, London, p. 145.

WEBER, M. (1949), 'Critical Studies in the Logic of the Cultural Sciences I: A Critique of Eduard Meyer's Methodological Views', in *Max Weber on the Methodology of the Social Sciences*, ed. and tr. Edward A. Shils and Henry A. Finch, Free Press, Glencoe, U.S.A.

WEYL, H. (1927), 'Philosophie der Naturwissenschaft', in *Handbuch der Philosophie*, Part 2, Munich-Berlin, 1927, pp. 118 ff.

11 Friedrich Pollock

Empirical Research into Public Opinion

Excerpt from Friedrich Pollock, *Gruppenexperiment – Ein Studienbericht*, Frankfurter Beiträge zur Soziologie, ed. T. W. Adorno and W. Dirks, Bd. 2., Europäische Verlagsanstalt, Frankfurt, 1955, pp. 15–32. Translated by Thomas Hall.

The object and procedure of empirical research

In the course of the last two decades empirical sociology has taken an extraordinary turn for the better through the systematic development and refinement of its methods of definition. Nowadays it can claim to be able to make pronouncements in areas which in the past had been to a great extent left to theoretical constructions if not to pure speculation. This is particularly true of the investigation of opinions, attitudes and patterns of behaviour, whether of the population as a whole or of specific groups. Not only objective sociological data but also the way in which people refer to that data are supposed nowadays to be susceptible to reliable investigation.[1] Associated with this is the hope of understanding modern industrial mass society better according to a model of knowledge based on those of the natural sciences, and of thereby bringing the problems which exist between men and their society nearer to a practical solution.

Social scientists of all disciplines and practical men from all areas of business, management and social welfare were exceptionally impressed by the achievements of modern methods of inquiry. While these methods promised to place a severe limitation on the idiosyncrasy and prejudice of the researcher by confronting him with hard facts, at the same time they appeared to have a democratic potential, by contrast with the kind of sociology that was still oriented towards old-fashioned institutional analysis. The process of sample analysis treats everyone equally. It opens up the possibility of revealing the distribution of opinion within the

1. Cf. S. A. Rice's foreword to Young (1960).

population far beyond the abstract process of elections, and of directing government policy accordingly. And at the same time it indicates a way of overcoming the difficulty which has been a constant bugbear to German sociology in the past: how to ascertain subjective opinion not subjectively but objectively. In place of the widely ramifying problems of 'interpretative' sociology, which is directed towards complexes of meaning, there arose a procedure which claims to make tangible realities of the phenomena of consciousness as recordable, measurable and mathematically classifiable facts. A procedure of this kind was all the more attractive in that in the web of life of a thoroughly socially organized mankind, a larger and larger number of structures and contexts confront the individual no longer as a comprehensible, but as an overwhelming, fact: as blind, merciless existence. The more contemporary society appears as a 'second nature' to the people of whom it is composed, the more appropriate it seems to analyse it with methods borrowed from the natural sciences.

The progress of a science is undeniable when it is able to develop methods with the help of which it can register, and conditionally predict, men's opinions, desires, and even their subtlest ways of reacting. And equally undeniable is the gain which is involved in the ability to test political and economic decisions by the reactions of the electorate. Yet this should not lead us to ignore the fact that the approach of sociological methods to those of the natural sciences is itself the offspring of a society which has solidified into a thing-like entity confronting the men who form part of it. Hence the democratic potential of the new methods is not so unquestionable as it is popularly believed to be in Germany, after the muzzling of public opinion under the Hitler régime. It is not an insignificant fact that modern 'opinion research' grew out of market and consumer research.[2] It tacitly posits the universe of the customer as that of mankind as a whole. Thus the various tendencies towards social control and manipulation which may be observed in the wake of modern empirical sociology – for instance in the field of consumer analysis or in the

2. Cf. Cantril (1947); Noelle (1940); Albig (1939).

analysis of 'human relations' – are not extrinsic to the method itself. While it may be directed by the notion of the equality of men and recognizes no special privileges in its evaluation of the opinions of individuals, it nonetheless accepts these individuals as they are formed by the prevailing economic and social conditions, without itself penetrating this formation. The difficulty becomes striking when it is a matter of discovering, by means of representative sample questionnaires, the opinions and attitudes of people to questions of general public interest – that is, as soon as attempts are made to treat the problem of so-called public opinion with the techniques of empirical social research.

The concept of public opinion and its problematic

Individual opinion and public opinion

According to older ways of thinking it was certainly not taken for granted that *public opinion* on a particular question could be determined with mathematical reliability. Today, on the other hand, it is assumed that public opinion may everywhere be investigated and measured.[3] This relies on a technique which has been evolved in the meantime. A number of questions are put by the interviewers of the institutes for public opinion to a statistically representative cross-section of the population. The answers received are grouped according to content and in the process of interpretation are related to a series of objective qualities of the interviewees. The results are then presented in tabulated form, the tables are interpreted and the product regarded as public opinion. According to the method employed and the size of the statistical sample this is accepted within an exactly determinable margin of error as a reliable result.[4] Hardly any consideration is given to the problem of the very concept 'public opinion', but it is tacitly postulated that this is known if it is possible to state what percentage of the sample – and with it, of the population as a whole, which it represents – answers a particular question in one way or another. Yet it is obvious that the legitimacy of this procedure is itself dependent on the concept of public opinion. The problem is

3. Cf. Doob (1949); Albig, op. cit. 4. Cf. Parten (1950).

excluded, not solved, if this concept is defined in advance in such a way as to be applicable to the possible results of sample questioning.

The concept of *individual opinion*, which must be clarified if that of public opinion is to be given a precise formulation, already presents considerable difficulties. Traditionally, opinion means the content of a person's consciousness, without any judgement being made as to its truth or untruth. If someone thinks two and two make four that is as much his opinion as if he thinks two and two make five. But both types of judgement are distinguished from one another not only according to an objective context independent of individual thought but also by their internal structure. In one kind of judgement there is an adequate relationship to the objective state of affairs; in the other there is not. The acts of thinking vary correspondingly. In the first case they are genuine syntheses, logically legitimate operations; while in the second case psychological, if not pathogenic, determinants predominate. The concept of opinion which lies at the basis of opinion research takes no account of this distinction. The relationship of consciousness to objectivity does not enter into consideration and the contents of consciousness are treated as if the furthest, ultimate source of their justification were the individual's thoughts of the moment; whereas all thinking of that sort is dependent on the impulses provoking what is thought, which are not simply a part of what the individual thinks. The concept of opinion held by current opinion research, which believes itself to be scientific without presuppositions, in fact presupposes a nominalist epistemology. It operates with a subjective concept of truth,[5] without even a glance at the problem of the objective. Objectivity, on which it prides itself so much, is nothing but a generality abstracted from subjectivities of this kind – the common denominator of opinions, as it were, unrelated to their objective validity.

But the concept of opinion is problematical not merely because it cannot be separated from what is thought and from the truth of what is thought. Rather, the very assumption that there exists the opinion of every individual is dubious. It is a contemporary cliché that everyone has his own opinion about everything. On the other

5. Cf. Horkheimer (1947).

hand, in earlier ages of society the spiritual cosmos was far too firmly fixed and strictly controlled to allow every individual to form a personal opinion about everything, or even to want to do so – the very opinion itself is a specifically liberal one – while on the other hand the possibilities of information and communication were too limited ever to place the overwhelming majority of people in a position to have an opinion about everything under the sun. Nowadays, when in the great industrial nations information about practically everything is widely available, the mass of information and the complexity of all social relationships has expanded to such an extent that sometimes it is difficult even for a specialist to form a personal opinion about his own subject. That lack of interest in public affairs on the part of the individual who enjoys democratic rights, which is the subject of so much lamentation, may in part result from the fact that when confronted with these matters he feels helpless, having neither the time, the energy, nor the education to put together the data necessary to form a personal opinion. By proceeding on the assumption that it is necessary to have an opinion about everything, opinion research runs the risk of seducing people in the interviews it conducts to express opinions they do not instinctively hold, opinions which are not theirs at all.[6] Precisely the contradiction between the compulsion to have an opinion and the incapacity to form an opinion leads many people to accept stereotypes which relieve them of the thankless task of forming their own opinions and yet enable them to enjoy the prestige of being in touch with things.[7] This contradiction applies to the discussion of general questions at all levels of society. Still, modern methods of transport and information have promoted the formation of opinion, however this may come about. Yet it is precisely the effect of this immeasurably expanded possibility of communication which no longer allows us to think of every individual as a monad, whose opinions crystallize and take on permanent existence in isolation, in a vacuum as it were. Realistic opinion research would have to come as close as possible in its methods of research to those con-

6. Frequent reference is made to this point in specialist literature, but the necessary conclusions have not always been drawn in practice.

7. Cf. Lippmann (1947); Hofstätter (1949).

ditions in which actual opinions are formed, held and modified. It must liberate itself from the prejudice that an opinion is to a great extent stable, like some possession owned by the individual, and that its modification is a secondary matter. However problematic the notion of an individual firmly established within himself has become in modern society, in the light of the discoveries of modern social psychology, the conception which views an individual's opinion as a substratum present at one moment and then in certain situations moving in one direction or another, has become equally problematic. Opinion research should take due account of the dynamic impulse not only in retrospect, for instance by repeated questioning of the same individuals, but in the original design of the research. It should take its cue from the fact that in socialized society the objective situation in which it is at any given moment plays a decisive part in the formation and content of the individual's opinions,[8] without this eliminating the subjective impulse which addresses itself to the objective facts of society.[9]

Public opinion – a phenomenon of quantities?

All these questions connected with apparently so elementary a concept as that of individual opinion are preliminary to the real problem of public opinion. In empirical social research there fre-

8. The complicated relationship of opinion and attitude has been thoroughly discussed by C. D. Wiebe in 'Some Implications of Separating Opinion from Attitudes', *Public Opinion Quarterly*, Autumn 1953, pp. 328 ff.

9. In the interest of better comprehensibility we depart somewhat from the usual, but by no means uniform, terminology employed in the specialist literature. On the other hand it is not always possible to maintain one terminology. Departures from normal usage will be noted. In the following passage we shall as a rule express the problems discussed in the following terms: by individual or group *opinion* we mean the specifically formulated and therefore conscious view about a subject. *Attitude* is the view of a subject which underlies an opinion and its judgement. *Views and judgements* can be latent or conscious, fixed and generalized or more or less fluid and therefore more or less susceptible to influence from subjective and external factors. *Outlook*, *Behaviour*, *Mode of Behaviour*: preparedness to judge and act, voting on deposited and to some extent generalized views and ways of reacting. By *mode of reaction* we mean the formal character of an expression

quently prevails the notion that public opinion is the essence of all individual opinions. Since it is impossible to discover the opinion held by all elements of the statistical universe – all the individuals of a population – the intention is to employ a process of reliable selection by taking samples which permit valid conclusions to be drawn about the whole. However, it is not beyond question whether public opinion is the opinion of all individuals or even of the majority. In German tradition, at least, the concept is by no means always understood in the way it is by present-day opinion research. Let us first of all recall that neither the significance of minority groups in the shaping of majority opinions, nor even the extremely important tensions between majority and minority in the formation of opinions, is taken into account by the usual methods of counting and measuring. Above all, from the standpoint of theoretical sociology the objection may be raised which is becoming more and more important in current American work: the objection, that is, that the procedure of opinion research which enumerates and appraises all individuals as having equal rights, as dots without qualities so to speak, ignores the real differences of social power and social impotence.[10]

The debate about the concept of public opinion has for the most part found naïve solutions for these difficulties in the theory of the élite and in cultural prestige. Thus, for instance, W. A. MacKinnon designated as public opinion that held by the best-informed, most intelligent and morally best members of a group, on the grounds that this opinion would establish itself, although very slowly, and be accepted at least by the majority of the group. Other authors supplement their concept of public opinion by formal sociological criteria. Thus Leonhard W. Doob states that it is possible to speak of public opinion only insofar as the attitudes of members of equal social groups agree with one another. The concept of public opinion presupposes a social organization or group the members of which have to have more or less common experience. Here the attempt is being made to differentiate

of opinion, e.g. whether the opinion is asserting, limitedly asserting (ambivalent) or dissenting. The word *disposition* is used as a general term for attitude and modes of behaviour.

10. Cf. P. F. Lazarsfeld *et al.* (1949).

the concept of public opinion by taking into consideration the structure of opinion-forming groups. This is the first sign of the awareness that public opinion does not represent merely a collection of individual opinions, but contains a blanket collective component. Reference may be made to public opinion only where there is something like a group structure which is of one voice. The objection may be made, though, that even in a totalitarian, and therefore atomized, society, there is something like public opinion.

Finally, other authors take their cue mainly from that linguistic usage according to which opinions disseminated through newspapers and radio broadcasts are viewed as public.[11] It cannot be denied that there is some justification in this. Not only are the organs of public opinion inclined to regard themselves as the only public opinion as such, and not only are they often regarded, especially in politics, as the voices of public opinion, but official channels of communication do often enough disseminate views which are commonly held by the public, views which are 'in the air', so to speak. Their centralization and concentration, the standardization inherent in their technology, exercises an almost inconceivable influence on the consciousness of the consumers; and what the consumer considers to be his own ideas are to a great extent merely a reflection of what he receives from the power of society which lies behind the communications media. Still, necessary though it is to take social power into account in the analysis of public opinion, it is not enough to regard the expressions of social power as the sole object of this analysis.

All the theories we have so far discussed have in common the fact that ultimately they regard public opinion either as the sum of all individual opinions, or as separate sectors, but never as a totality. The difference between this whole and the results of the definitions of public opinion already mentioned bears some likeness to Rousseau's celebrated distinction between 'volonté générale' and 'volonté de tous'. The 'volonté de tous' corresponds to the currently predominant view which regards public opinion as the sum of individual opinions, while the 'volonté générale' tends towards that whole which is more than the sum

11. Cf. W. Bauer (1950).

of its parts.[12] Tönnies has indicated the problem and pointed out that public opinion as a homogeneously effective force should be clearly and sharply distinguished from the publicly proclaimed mass of manifold contradictory opinions. The conception of public opinion as analogous to the 'volonté de tous' is built on the model of a purely competitive society. Every individual must enter the life of society equipped, as it were, with nothing but his own head, and form his opinions as an autonomous being. However, just as *homo oeconomicus* does not enter the competitive race with nothing but the cunning of his hands, so it is impossible for the critical intellect of the individual to be a *tabula rasa*. From his childhood on every individual is possessed of innumerable views, in the first instance ones acquired uncritically, the greater part of which are themselves in turn condensations of the prevailing atmosphere. Later in life the individual is all the more subject to the pressure of this intellectual atmosphere in that resistance to it presupposes a strong ego which but few men possess. Individual opinion, which appears to current opinion research to be the elementary unit, is in actual fact an extremely derivative, mediated thing. On the other hand, what has just been mentioned here as 'intellectual atmosphere' – classical German philosophy calls it 'objective spirit' – is, by contrast with individual opinion, something primary. This is true not in the sense of a speculative construction, but in the much more tangible sense of the primacy of the means of economic and social production over consumption – even over what is called intellectual consumption. It is this, and not a conception along the lines of Gestalt theory, which lies behind the 'wholeness' of public opinion, Tönnies' 'homogeneously effective force', which other writers designate as a collective power or as a group opinion with its own essence.[13] While it is sustained by individuals and based on their thoughts and emotions, it is not the sum total of their opinions, but confronts each

12. 'Il y a souvent bien de la différence entre la volonté de tous et la volonté générale: celle-ci ne regarde qu'à l'intérêt commun, l'autre regarde l'intérêt privé, et n'est qu'une somme de volontés particulières; mais ôtez de ces mêmes volontés les plus et les moins qui s'entre-détruisent, reste pour somme des différences la volonté générale'. Rousseau.

13. Cf. Albig, op. cit.; Doob, op. cit.; Lowell.

individual as something pre-formed, pre-established, and often of overwhelming force. The objectification of public opinion as a kind of 'thing-in-itself' is a reflection of a social condition in which relationships themselves are experienced by the individual as having an independent existence, and compel him to conform to them.

Public opinion may be regarded as the essence of this objective spirit which mirrors social relationships and dispositions of power, the form of consciousness which is characteristic for society as a whole. Insofar as this consciousness asserts itself over the heads of individuals, it is not identical with the contents of the consciousness of all individual men, and it contradicts those held by many. It is modified in its attitudes and opinions, and sometimes shattered beyond recognition by the subjective factor in the individual's intellectual destiny. Nevertheless, public opinion proves to be something objective with regard to individuals, the expression of the social totality; yet it is at the same time the expression of a social fate which takes its course over and above the lives of individuals.

This view of public opinion links up with that which is given in reality, with the decisive power-relationships of society. And yet it is not accepted by an empirical and positivistic science which constantly appeals to the factual. It is indeed frequently conceded that public opinion is supra-individual in nature. It is admitted that there exist in the public world notions, feelings and thoughts conditioned by tradition, traditional usages and modes of behaviour, which play a continual role in the way people form opinions. Nor does anyone deny the interrelation between these institutional intellectual forces and individuals, and between one individual and another. But in the end public opinion is still the name given to the sum of individual opinions which result from all these influences. This, and not the objective spirit, forms the substratum of opinion research, because only individual opinions can be counted and measured. Although the principle that 'science is measurement' in all its crudeness is hardly accepted by any American scholar nowadays, it still exerts an influence as an implicit criterion of scientific validity. And yet nobody can simply ignore the fact that the positivistic-atomistic conception of public opinion does not give an adequate account of the facts. The uneasiness produced by this is countered by agnosticism: 'The nature of public opinion must not be defined, but studied.'[14] Comfort is sought in a future in which so much empirical data will have been assembled that the question of the nature of public opinion will solve itself; and, in thus choosing not to consider the direction taken by the fact-collecting which it is hoped will produce insight, researchers presuppose a concept of public opinion which does not correspond to reality. If theory is referred to, the word is used not to denote some theoretical conception of society as a whole – in which the concept of public opinion would find its proper place – but is restricted to the formulation and testing of hypotheses which can be verified or falsified only by the criterion of the atomistic-quantitative procedure. This weakness in the 'philosophy' which underlies opinion research and which rests on a questionable notion of society brings into question the reliability of these seemingly objective methods of research.

References

ALBIG, W. (1939), *Public Opinion*, New York, pp. 1 ff., 181 ff.
BAUER, W. (1950), *Die öffentliche Meinung in der Weltgeschichte*, Potsdam.
CANTRIL, H. (1944), *Gauging Public Opinion*, Princeton, U.S.A.
CHILD, H. L. (1939), 'By Public Opinion I Mean', *Public Opinion Quarterly*.
DOOB, L. W. (1949), *Public Opinion and Propaganda*, New York, pp. 31 ff., 33 ff.
HOFSTÄTTER, P. R. (1949), *Die Psychologie der öffentlichen Meinung*, Vienna, pp. 64 ff.
HORKHEIMER, M. (1947), *Eclipse of Reason*, New York, pp. 3 ff., 128 ff.
LAZARSFELD, P. F., *et al*. (1949), *The People's Choice*, New York, pp. xix ff., 40 ff., 65 ff.
LIPPMANN, W. (1922), *Public Opinion*, New York, pp. 3 ff.
LOWELL, A. L. (1953), 'The Nature of Public Opinion', in B. Berelson and M. Janowitz, *Reader in Public Opinion and Communication*, Free Press, Glencoe, pp. 21 ff.
MACKINNON, W. A. (1888), *On the Rise, Progress and Present State of Public Opinion in Great Britain*, London, p. 15.
NOELLE, E. (1940), *Amerikanische Massenbefragung über Politik und Presse*, Limburg, p. 36.
PARTEN, M. (1950), *Surveys, Polls and Samples*, New York, pp. 290 ff.

14. Child (1939).

RICE, S. A. (1960), foreword to P. V. Young, *Scientific Social Surveys and Research*, New York.
ROUSSEAU, J. J., *Du Contrat Social*, Paris, 1834, p. 48.
TÖNNIES, F. (1922), *Kritik der öffentlichen Meinung*, Berlin, pp. 131 ff.
WIEBE, C. D. (1953), 'Some Implications of Separating Opinion from Attitudes', *Public Opinion Quarterly*, pp. 328 ff.

12 Theodor W. Adorno

Sociology and Empirical Research

Excerpt from Theodor W. Adorno, 'Soziologie und empirische Forschung', in Max Horkheimer and Theodor W. Adorno, *Sociologica II*, Europäische Verlagsanstalt, Frankfurt, 1962, pp. 205–22. First published in 1957. Translated by Graham Bartram.

The connection between the various approaches classed together as an academic discipline under the name of sociology is at best a highly abstract one: namely, the fact that they all, in one way or another, deal with social phenomena. They are unified neither in the subject of their investigations nor in their method. Some are applied to the totality of society and its dynamics, others, in emphatic opposition to the first, devote themselves to individual social phenomena, decrying as speculative any attempt to relate these to a general concept of society. Methods vary accordingly. In the former case, by focusing on basic structural determinants, such as the exchange relationship, it is hoped to gain insight into the total social context; in the latter, such an endeavour, innocent though it be of any tyrannical designs on the realm of facticity, is dismissed as a philosophical relic in the evolution of science, to be replaced by the simple determination of what is the case. The two conceptions are based on historically divergent models. The theory of society springs from philosophy, but at the same time attempts to place the latter's inquiries in a different functional context, by situating in society that fundamental reality which in traditional philosophy had been constituted by eternal essences or Mind. Just as philosophy mistrusted deceptive appearances, and made it its business to interpret them, so does theory's suspicion of society's façade grow in proportion to the latter's bland impenetrability. Theory wants to discover the hidden spring that keeps the whole mechanism going. The yearning of thought, which once found intolerable the meaninglessness of that which simply exists, has secularized its longing in the striving for disenchantment. It wants to raise the stone and expose the teeming confusion underneath, seeing in the understanding of the latter the only way to preserve meaning.

This impulse is resisted by factual social research, which sees disenchantment, even of the kind accepted by Max Weber, as simply a specific type of mystification, and regards its concern with a latent driving force, and with the possibility of intervening in its operation, as nothing but an unnecessary delay in the process of changing what is already exposed to view. In particular, what is generally known nowadays as empirical social research has, since Comte's positivism, more or less explicitly taken the natural sciences as its model. The two tendencies have no common denominator.

Theoretical speculations on society cannot be confirmed by precisely corresponding sets of empirical data: they elude the latter as persistently as spirits elude the experimental apparatus of parapsychology. Any and every view of society as a whole necessarily transcends the scatter of social facts. The construction of the whole has as its first pre-condition an overall concept according to which the disparate data can be organized. From a living experience that has not adapted itself to social control mechanisms, from the recollection of its previous thinking, and from the unwavering consistency of its own reflection, it must form that concept, bring it to bear on the material, and in turn modify the former through its contact with the latter. If, however, theory does not wish to succumb to dogmatism – that dogmatism which scepticism, which has grown into a total censorship of thought, will at every possible opportunity claim to have detected – it cannot afford to rest there. It must transform the concepts that it brings in from outside into those which the object by itself has, into that which the object would itself like to be, and confront it with what it is. It must dissolve the rigidity of an object frozen in the here-and-now into a field of tensions between the possible and the actual; for each of these two – the possible and the actual – depends on the other for its very existence. In other words, theory is inalienably critical. But for this reason, hypotheses deduced from it, predictions of what may be expected according to the rules, are not fully adequate to it. The merely predictable is itself a part of the social mechanism, and has nothing to do with the real aim of criticism. Smug satisfaction at the fact that things have turned out just as they were forecast must not be allowed to blind social theory to the realization that by presenting itself as hypothesis it is changing its inner structure. The particular observation by which it is verified immediately becomes a part of that deceptive façade that it is attempting to break through. What is gained by way of concretization and irrefutability is paid for by a loss of penetrating force; the fundamental proposition is reduced to the dimensions of the phenomenon that is used to test it. If, on the other hand, one follows customary scientific procedure and ascends from particular investigations to a total view of society, what one gains are at best general classificatory categories which are never capable of giving expression to the life of the society itself. The category 'societies with a division of labour' is of a higher and more general order than the category 'capitalist society'; but it is a less, not a more essential one, with less to say about the lives of human beings and what threatens them – without this implying that a lower order category such as 'urbanism' has correspondingly more to say on the subject. The degree of abstraction of sociological categories varies neither directly nor inversely with their contribution to the understanding of society. It is for this reason that so little is to be gained from the systematic unification of these categories in a model like the functionalist one of Parsons.

Even less, however, is to be expected from those promises of a synthesis of theory and empiricism – promises made time and time again since the very beginnings of sociology but as yet unfulfilled – which falsely equate theory with formal unity, and refuse to acknowledge the fact that a social theory purified of real social content puts all its emphases in the wrong place. One need only point out how totally inconsequential has been the recourse to the 'group' compared with the recourse to 'industrial society'. The construction of social theory according to the model of classificatory systems substitutes the thinnest conceptual remnants for what the immanent laws of society dictate. Empiricism and theory cannot be accommodated in a single continuum. Compared with the projected insight into the essence of modern society, the contributions of empiricism are drops of water on a hot stone; but empirical evidence for fundamental structural laws will always, according to the rules of empiricism, remain open to disputation. It is not a question of smoothing out and harmonizing these divergencies: only a harmonistic view of society allows itself to be thus misled. The tensions must be developed and made fruitful.

Today, in the wake of the disillusionment both with cultural (*geisteswissenschaftlich*) and formal sociology, there is a general tendency to accord primacy to empirical sociology. The immediate practical use to which it can be put, its affinity with any and every form of administration, is no doubt a contributory factor. But the reaction against arbitrary or simply meaningless pronouncements from above on the nature of society is a legitimate one. Nevertheless, this does not mean that empirical methods automatically take pride of place. To begin with, there are others apart from them: the simple existence of disciplines and modes of thought does not amount to their justification. But their limits are also set by the subject-matter itself. The empirical methods, whose attraction lies in the claims they make for their objectivity, show a paradoxical preference – explained by their origins in market research – for the subjective: that is to say (apart from census-type statistical data such as sex, age, legal status, income, education, etc.) for things such as opinions and attitudes, seen always as behavioural tendencies of individual subjects. It is in any case only in this sphere that their specific contribution has so far stood the test: as inventories of so-called objective facts it would be difficult to distinguish them from pre-scientific information geared to administrative ends.

In general, the objectivity of empirical social research is one of method, not of subject-matter. Through statistical processing, information on a greater or lesser number of individuals is turned into statements which, following the laws of probability, are generalizable and independent of individual variations. But the resultant mean values, objectively valid though they be, nevertheless remain for the most part objective statements about individual subjects; in fact, about how these subjects see themselves in reality. Society in its objectivity, the aggregate of all the relationships, institutions and forces, within whose context men act, is something which the empirical methods of questionnaire and interview, with all their possible combinations and variations, have ignored or at least regarded as purely accidental. The fault lies in part with project-sponsors with vested interests, who wittingly or unwittingly hinder the clarification of those relationships and who in America, when research projects on, for example, the mass-media are being assigned, make sure from the start that they are limited to the recording of reactions coming from within the dominant commercial systems and exclude any analysis of the structure and implications of the system itself. But, in addition to this, the empirical methods themselves are already tailored to this kind of approach. By taking more or less standardized surveys of numbers of individuals and processing the results into statistics, they tend to enshrine already widespread – and as such pre-formed – attitudes as the foundation for their perspective on the subject of their investigations. Objective realities are admittedly reflected in these attitudes, but the reflection is bound to be incomplete and marred by multiple distortions. And in any case, the most cursory glance at the functioning of people at work shows that, compared with these objective realities, the significance of subjective opinions, attitudes and patterns of behaviour is entirely secondary. However positivist they make themselves out to be, these methodologies are implicitly based on the presupposition – derived probably from an over-hasty generalization from the rules of the game in democratic elections – that the sum of conscious and unconscious human experiences, formed into a statistical universe, provides an immediate key to the social process. In spite of, or rather because of, their objectification, these methods are unable to penetrate the objectification of whatever they are focused on, particularly the concrete determinisms of economics. All attitudes possess for them virtually equal weight, and such elementary distinctions as the variations in the importance of these attitudes according to the measure of social power they represent are only taken into account in additional refinements such as the selection of key groups. The primary becomes secondary. But such dislocations within the method are not without effect on the objects to which it is applied. In spite of its aversion to the philosophical anthropologies whose rise to prominence dates from the same time as its own, empirical sociology shares with them an orientation that already in the here-and-now gives primacy of significance to human beings as individuals, instead of defining socialized man today first and foremost as a moment – and, above all, the object – of the social totality. The method's unreflecting approach to phenomena, its ceaseless endeavour to nail down hard facts, is transferred to its objects – the subjective facts that have thus been obtained – as if these things existed in themselves and not, as they really are, reified.

The method threatens both to make a fetish of its object and to degenerate into a fetish itself. Not without significance – and, indeed, fully consonant with the logic of the procedures involved – is the fact that in discussions on empirical social research, questions of method predominate over those of content. The intrinsic interest of what is to be studied is frequently replaced as a criterion by the objectivity of the results obtained with this or that method, and in the pursuit of empirical science the selection of the material and the general orientation of the investigation, insofar as they are not dictated by practical desiderata of an administrative kind, depend to a far greater extent on the procedures lying to hand and offering unfailing opportunities for further development, than on the specific nature of the subject of the research.

Hence the indisputable irrelevance of so many empirical studies. The widely used empirical technique of operational or instrumental definition, which delimits a category such as 'conservatism' by attaching numerical values to questions posed within the context of the survey itself, places a seal of approval on the primacy of the method over the subject-matter and on the arbitrary way in which the scientific procedure has been devised. The technique sets out to investigate an object with an instrument which, through its own construction, decides in advance just what that object is: a simple case of circularity. The refusal, for reasons of scientific integrity, to work with any concepts other than clear and unambiguous ones, becomes a pretext for putting the interests of a self-legitimizing research industry before those of the subject-matter itself. With an arrogance born of ignorance the objections of classical philosophy to the practice of definition are consigned to oblivion;[1] what that philosophy banished as a remnant of scholasticism is still being perpetuated by unreflecting individual sciences in the name of scientific exactitude. As soon as the almost inevitable extrapolation is made from the instrumentally defined concepts to those of conventional usage, research becomes guilty of that very contamination which through its definitions it sought to eradicate.

The fact that we cannot just cheerfully transfer the scientific model *in toto* to the study of society is due to the nature of the latter. But not for the ideological reasons which German reactionaries in particular use to rationalize their opposition to the new techniques: namely, the pretext that human dignity, which humanity is at present busy demolishing, is somehow beyond the reach of methods that regard man as a part of nature. Mankind commits more of a sacrilege by permitting its claim to supremacy to repress all thought of its nature as a species, and thus causing crude nature to flourish blind and unchecked, than by reminding itself that it is a part of nature.[2]

'Sociology is not a cultural science (*Geisteswissenschaft*).' To the extent that the hardening of society reduces men increasingly to the condition of objects and transforms this condition into a 'second nature', there is no need to treat as sacrilegious those methods which are themselves a testimony to this very process. The unfreedom of the methods serves the cause of freedom by bearing silent witness to the unfreedom that prevails in reality. The cries of heartfelt rage and the more sophisticated defensive reactions elicited by Kinsey's investigations provide the strongest argument in Kinsey's favour. In cases where under the pressure of their situation men are indeed reduced to 'reacting like batrachians'[3] – as in their role as captive consumers of the products of the

1. Compare for example Kant, *Kritik der reinen Vernunft*, 553 f; Hegel, *Wissenschaft der Logik*, Stuttgart, 1949, 11 Teil, p. 289 ff, p. 292 ff.
2. 'Soziologie und empirische Forschung', in: *Frankfurter Beitrage zur Soziologie*, Bd. 4: Exkurse, Frankfurt-am-Main, 1956, p. 112.
3. Compare M. Horkheimer, T. W. Adorno, *Dialektik der Aufklärung*, Amsterdam, 1947, p. 50.

mass media and other regimented pleasures – they are more adequately described by the opinion poll, that *bête noire* of an enfeebled humanism, than by a sociology that sees itself as 'interpretative': for the substratum of interpretative understanding – meaningful and internally consistent human behaviour – has already been displaced in the subjects themselves by a purely reactive form of existence. A social science that is atomistic, and which at the same time works upwards from these atoms to general syntheses by means of a classificatory system, holds a Medusa-like mirror to a society similarly atomized and organized according to abstract classificatory categories – in this case administrative ones.

But this *adequatio rei atque cogitationis* only attains its full truth-value when it reflects on itself. Its sole right is that of criticism. As soon as one hypostatizes the state of affairs which these research methods both describe and embody, as the rationale inherent in science itself, instead of making it the object of critical reflection, one is contributing willy-nilly to its perpetuation. In so doing, empirical social research confuses the epiphenomenon – what the world has made of us – with the thing itself. Its procedure contains a presupposition rooted less in the demands of the method than in the state of society, i.e. historical factors. The thing-like method postulates a reified consciousness in those whom it subjects to its experiments. If a questionnaire asking members of the public about their musical tastes gives them the choice of the categories 'classical' and 'popular', it is with the justifiable certainty that the people concerned listen according to these categories, just as when switching on the radio they automatically and without thinking register whether the programme they have tuned into is one of popular hits, so-called serious music, or a religious service with its musical accompaniment. But as long as the social determinants of this sort of reaction are omitted from the survey, the conclusions it comes to, though correct, are at the same time misleading; they suggest that the division of musical experience into 'classical' and 'popular' is a final one, somehow part of the natural order of things.

The inquiry does not achieve social relevance, however, until it directs itself at this very dichotomy and its fossilization into something taken entirely for granted, and poses as a necessary corollary the question whether the spontaneity of our experience of music is not seriously affected by this *a priori* classification of what we hear. Only an insight into the genesis of the present patterns of response and their relationship to the intrinsic meaning of what is experienced would permit a true interpretation of the phenomenon registered. Prevailing empirical practice, however, would reject any inquiry into the objective meaning of the work of art, dismiss that meaning as a mere subjective projection on the part of the listeners and demote the artistic structure to the status of the 'stimulus' of experimental psychology. In so doing it would deprive itself in advance of the opportunity of investigating the relationship of the masses to the commodities forced on them by the culture-industry; the commodities themselves would, after all, be defined in terms of precisely those mass reactions whose relation to the commodities was supposed to be under discussion. Today, however, there is an even greater need to progress beyond the isolated study in that, with populations becoming increasingly subject to the power of mass communications, the pre-formation of people's minds has increased to a degree that scarcely allows room for an awareness of it on the part of the people themselves. Even a positivist sociologist like Durkheim, who was at one with Social Research in his rejection of 'interpretative understanding', rightly linked the statistical laws, for which he too had a certain fondness, with the *constrainte sociale*,[4] and indeed saw in the latter the criterion of a universally valid law of society. Contemporary social research denies this link, but in so doing sacrifices any connection between its own generalizations and the concrete determinants of social structure.

But once such perspectives are dispensed with, their construction relegated to some future special investigation, the image of society created by science does in fact remain a mere duplicate, a reified apperception of the thing-like object, and distorts this object by the very act of duplication, transforming the mediated into the immediate. To correct this it is not sufficient, as Durkheim hoped, simply to make a descriptive distinction between the realms of the collective and the individual. A relationship has to

4. Durkheim (1950), p. 6.

be established between the two, and given a theoretical basis. The opposition of quantitative and qualitative analysis is not an absolute one: it finds no ultimate support in the subject-matter itself. It is well known that, in order to quantify, one has always to begin by ignoring qualitative differences between the various elements; and every individual social phenomenon bears within itself the general determinisms to which the quantitative generalizations apply. But the categories of the latter are themselves of course qualitative. A method that fails to do justice to this and which, for example, rejects qualitative analysis as incompatible with the nature of the collective, is doing violence to its subject. Society is a unity; even in areas as yet beyond the reach of its powerful forces, there is a functional connection between the 'undeveloped' segments and those that have advanced to a state of rationality and homogeneous socialization. A sociology which ignores that and contents itself with a methodological pluralism, which it then justifies with such threadbare and inadequate concepts as induction and deduction,[5] bolsters up what exists through its over-zealous attempts to describe it. It becomes an ideology in the strictest sense of the word, a necessary illusion.

Illusion, because the multiplicity of methods fails to capture the oneness of the object but instead conceals it behind the so-called factors into which, for the sake of tractability, it has been split up; necessary, because the object, society, fears nothing so much as being exposed for what it is, and thus automatically furthers or permits only those understandings of itself that fail to penetrate its protective shell. The pair of concepts 'induction' and 'deduction' is the scientistic substitute for dialectics. But just as social theory, if it is to have any binding force, must absorb all the material it can, so must the single fact that is being assimilated use the process that selects it as a means of pointing beyond itself to the social totality. Once the method has instead served it up as a 'brute fact', no subsequent efforts will succeed in injecting any light into its opacity. Through this static opposition and mutual complementing of formal sociology and the blind registration of fact, there is lost that relationship of the universal to the particular

5. Compare Erich Reigrotzki, *Soziale Verflechtungen in der Bundesrepublik*, Tübingen, 1956, p. 4.

by virtue of which society has its life and sociology its one object worthy of human attention. But even if one adds together afterwards these separated fragments, the real state of affairs is still stood on its head by the order in which the method proceeds. The eagerness to turn any qualitative results back into quantities is thus no coincidence. Science wishes with the aid of a single harmonious system to remove the tension between the universal and the particular from a world whose unity is founded in inconsistency.

It is because of this inconsistency that the subject of sociology – society and its phenomena – lacks the kind of homogeneity that the natural sciences could count on. One cannot in sociology advance from partially valid statements concerning social phenomena to ones of a broader – even if still limited – application, in the way that one could deduce from observations on the properties of a single piece of lead the properties of lead in general. The general validity of sociological laws is not in any sense that of a conceptual framework in which the individual fragments can be neatly slotted into place, but is always and essentially concerned with the relationship between the universal and the particular in its historical concretion. This bears testimony both negatively, to the inhomogeneous state of society, the 'anarchy' of all history up to the present, and positively, to the moment of spontaneity that cannot be captured by the law of averages.

To make a distinction between the human world and the relative regularity and constancy that characterize the objects of the mathematical sciences, at least on the macrocosmic scale, is not to glorify the former. Of central importance is the antagonistic nature of society, and simple generalizations do away with this. What demands elucidation is homogeneity, insofar as it subjects human behaviour to the law of averages, rather than its absence. The applicability of that law contradicts the *principium individuationis*, the assertion – not to be lightly cast aside – that men are more than just members of a species. Their modes of behaviour are mediated through their reason. The latter admittedly contains a moment of the universal, which is quite capable of surfacing again in the statistical generalization; but this moment is at the same time specified by the interests of individuals, which in bourgeois society tend to diverge and, notwithstanding their uniformity, to come in conflict with each other; not to mention the irrationality socially perpetuated in individuals. Only the unifying principle of an individualistic society reduces the diffuse interests of individuals to the unified formula of their 'opinion'. The currently widespread talk of the social atom admittedly does justice to the impotence of the individual *vis-à-vis* the totality, but, compared with the scientific concept of the atom, it possesses of necessity only a metaphorical force.

The similarity to each other of the smallest units of society – individuals – cannot be asserted, even in front of the TV screen, with quite the same seriousness and stringency as in the case of physical or chemical matter. Empirical social research, however, proceeds as though it took the idea of the social atom literally. That it more or less manages with such an approach constitutes a critical reflection on society itself. The construction of general laws, and the consequent demotion of the entities subsumed under them, clearly show that the universal and the particular are not reconciled, that it is precisely in the individualistic society that the individual is reduced to the status of an object blindly subjugated to generality. This has been previously recognized in references to the social 'character-mask'; present-day empiricism has forgotten about it. What social responses have in common is essentially the product of common social pressures. The only reason why empirical social research in its conception of the collective can treat individuation with such sovereign disdain, is that the latter has so far remained an ideology, insofar as human beings have yet to realize their humanity.

In a liberated society statistics would become in a positive sense what they are at the moment in a negative sense, an administrative science, but one concerned genuinely with the administration of things, namely consumer goods, and not of people. In spite of its unfortunate basis in the social structure, however, empirical social research should remain capable of self-criticism to the extent that the generalizations that it succeeds in formulating are derived, not solely and straightforwardly from the subject-matter, the standardized world, but also from the method, which by the generality or the limited 'cafeteria' choice of the questions it puts to individuals, from the very start forces the subject of the investigation – the opinions it seeks to ascertain – into an atomistic mould.

To be aware of the inhomogeneity of sociology as a scientific framework, of the categorical rather than gradual and easily bridgeable divergence of disciplines such as theory of society, analysis of objective social relations and institutions, and subjectively-directed social research in the narrower sense, does not mean that one allows things to remain at this sterile separation of disciplines. One need have no respect for the formal demand for unity coming from a science which itself bears the marks of an arbitrary division of labour, and whose claim to have a privileged and unhampered view of those much-cherished totalities – whose social existence is in any case rather dubious – is therefore hardly a plausible one.

But the critical interconnection of these diverging sociological methods is a healthy one, in spite of the extent to which the latter, in accordance with their 'administrative' structure, are themselves entwined with particular interest-groups. Innumerable substantive propositions advanced by this or that social theory – those of Max Scheler on the typical forms of consciousness provide a ready example[6] – can be tested and refuted by stringently controlled investigations. Conversely, social research depends upon the confrontation with theory and upon the cognizance of objective social structures, if it is not to become the willing tool of obsolescent or apologetical catchwords, like the references to the family that enjoy an occasional vogue. Isolated social research becomes false as soon as it conceives the wish to eradicate totality as a crypto-metaphysical superstition, simply because that totality systematically eludes its methodology. Science then takes its oath on the phenomenon pure and simple.

In tabooing the inquiry into the essence of things as an illusion, as a demand that the method is incapable of fulfilling, one is *a priori* shielding the essential relationships, those which really

6. Compare 'Ideologie und Handeln', p. 41 f.

determine the nature of society, from cognitive analysis. It is pointless to ask whether these essential relationships are 'real' or simply conceptual constructs. To consider the conceptual as part of social reality itself is not necessarily to lay oneself open to the charge of idealism. What is meant here is not so much the constitutive conceptuality of the cognitive subject, as the conceptuality prevailing in the object itself: even in his theory of the conceptual mediation of all existing things Hegel was attempting to focus on a real and decisive moment. The law that governs the unfolding destiny of mankind is that of exchange. This, however, is not an immediate given but conceptually mediated: the act of exchange implies the reduction of the goods to be exchanged to something which is equivalent to them, and thus not material, as has traditionally been supposed, but abstract. This mediating conceptuality, however, is not a general formulation of average expectations, nor a time-saving addition bestowed by an ordering science, but something which society as it is conforms to, and which provides the objectively valid model – independent of the consciousness both of the individuals subjected to that conceptuality and of the researchers themselves – of all essential societal events. In the face of solid reality and concrete data one might call this conceptual essence an illusion, since the exchange of equivalents, though straightforward, has at the same time something devious about it; and yet it is not an illusion, a sublimation of reality by ordering science, but is, rather, immanent in reality itself. Even the talk of the unreality of social laws is correct only in a critical sense, with reference to the fetishism of commodities. The exchange-value, a purely notional one compared with the use-value, prevails over and in the place of human needs; illusion governs reality. To that extent society is still myth and the enlightenment of myth is as pressing as ever.

At the same time, that illusion is the most efficacious reality, the spell that holds the world bewitched. Criticism of it has nothing to do with the positivistic criticism of science, according to which the objective exchange relationship, whose validity is continually being confirmed by reality, is dismissed as not really valid. When sociological empiricism has recourse to the proposition that laws do not in themselves possess any form of real existence, it is wrongly ascribing to the method an element of social unreality that it has, without knowing it, discovered in the thing itself. It is precisely the would-be anti-idealism of the scientific mentality that is here contributing to the perpetuation of ideology. This latter is supposed to be inaccessible to science, since it is not a fact; whereas the truth is that nothing has more power than the conceptual mediation that dangles the being-for-the-other in front of men as a being-for-itself, and thus hinders them in their awareness of the conditions in which they are living. As soon as sociology shuts itself off from the recognition of this, contents itself with registering and organizing what it terms facts, and confuses the rules distilled from this activity with the law that governs the facts and determines their incidence, it has already, albeit unsuspectingly, forfeited its own right to existence. The reason why in the social sciences one cannot progress as in the natural sciences from a segment to the whole, is that in the case of the former, the whole is constituted by a conceptuality completely different from the logical compass and characteristic unity of any of its individual elements. Equally, because of its mediated conceptual nature, this whole has nothing in common with 'totalities' and configurations which are necessarily always presented as immediately given; society is more like a system than an organism. Empirical social research, devoid of theory and budgeting with pure hypotheses, screens itself off from its true object – society as a system – since this object does not coincide with the sum of all the segments, does not subsume them, and cannot even be constituted by juxtaposing them all simultaneously to form an entity like the geographical map's 'country and its inhabitants'. No social atlas, either in a literal or in a figurative sense, represents society.

Inasmuch as the latter consists of more than the immediate existence of its members and the subjective and objective facts related to that existence, a line of research that devotes its whole effort to the investigation of such immediacy remains wide of the mark. In spite of the thing-like nature of the method, and indeed by virtue of that very thing-likeness – the idol of the straightforwardly ascertainable – it produces an illusion of life, of neighbourly face-to-face encounter, whose dissolution would constitute by no means the last task of social science, were it not already a long-accomplished fact. Today, however, such research is being elbowed aside. For this, the glorifying metaphysic of existence and the dogged description of what is the case are equally to blame. Apart from that, however, the praxis of empirical sociology over a wide front does not even correspond to its own theoretical admission of the necessity of hypotheses. While grudgingly conceding the need for these latter, it encounters each individual one with suspicion, on the grounds that it would produce a 'bias' prejudicial to the research's impartiality.[7] At the basis of this lies a 'theory of truth-as-residuum' – the idea that truth consists of what remains after the removal of the supposedly purely subjective additions, the substratum of the production costs, as it were. The knowledge, familiar to psychology since the time of Georg Simmel and Freud, that the validity of a person's experience of objects – insofar as the latter, like society, are essentially mediated through the subject – increases rather than decreases with the extent of the person's subjective share, has yet to be digested by the social sciences. Having sent intelligent common-sense packing and adopted in its stead the pose of the responsible researcher, they immediately turn for salvation to procedures as devoid of hypotheses as possible. The superstition that research has to begin with a *tabula rasa*, upon which data gathered without any preconceived plan are then assembled into some kind of pattern, is one that empirical social research should rid itself of once and for all. This, admittedly, would mean the resurrection of epistemological controversies that were fought out long ago, but which short-winded intellects, pleading the prior claims of present activity, are all too ready to forget. It behoves a sceptical science to adopt an attitude of scepticism towards its own ascetic ideals. The readily-quoted maxim to the effect that a researcher needs 10 per cent inspiration and 90 per cent perspiration betrays intellectual mediocrity and hints at censorship of thought. For a long while the self-denying work of the scholar consisted in his receiving a miserable remuneration in

7. Compare, for instance, René König, 'Beobachtung und Experiment in der Sozialforschung', in *Praktische Sozialforschung*, vol. 2, Cologne, 1956, p. 27.

exchange for which he renounced thoughts that he had not got in the first place. Today, now that the better-paid office-boss has replaced the scholar, the lack of intelligence is not only celebrated as the virtue of the unassuming, well-adjusted team-member, but is institutionalized in the structure of the research process, which recognizes individual spontaneity only as a coefficient of friction. There is however something intrinsically small-minded about the antithesis of high-flown inspiration and solid research-work. Thoughts do not arrive out of thin air, but – even when their actual appearance is unexpected – have been crystallizing in long-drawn-out underground processes. The suddenness of what research technicians patronizingly refer to as intuition marks the eruption of living experience through the hardened crust of *communis opinio*; it is the sustained opposition to the latter – not the privileged moments of inspiration – which permits the un-regimented mind that contact with the essence of things which the interposition of an over-inflated apparatus so often relentlessly sabotages. Conversely, the necessary routine-work of science always brings with it a ceaseless adjustment of and wrestling with the conceptual framework – the very opposite of that mechanical, doggedly unthinking procedure with which such work is customarily equated. One might define science thus: the process of becoming aware of the truth and untruth of the self-image that the observed object is attempting to realize. Cognition is not true cognition without the critical impulse arising from its inherent power to distinguish between true and false. Not until sociology brings the fossilized antitheses of its own structure into dynamic interplay can it realize its own potential.

The categorical differentiation of the disciplines is underlined by the fact that what ought to be the central concern of sociology – the linking of empirical investigations with central theoretical questions – has, in spite of isolated attempts, so far not been achieved. The most modest task for empirical social research – and also one which, from the standpoint of immanent critique, i.e. according to the method's own rules of 'objectivity', possesses the greatest plausibility – would be for it to confront all its statements on the subjective experience, conscious and unconscious, of human beings and human groups, with the objective factors determining their existence. What appears to social research to be purely incidental, mere 'background study', is in fact the necessary pre-condition for its achieving anything of real importance. Inevitably, it will emphasize first and foremost those determining factors that are connected with the subjective thoughts, feelings and behaviour of those whom it is investigating, even though these connections are themselves so extensive that such a confrontation ought not to content itself with the analysis of isolated institutions, but refer back again to the social structure – the categorical difficulty is not removed by the comparison of a given set of attitudes with a given set of objective conditions.

But even with this considerable reservation, the results of attitude measurement acquire a different function and value as soon as they can be juxtaposed with the real nature of whatever it is those attitudes are concerned with. The differences which thereby become apparent between social objectivity and the consciousness – however widespread it be – of that objectivity, mark a point at which empirical social research breaks through to the analysis of society – to the analysis of ideologies, their genesis and function. Such an analysis would seem to be the main object, though by no means the sole one, of empirical social research. Taken by itself, however, the latter has not the substantive force of social analysis: the market forces, within whose system it is confined in unreflecting isolation, are themselves a façade. Even if a survey were to produce overwhelming statistical evidence that the workers no longer considered themselves as workers and denied that there was any such thing as a proletariat, that would by no means suffice as proof of the non-existence of the proletariat. Rather, such subjective findings would have to be compared with objective ones, like the position of the respondents in the productive process, their social power or impotence. At the same time, the empirical facts concerning the individual subjects would retain their importance. Not only would the theory of ideologies have to ask how such forms of consciousness arose in the first place, but one would have to inquire whether their existence had not brought about an essential change in the objective reality of society.

The role played in the latter by the make-up and the self-image of human beings, however they be produced and reproduced, can be ignored only by a dogmatism amounting to self-delusion. They, too, are moments of the social totality – either as part of the affirmation of the *status quo*, or as a potential for change. Not only theory, but also its absence becomes a material force as soon as it takes a hold on the masses. Empirical social research provides a corrective, not only in preventing blind system-building from above, but also in the relationship between appearance and reality. If the theory of society has the job of critically relativizing the cognitive value of appearance, then empirical research has conversely to protect the idea of essential laws from being mythologized. Appearance is always the appearance of reality, never pure illusion. Its changes do not leave that reality untouched. If indeed nobody realizes any more that he is a worker, then that affects the composition of the concept 'worker', even when the objective criterion of separation from the means of production remains fulfilled.

Empirical social research cannot get round the fact that all the data it investigates, the subjective no less than the objective, are mediated by society. The given, the facts which, according to its methodology, it encounters as its ultimate, are themselves not ultimate but conditional. Hence, it must not confuse its cognitive basis – the given-ness of the facts that its method concerns itself with – with the ground of reality, with facts as things-in-themselves, their immediacy and fundamental nature. It can protect itself against this confusion insofar as it is able, by refining its methods, to break down the immediacy of the data. Hence the importance of motivational studies, although they remain confined to the sphere of subjective response. Admittedly, they can hardly ever base themselves on direct questions, and correlations only point to functional connections without clarifying the causal relationships involved. The development of indirect methods thus represents in principle the chance for empirical social research to progress beyond the simple registering and processing of a façade of facts. The cognitive problem hindering the development of its critical self-awareness remains the fact that the data thus obtained do not truly mirror the underlying social realities, but rather constitute the veil that the latter use, and indeed need, to conceal themselves. Consequently, one can apply to the findings of what are known – not without reason – as 'opinion surveys', the judgement on public opinion in general formulated by Hegel in his *Philosophy of Right*: it deserves equally to be respected and despised.[8] Respected, because even ideologies, the necessarily false consciousness, are an element of social reality, with which anyone who desires knowledge of the reality itself must be acquainted. But despised: that is, their claim to truth criticized. Empirical social research becomes an ideology itself as soon as it gives public opinion absolute status. It is induced to do this by an unreflectingly nominalist concept of truth, which, because no other definition is readily available, smuggles in the *volonté de tous* as the truth pure and simple. This tendency is especially marked in American empirical social research.

But it should not be dogmatically opposed by the simple assertion of a *volonté générale* as a truth-in-itself, for example in the form of postulated 'values'. Such a procedure would be vitiated by the same arbitrariness as the enthroning of the commonly accepted opinion as the one which is objectively valid: history since Robespierre has possibly seen more mischief brought about through the officially decreed establishment of the *volonté générale* than through the unthinking acceptance of the *volonté de tous*. The only way to escape this fateful pair of alternatives is that of immanent analysis: analysis, that is, of the internal consistency or inconsistency of the opinion itself, and of its relationship to its object, not the abstract opposition of the opinion to something postulated as objectively valid. It is not a question of dismissing the opinion with a Platonic disdain, but of deducing its untruth from the truth – the social structure that undergirds it – and finally from the untruth inherent in the latter. On the other hand, the cross-section of attitudes represents, not an approximation to the truth, but a cross-section of social illusion. Participating in this is that *ens realissimum* of unreflecting social research – the respondents, the subjects. Their own being, their existence as subjects, depends on the objectivity, the mechanisms that they

8. Hegel, Leipzig, 1921, pp. 257, 318.

obey and which constitute the conceptual framework in which they are to be situated. This latter, however, can only be determined by discovering in the facts themselves the tendency that points beyond them. That is the function of philosophy in empirical social research. If it fails to fulfil it or allows it to be suppressed, so that mere facts are reproduced, such a reproduction immediately falsifies the facts and creates out of them an ideology.

References

ADORNO, T. W. (1956), 'Soziologie und empirische Forschung', *Frankfurter Beiträge zür Sociologie*, Bd. 4, Exkurse, Frankfurt-am-Main, p. 112.

DURKHEIM, E. (1950), *Les Règles de la Méthode Sociologique*, Paris, p. 6 ff.

HEGEL, G. W. F. (1811), *Wissenschaft der Logik* (*The Science of Logic*). This edition published in Stuttgart, 1949.

HEGEL, G. W. F. (1821), *Grundlinien der Philosophie des Rechts* (*Philosophy of Right*). This edition edited by Lasson and published in Leipzig, 1921, section 318, p. 257.

HORKHEIMER, M. (1962), 'Ideologie und Handeln', in M. Horkheimer, T. W. Adorno, *Sociologica II*, Europäische Verlagsanstalt, Frankfurt, pp. 41 ff.

HORKHEIMER, M., ADORNO, T. W. (1947), *Dialektik der Aufklärung*, Amsterdam, p. 50.

KANT, I. (1781), *Kritik der reinen Vernunft* (*Critique of Pure Reason*). This edition published in 1955, Inselausgabe, pp. 553 et seq.

KÖNIG, R. (1956), 'Beobachtung und Experiment in der Sozialforschung', *Praktische Sozialforschung*, vol. 2, Cologne, p. 27.

REIGROTZKI, E. (1956), *Soziale Verflechtungen in der Bundesrepublik*, Tübingen, p. 4.

13 Theodor W. Adorno

Cultural Criticism and Society

Excerpt from Theodor W. Adorno, 'Cultural Criticism and Society', in *Prisms*, Neville Spearman, London, 1967, pp. 19–34. First published in 1951.

To anyone in the habit of thinking with his ears, the words 'cultural criticism' (*Kulturkritik*) must have an offensive ring, not merely because, like 'automobile', they are pieced together from Latin and Greek. The words recall a flagrant contradiction. The cultural critic is not happy with civilization, to which alone he owes his discontent. He speaks as if he represented either unadulterated nature or a higher historical stage. Yet he is necessarily of the same essence as that to which he fancies himself superior. The insufficiency of the subject – criticized by Hegel in his apology for the *status quo* – which in its contingency and narrowness passes judgement on the might of the existent, becomes intolerable when the subject itself is mediated down to its innermost make-up by the notion to which it opposes itself as independent and sovereign. But what makes the content of cultural criticism inappropriate is not so much lack of respect for that which is criticized as the dazzled and arrogant recognition which criticism surreptitiously confers on culture. The cultural critic can hardly avoid the imputation that he has the culture which culture lacks. His vanity aids that of culture: even in the accusing gesture, the critic clings to the notion of culture, isolated, unquestioned, dogmatic. He shifts the attack. Where there is despair and measureless misery, he sees only spiritual phenomena, the state of man's consciousness, the decline of norms. By insisting on this, criticism is tempted to forget the unutterable, instead of striving, however impotently, so that man may be spared.

The position of the cultural critic, by virtue of its difference from the prevailing disorder, enables him to go beyond it theoretically, although often enough he merely falls behind. But he incorporates this difference into the very culture industry which he seeks to leave behind and which itself needs the difference in order to fancy itself culture. Characteristic of culture's pretension to distinction, through which it exempts itself from evaluation against the material conditions of life, is that it is insatiable. The exaggerated claims of culture, which in turn inhere in the movement of the mind, remove it ever further from those conditions as the worth of sublimation becomes increasingly suspect when confronted both by a material fulfilment near enough to touch and by the threatening annihilation of uncounted human beings. The cultural critic makes such distinction his privilege and forfeits his legitimation by collaborating with culture as its salaried and honoured nuisance. This, however, affects the substance of criticism. Even the implacable rigour with which criticism speaks the truth of an untrue consciousness remains imprisoned within the orbit of that against which it struggles, fixated on its surface manifestations. To flaunt one's superiority is, at the same time, to feel in on the job. Were one to study the profession of critic in bourgeois society as it progressed towards the rank of cultural critic, one would doubtless stumble on an element of usurpation in its origins, an element of which a writer like Balzac was still aware. Professional critics were first of all 'reporters': they oriented people in the market of intellectual products. In so doing, they occasionally gained insights into the matter at hand, yet remained continually traffic agents, in agreement with the sphere as such if not with its individual products. Of this they bear the mark even after they have discarded the role of agent. That they should have been entrusted with the roles of expert and then of judge was economically inevitable although accidental with respect to their objective qualifications. Their agility, which gained them privileged positions in the general competition – privileged, since the fate of those judged depends largely on their vote – invests their judgements with the semblance of competence. While they adroitly slipped into gaps and won influence with the expansion of the press, they attained that very authority which their profession already presupposed. Their arrogance derives from the fact that, in the forms of competitive society in which all being is merely there *for* something else, the critic himself is also measured only in terms of his marketable success – that is, in terms of his *being for* something else. Knowledge and understanding were not primary, but at most by-products, and the more they are lacking, the more they are replaced by Oneupmanship and conformity. When the critics in their playground – art – no longer understand what they judge and enthusiastically permit themselves to be degraded to propagandists or censors, it is the old dishonesty of trade fulfilling itself in their fate. The prerogatives of information and position permit them to express their opinion as if it were objectivity. But it is solely the objectivity of the ruling mind. They help to weave the veil.

The notion of the free expression of opinion, indeed, that of intellectual freedom itself in bourgeois society, upon which cultural criticism is founded, has its own dialectic. For while the mind extricated itself from a theological-feudal tutelage, it has fallen increasingly under the anonymous sway of the *status quo*. This regimentation, the result of the progressive societalization of all human relations, did not simply confront the mind from without; it immigrated into its immanent consistency. It imposes itself as relentlessly on the autonomous mind as heteronomous orders were formerly imposed on the mind which was bound. Not only does the mind mould itself for the sake of its marketability, and thus reproduce the socially prevalent categories. Rather, it grows to resemble ever more closely the *status quo* even where it subjectively refrains from making a commodity of itself. The network of the whole is drawn ever tighter, modelled after the act of exchange. It leaves the individual consciousness less and less room for evasion, preforms it more and more thoroughly, cuts it off *a priori* as it were from the possibility of differencing itself as all difference degenerates to a nuance in the monotony of supply. At the same time, the semblance of freedom makes reflection upon one's own unfreedom incomparably more difficult than formerly when such reflection stood in contradiction to manifest unfreedom, thus strengthening dependence. Such moments, in conjunction with the social selection of the 'spiritual and intellectual leaders', result in the regression of spirit and intellect. In accordance with the predominant social tendency, the integrity of the mind becomes a fiction. Of its freedom it develops only the negative moment, the heritage of the planless-monadological condition, irresponsibility. Otherwise, however, it clings ever more closely as a mere ornament to the material base which it claims to transcend. The strictures of Karl Kraus against freedom of the press are certainly not to be taken literally. To invoke seriously the censors against hack-writers would be to drive out the devil with Beelzebub. Nevertheless, the brutalization and deceit which flourish under the aegis of freedom of the press are not accidental to the historical march of the mind. Rather, they represent the stigma of that slavery within which the liberation of the mind – a false emancipation – has taken place. This is nowhere more striking than where the mind tears at its bonds: in criticism. When the German fascists defamed the word and replaced it with the inane notion of 'art appreciation', they were led to do so only by the rugged interests of the authoritarian state which still feared the passion of a Marquis Posa in the impertinence of the journalist. But the self-satisfied cultural barbarism which clamoured for the abolition of criticism, the incursion of the wild horde into the preserve of the mind, unawares repaid kind in kind. The bestial fury of the Brownshirt against 'carping critics' arises not merely from his envy of a culture which excludes him and against which he blindly rebels; nor is it merely his resentment of the person who can speak out the negative moment which he himself must repress. Decisive is that the critic's sovereign gesture suggests to his readers an autonomy which he does not have, and arrogates for itself a position of leadership which is incompatible with his own principle of intellectual freedom. This is innervated by his enemies. Their sadism was idiosyncratically attracted by the weakness, cleverly disguised as strength, of those who, in their dictatorial bearing, would have willingly excelled the less clever tyrants who were to succeed them. Except that the fascists succumbed to the same naïveté as the critics, the faith in culture as such, which reduced it to pomp and approved spiritual giants. They regarded themselves as physicians of culture and removed the thorn of criticism from it. They thus not only degraded culture to the Official, but in addition, failed to recognize the extent to which culture and criticism, for better or for worse, are intertwined. Culture is only true when implicitly critical, and the mind which forgets this revenges itself in the critics it breeds. Criticism is an indispensable element of culture which is itself contradictory: in all its untruth still as true as culture is untrue. Criticism is not unjust when it dissects – this can be its greatest virtue – but rather when it parries by not parrying.

The complicity of cultural criticism with culture lies not in the mere mentality of the critic. Far more, it is dictated by his relation to that with which he deals. By making culture his object, he objectifies it once more. Its very meaning, however, is the suspension of objectification. Once culture itself has been debased to 'cultural goods', with its hideous philosophical rationalization, 'cultural values', it has already defamed its *raison d'être*. The distillation of such 'values' – the echo of commercial language is by no means accidental – places culture at the will of the market. Even the enthusiasm for foreign cultures includes the excitement over the rarity in which money may be invested. If cultural criticism, even at its best with Valéry, sides with conservatism, it is because of its unconscious adherence to a notion of culture which, during the era of late capitalism, aims at a form of property which is stable and independent of stock-market fluctuations. This idea of culture asserts its distance from the system in order, as it were, to offer universal security in the middle of a universal dynamic. The model of the cultural critic is no less the appraising collector than the art critic. In general, cultural criticism recalls the gesture of bargaining, of the expert questioning the authenticity of a painting or classifying it among the Master's lesser works. One devaluates in order to get more. The cultural critic evaluates and hence is inevitably involved in a sphere stained with 'cultural values', even when he rants against the mortgaging of culture. His contemplative stance towards culture necessarily entails scrutinizing, surveying, balancing, selecting: this piece suits him, that he rejects. Yet his very sovereignty, the claim to a more profound knowledge of the object, the separation of the idea from its object through the independence of the critical judgement threatens to succumb to the thing-like form of the object when cultural criticism appeals to a collection of ideas on display, as it were, and fetishizes isolated categories such as mind, life and the individual.

But the greatest fetish of cultural criticism is the notion of culture as such. For no authentic work of art and no true philosophy, according to their very meaning, has ever exhausted itself in itself alone, in its being-in-itself. They have always stood in relation to the actual life-process of society from which they distinguished themselves. Their very rejection of the guilt of a life which blindly and callously reproduces itself, their insistence on independence and autonomy, on separation from the prevailing realm of purposes, implies, at least as an unconscious element, the promise of a condition in which freedom were realized. This remains an equivocal promise of culture as long as its existence depends on a bewitched reality and, ultimately, on control over the work of others. That European culture in all its breadth – that which reached the consumer and which today is prescribed for whole populations by managers and psycho-technicians – degenerated to mere ideology resulted from a change in its function with regard to material *praxis*: its renunciation of interference. Far from being culture's 'sin', the change was forced upon culture by history. For it is only in the process of withdrawing into itself, only indirectly that is, that bourgeois culture conceives of a purity from the corrupting traces of a totalitarian disorder which embraces all areas of existence. Only insofar as it withdraws from a *praxis* which has degenerated into its opposite, from the ever-changing production of what is always the same, from the service of the customer who himself serves the manipulator – only insofar as it withdraws from Man can culture be faithful to man. But such concentration on substance which is absolutely one's own, the greatest example of which is to be found in the poetry and theoretical writings of Paul Valéry, contributes at the same time to the impoverishment of that substance. Once the mind is no longer directed at reality, its meaning is changed despite the strictest preservation of meaning. Through its resignation before the facts of life and, even more, through its isolation as one 'field' among others, the mind aids the existing order and takes its place within it. The emasculation of culture has angered philosophers since the time of Rousseau and the 'ink-splattering age' of Schiller's *Robbers*, to Nietzsche and, finally, to the preachers of commitment for its own sake. This is the result of culture's becoming self-consciously cultural, which in turn places culture in vigorous and consistent opposition to the growing barbarism of economic hegemony. What appears to be the decline of culture is its coming to pure self-consciousness. Only when neutralized and reified, does Culture allow itself to be idolized. Fetishism gravitates towards mythology. In general, cultural critics become intoxicated with idols drawn from antiquity to the dubious, long-evaporated warmth of the liberalist era, which recalled the origins of culture in its decline. Cultural criticism rejects the progressive integration of all aspects of consciousness within the apparatus of material production. But because it fails to see through the apparatus, it turns towards the past, lured by the promise of immediacy. This is necessitated by its own momentum and not merely by the influence of an order which sees itself obliged to drown out its progress in dehumanization with cries against dehumanization and progress. The isolation of the mind from material production heightens its esteem but also makes it a scapegoat in the general consciousness for that which is perpetrated in practice. Enlightenment as such – not as an instrument of actual domination – is held responsible. Hence, the irrationalism of cultural criticism. Once it has wrenched the mind out of its dialectic with the material conditions of life, it seizes it unequivocally and straightforwardly as the principle of fatality, thus undercutting the mind's own resistance. The cultural critic is barred from the insight that the reification of life results not from too much enlightenment but from too little, and that the mutilation of man which is the result of the present particularistic rationality is the stigma of the total irrationality. The abolition of this irrationality, which would coincide with the abolition of the divorce between mental and physical work, appears as chaos to the blindness of cultural criticism: whoever glorifies order and form as such, must see in the petrified divorce an archetype of the Eternal. That the fatal fragmentation of society might some day end is, for the cultural critic, a fatal destiny. He would rather that everything end than for mankind to put an end to reification. This fear harmonizes with the interests of those interested in the perpetuation of material denial. Whenever cultural criticism complains of 'materialism', it furthers the belief that the sin lies in man's desire for consumer goods, and not in the organization of the whole which withholds these goods from man: for the cultural critic, the sin is satiety, not hunger. Were mankind to possess the wealth of goods, it would shake off the chains of that civilized barbarism which cultural critics ascribe to the advanced state of the human spirit rather than to the retarded state of society. The 'eternal values' of which cultural criticism is so fond reflect the perennial catastrophe. The cultural critic thrives on the mythical obduracy of culture.

Because the existence of cultural criticism, no matter what its content, depends on the economic system, it is involved in the fate of the system. The more completely the life-process, including leisure, is dominated by modern social orders – those in the East, above all – the more all spiritual phenomena bear the mark of the order. Either, they may contribute directly to the perpetuation of the system as entertainment or edification, and are enjoyed as exponents of the system precisely because of their socially preformed character. Familiar, stamped and Approved by Good Housekeeping as it were, they insinuate themselves into a regressive consciousness, present themselves as 'natural', and permit identification with powers whose preponderance leaves no alternative but that of false love. Or, by being different, they become rarities and once again marketable. Throughout the liberalist era, culture fell within the sphere of circulation. Hence, the gradual withering away of this sphere strikes culture to the quick. With the elimination of trade and its irrational loopholes by the calculated distributive apparatus of industry, the commercialization of culture culminates in absurdity. Completely subdued, administered, thoroughly 'cultivated' in a sense, it dies out. Spengler's denunciation: that mind and money go together, proves correct. But because of his sympathy with direct rule, he advocated a structure of existence divested of all economic as well as spiritual mediations. He maliciously threw the mind together with an economic type which was in fact obsolete. What Spengler failed to understand was that no matter to what extent the mind is a product of that type, it implies at the same time the objective possibility of overcoming it. Just as culture sprang up in the market-place, in the traffic of trade, in communication and negotiation, as something distinct from the immediate struggle for individual self-preservation, just as it was closely tied to trade in the era of mature capitalism, just as its representatives were counted among the class of 'third persons' who supported themselves in life as middlemen, so culture, considered 'socially necessary' according to classical rules, in the sense of reproducing itself economically, is in the end reduced to that as which it began, to mere communication. Its alienation from human affairs terminates in its absolute docility before a humanity which has been enchanted and transformed into clientele by the suppliers. In the name of the consumer, the manipulators suppress everything in culture which enables it to go beyond the total immanence in the existing society and allow only that to remain which serves society's unequivocal purpose. Hence, 'consumer culture' can boast of being not a luxury but rather the simple extension of production. Political slogans, designed for mass manipulation, unanimously stigmatize, as 'luxury', 'snobbism', and 'highbrow', everything cultural which displeases the commissars. Only when the established order has become the measure of all things does its mere reproduction in the realm of consciousness become truth. Cultural criticism points to this and rails against 'superficiality' and 'loss of substance'. But by limiting its attention to the entanglement of culture in commerce, such criticism itself becomes superficial. It follows the pattern of reactionary social critics who pit 'productive' against 'predatory' capital. In fact, all culture shares the guilt of society. It ekes out its existence only by virtue of injustice already perpetrated in the sphere of production, much as does commerce (cf. *Dialektik der Aufklärung*). Consequently, cultural criticism shifts the guilt: such criticism is ideology as long as it remains mere criticism of ideology. Totalitarian régimes of both kinds, seeking to protect the *status quo* from even the last traces of insubordination which they ascribe to culture even at its most servile, can conclusively convict culture and its introspection of servility. They suppress the mind, in itself already grown intolerable, and so feel themselves to be purifiers and revolutionaries. The ideological function of cultural criticism bridles its very truth which lies in its opposition to ideology. The struggle against deceit works to the advantage of naked terror. 'When I hear the word "culture", I reach for my gun,' said the spokesman of Hitler's Imperial Chamber of Culture.

Cultural criticism is, however, only able to reproach culture so penetratingly for prostituting itself, for violating in its decline the pure autonomy of the mind, because culture originates in the radical separation of mental and physical work. It is from this separation, the original sin as it were, that culture draws its strength. When culture simply denies the separation and feigns harmonious union, it falls back behind its own notion. Only the mind which, in the delusion of being absolute, removes itself entirely from the merely existent, truly defines the existent in its negativity. As long as even the least part of the mind remains engaged in the reproduction of life, it is its sworn bondsman. The anti-philistinism of Athens was both the most arrogant contempt of the man who need not soil his hands for the man from whose work he lives, and the preservation of an image of existence beyond the constraint which underlies all work. In projecting its own uneasy conscience on to its victims as their 'baseness', such an attitude also accuses that which they endure: the subjugation of men to the prevailing form in which their lives are reproduced. All 'pure culture' has always been a source of discomfort to the spokesmen of power. Plato and Aristotle knew why they would not permit the notion to arise. Instead, in questions concerning the evaluation of art, they advocated a pragmatism which contrasts curiously with the *pathos* of the two great metaphysicians. Modern bourgeois cultural criticism has, of course, been too prudent to follow them openly in this respect. But such criticism secretly finds a source of comfort in the divorce between 'high' and 'popular' culture, art and entertainment, knowledge and non-committal *Weltanschauung*. Its anti-philistinism exceeds that of the Athenian upper class to the extent that the proletariat is more dangerous than the slaves. The modern notion of a pure, autonomous culture indicates that the antagonism has become irreconcilable. This is the result both of an uncompromising opposition to being-for-something else, and of an ideology which in its hubris enthrones itself as being-in-itself.

Cultural criticism shares the blindness of its object. It is incapable of allowing the recognition of its frailty to arise, a frailty set in the division of mental and physical work. No society which contradicts its very notion – that of mankind – can have full consciousness of itself. A display of subjective ideology is not required to obstruct this consciousness, although in times of historical upheaval it tends to contribute to the objective blindness. Rather, the fact that every form of repression, depending on the level of technology, has been necessary for the survival of society, and that society as it is, despite all absurdity, does indeed reproduce its life under the existing conditions, objectively produces the semblance of society's legitimation. As the epitome of the self-consciousness of an antagonistic society, culture can no more divest itself of this semblance than can cultural criticism, which measures culture against culture's own ideal. The semblance has become total in a phase in which irrationality and objective falsity hide behind rationality and objective necessity. Nevertheless, by virtue of their real force, the antagonisms reassert themselves in the realm of consciousness. Just because culture affirms the validity of the principle of harmony within an antagonistic society, albeit in order to glorify that society, it cannot avoid confronting society with its own notion of harmony and thereby stumbling on discord. The ideology which affirms life is forced into opposition to life by the immanent drive of the ideal. The mind which sees that reality does not resemble it in every respect but is instead subject to an unconscious and fatal dynamic, is impelled even against its will beyond apologetics. The fact that theory becomes real force when it moves men is founded in the objectivity of the mind itself which, through the fulfilment of its ideological function, must lose faith in ideology. Prompted by the incompatibility of ideology and existence, the mind, in displaying its blindness, also displays its effort to free itself of ideology. Disenchanted, the mind perceives naked existence in its nakedness and delivers it up to criticism. The mind either damns the material base, in accordance with the ever-questionable criterion of its 'pure principle', or it becomes aware of its own questionable position, by virtue of its incompatibility with the base. As a result of the social dynamic, culture becomes cultural criticism, which preserves the notion of culture while demolishing its present manifestations as mere commodities and means of brutalization. Such critical consciousness remains subservient to culture insofar as its concern with culture distracts from the true horrors. From this arises the ambivalent attitude of social theory towards cultural criticism. The procedure of cultural criticism is itself the object of permanent criticism, both in its general presuppositions – its immanence in the existing society – and in its concrete udgements. For the subservience of cultural criticism is revealed in its specific content, and only in this may it be grasped conclusively. At the same time, a dialectical theory which does not wish to succumb to 'Economism', the sentiment which holds that the transformation of the world is exhausted in the increase of production, must absorb cultural criticism, the truth of which consists in bringing untruth to consciousness of itself. A dialectical theory which is uninterested in culture as a mere epiphenomenon, aids pseudo-culture to run rampant and collaborates in the reproduction of the evil. Cultural traditionalism and the terror of the new Russian despots are in basic agreement. Both affirm culture as a whole, sight-unseen, while at the same time proscribing all forms of consciousness which are not made-to-order. They are thus no less ideological than is criticism when it calls a disembodied culture before its tribunal, or holds the alleged negativity of culture responsible for real catastrophes. To accept culture as a whole is to deprive it of the ferment which is its very truth – negation. The joyous appropriation of culture harmonizes with a climate of military music and paintings of battle-scenes. What distinguishes dialectical from cultural criticism is that it heightens cultural criticism until the notion of culture is itself negated, fulfilled and surmounted in one.

Immanent criticism of culture, it may be argued, overlooks what is decisive: the role of ideology in social conflicts. To suppose, if only methodologically, anything like an independent logic of culture is to collaborate in the hypostasis of culture, the ideological *proton pseudos*. The substance of culture, according to this argument, resides not in culture alone but in its relation to something external, to the material life-process. Culture, as Marx observed of juridical and political systems, cannot be fully 'understood either in terms of itself . . . or in terms of the so-called universal development of the mind'. To ignore this, the argument concludes, is to make ideology the basic matter and thus to establish it firmly. And in fact, having taken a dialectical turn, cultural criticism must not hypostasize the criteria of culture. Criticism retains its mobility in regard to culture by recognizing the latter's position within the whole. Without such freedom, without consciousness transcending the immanence of culture, immanent criticism itself would be inconceivable: the spontaneous movement of the object can be followed only by someone who is not entirely engulfed by it. But the traditional demand of the ideology-critique is itself subject to a historical dynamic. The critique was conceived against idealism, the philosophical form which reflects the fetishization of culture. Today, however, the definition of consciousness in terms of being has become a means of dispensing with all consciousness which does not conform to existence. The objectivity of truth, without which the dialectic is inconceivable, is tacitly replaced by vulgar positivism and pragmatism – ultimately, that is, by bourgeois subjectivism. During the bourgeois era, the prevailing theory was the ideology and the opposing *praxis* was in direct contradiction. Today, theory hardly exists any longer and the ideology drones, as it were, from the gears of an irresistible *praxis*. No notion dares to be conceived any more which does not cheerfully include, in all camps, explicit instructions as to who its beneficiaries are – exactly what the polemics once sought to expose. But the unideological thought is that which does not permit itself to be reduced to 'operational terms' and instead strives solely to help the things themselves to that articulation from which they are otherwise cut off by the prevailing language. Since the moment arrived when every advanced economic and political council agreed that what was important was to change the world and that to interpret it was *allotria*, it has become difficult simply to invoke the *Theses* against Feuerbach. Dialectics also includes the relation between action and contemplation. In an epoch in which bourgeois social science has, in Scheler's words, 'plundered' the Marxian notion of ideology and diluted it to universal relativism, the danger involved in overlooking the function of ideologies has become less than that of judging intellectual phenomena in a subsumptive, uninformed and administrative manner and assimilating them into the prevailing constellations of power which the intellect ought to expose. As with many other elements of dialectical materialism, the notion of ideology has changed from an instrument of knowledge into its strait-jacket. In the name of the dependence of superstructure on base, all use of ideology is controlled instead of criticized. No one is concerned with the objective substance of an ideology as long as it is expedient.

Yet the very function of ideologies becomes increasingly abstract. The suspicion held by earlier cultural critics is confirmed: in a world which denies the mass of human beings the authentic experience of intellectual phenomena by making genuine education a privilege and by shackling consciousness, the specific ideological content of these phenomena is less important than the fact that there should be anything at all to fill the vacuum of the expropriated consciousness and to distract from the open secret. Within the context of its social effect, the particular ideological doctrine which a film imparts to its audience is presumably far less important than the interest of the homeward bound movie-goer in the names and marital affairs of the stars. Vulgar notions such as 'amusement' and 'diversion' are more appropriate than pretentious explanations which designate one writer as a representative of the lower-middle class, another of the upper-middle. Culture has become ideological not only as the quintessence of subjectively devised manifestations of the objective mind, but even more as the sphere of private life. The illusory importance and autonomy of private life conceals the fact that private life drags on only as an appendage of the social process. Life transforms itself into the ideology of reification – a death mask. Hence, the task of criticism must be not so much to search for the particular interest-groups to which cultural phenomena are to be assigned, but rather to decipher the general social tendencies which are expressed in these phenomena and through which the most powerful interests realize themselves. Cultural criticism must become social physiognomy. The more the whole divests itself of all spontaneous elements, is socially mediated and filtered, is 'consciousness', the more it becomes 'culture'. In addition to being the means of subsistence, the material process of production finally unveils itself as that which it always was, from its origins in the exchange-relationship as the false consciousness which the two contracting parties have of each other: ideology. Inversely, however, consciousness becomes at the same time increasingly a mere transitional moment in the functioning of the whole. Today, ideology means society as appearance. Although mediated by the totality behind which stands the rule of partiality, ideology is not simply reducible to a partial interest. It is, as it were, equally near the centre in all its pieces.

The alternatives – either calling culture as a whole into question from outside under the general notion of ideology, or confronting it with the norms which it itself has crystallized – cannot be accepted by critical theory. To insist on the choice between immanence and transcendence is to revert to the traditional logic criticized in Hegel's polemic against Kant. As Hegel argued, every method which sets limits and restricts itself to the limits of its object thereby goes beyond them. The position transcending culture is in a certain sense presupposed by dialectics as the consciousness which does succumb in advance to the fetishization of the intellectual sphere. Dialectics means intransigence towards all reification. The transcendent method, which aims at totality, seems more radical than the immanent method, which presupposes the questionable whole. The transcendent critic assumes an, as it were, Archimedean position above culture and the blindness of society, from which consciousness can bring the totality, no matter how massive, into flux. The attack on the whole draws strength from the fact that the semblance of unity and wholeness in the world grows with the advance of reification; that is, with division. But the summary dismissal of ideology which in the Soviet sphere has already become a pretext for cynical terror, taking the form of a ban on 'objectivism', pays that wholeness too high an honour. Such an attitude buys up culture *en bloc* from society, regardless of the use to which it is put. If ideology is defined as socially necessary appearance, then the ideology today is society itself insofar as its integral power and inevitability, its overwhelming existence-in-itself, surrogates the meaning which that existence has exterminated. The choice of a standpoint outside the sway of existing society is as fictitious as only the construction of abstract utopias can be. Hence, the transcendent criticism of culture, much like bourgeois cultural criticism, sees itself obliged to fall back upon the idea of 'naturalness', which itself forms a central element of bourgeois ideology. The transcendent attack on culture regularly speaks the language of false escape, that of the 'nature boy'. It despises the mind and its works, contending that they are, after all, only man-made and serve only to cover up 'natural' life. Because of this alleged worthlessness, the phenomena allow themselves to be manipulated and degraded for purposes of domination.

This explains the inadequacy of most socialist contributions to cultural criticism: they lack the experience of that with which they deal. In wishing to wipe away the whole as if with a sponge, they develop an affinity to barbarism. Their sympathies are inevitably with the more primitive, more undifferentiated, no matter how much it may contradict the level of intellectual productive forces. The blanket rejection of culture becomes a pretext for promoting what is crudest, 'healthiest', even repressive; above all, the perennial conflict between individual and society, both drawn in like manner, which is obstinately resolved in favour of society according to the criteria of the administrators who have appropriated it. From there it is only a step to the official reinstatement of culture. Against this struggles the immanent procedure as the more essentially dialectical. It takes seriously the principle that it is not ideology in itself which is untrue but rather its pretension to correspond to reality. Immanent criticism of intellectual and artistic phenomena seeks to grasp, through the analysis of their form and meaning, the contradiction between their objective idea and that pretension. It names what the consistency or inconsistency of the work itself expresses of the structure of the existent. Such criticism does not stop at a general recognition of the servitude of the objective mind, but seeks rather to transform this knowledge into a heightened perception of the thing itself. Insight into the negativity of culture is binding only when it reveals the truth or untruth of a perception, the consequence or lameness of a thought, the coherence or incoherence of a structure, the substantiality or emptiness of a figure of speech. Where it finds inadequacies it does not ascribe them hastily to the individual and his psychology, which are merely the façade of the failure, but instead seeks to derive them from the irreconcilability of the object's moments. It pursues the logic of its aporias, the insolubility of the task itself. In such antinomies criticism perceives those of society. A successful work, according to immanent criticism, is not one which resolves objective contradictions in a spurious harmony, but one which expresses the idea of harmony negatively by embodying the contradictions, pure and uncompromised, in its innermost structure. Confronted with this kind of work, the verdict 'mere ideology' loses its meaning. At the same time, however, immanent criticism holds in evidence the fact that the mind has always been under a spell. On its own it is unable to resolve the contradictions under which it labours. Even the most radical reflection of the mind on its own failure is limited by the fact that it remains only reflection, without altering the existence to which its failure bears witness. Hence immanent criticism cannot take comfort in its own idea. It can neither be vain enough to believe that it can liberate the mind directly by immersing itself in it, nor naïve enough to believe that unflinching immersion in the object will inevitably lead to truth by virtue of the logic of things if only the subjective knowledge of the false whole is kept from intruding from the outside, as it were, in the determination of the object. The less the dialectical method can today presuppose the Hegelian identity of subject and object, the more it is obliged to be mindful of the duality of the moments. It must relate the knowledge of society as a totality and of the mind's involvement in it to the claim inherent in the specific content of the object that it be apprehended as such. Dialectics cannot, therefore, permit any insistence on logical neatness to encroach on its right to go from one *genus* to another, to shed light on an object in itself hermetic by casting a glance at society, to present society with the bill which the object does not redeem. Finally, the very opposition between knowledge which penetrates from without and that which bores from within becomes suspect to the dialectical method, which sees in it a symptom of precisely that reification which the dialectic is obliged to accuse. The abstract categorizing and, as it were, administrative thinking of the former corresponds in the latter to the fetishism of an object blind to its genesis, which has become the prerogative of the expert. But if stubbornly immanent contemplation threatens to revert to idealism, to the illusion of the self-sufficient mind in command of both itself and of reality, transcendent contemplation threatens to forget the effort of conceptualization required and content itself instead with the prescribed label, the petrified invective, most often 'petty bourgeois', the ukase dispatched from above. Topological thinking, which knows the place of every phenomenon and the essence of none, is secretly related to the paranoic system of delusions which is cut off from experience of the object. With the aid of mechanically functioning categories, the world is divided into black and white and thus made ready for the very domination against which concepts were once conceived. No theory, not even that which is true, is safe from perversion into delusion once it has renounced a spontaneous relation to the object. Dialectics must guard against this no less than against enthralment in the cultural object. It can subscribe neither to the cult of the mind nor to hatred of it. The dialectical critic of culture must both participate in culture and not participate. Only then does he do justice to his object and to himself.

The traditional transcendent critique of ideology is obsolete. In principle, the method succumbs to the very reification which is its critical theme. By transferring the notion of causality directly from the realm of physical nature to society, it falls back behind its own object. Nevertheless, the transcendent method can still appeal to the fact that it employs reified notions only insofar as society itself is reified. Through the crudity and severity of the notion of causality, it claims to hold up a mirror to society's own crudity and severity, to its debasement of the mind. But the sinister, integrated society of today no longer tolerates even those relatively independent, distinct moments to which the theory of the causal dependence of superstructure on base once referred. In the open-air prison which the world is becoming, it is no longer so important to know what depends on what, such is the extent to which everything is one. All phenomena rigidify, become insignias of the absolute rule of that which is. There are no more ideologies in the authentic sense of false consciousness, only advertisements for the world through its duplication and the provocative lie which does not seek belief but commands silence. Hence, the question of the causal dependence of culture, a question which seems to embody the voice of that on which culture is thought only to depend, takes on a backwoods ring. Of course, even the immanent method is eventually overtaken by this. It is dragged into the abyss by its object. The materialistic transparency of culture has not made it more honest, only more vulgar. By relinquishing its own particularity, culture has also relinquished the salt of truth, which once consisted in its opposition to other particularities. To call it to account before a responsibility which it denies is only to confirm cultural pomposity. Neutralized and ready-made, traditional culture has become worthless today. Through an irrevocable process its heritage, hypocritically reclaimed by the Russians, has become expendable to the highest degree, superfluous, trash. And the hucksters of mass culture can point to it with a grin, for they treat it as such. The more total society becomes, the greater the reification of the mind and the more paradoxical its effort to escape reification on its own. Even the most extreme consciousness of doom threatens to degenerate into idle chatter. Cultural criticism finds itself faced with the final stage of the dialectic of culture and barbarism. To write poetry after Auschwitz is barbaric. And this corrodes even the knowledge of why it has become impossible to write poetry today. Absolute reification, which presupposed intellectual progress as one of its elements, is now preparing to absorb the mind entirely. Critical intelligence cannot be equal to this challenge as long as it confines itself to self-satisfied contemplation.

14 Walter Benjamin

The Storyteller and Artisan Cultures

Excerpt from Walter Benjamin, *Illuminations*, tr. Harry Zohn, ed. Hannah Arendt, Cape, 1970, pp. 83–109. First published in 1936.

Familiar though his name may be to us, the storyteller in his living immediacy is by no means a present force. He has already become something remote from us and something that is getting even more distant. To present something like Nikolai Leskov as a storyteller does not mean bringing him closer to us but, rather, increasing our distance from him. Viewed from a certain distance, the great, simple outlines which define the storyteller stand out in him, or rather, they become visible in him, just as in a rock a human head or an animal's body may appear to an observer at the proper distance and angle of vision. This distance and this angle of vision are prescribed for us by an experience which we may have almost every day. It teaches us that the art of storytelling is coming to an end. Less and less frequently do we encounter people with the ability to tell a tale properly. More and more often there is embarrassment all around when the wish to hear a story is expressed. It is as if something that seemed inalienable to us, the securest among our possessions, were taken from us: the ability to exchange experiences.

One reason for this phenomenon is obvious: experience has fallen in value. And it looks as if it is continuing to fall into bottomlessness. Every glance at a newspaper demonstrates that it has reached a new low, that our picture, not only of the external world but of the moral world as well, overnight has undergone changes which were never thought possible. With the [First] World War a process began to become apparent which has not halted since then. Was it not noticeable at the end of the war that men returned from the battlefield grown silent – not richer, but poorer in communicable experience? What ten years later was poured out in the flood of war books was anything but experience that goes from mouth to mouth. And there was nothing remarkable about that. For never has experience been contradicted more thoroughly than strategic experience by tactical warfare, economic experience by inflation, bodily experience by mechanical warfare, moral experience by those in power. A generation that had gone to school on a horse-drawn streetcar now stood under the open sky in a countryside in which nothing remained unchanged but the clouds; and beneath these clouds, in a field of force of destructive torrents and explosions, was the tiny, fragile human body.

Experience which is passed on from mouth to mouth is the source from which all storytellers have drawn. And among those who have written down the tales, it is the great ones whose written version differs least from the speech of the many nameless storytellers. Incidentally, among the last named there are two groups which, to be sure, overlap in many ways. And the figure of the storyteller gets its full corporeality only for the one who can picture them both. 'When someone goes on a trip, he has something to tell about', goes the German saying, and people imagine the storyteller as someone who has come from afar. But they enjoy no less listening to the man who has stayed at home, making an honest living, and who knows the local tales and traditions. If one wants to picture these two groups through their archaic representatives, one is embodied in the resident tiller of the soil, and the other in the trading seaman. Indeed, each sphere of life has, as it were, produced its own tribe of storytellers. Each of these tribes preserves some of its characteristics centuries later. Thus, among nineteenth-century German storytellers, writers like Hebel and Gotthelf stem from the first tribe, writers like Sealsfield and Gerstäcker from the second. With these tribes, however, as stated above, it is only a matter of basic types. The actual extension of the realm of storytelling in its full historical breadth is inconceivable without the most intimate interpenetration of these two archaic types. Such an interpenetration was achieved particularly by the Middle Ages in their trade structure. The resident master craftsman and the travelling journeyman worked together in the same rooms; and every master had been a travelling journeyman before he settled down in his home town or somewhere else. If peasants and seamen were past masters of storytelling, the artisan class was its university. In it was combined the lore of faraway places, such as a much-travelled man brings home, with the lore of the past, as it best reveals itself to natives of a place.

Leskov was at home in distant places as well as distant times. He was a member of the Greek Orthodox Church, a man with genuine religious interests. But he was a no less sincere opponent of ecclesiastic bureaucracy. Since he was not able to get along any better with secular officialdom, the official positions he held were not of long duration. Of all his posts, the one he held for a long time as Russian representative of a big English firm was presumably the most useful one for his writing. For this firm he travelled through Russia, and these trips advanced his worldly wisdom as much as they did his knowledge of conditions in Russia. In this way he had an opportunity of becoming acquainted with the organization of the sects in the country. This left its mark on his works of fiction. In the Russian legends Leskov saw allies in his fight against Orthodox bureaucracy. There are a number of his legendary tales whose focus is a righteous man, seldom an ascetic, usually a simple, active man who becomes a saint apparently in the most natural way in the world. Mystical exaltation is not Leskov's forte. Even though he occasionally liked to indulge in the miraculous, even in piousness he prefers to stick with a sturdy nature. He sees the prototype in the man who finds his way about the world without getting too deeply involved with it.

He displayed a corresponding attitude in worldly matters. It is in keeping with this that he began to write late, at the age of twenty-nine. That was after his commercial travels. His first printed work was entitled *Why Are Books Expensive in Kiev?* A number of other writings about the working class, alcoholism, police doctors, and unemployed salesmen are precursors of his works of fiction.

An orientation toward practical interests is characteristic of many born storytellers. More pronouncedly than in Leskov this trait can be recognized, for example, in Gotthelf, who gave his peasants agricultural advice; it is found in Nodier, who concerned himself with the perils of gas light; and Hebel, who slipped bits of scientific instruction for his readers into his *Schatzkästlein*, is in this line as well. All this points to the nature of every real story. It contains, openly or covertly, something useful. The usefulness may, in one case, consist in a moral; in another, in some practical advice; in a third, in a proverb or maxim. In every case the storyteller is a man who has counsel for his readers. But if today 'having counsel' is beginning to have an old-fashioned ring, this is because the communicability of experience is decreasing. In consequence we have no counsel either for ourselves or for others. After all, counsel is less an answer to a question than a proposal concerning the continuation of a story which is just unfolding. To seek this counsel one would first have to be able to tell the story. (Quite apart from the fact that a man is receptive to counsel only to the extent that he allows his situation to speak.) Counsel woven into the fabric of real life is wisdom. The art of storytelling is reaching its end because the epic side of truth, wisdom, is dying out. This, however, is a process that has been going on for a long time. And nothing would be more fatuous than to want to see in it merely a 'symptom of decay', let alone a 'modern' symptom. It is, rather, only a concomitant symptom of the secular productive forces of history, a concomitant that has quite gradually removed narrative from the realm of living speech and at the same time is making it possible to see a new beauty in what is vanishing.

The earliest symptom of a process whose end is the decline of storytelling is the rise of the novel at the beginning of modern times. What distinguishes the novel from the story (and from the epic in the narrower sense) is its essential dependence on the book. The dissemination of the novel became possible only with the invention of printing. What can be handed on orally, the wealth of the epic, is of a different kind from what constitutes the stock in trade of the novel. What differentiates the novel from all other forms of prose literature – the fairy tale, the legend, even the novella – is that it neither comes from oral tradition nor goes into it. This distinguishes it from storytelling in particular. The storyteller takes what he tells from experience – his own or that reported by others. And he in turn makes it the experience of those who are listening to his tale. The novelist has isolated himself. The birthplace of the novel is the solitary individual, who is no longer able to express himself by giving examples of his most important concerns, is himself uncounselled, and cannot counsel others. To write a novel means to carry the incommensurable to extremes in the representation of human life. In the midst of life's fullness, and through the representation of this fullness, the novel gives evidence of the profound perplexity of the living. Even the first great book of the genre, *Don Quixote*, teaches how the spiritual greatness, the boldness, the helpfulness of one of the noblest of men, Don Quixote, are completely devoid of counsel and do not contain the slightest scintilla of wisdom. If now and then, in the course of the centuries, efforts have been made – most effectively, perhaps, in *Wilhelm Meisters Wanderjahre* – to implant instruction in the novel, these attempts have always amounted to a modification of the novel form. The *Bildungsroman*, on the other hand, does not deviate in any way from the basic structure of the novel. By integrating the social process with the development of a person, it bestows the most frangible justification on the order determining it. The legitimacy it provides stands in direct opposition to reality. Particularly in the *Bildungsroman*, it is this inadequacy that is actualized.

One must imagine the transformation of epic forms occurring in rhythms comparable to those of the change that has come over the earth's surface in the course of thousands of centuries. Hardly any other forms of human communication have taken shape more slowly, been lost more slowly. It took the novel, whose beginnings go back to antiquity, hundreds of years before it encountered in the evolving middle class those elements which were favourable to its flowering. With the appearance of these elements, storytelling began quite slowly to recede into the archaic; in many ways, it is true, it took hold of the new material, but it was not really determined by it. On the other hand, we recognize that with the full control of the middle class, which has the press as one of its most important instruments in fully developed capitalism, there emerges a form of communication which, no matter how far back its origin may lie, never before influenced the epic form in a decisive way. But now it does exert such an influence. And it turns out that it confronts storytelling as no less of a stranger than did the novel, but in a more menacing way, and that it also brings about a crisis in the novel. This new form of communication is information.

Villemessant, the founder of *Le Figaro*, characterized the nature of information in a famous formulation. 'To my readers,' he used to say, 'an attic fire in the Latin Quarter is more important than a revolution in Madrid.' This makes strikingly clear that it is no longer intelligence coming from afar, but the information which supplies a handle for what is nearest that gets the readiest hearing. The intelligence that came from afar – whether the spatial kind from foreign countries or the temporal kind of tradition – possessed an authority which gave it validity, even when it was not subject to verification. Information, however, lays claim to prompt verifiability. The prime requirement is that it appear 'understandable in itself'. Often it is no more exact than the intelligence of earlier centuries was. But while the latter was inclined to borrow from the miraculous, it is indispensable for information to sound plausible. Because of this it proves incompatible with the spirit of storytelling. If the art of storytelling has become rare, the dissemination of information has had a decisive share in this state of affairs.

Every morning brings us the news of the globe, and yet we are poor in noteworthy stories. This is because no event any longer comes to us without already being shot through with explanation. In other words, by now almost nothing that happens benefits storytelling; almost everything benefits information. Actually, it is half the art of storytelling to keep a story free from explanation as one reproduces it. Leskov is a master at this (compare pieces like *The Deception* and *The White Eagle*). The most extraordinary things, marvellous things, are related with the greatest accuracy, but the psychological connection of the events is not forced on the reader. It is left up to him to interpret things the way he understands them, and thus the narrative achieves an amplitude that information lacks.

Leskov was grounded in the classics. The first storyteller of the Greeks was Herodotus. In the fourteenth chapter of the third book of his *Histories* there is a story from which much can be learned. It deals with Psammenitus.

When the Egyptian king Psammenitus had been beaten and captured by the Persian king Cambyses, Cambyses was bent on humbling his prisoner. He gave orders to place Psammenitus on the road along which the Persian triumphal procession was to pass. And he further arranged that the prisoner should see his daughter pass by as a maid going to the well with her pitcher. While all the Egyptians were lamenting and bewailing this spectacle, Psammenitus stood alone, mute and motionless, his eyes fixed on the ground; and when presently he saw his son, who was being taken along in the procession to be executed, he likewise remained unmoved. But when afterwards he recognized one of his servants, an old, impoverished man, in the ranks of the prisoners, he beat his fists against his head and gave all the signs of deepest mourning.

From this story it may be seen what the nature of true storytelling is. The value of information does not survive the moment in which it was new. It lives only at that moment; it has to surrender to it completely and explain itself to it without losing any time. A story is different. It does not expend itself. It preserves and concentrates its strength and is capable of releasing it even after a long time. Thus Montaigne referred to this Egyptian king and asked himself why he mourned only when he caught sight of his servant. Montaigne answers: 'Since he was already overfull of grief, it took only the smallest increase for it to burst through its dams.' Thus Montaigne. But one could also say: The king is not moved by the fate of those of royal blood, for it is his own fate. Or: We are moved by much on the stage that does not move us in real life; to the king, this servant is only an actor. Or: Great grief is pent up and breaks forth only with relaxation. Seeing this servant was the relaxation. Herodotus offers no explanations. His report is the driest. That is why this story from ancient Egypt is still capable after thousands of years of arousing astonishment and thoughtfulness. It resembles the seeds of grain which have lain for centuries in the chambers of the pyramids shut up air-tight and have retained their germinative power to this day.

There is nothing that commends a story to memory more effectively than that chaste compactness which precludes psychological analysis. And the more natural the process by which the storyteller forgoes psychological shading, the greater becomes the story's claim to a place in the memory of the listener, the more completely is it integrated into his own experience, the greater will be his inclination to repeat it to someone else some day, sooner or later. This process of assimilation, which takes place in depth, requires a state of relaxation which is becoming rarer and rarer. If sleep is the apogee of physical relaxation, boredom is the apogee of mental relaxation. Boredom is the dream bird that hatches the egg of experience. A rustling in the leaves drives him away. His nesting places – the activities that are intimately associated with boredom – are already extinct in the cities and are declining in the country as well. With this the gift for listening is lost and the community of listeners disappears. For storytelling is always the art of repeating stories, and this art is lost when the stories are no longer retained. It is lost because there is no more weaving and spinning to go on while they are being listened to. The more self-forgetful the listener is, the more deeply is what he listens to impressed upon his memory. When the rhythm of work has seized him, he listens to the tales in such a way that the gift of retelling them comes to him all by itself. This, then, is the nature of the web in which the gift of storytelling is cradled. This is how today it is becoming unravelled at all its ends after being woven thousands of years ago in the ambience of the oldest forms of craftsmanship.

The storytelling that thrives for a long time in the milieu of work – the rural, the maritime, and the urban – is itself an artisan form of communication, as it were. It does not aim to convey the pure essence of the thing, like information or a report. It sinks the thing into the life of the storyteller, in order to bring it out of him again. Thus traces of the storyteller cling to the story the way the handprints of the potter cling to the clay vessel. Storytellers tend to begin their story with a presentation of the circumstances in which they themselves have learned what is to follow, unless they simply pass it off as their own experience. Leskov begins his *Deception* with the description of a train trip on which he supposedly heard from a fellow passenger the events which he then goes on to relate; or he thinks of Dostoevsky's funeral, where he sets his acquaintance with the heroine of his story *À Propos of the Kreutzer Sonata*; or he evokes a gathering of a reading circle in which we are told the events that he reproduces for us in his *Interesting Men*. Thus his tracks are frequently evident in his narratives, if not as those of the one who experienced it, then as those of the one who reports it.

This craftsmanship, storytelling, was actually regarded as a craft by Leskov himself. 'Writing,' he says in one of his letters, 'is to me no liberal art, but a craft.' It cannot come as a surprise that he felt bonds with craftsmanship, but faced industrial technology as a stranger. Tolstoy, who must have understood this, occasionally touches this nerve of Leskov's storytelling talent when he calls him the first man 'who pointed out the inadequacy of economic progress . . . It is strange that Dostoevsky is so widely read . . . But I simply cannot comprehend why Leskov is not read. He is a truthful writer.' In his artful and high-spirited story *The Steel Flea*, which is midway between legend and farce, Leskov glorifies native craftsmanship through the silversmiths of Tula. Their masterpiece, the steel flea, is seen by Peter the Great and convinces him that the Russians need not be ashamed before the English.

The intellectual picture of the atmosphere of craftsmanship from which the storyteller comes has perhaps never been sketched in such a significant way as by Paul Valéry. 'He speaks of the perfect things in nature, flawless pearls, full-bodied, matured wines, truly developed creatures, and calls them "the precious product of a long chain of causes similar to one another".' The accumulation of such causes has its temporal limit only at perfection. 'This patient process of Nature,' Valéry continues, was once imitated by men. Miniatures, ivory carvings, elaborated to the point of greatest perfection, stones that are perfect in polish and engraving, lacquer work or paintings in which a series of thin, transparent layers are placed one on top of the other – all these products of sustained, sacrificing effort are vanishing, and the time is past in which time did not matter. Modern man no longer works at what cannot be abbreviated.

In point of fact, he has succeeded in abbreviating even storytelling. We have witnessed the evolution of the 'short story', which has removed itself from oral tradition and no longer permits that slow piling one on top of the other of thin, transparent layers which constitutes the most appropriate picture of the way in which the perfect narrative is revealed through the layers of a variety of retellings.

Valéry concludes his observations with this sentence: 'It is almost as if the decline of the idea of eternity coincided with the increasing aversion to sustained effort.' The idea of eternity has ever had its strongest source in death. If this idea declines, so we reason, the face of death must have changed. It turns out that this change is identical with the one that has diminished the communicability of experience to the same extent as the art of storytelling has declined.

It has been observable for a number of centuries how in the general consciousness the thought of death has declined in omnipresence and vividness. In its last stages this process is accelerated. And in the course of the nineteenth century bourgeois society has, by means of hygienic and social, private and public institutions, realized a secondary effect which may have been its subconscious main purpose: to make it possible for people to avoid the sight of the dying. Dying was once a public process in the life of the individual and a most exemplary one; think of the medieval pictures in which the deathbed has turned into a throne toward which the people press through the wide-open doors of the death house. In the course of modern times dying has been pushed further and further out of the perceptual world of the living. There used to be no house, hardly a room, in which someone had not once died.

(The Middle Ages also felt spatially what makes that inscription on a sun dial of Ibiza, *Ultima multis* [the last day for many], significant as the temper of the times.) Today people live in rooms that have never been touched by death, dry dwellers of eternity, and when their end approaches they are stowed away in sanatoria or hospitals by their heirs. It is, however, characteristic that not only a man's knowledge or wisdom, but above all his real life – and this is the stuff that stories are made of – first assumes transmissible form at the moment of his death. Just as a sequence of images is set in motion inside a man as his life comes to an end – unfolding the views of himself under which he has encountered himself without being aware of it – suddenly in his expressions and looks the unforgettable emerges and imparts to everything that concerned him that authority which even the poorest wretch in dying possesses for the living around him. This authority is at the very source of the story.

Death is the sanction of everything that the storyteller can tell. He has borrowed his authority from death. In other words, it is natural history to which his stories refer back. This is expressed in exemplary form in one of the most beautiful stories we have by the incomparable Johann Peter Hebel. It is found in the *Schatzkästlein des rheinischen Hausfreundes*, is entitled *Unexpected Reunion*, and begins with the betrothal of a young lad who works in the mines of Falun. On the eve of his wedding he dies a miner's death at the bottom of his tunnel. His bride keeps faith with him after his death, and she lives long enough to become a wizened old woman; one day a body is brought up from the abandoned tunnel which, saturated with iron vitriol, has escaped decay, and she recognizes her betrothed. After this reunion she too is called away by death. When Hebel, in the course of this story, was confronted with the necessity of making this long period of years graphic, he did so in the following sentences:

In the meantime the city of Lisbon was destroyed by an earthquake, and the Seven Years' War came and went, and Emperor Francis I died, and the Jesuit Order was abolished, and Poland was partitioned, and Empress Maria Theresa died, and Struensee was executed. America became independent, and the united French and Spanish forces were unable to capture Gibraltar. The Turks locked up General Stein in the Veteraner Cave in Hungary, and Emperor Joseph died also. King Gustavus of Sweden conquered Russian Finland, and the French Revolution and the long war began, and Emperor Leopold II went to his grave too. Napoleon captured Prussia, and the English bombarded Copenhagen, and the peasants sowed and harvested. The millers ground, the smiths hammered, and the miners dug for veins of ore in their underground workshops. But when in 1809 the miners at Falun . . .

Never has a storyteller embedded his report deeper in natural history than Hebel manages to do in this chronology. Read it carefully. Death appears in it with the same regularity as the Reaper does in the processions that pass around the cathedral clock at noon.

Any examination of a given epic form is concerned with the relationship of this form to historiography. In fact, one may go even further and raise the question whether historiography does not constitute the common ground of all forms of the epic. Then written history would be in the same relationship to the epic forms as white light is to the colours of the spectrum. However this may be, among all forms of the epic there is not one whose incidence in the pure, colourless light of written history is more certain than the chronicle. And in the broad spectrum of the chronicle the ways in which a story can be told are graduated like shadings of one and the same colour. The chronicler is the history-teller. If we think back to the passage from Hebel, which has the tone of a chronicle throughout, it will take no effort to gauge the difference between the writer of history, the historian, and the teller of it, the chronicler. The historian is bound to explain in one way or another the happenings with which he deals; under no circumstances can he content himself with displaying them as models of the course of the world. But this is precisely what the chronicler does, especially in his classical representatives, the chroniclers of the Middle Ages, the precursors of the historians of today. By basing their historical tales on a divine plan of salvation – an inscrutable one – they have from the very start lifted the burden of demonstrable explanation from their own shoulders. Its place is taken by interpretation, which is not concerned with an accurate concatenation of definite events, but with the way these are embedded in the great inscrutable course of the world.

Whether this course is eschatologically determined or is a natural one makes no difference. In the storyteller the chronicler is preserved in changed form, secularized, as it were. Leskov is among those whose work displays this with particular clarity. Both the chronicler with his eschatological orientation and the storyteller with his profane outlook are so represented in his works that in a number of his stories it can hardly be decided whether the web in which they appear is the golden fabric of a religious view of the course of things, or the multi-coloured fabric of a worldly view.

Consider the story *The Alexandrite*, which transports the reader into

> that old time when the stones in the womb of the earth and the planets at celestial heights were still concerned with the fate of men, and not today when both in the heavens and beneath the earth everything has grown indifferent to the fates of the sons of men and no voice speaks to them from anywhere, let alone does their bidding. None of the undiscovered planets play any part in horoscopes any more, and there are a lot of new stones, all measured and weighed and examined for their specific weight and their density, but they no longer proclaim anything to us, nor do they bring us any benefit. Their time for speaking with men is past.

As is evident, it is hardly possible unambiguously to characterize the course of the world that is illustrated in this story of Leskov's. Is it determined eschatologically or naturalistically? The only certain thing is that in its very nature it is by definition outside all real historical categories. Leskov tells us that the epoch in which man could believe himself to be in harmony with nature has expired. Schiller called this epoch in the history of the world the period of naïve poetry. The storyteller keeps faith with it, and his eyes do not stray from that dial in front of which there moves the procession of creatures of which, depending on circumstances, Death is either the leader or the last wretched straggler.

It has seldom been realized that the listener's naïve relationship to the storyteller is controlled by his interest in retaining what he is told. The cardinal point for the unaffected listener is to assure himself of the possibility of reproducing the story. Memory is the epic faculty *par excellence.* Only by virtue of a comprehensive memory can epic writing absorb the course of events on the one hand and, with the passing of these, make its peace with the power of death on the other. It is not surprising that to a simple man of the people, such as Leskov once invented, the Czar, the head of the sphere in which his stories take place, has the most encyclopaedic memory at his command. 'Our Emperor,' he says, 'and his entire family have indeed a most astonishing memory.'

Mnemosyne, the rememberer, was the Muse of the epic art among the Greeks. This name takes the observer back to a parting of the ways in world history. For if the record kept by memory – historiography – constitutes the creative matrix of the various epic forms (as great prose is the creative matrix of the various metrical forms), its oldest form, the epic, by virtue of being a kind of common denominator includes the story and the novel. When in the course of centuries the novel began to emerge from the womb of the epic, it turned out that in the novel the element of the epic mind that is derived from the Muse – that is, memory – manifests itself in a form quite different from the way it manifests itself in the story.

Memory creates the chain of tradition which passes a happening on from generation to generation. It is the Muse-derived element of the epic art in a broader sense and encompasses its varieties. In the first place among these is the one practised by the storyteller. It starts the web which all stories together form in the end. One ties on to the next, as the great storytellers, particularly the Oriental ones, have always readily shown. In each of them there is a Scheherazade who thinks of a fresh story whenever her tale comes to a stop. This is epic remembrance and the Muse-inspired element of the narrative. But this should be set against another principle, also a Muse-derived element in a narrower sense, which as an element of the novel in its earliest form – that is, in the epic – lies concealed, still undifferentiated from the similarly derived element of the story. It can, at any rate, occasionally be divined in the epics, particularly at moments of solemnity in the Homeric epics, as in the invocations to the Muse at their beginning. What announces itself in these passages is the perpetuating remembrance of the novelist as contrasted with the short-lived reminiscences of the storyteller. The first is dedicated to *one* hero, *one* odyssey, *one* battle; the second, to *many* diffuse occurrences. It is, in other words, *remembrance* which, as the Muse-derived element of the novel, is added to reminiscence, the corresponding element of the story, the unity of their origin in memory having disappeared with the decline of the epic.

'No one,' Pascal once said, 'dies so poor that he does not leave something behind.' Surely it is the same with memories, too – although these do not always find an heir. The novelist takes charge of this bequest, and seldom without profound melancholy. For what Arnold Bennett says about a dead woman in one of his novels – that she had had almost nothing in the way of real life – is usually true of the sum total of the estate which the novelist administers. Regarding this aspect of the matter we owe the most important elucidation to Georg Lukács, who sees in the novel 'the form of transcendental homelessness'. According to Lukács, the novel is at the same time the only art form which includes time among its constitutive principles.

'Time,' he says in his *Theory of the Novel*,

> can become constitutive only when connection with the transcendental home has been lost. Only in the novel are meaning and life, and thus the essential and the temporal, separated; one can almost say that the whole inner action of a novel is nothing else but a struggle against the power of time . . . And from this . . . arise the genuinely epic experiences of time: hope and memory . . . Only in the novel . . . does there occur a creative memory which transfixes the object and transforms it . . . The duality of inwardness and outside world can here be overcome for the subject 'only' when he sees the . . . unity of his entire life . . . out of the past life-stream which is compressed in memory . . . The insight which grasps this unity . . . becomes the divinatory-intuitive grasping of the unattained and therefore inexpressible meaning of life.

The 'meaning of life' is really the centre about which the novel moves. But the quest for it is no more than the initial expression of perplexity with which its reader sees himself living this written life. Here 'meaning of life' – there 'moral of the story': with these slogans novel and story confront each other, and from them the totally different historical co-ordinates of these art forms may be discerned. If *Don Quixote* is the earliest perfect specimen of the novel, its latest exemplar is perhaps the *Éducation sentimentale*.

In the final words of the last-named novel, the meaning which the bourgeois age found in its behaviour at the beginning of its decline has settled like sediment in the cup of life. Frédéric and Deslauriers, the boyhood friends, think back to their youthful friendship. This little incident then occurred: one day they showed up in the bordello of their home town, stealthily and timidly, doing nothing but presenting the *patronne* with a bouquet of flowers which they had picked in their own gardens.

This story was still discussed three years later. And now they told it to each other in detail, each supplementing the recollection of the other. 'That may have been,' said Frédéric when they had finished, 'the finest thing in our lives.' 'Yes, you may be right,' said Deslauriers, 'that was perhaps the finest thing in our lives.'

With such an insight the novel reaches an end which is more proper to it, in a stricter sense, than to any story. Actually there is no story for which the question as to how it continued would not be legitimate. The novelist, on the other hand, cannot hope to take the smallest step beyond that limit at which he invites the reader to a divinatory realization of the meaning of life by writing 'Finis'.

A man listening to a story is in the company of the storyteller; even a man reading one shares this companionship. The reader of a novel, however, is isolated, more so than any other reader. (For even the reader of a poem is ready to utter the words, for the benefit of the listener.) In this solitude of his, the reader of a novel seizes upon his material more jealously than anyone else. He is ready to make it completely his own, to devour it, as it were. Indeed, he destroys, he swallows up the material as the fire devours logs in the fireplace. The suspense which permeates the novel is very much like the draught which stimulates the flame in the fireplace and enlivens its play.

It is a dry material on which the burning interest of the reader feeds. 'A man who dies at the age of 35,' said Moritz Heimann once, 'is at every point of his life a man who dies at the age of 35.' Nothing is more dubious than this sentence – but for the sole reason that the tense is wrong. A man – so says the truth that was meant here – who died at 35 will appear to *remembrance* at every point in his life as a man who dies at the age of 35. In other words, the statement that makes no sense for real life becomes indisputable for remembered life. The nature of the character in a novel cannot be presented any better than is done in this statement, which says that the 'meaning' of his life is revealed only in his death. But the reader of a novel actually does look for human beings from whom he derives the 'meaning of life'. Therefore he must, no matter what, know in advance that he will share their experience of death: if need be their figurative death – the end of the novel – but preferably their actual one. How do the characters make him understand that death is already waiting for them – a very definite death and at a very definite place? That is the question which feeds the reader's consuming interest in the events of the novel.

The novel is significant, therefore, not because it presents someone else's fate to us, perhaps didactically, but because this stranger's fate by virtue of the flame which consumes it yields us the warmth which we never draw from our own fate. What draws the reader to the novel is the hope of warming his shivering life with a death he reads about.

'Leskov,' writes Gorky, 'is the writer most deeply rooted in the people and is completely untouched by any foreign influences.' A great storyteller will always be rooted in the people, primarily in a milieu of craftsmen. But just as this includes the rural, the maritime, and the urban elements in the many stages of their economic and technical development, there are many gradations in the concepts in which their store of experience comes down to us. (To say nothing of the by no means insignificant share which traders had in the art of storytelling; their task was less to increase its didactic content than to refine the tricks with which the attention of the listener was captured. They have left deep traces in the narrative cycle of *The Arabian Nights*.) In short, despite the primary role which storytelling plays in the household of humanity, the concepts through which the yield of the stories may be garnered are manifold. What may most readily be put in religious terms in Leskov seems almost automatically to fall into place in the pedagogical perspectives of the Enlightenment in Hebel, appears as hermetic tradition in Poe, finds a last refuge in Kipling in the life of British seamen and colonial soldiers. All great storytellers have in common the freedom with which they move up and down the rungs of their experience as on a ladder. A ladder extending downward to the interior of the earth and disappearing into the clouds is the image for a collective experience to which even the deepest shock of every individual experience, death, constitutes no impediment or barrier.

'And they lived happily ever after,' says the fairy tale. The fairy tale, which to this day is the first tutor of children because it was once the first tutor of mankind, secretly lives on in the story. The first true storyteller is, and will continue to be, the teller of fairy tales. Whenever good counsel was at a premium, the fairy tale had it, and where the need was greatest, its aid was nearest. This need was the need created by the myth. The fairy tale tells us of the earliest arrangements that mankind made to shake off the nightmare which the myth had placed upon its chest. In the figure of the fool it shows us how mankind 'acts dumb' towards the myth; in the figure of the youngest brother it shows us how one's chances increase as the mythical primitive times are left behind; in the figure of the man who sets out to learn what fear is it shows us that the things we are afraid of can be seen through; in the figure of the wiseacre it shows us that the questions posed by the myth are simple-minded, like the riddle of the Sphinx; in the shape of the animals which come to the aid of the child in the fairy tale it shows that nature not only is subservient to the myth, but much prefers to be aligned with man. The wisest thing – so the fairy tale taught mankind in olden times, and teaches children to this day – is to meet the forces of the mythical world with cunning and with high spirits. (This is how the fairy tale polarizes *Mut*, courage, dividing it dialectically into *Untermut*, that is, cunning, and *Übermut*, high spirits.) The liberating magic which the fairy tale has at its disposal does not bring nature into play in a mythical way, but points to its complicity with liberated man. A mature man feels this complicity only occasionally, that is, when he is happy; but the child first meets it in fairy tales, and it makes him happy.

Few storytellers have displayed so profound a kinship with the spirit of the fairy tale as did Leskov. This involves tendencies that were promoted by the dogmas of the Greek Orthodox Church. As is well known, Origen's speculation about *apokatastasis* – the entry of all souls into Paradise – which was rejected by the Roman Church plays a significant part in these dogmas. Leskov was very much influenced by Origen and planned to translate his work *On First Principles*. In keeping with Russian folk belief he interpreted the Resurrection less as a transfiguration than as a disenchantment, in a sense akin to the fairy tale. Such an interpretation of Origen is at the bottom of *The Enchanted Pilgrim*. In this, as in many other tales by Leskov, a hybrid between fairy tale and legend is involved, not unlike that hybrid which Ernst Bloch mentions in a connection in which he utilizes our distinction between myth and fairy tale in his fashion.

'A hybrid between fairy tale and legend,' he says,

> contains figuratively mythical elements, mythical elements whose effect is certainly captivating and static, and yet not outside man. In the legend there are Taoist figures, especially very old ones, which are 'mythical' in this sense. For instance, the couple Philemon and Baucis: magically escaped though in natural repose. And surely there is a similar relationship between fairy tale and legend in the Taoist climate of Gotthelf, which, to be sure, is on a much lower level. At certain points it divorces the legend from the locality of the spell, rescues the flame of life, the specifically human flame of life, calmly burning, within as without.

'Magically escaped' are the beings that lead the procession of Leskov's creations: the righteous ones. Pavlin, Figura, the toupée artiste, the bear keeper, the helpful sentry – all of them embodiments of wisdom, kindness, comfort the world, crowd about the storyteller. They are unmistakably suffused with the *imago* of his mother.

This is how Leskov describes her:

She was so thoroughly good that she was not capable of harming any man, nor even an animal. She ate neither meat nor fish, because she had such pity for living creatures. Sometimes my father used to reproach her with this. But she answered: 'I have raised the little animals myself, they are like my children to me. I can't eat my own children, can I?' She would not eat meat at a neighbor's house either. 'I have seen them alive,' she would say; 'they are my acquaintances. I can't eat my acquaintances, can I?'

The righteous man is the advocate for created things and at the same time he is their highest embodiment. In Leskov he has a maternal touch which is occasionally intensified into the mythical (and thus, to be sure, endangers the purity of the fairy tale). Typical of this is the protagonist of his story 'Kotin the Provider and Platonida'. This figure, a peasant named Pisonski, is a hermaphrodite. For twelve years his mother raised him as a girl. His male and female organs mature simultaneously, and his bisexuality 'becomes the symbol of God incarnate'.

In Leskov's view, the pinnacle of creation has been attained with this, and at the same time he presumably sees it as a bridge established between this world and the other. For these earthily powerful, maternal male figures which again and again claim Leskov's skill as a storyteller have been removed from obedience to the sexual drive in the bloom of their strength. They do not, however, really embody an ascetic ideal; rather, the continence of these righteous men has so little privative character that it becomes the elemental counterpoise to uncontrolled lust which the storyteller has personified in *Lady Macbeth of Mzensk*. If the range between a Pavlin and this merchant's wife covers the breadth of the world of created beings, in the hierarchy of his characters Leskov has no less plumbed its depth.

The hierarchy of the world of created things, which has its apex in the righteous man, reaches down into the abyss of the inanimate by many gradations. In this connection one particular has to be noted. This whole created world speaks not so much with the human voice as with what could be called 'the voice of Nature' in the title of one of Leskov's most significant stories.

This story deals with the petty official Philip Philipovich who leaves no stone unturned to get the chance to have as his house guest a field marshal passing through his little town. He manages to do so. The guest, who is at first surprised at the clerk's urgent invitation, gradually comes to believe that he recognizes in him someone he must have met previously. But who is he? He cannot remember. The strange thing is that the host, for his part, is not willing to reveal his identity. Instead, he puts off the high personage from day to day, saying that the 'voice of Nature' will not fail to speak distinctly to him one day. This goes on until finally the guest, shortly before continuing on his journey, must grant the host's public request to let the 'voice of Nature' resound. Thereupon the host's wife withdraws. She

returned with a big, brightly polished, copper hunting horn which she gave to her husband. He took the horn, put it to his lips, and was at the same instant as though transformed. Hardly had he inflated his cheeks and produced a tone as powerful as the rolling of thunder when the field marshal cried: 'Stop, I've got it now, brother. This makes me recognize you at once! You are the bugler from the regiment of jaegers, and because you were so honest I sent you to keep an eye on a crooked supplies supervisor.' 'That's it, Your Excellency ' answered the host. 'I didn't want to remind you of this myself, but wanted to let the voice of Nature speak.'

The way the profundity of this story is hidden beneath its silliness conveys an idea of Leskov's magnificent humour. This humour is confirmed in the same story in an even more cryptic way. We have heard that because of his honesty the official was assigned to watch a crooked supplies supervisor. This is what we are told at the end, in the recognition scene. At the very beginning of the story, however, we learn the following about the host:

All the inhabitants of the town were acquainted with the man, and they knew that he did not hold a high office, for he was neither a state official nor a military man, but a little supervisor at the tiny supply depot, where together with the rats he chewed on the state rusks and boot soles, and in the course of time had chewed himself together a nice little frame house.

It is evident that this story reflects the traditional sympathy which storytellers have for rascals and crooks. All the literature of farce bears witness to it. Nor is it denied on the heights of art; of all Hebel's characters, the Brassenheim Miller, Tinder Frieder, and Red Dieter have been his most faithful companions. And yet for Hebel, too, the righteous man has the main role in the *theatrum mundi*. But because no one is actually up to this role, it keeps changing hands. Now it is the tramp, now the haggling Jewish peddler, now the man of limited intelligence who steps in to play this part. In every single case it is a guest performance, a moral improvisation. Hebel is a casuist. He will not for anything take a stand with any principle, but he does not reject it either, for any principle can at some time become the instrument of the righteous man. Compare this with Leskov's attitude. 'I realize,' he writes in his story *À Propos of the Kreutzer Sonata*, 'that my thinking is based much more on a practical view of life than on abstract philosophy or lofty morality; but I am nevertheless used to thinking the way I do.' To be sure, the moral catastrophes that appear in Leskov's world are to the moral incidents in Hebel's world as the great, silent flowing of the Volga is to the babbling, rushing little millstream. Among Leskov's historical tales there are several in which passions are at work as destructively as the wrath of Achilles or the hatred of Hagen. It is astonishing how fearfully the world can darken for this author and with what majesty evil can raise its sceptre. Leskov has evidently known moods – and this is probably one of the few characteristics he shares with Dostoevsky – in which he was close to antinomian ethics. The elemental natures in his *Tales from Olden Times* go to the limit in their ruthless passion. But it is precisely the mystics who have been inclined to see this limit as the point at which utter depravity turns into saintliness.

The lower Leskov descends on the scale of created things the more obviously does his way of viewing things approach the mystical. Actually, as will be shown, there is much evidence that in this, too, a characteristic is revealed which is inherent in the nature of the storyteller. To be sure, only a few have ventured into the depths of inanimate nature, and in modern narrative literature there is not much in which the voice of the anonymous storyteller, who was prior to all literature, resounds so clearly as it does in Leskov's story *The Alexandrite*. It deals with a semi-precious stone, the chrysoberyl. The mineral is the lowest stratum of created things. For the storyteller, however, it is directly joined to the highest. To him it is granted to see in this chrysoberyl a natural prophecy of petrified, lifeless nature concerning the historical world in which he himself lives. This world is the world of Alexander II. The storyteller – or rather, the man to whom he attributes his own knowledge – is a gem engraver named Wenzel who has achieved the greatest conceivable skill in his art. One can juxtapose him with the silversmiths of Tula and say that – in the spirit of Leskov – the perfect artisan has access to the innermost chamber of the realm of created things. He is an incarnation of the devout. We are told of this gem cutter:

He suddenly squeezed my hand on which was the ring with the alexandrite, which is known to sparkle red in artificial light, and cried: 'Look, here it is, the prophetic Russian stone! O crafty Siberian. It was always green as hope and only toward evening was it suffused with blood. It was that way from the beginning of the world, but it concealed itself for a long time, lay hidden in the earth, and permitted itself to be found only on the day when Czar Alexander was declared of age, when a great sorcerer had come to Siberia to find the stone, a magician . . .' 'What nonsense are you talking,' I interrupted him; 'this stone wasn't found by a magician at all, it was a scholar named Nordenskjöld!' 'A magician! I tell you, a magician!' screamed Wenzel in a loud voice. 'Just look; what a stone! A green morning is in it and a bloody evening . . . This is fate, the fate of noble Czar Alexander!' With these words old Wenzel turned to the wall, propped his head on his elbows, and . . . began to sob.

One can hardly come any closer to the meaning of this significant story than by some words which Paul Valéry wrote in a very remote context. 'Artistic observation,' he says in reflection on a woman artist whose work consisted in the silk embroidery of figures,

can attain an almost mystical depth. The objects on which it falls lose their names. Light and shade form very particular systems, present very individual questions which depend upon no knowledge and are derived from no practice, but get their existence and value exclusively from a certain accord of the soul, the eye, and the hand of someone who was born to perceive them and evoke them in his own inner self.

With these words, soul, eye, and hand are brought into connection. Interacting with one another, they determine a practice. We are no longer familiar with this practice. The role of the hand in production has become more modest, and the place it filled in storytelling lies waste. (After all, storytelling, in its sensory aspect, is by no means a job for the voice alone. Rather, in genuine storytelling the hand plays a part which supports what is expressed in a hundred ways with its gestures trained by work.) That old coordination of the soul, the eye, and the hand which emerges in Valéry's words is that of the artisan which we encounter wherever the art of storytelling is at home. In fact, one can go on and ask oneself whether the relationship of the storyteller to his material, human life, is not in itself a craftsman's relationship, whether it is not his very task to fashion the raw material of experience, his own and that of others, in a solid, useful, and unique way. It is a kind of procedure which may perhaps most adequately be exemplified by the proverb if one thinks of it as an ideogram of a story. A proverb, one might say, is a ruin which stands on the site of an old story and in which a moral twines about a happening like ivy around a wall.

Seen in this way, the storyteller joins the ranks of the teachers and sages. He has counsel – not for a few situations, as the proverb does, but for many, like the sage. For it is granted to him to reach back to a whole lifetime (a life, incidentally, that comprises not only his own experience but no little of the experience of others; what the storyteller knows from hearsay is added to his own). His gift is the ability to relate his life; his distinction, to be able to tell his entire life. The storyteller: he is the man who could let the wick of his life be consumed completely by the gentle flame of his story. This is the basis of the incomparable aura about the storyteller, in Leskov as in Hauff, in Poe as in Stevenson. The storyteller is the figure in which the righteous man encounters himself.

15 Herbert Marcuse

Repressive Tolerance

Excerpt from Robert Paul Wolff, Barrington Moore Jr, and Herbert Marcuse, *A Critique of Pure Tolerance*, Beacon Press, Boston, pp. 81–123. First published 1965.

This essay is dedicated to my students at Brandeis University.

This essay examines the idea of tolerance in our advanced industrial society. The conclusion reached is that the realization of the objective of tolerance would call for intolerance toward prevailing policies, attitudes, opinions, and the extension of tolerance to policies, attitudes, and opinions which are outlawed or suppressed. In other words, today tolerance appears again as what it was in its origins, at the beginning of the modern period – a partisan goal, a subversive liberating notion and practice. Conversely, what is proclaimed and practised as tolerance today, is in many of its most effective manifestations serving the cause of oppression.

The author is fully aware that, at present, no power, no authority, no government exists which would translate liberating tolerance into practice, but he believes that it is the task and duty of the intellectual to recall and preserve historical possibilities which seem to have become utopian possibilities – that it is his task to break the concreteness of oppression in order to open the mental space in which this society can be recognized as what it is and does.

Tolerance is an end in itself. The elimination of violence, and the reduction of suppression to the extent required for protecting man and animals from cruelty and aggression are pre-conditions for the creation of a humane society. Such a society does not yet exist; progress toward it is, perhaps more than before, arrested by violence and suppression on a global scale. As deterrents against nuclear war, as police action against subversion, as technical aid in the fight against imperialism and communism, as methods of pacification in neo-colonial massacres, violence and suppression are promulgated, practised, and defended by democratic and authoritarian governments alike, and the people subjected to these governments are educated to sustain such practices as necessary for the preservation of the *status quo*. Tolerance is extended to policies, conditions, and modes of behaviour which should not be tolerated because they are impeding, if not destroying, the chances of creating an existence without fear and misery.

This sort of tolerance strengthens the tyranny of the majority against which authentic liberals protested. The political locus of tolerance has changed: while it is more or less quietly and constitutionally withdrawn from the opposition, it is made compulsory behaviour with respect to established policies. Tolerance is turned from an active into a passive state, from practice to non-practice: *laissez-faire* the constituted authorities. It is the people who tolerate the government, which in turn tolerates opposition within the framework determined by the constituted authorities.

Tolerance toward that which is radically evil now appears as good because it serves the cohesion of the whole on the road to affluence or more affluence. The toleration of the systematic moronization of children and adults alike by publicity and propaganda, the release of destructiveness in aggressive driving, the recruitment for and training of special forces, the impotent and benevolent tolerance toward outright deception in merchandizing, waste, and planned obsolescence are not distortions and aberrations, they are the essence of a system which fosters tolerance as a means for perpetuating the struggle for existence and suppressing the alternatives. The authorities in education, morals, and psychology are vociferous against the increase in juvenile delinquency; they are less vociferous against the proud presentation, in word and deed and pictures, of ever more powerful missiles, rockets, bombs – the mature delinquency of a whole civilization.

According to a dialectical proposition it is the whole which determines the truth – not in the sense that the whole is prior or superior to its parts, but in the sense that its structure and function determine every particular condition and relation. Thus, within a repressive society, even progressive movements threaten to turn into their opposite to the degree to which they accept the rules of the game. To take a most controversial case: the exercise of political rights (such as voting, letter-writing to the press, to Senators, etc., protest-demonstrations with *a priori* renunciation of counter-violence) in a society of total administration serves to strengthen this administration by testifying to the existence of democratic liberties which, in reality, have changed their content and lost their effectiveness. In such a case, freedom (of opinion, of assembly, of speech) becomes an instrument for absolving servitude. And yet (and only here the dialectical proposition shows its full intent) the existence and practice of these liberties remain a pre-condition for the restoration of their original oppositional function, provided that the effort to transcend their (often self-imposed) limitations is intensified. Generally, the function and value of tolerance depend on the equality prevalent in the society in which tolerance is practised. Tolerance itself stands subject to overriding criteria: its range and its limits cannot be defined in terms of the respective society. In other words, tolerance is an end in itself only when it is truly universal, practised by the rulers as well as by the ruled, by the lords as well as by the peasants, by the sheriffs as well as by their victims. And such universal tolerance is possible only when no real or alleged enemy requires in the national interest the education and training of people in military violence and destruction. As long as these conditions do not prevail, the conditions of tolerance are 'loaded': they are determined and defined by the institutionalized inequality (which is certainly compatible with constitutional equality), i.e., by the class structure of society. In such a society, tolerance is *de facto* limited on the dual ground of legalized violence or suppression (police, armed forces, guards of all sorts) and of the privileged position held by the predominant interests and their 'connections'.

These background limitations of tolerance are normally prior to the explicit and judicial limitations as defined by the courts, custom, governments, etc. (for example, 'clear and present danger', threat to national security, heresy). Within the framework of such a social structure, tolerance can be safely practised and proclaimed. It is of two kinds: (1) the passive toleration of entrenched and established attitudes and ideas even if their damaging effect on man and nature is evident; and (2) the active, official tolerance granted to the Right as well as to the Left, to movements of aggression as well as to movements of peace, to the party of hate as well as to that of humanity. I call this non-partisan tolerance 'abstract' or 'pure' inasmuch as it refrains from taking sides – but in doing so it actually protects the already established machinery of discrimination.

The tolerance which enlarged the range and content of freedom was always partisan – intolerant toward the protagonists of the repressive *status quo*. The issue was only the degree and extent of intolerance. In the firmly established liberal society of England and the United States, freedom of speech and assembly was granted even to the radical enemies of society, provided they did not make the transition from word to deed, from speech to action.

Relying on the effective background limitations imposed by its class structure, the society seemed to practise general tolerance. But liberalist theory had already placed an important condition on tolerance: it was 'to apply only to human beings in the maturity of their faculties'. John Stuart Mill does not only speak of children and minors; he elaborates: 'Liberty, as a principle, has no application to any state of things anterior to the time when mankind have become capable of being improved by free and equal discussion.' Anterior to that time, men may still be barbarians, and 'despotism is a legitimate mode of government in dealing with barbarians, provided the end be their improvement, and the means justified by actually effecting that end'. Mill's often-quoted words have a less familiar implication on which their meaning depends: the internal connection between liberty and truth. There is a sense in which truth is the end of liberty, and liberty must be defined and confined by truth. Now in what sense can liberty be for the sake of truth? Liberty is self-determination, autonomy – this is almost a tautology, but a tautology which results from a whole series of synthetic judgements. It stipulates the ability to determine one's own life: to be able to determine what to do and what not to do, what to suffer and what not. But the subject of this autonomy is never the contingent, private individual as that which he actually is or happens to be; it is rather the individual as a human being who is capable of being free with the others. And the problem of making possible such a harmony between every individual liberty and the other is not that of finding a compromise between competitors, or between freedom and law, between general and individual interest, common and private welfare in an *established* society, but of *creating* the society in which man is no longer enslaved by institutions which vitiate self-determination from the beginning. In other words, freedom is still to be created even for the freest of the existing societies. And the direction in which it must be sought, and the institutional and cultural changes which may help to attain the goal are, at least in developed civilization, *comprehensible*, that is to say, they can be identified and projected, on the basis of experience, by human reason.

In the interplay of theory and practice, true and false solutions become distinguishable – never with the evidence of necessity, never as the positive, only with the certainty of a reasoned and reasonable chance, and with the persuasive force of the negative. For the true positive is the society of the future and therefore beyond definition and determination, while the existing positive is that which must be surmounted. But the experience and understanding of the existent society may well be capable of identifying what is *not* conducive to a free and rational society, what impedes and distorts the possibilities of its creation. Freedom is liberation, a specific historical process in theory and practice, and as such it has its right and wrong, its truth and falsehood.

The uncertainty of chance in this distinction does not cancel the historical objectivity, but it necessitates freedom of thought and expression as pre-conditions of finding the way to freedom – it necessitates *tolerance*. However, this tolerance cannot be indiscriminate and equal with respect to the contents of expression, neither in word nor in deed; it cannot protect false words and wrong deeds which demonstrate that they contradict and counteract the possibilities of liberation. Such indiscriminate tolerance is justified in harmless debates, in conversation, in academic discussion; it is indispensable in the scientific enterprise, in private religion. But society cannot be indiscriminate where the pacification of existence, where freedom and happiness themselves are at stake: here, certain things cannot be said, certain ideas cannot be expressed, certain policies cannot be proposed, certain behaviour cannot be permitted without making tolerance an instrument for the continuation of servitude.

The danger of 'destructive tolerance' (Baudelaire), of 'benevolent neutrality' toward *art* has been recognized: the market, which absorbs equally well (although with often quite sudden fluctuations) art, anti-art, and non-art, all possible conflicting styles, schools, forms, provides a 'complacent receptacle, a friendly abyss'[1] in which the radical impact of art, the protest of art against the established reality is swallowed up. However, censorship of art and literature is regressive under all circumstances. The authentic *œuvre* is not and cannot be a prop of oppression, and pseudo-art (which can be such a prop) is not art. Art stands against history, withstands history which has been the history of oppression, for art subjects reality to laws other than the established ones: to the laws of the Form which creates a different reality – negation of the established one even where art depicts the established reality. But in its struggle with history, art subjects itself to history: history enters the definition of art and enters into the distinction between art and pseudo-art. Thus it happens that what was once art becomes pseudo-art. Previous forms, styles, and qualities, previous modes of protest and refusal cannot be recaptured in or against a different society. There are cases where an authentic *œuvre* carries a regressive political message – Dostoevsky is a case in point. But then, the message is cancelled by the *œuvre* itself: the regressive political content is absorbed, *aufgehoben* in the artistic form: in the work as literature.

Tolerance of free speech is the way of improvement, of progress in liberation, *not* because there is no objective truth, and improvement must necessarily be a compromise between a variety of opinions, but because there *is* an objective truth which can be discovered, ascertained only in learning and comprehending that which is and that which can be and ought to be done for the sake of improving the lot of mankind. This common and historical 'ought' is not immediately evident, at hand: it has to be uncovered by 'cutting through', 'splitting', 'breaking asunder'

1. Wind (1963).

(*dis-cutio*) the given material – separating right and wrong, good and bad, correct and incorrect. The subject whose 'improvement' depends on a progressive historical practice is each man as man, and this universality is reflected in that of the discussion, which *a priori* does not exclude any group or individual. But even the all-inclusive character of liberalist tolerance was, at least in theory, based on the proposition that men were (potential) *individuals* who could learn to hear and see and feel by themselves, to develop their own thoughts, to grasp their true interests and rights and capabilities, also against established authority and opinion. This was the rationale of free speech and assembly. Universal toleration becomes questionable when its rationale no longer prevails, when tolerance is administered to manipulated and indoctrinated individuals who parrot, as their own, the opinion of their masters, for whom heteronomy has become autonomy.

The telos of tolerance is truth. It is clear from the historical record that the authentic spokesmen of tolerance had more and other truth in mind than that of propositional logic and academic theory. John Stuart Mill speaks of the truth which is persecuted in history and which does *not* triumph over persecution by virtue of its 'inherent power', which in fact has no inherent power 'against the dungeon and the stake'. And he enumerates the 'truths' which were cruelly and successfully liquidated in the dungeons and at the stake: that of Arnold of Brescia, of Fra Dolcino, of Savonarola, of the Albigensians, Waldensians, Lollards, and Hussites. Tolerance is first and foremost for the sake of the heretics – the historical road toward *humanitas* appears as heresy: target of persecution by the powers that be. Heresy by itself, however, is no token of truth.

The criterion of progress in freedom according to which Mill judges these movements is the Reformation. The evaluation is *ex post facto*, and his list includes opposites (Savonarola too would have burned Fra Dolcino). Even the *ex post facto* evaluation is contestable as to its truth: history corrects the judgement – too late. The correction does not help the victims and does not absolve their executioners. However, the lesson is clear: intolerance has delayed progress and has prolonged the slaughter and torture of innocents for hundreds of years. Does this clinch the case for indiscriminate, 'pure' tolerance? Are there historical conditions in which such toleration impedes liberation and multiplies the victims who are sacrificed to the *status quo*? Can the indiscriminate guaranty of political rights and liberties be repressive? Can such tolerance serve to contain qualitative social change?

I shall discuss this question only with reference to political movements, attitudes, schools of thought, philosophies which are 'political' in the widest sense – affecting the society as a whole, demonstrably transcending the sphere of privacy. Moreover, I propose a shift in the focus of the discussion: it will be concerned not only, and not primarily, with tolerance toward radical extremes, minorities, subversives, etc., but rather with tolerance toward majorities, toward official and public opinion, toward the established protectors of freedom. In this case, the discussion can have as a frame of reference only a democratic society, in which the people, as individuals and as members of political and other organizations, participate in the making, sustaining, and changing of policies. In an authoritarian system, the people do not tolerate – they suffer established policies.

Under a system of constitutionally guaranteed and (generally and without too many and too glaring exceptions) practised civil rights and liberties, opposition and dissent are tolerated unless they issue in violence and/or in exhortation to and organization of violent subversion. The underlying assumption is that the established society is free, and that any improvement, even a change in the social structure and social values, would come about in the normal course of events, prepared, defined, and tested in free and equal discussion, on the open market-place of ideas and goods.[2] Now in recalling John Stuart Mill's passage, I drew attention to the premise hidden in this assumption: free and equal discussion can fulfil the function attributed to it only if it is *rational* – expression and development of independent thinking,

2. I wish to reiterate for the following discussion that, *de facto*, tolerance is *not* indiscriminate and 'pure' even in the most democratic society. The 'background limitations' stated on page 304 restrict tolerance before it begins to operate. The antagonistic structure of society rigs the rules of the game. Those who stand against the established system are *a priori* at a disadvantage, which is not removed by the toleration of their ideas, speeches, and newspapers.

free from indoctrination, manipulation, extraneous authority. The notion of pluralism and countervailing powers is no substitute for this requirement. One might in theory construct a state in which a multitude of different pressures, interests, and authorities balance each other out and result in a truly general and rational interest. However, such a construction badly fits a society in which powers are and remain unequal and even increase their unequal weight when they run their own course. It fits even worse when the variety of pressures unifies and coagulates into an overwhelming whole, integrating the particular countervailing powers by virtue of an increasing standard of living and an increasing concentration of power. Then, the labourer, whose real interest conflicts with that of management, the common consumer whose real interest conflicts with that of the producer, the intellectual whose vocation conflicts with that of his employer find themselves submitting to a system against which they are powerless and appear unreasonable. The idea of the available alternatives evaporates into an utterly utopian dimension in which it is at home, for a free society is indeed unrealistically and undefinably different from the existing ones. Under these circumstances, whatever improvement may occur 'in the normal course of events' and without subversion is likely to be an improvement in the direction determined by the particular interests which control the whole.

By the same token, those minorities which strive for a change of the whole itself will, under optimal conditions which rarely prevail, be left free to deliberate and discuss, to speak and to assemble – and will be left harmless and helpless in the face of the overwhelming majority, which militates against qualitative social change. This majority is firmly grounded in the increasing satisfaction of needs, and technological and mental co-ordination, which testify to the general helplessness of radical groups in a well-functioning social system.

Within the affluent democracy, the affluent discussion prevails and, within the established framework, it is tolerant to a large extent. All points of view can be heard: the Communist and the Fascist, the Left and the Right, the white and the Negro, the crusaders for armament and for disarmament. Moreover, in endlessly dragging debates over the media, the stupid opinion is treated with the same respect as the intelligent one, the misinformed may talk as long as the informed, and propaganda rides along with education, truth and falsehood. This pure toleration of sense and nonsense is justified by the democratic argument that nobody, neither group nor individual, is in possession of the truth and capable of defining what is right and wrong, good and bad. Therefore, all contesting opinions must be submitted to 'the people' for its deliberation and choice. But I have already suggested that the democratic argument implies a necessary condition, namely, that the people must be capable of deliberating and choosing on the basis of knowledge, that they must have access to authentic information, and that, on this basis, their evaluation must be the result of autonomous thought.

In the contemporary period, the democratic argument for abstract tolerance tends to be invalidated by the invalidation of the democratic process itself. The liberating force of democracy was the chance it gave to effective dissent, on the individual as well as social scale, its openness to qualitatively different forms of government, of culture, education, work – of the human existence in general. The toleration of free discussion and the equal right of opposites was to define and clarify the different forms of dissent: their direction, content, prospect. But with the concentration of economic and political power and the integration of opposites in a society which uses technology as an instrument of domination, effective dissent is blocked where it could freely emerge; in the formation of opinion, in information and communication, in speech and assembly. Under the rule of monopolistic media – themselves the mere instruments of economic and political power – a mentality is created for which right and wrong, true and false are pre-defined wherever they affect the vital interests of the society. This is, prior to all expression and communication, a matter of semantics: the blocking of effective dissent, of the recognition of that which is not of the Establishment which begins in the language that is publicized and administered. The meaning of words is rigidly stabilized. Rational persuasion, persuasion to the opposite is all but precluded. The avenues of entrance are closed to the meaning of words and ideas other than the established one – established by the publicity of the powers that be, and verified in their practices. Other words can be spoken and heard, other ideas can be expressed, but, at the massive scale of the conservative majority (outside such enclaves as the intelligentsia), they are immediately 'evaluated' (i.e. automatically understood) in terms of the public language – a language which determines *a priori* the direction in which the thought process moves. Thus the process of reflection ends where it started: in the given conditions and relations. Self-validating, the argument of the discussion repels the contradiction because the antithesis is re-defined in terms of the thesis. For example, thesis: we work for peace; antithesis: we prepare for war (or even: we wage war); unification of opposites; preparing for war *is* working for peace. Peace is re-defined as necessarily, in the prevailing situation, including preparation for war (or even war) and in this Orwellian form, the meaning of the word 'peace' is stabilized. Thus, the basic vocabulary of the Orwellian language operates as *a priori* categories of understanding: preforming all content. These conditions invalidate the logic of tolerance which involves the rational development of meaning and precludes the closing of meaning. Consequently, persuasion through discussion and the equal presentation of opposites (even where it is really equal) easily lose their liberating force as factors of understanding and learning; they are far more likely to strengthen the established thesis and to repel the alternatives.

Impartiality to the utmost, equal treatment of competing and conflicting issues is indeed a basic requirement for decision-making in the democratic process – it is an equally basic requirement for defining the limits of tolerance. But in a democracy with totalitarian organization, objectivity may fulfil a very different function, namely, to foster a mental attitude which tends to obliterate the difference between true and false, information and indoctrination, right and wrong. In fact, the decision between opposed opinions has been made before the presentation and discussion get under way – made, not by a conspiracy or a sponsor or a publisher, not by any dictatorship, but rather by the 'normal course of events', which is the course of administered events, and by the mentality shaped in this course. Here, too, it is the whole which determines the truth. Then the decision asserts itself, without any open violation of objectivity, in such things as the make-up of a newspaper (with the breaking up of vital information into bits interspersed between extraneous material, irrelevant items, relegating of some radically negative news to an obscure place), in the juxtaposition of gorgeous ads with unmitigated horrors, in the introduction and interruption of the broadcasting of facts by overwhelming commercials. The result is a *neutralization* of opposites, a neutralization, however, which takes place on the firm grounds of the structural limitation of tolerance and within a pre-formed mentality. When a magazine prints side by side a negative and a positive report on the F.B.I., it fulfils honestly the requirements of objectivity: however, the chances are that the positive wins because the image of the institution is deeply engraved in the mind of the people. Or, if a newscaster reports the torture and murder of civil rights workers in the same unemotional tone he uses to describe the stock market or the weather, or with the same great emotion with which he says his commercials, then such objectivity is spurious – more, it offends against humanity and truth by being calm where one should be enraged, by refraining from accusation where accusation is in the facts themselves. The tolerance expressed in such impartiality serves to minimize or even absolve prevailing intolerance and suppression. If objectivity has anything to do with truth, and if truth is more than a matter of logic and science, then this kind of objectivity is false, and this kind of tolerance inhuman. And if it is necessary to break the established universe of meaning (and the practice enclosed in this universe) in order to enable man to find out what is true and false, this deceptive impartiality would have to be abandoned. The people exposed to this impartiality are no *tabulae rasae*, they are indoctrinated by the conditions under which they live and think and which they do not transcend. To enable them to become autonomous, to find by themselves what is true and what is false for man in the existing society, they would have to be freed from the prevailing indoctrination (which is no longer recognized as indoctrination). But this means that the trend would have to be reversed: they would have to get information slanted in the opposite direction. For the facts are never given immediately and never accessible immediately; they are established, 'mediated' by those who made them; the truth, 'the whole truth' surpasses these facts and requires the rupture with their appearance. This rupture – prerequisite and token of all freedom of thought and of speech – cannot be accomplished within the established framework of abstract tolerance and spurious objectivity because these are precisely the factors which pre-condition the mind *against* the rupture.

The factual barriers which totalitarian democracy erects against the efficacy of qualitative dissent are weak and pleasant enough compared with the practices of a dictatorship which claims to educate the people in the truth. With all its limitations and distortions, democratic tolerance is under all circumstances more humane than an institutionalized intolerance which sacrifices the rights and liberties of the living generations for the sake of future generations. The question is whether this is the only alternative. I shall presently try to suggest the direction in which an answer may be sought. In any case, the contrast is not between democracy in the abstract and dictatorship in the abstract.

Democracy is a form of government which fits very different types of society (this holds true even for a democracy with universal suffrage and equality before the law), and the human costs of a democracy are always and everywhere those exacted by the society whose government it is. Their range extends all the way from normal exploitation, poverty and insecurity to the victims of wars, police actions, military aid, etc., in which the society is engaged – and not only to the victims within its own frontiers. These considerations can never justify the exacting of different sacrifices and different victims on behalf of a future better society, but they do allow weighing the costs involved in the perpetuation of an existing society against the risk of promoting alternatives which offer a reasonable chance of pacification and liberation. Surely, no government can be expected to foster its own subversion, but in a democracy such a right is vested in the people (i.e. in the majority of the people). This means that the ways should not be blocked on which a subversive majority could develop, and if they are blocked by organized repression and indoctrination, their reopening may require apparently undemocratic means. They would include the withdrawal of toleration of speech and assembly from groups and movements which promote aggressive policies, armament, chauvinism, discrimination on the grounds of race and religion, or which oppose the extension of public services, social security, medical care, etc. Moreover, the restoration of freedom of thought may necessitate new and rigid restrictions on teachings and practices in the educational institutions which, by their very methods and concepts, serve to enclose the mind within the established universe of discourse and behaviour – thereby precluding *a priori* a rational evaluation of the alternatives. And to the degree to which freedom of thought involves the struggle against inhumanity, restoration of such freedom would also imply intolerance toward scientific research in the interest of deadly 'deterrents', of abnormal human endurance under inhuman conditions, etc. I shall presently discuss the question as to who is to decide on the distinction between liberating and repressive, human and inhuman teachings and practices; I have already suggested that this distinction is not a matter of value-preference but of rational criteria.

While the reversal of the trend in the educational enterprise at least could conceivably be enforced by the students and teachers themselves, and thus be self-imposed, the systematic withdrawal of tolerance toward regressive and repressive opinions and movements could only be envisaged as results of large-scale pressure which would amount to an upheaval. In other words, it would presuppose that which is still to be accomplished: the reversal of the trend. However, resistance at particular occasions, boycott, non-participation at the local and small-group level may perhaps prepare the ground. The subversive character of the restoration of freedom appears most clearly in that dimension of society where false tolerance and free enterprise do perhaps the most serious and lasting damage, namely in business and publicity. Against the emphatic insistence on the part of spokesmen for labour, I maintain that practices such as planned obsolescence, collusion between union leadership and management, slanted publicity are not simply imposed from above on a powerless rank and file, but are *tolerated* by them – and the consumer at large.

However, it would be ridiculous to speak of a possible withdrawal of tolerance with respect to these practices and to the ideologies promoted by them. For they pertain to the basis on which the repressive affluent society rests and reproduces itself and its vital defences – their removal would be that total revolution which this society so effectively repels.

To discuss tolerance in such a society means to re-examine the issue of violence and the traditional distinction between violent and non-violent action. The discussion should not, from the beginning, be clouded by ideologies which serve the perpetuation of violence. Even in the advanced centres of civilization, violence actually prevails: it is practised by the police, in the prisons and mental institutions, in the fight against racial minorities; it is carried, by the defenders of metropolitan freedom, into the backward countries. This violence indeed breeds violence. But to refrain from violence in the face of vastly superior violence is one thing, to renounce *a priori* violence against violence, on ethical or psychological grounds (because it may antagonize sympathizers) is another. Non-violence is normally not only preached to but exacted from the weak – it is a necessity rather than a virtue, and normally it does not seriously harm the case of the strong. (Is the case of India an exception? There, passive resistance was carried through on a massive scale, which disrupted, or threatened to disrupt, the economic life of the country. Quantity turns into quality: on such a scale, passive resistance is no longer passive – it ceases to be non-violent. The same holds true for the General Strike.) Robespierre's distinction between the terror of liberty and the terror of despotism, and his moral glorification of the former belongs to the most convincingly condemned aberrations, even if the white terror was more bloody than the red terror. The comparative evaluation in terms of the number of victims is the quantifying approach which reveals the man-made horror throughout history that made violence a necessity. In terms of historical function, there is a difference between revolutionary and reactionary violence, between violence practised by the oppressed and by the oppressors. In terms of ethics, both forms of violence are inhuman and evil – but since when is history made in accordance with ethical standards? To start applying them at the point where the oppressed rebel against the oppressors, the have-nots against the haves is serving the cause of actual violence by weakening the protest against it.

Comprenez enfin ceci: si la violence a commencé ce soir, si l'exploitation ni l'oppression n'ont jamais existé sur terre, peut-être la non-violence affichée peut apaiser la querelle. Mais si le régime tout entier et jusqu'à vos non-violentes pensées sont conditionnées par une oppression millénaire, votre passivité ne sert qu'à vous ranger du côté des oppresseurs.[3]

The very notion of false tolerance, and the distinction between right and wrong limitations on tolerance, between progressive and regressive indoctrination, revolutionary and reactionary violence demands the statement of criteria for its validity. These standards must be prior to whatever constitutional and legal criteria are set up and applied in an existing society (such as 'clear and present danger', and other established definitions of civil rights and liberties), for such definitions themselves presuppose standards of freedom and repression as applicable or not applicable in the respective society: they are specifications of more general concepts. By whom, and according to what standards, can the political distinction between true and false, progressive and regressive (for in this sphere, these pairs are equivalent) be made and its validity be justified? At the outset, I propose that the question cannot be answered in terms of the alternative between democracy and dictatorship, according to which, in the latter, one individual or group, without any effective control from below, arrogate to themselves the decision. Historically, even in the most democratic democracies, the vital and final decisions affecting the society as a whole have been made, constitutionally or in fact, by one or several groups without effective control by the people themselves. The ironical question: who educates the educators (i.e. the political leaders) also applies to democracy. The only authentic alternative and negation of dictatorship (with respect to this question) would be a society in which 'the people' have become autonomous individuals, freed from the repressive requirements of a struggle for existence in the interest of domination, and as such human beings choosing their government and

3. Sartre (1961), Preface to Frantz Fanon.

determining their life. Such a society does not yet exist anywhere. In the meantime, the question must be treated *in abstracto* – abstraction, not from the historical possibilities, but from the realities of the prevailing societies.

I suggested that the distinction between true and false tolerance, between progress and regression can be made rationally on empirical grounds. The real possibilities of human freedom are relative to the attained stage of civilization. They depend on the material and intellectual resources available at the respective stage, and they are quantifiable and calculable to a high degree. So are, at the stage of advanced industrial society, the most rational ways of using these resources and distributing the social product with priority on the satisfaction of vital needs and with a minimum of toil and injustice. In other words, it is possible to define the direction in which prevailing institutions, policies, opinions would have to be changed in order to improve the chance of a peace which is not identical with cold war and a little hot war, and a satisfaction of needs which does not feed on poverty, oppression and exploitation. Consequently, it is also possible to identify policies, opinions, movements which would promote this chance, and those which would do the opposite. Suppression of the regressive ones is a prerequisite for the strengthening of the progressive ones.

The question, who is qualified to make all these distinctions, definitions, identifications for the society as a whole, has now one logical answer, namely, everyone 'in the maturity of his faculties' as a human being, everyone who has learned to think rationally and autonomously. The answer to Plato's educational dictatorship is the democratic educational dictatorship of free men. John Stuart Mill's conception of the *res publica* is not the opposite of Plato's: the liberal too demands the authority of Reason not only as an intellectual but also as a political power. In Plato, rationality is confined to the small number of philosopher-kings; in Mill, every rational human being participates in the discussion and decision – but only as a rational being. Where society has entered the phase of total administration and indoctrination, this would be a small number indeed, and not necessarily that of the elected representatives of the people. The problem is not that of an educational dictatorship, but that of breaking the tyranny of public opinion and its makers in the closed society.

However, granted the empirical rationality of the distinction between progress and regression, and granted that it may be applicable to tolerance, and may justify strongly discriminatory tolerance on political grounds (cancellation of the liberal creed of free and equal discussion), another impossible consequence would follow. I said that, by virtue of its inner logic, withdrawal of tolerance from regressive movements, and discriminatory tolerance in favour of progressive tendencies would be tantamount to the 'official' promotion of subversion. The historical calculus of progress (which is actually the calculus of the prospective reduction of cruelty, misery, suppression) seems to involve the calculated choice between two forms of political violence: that on the part of the legally constituted powers (by their legitimate action, or by their tacit consent, or by their inability to prevent violence), and that on the part of potentially subversive movements. Moreover, with respect to the latter, a policy of unequal treatment would protect radicalism on the Left against that on the Right. Can the historical calculus be reasonably extended to the justification of one form of violence as against another? Or better (since 'justification' carries a moral connotation), is there historical evidence to the effect that the social origin and impetus of violence (from among the ruled or the ruling classes, the have or the have-nots, the Left or the Right) is in a demonstrable relation to progress (as defined above)?

With all the qualifications of a hypothesis based on an 'open' historical record, it seems that the violence emanating from the rebellion of the oppressed classes broke the historical continuum of injustice, cruelty, and silence for a brief moment, brief but explosive enough to achieve an increase in the scope of freedom and justice, and a better and more equitable distribution of misery and oppression in a new social system – in one word: progress in civilization. The English civil wars, the French Revolution, the Chinese and the Cuban Revolutions may illustrate the hypothesis. In contrast, the one historical change from one social system to another, marking the beginning of a new period in civilization, which was *not* sparked and driven by an effective movement 'from below', namely, the collapse of the Roman Empire in the West, brought about a long period of regression for long centuries, until a new, higher period of civilization was painfully born in the violence of the heretic revolts of the thirteenth century and in the peasant and labourer revolts of the fourteenth century.[4]

With respect to historical violence emanating from among ruling classes, no such relation to progress seems to obtain. The long series of dynastic and imperialist wars, the liquidation of Spartacus in Germany in 1919, Fascism and Nazism did not break but rather tightened and streamlined the continuum of suppression. I said emanating 'from among ruling classes': to be sure, there is hardly any organized violence from above that does not mobilize and activate mass support from below; the decisive question is, on behalf of and in the interest of which groups and institutions is such violence released? And the answer is not necessarily *ex post facto*: in the historical examples just mentioned, it could be and was anticipated whether the movement would serve the revamping of the old order or the emergence of the new.

Liberating tolerance, then, would mean intolerance against movements from the Right and toleration of movements from the Left. As to the scope of this tolerance and intolerance: . . . it would extend to the stage of action as well as of discussion and propaganda, of deed as well as of word. The traditional criterion of clear and present danger seems no longer adequate to a stage where the whole society is in the situation of the theatre audience when somebody cries: 'fire'. It is a situation in which the total catastrophe could be triggered off any moment, not only by a technical error, but also by a rational miscalculation of risks, or by a rash speech of one of the leaders. In past and different circumstances, the speeches of the Fascist and Nazi leaders were the immediate prologue to the massacre. The distance between the propaganda and the action, between the organization and its release on the people had become too short. But the spreading of the word could have been stopped before it was too late: if

4. In modern times, fascism has been a consequence of the transition to industrial society *without* a revolution. See Barrington Moore (1963).

democratic tolerance had been withdrawn when the future leaders started their campaign, mankind would have had a chance of avoiding Auschwitz and a world war.

The whole post-fascist period is one of clear and present danger. Consequently, true pacification requires the withdrawal of tolerance before the deed, at the stage of communication in word, print, and picture. Such extreme suspension of the right of free speech and free assembly is indeed justified only if the whole of society is in extreme danger. I maintain that our society is in such an emergency situation, and that it has become the normal state of affairs. Different opinions and 'philosophies' can no longer compete peacefully for adherence and persuasion on rational grounds: the 'market-place of ideas' is organized and delimited by those who determine the national and the individual interest. In this society, for which the ideologists have proclaimed the 'end of ideology', the false consciousness has become the general consciousness – from the government down to its last objects. The small and powerless minorities which struggle against the false consciousness and its beneficiaries must be helped: their continued existence is more important than the preservation of abused rights and liberties which grant constitutional powers to those who oppress these minorities. It should be evident by now that the exercise of civil rights by those who don't have them presupposes the withdrawal of civil rights from those who prevent their exercise, and that liberation of the Damned of the Earth presupposes suppression not only of their old but also of their new masters.

Withdrawal of tolerance from regressive movements *before* they can become active; intolerance even toward thought, opinion, and word, and finally, intolerance in the opposite direction, that is, toward the self-styled conservatives, to the political Right – these anti-democratic notions respond to the actual development of the democratic society which has destroyed the basis for universal tolerance. The conditions under which tolerance can again become a liberating and humanizing force have still to be created. When tolerance mainly serves the protection and preservation of a repressive society, when it serves to neutralize opposition and to render men immune against other and better forms of life, then tolerance has been perverted. And when this perversion starts in the mind of the individual, in his consciousness, his needs, when heteronomous interests occupy him before he can experience his servitude, then the efforts to counteract his dehumanization must begin at the place of entrance, there where the false consciousness takes form (or rather: is systematically formed) – it must begin with stopping the words and images which feed this consciousness. To be sure, this is censorship, even pre-censorship, but openly directed against the more or less hidden censorship that permeates the free media. Where the false consciousness has become prevalent in national and popular behaviour, it translates itself almost immediately into practice: the safe distance between ideology and reality, repressive thought and repressive action, between the word of destruction and the deed of destruction is dangerously shortened. Thus, the break through the false consciousness may provide the Archimedean point for a larger emancipation – at an infinitesimally small spot, to be sure, but it is on the enlargement of such small spots that the chance of change depends.

The forces of emancipation cannot be identified with any social class which, by virtue of its material condition, is free from false consciousness. Today, they are hopelessly dispersed throughout the society, and the fighting minorities and isolated groups are often in opposition to their own leadership. In the society at large, the mental space for denial and reflection must first be recreated. Repulsed by the concreteness of the administered society, the effort of emancipation becomes 'abstract'; it is reduced to facilitating the recognition of what is going on, to freeing language from the tyranny of the Orwellian syntax and logic, to developing the concepts that comprehend reality. More than ever, the preposition holds true that progress in freedom demands progress in the *consciousness* of freedom. Where the mind has been made into a subject-object of politics and policies, intellectual autonomy, the realm of 'pure' thought has become a matter of *political education* (or rather: counter-education).

This means that previously neutral, value-free, formal aspects of learning and teaching now become, on their own grounds and in their own right, political: learning to know the facts, the whole truth, and to comprehend it is radical criticism throughout, intellectual subversion. In a world in which the human faculties and needs are arrested or perverted, autonomous thinking leads into a 'perverted world': contradiction and counter-image of the established world of repression. And this contradiction is not simply stipulated, is not simply the product of confused thinking or phantasy, but is the logical development of the given, the existing world. To the degree to which this development is actually impeded by the sheer weight of a repressive society and the necessity of making a living in it, repression invades the academic enterprise itself, even prior to all restrictions on academic freedom. The pre-empting of the mind vitiates impartiality and objectivity: unless the student learns to think in the opposite direction, he will be inclined to place the facts into the predominant framework of values. Scholarship, i.e., the acquisition and communication of knowledge, prohibits the purification and isolation of facts from the context of the whole truth. An essential part of the latter is recognition of the frightening extent to which history is made and recorded by and for the victors, that is, the extent to which history was the development of oppression. And this oppression is in the facts themselves which it establishes; thus they themselves carry a negative value as part and aspect of their facticity. To treat the great crusades *against* humanity (like that against the Albigensians) with the same impartiality as the desperate struggles *for* humanity means neutralizing their opposite historical function, reconciling the executioners with their victims, distorting the record. Such spurious neutrality serves to reproduce acceptance of the dominion of the victors in the consciousness of man. Here, too, in the education of those who are not yet maturely integrated, in the mind of the young, the ground for liberating tolerance is still to be created.

Education offers still another example of spurious, abstract tolerance in the guise of concreteness and truth: it is epitomized in the concept of self-actualization. From the permissiveness of all sorts of licence to the child, to the constant psychological concern with the personal problems of the student, a large-scale movement is under way against the evils of repression and the need for being oneself. Frequently brushed aside is the question as to what has to be repressed before one can be a self, oneself.

The individual potential is first a negative one, a portion of the potential of his society: of aggression, guilt feeling, ignorance, resentment, cruelty which vitiate his life instincts. If the identity of the self is to be more than the immediate realization of this potential (undesirable for the individual as a human being), then it requires repression and sublimation, conscious transformation. This process involves at each stage (to use the ridiculed terms which here reveal their succinct concreteness) the negation of the negation, mediation of the immediate, and identity is no more and no less than this process. 'Alienation' is the constant and essential element of identity, the objective side of the subject – and not, as it is made to appear today, a disease, a psychological condition. Freud well knew the difference between progressive and regressive, liberating and destructive repression. The publicity of self-actualization promotes the removal of the one and the other, it promotes existence in that immediacy which, in a repressive society, is (to use another Hegelian term) bad immediacy (*schlechte Unmittelbarkeit*). It isolates the individual from the one dimension where he could 'find himself': from his political existence, which is at the core of his entire existence. Instead, it encourages nonconformity and letting-go in ways which leave the real engines of repression in the society entirely intact, which even strengthen these engines by substituting the satisfactions of private and personal rebellion for a more than private and personal, and therefore more authentic, opposition. The desublimation involved in this sort of self-actualization is itself repressive inasmuch as it weakens the necessity and the power of the intellect, the catalytic force of that unhappy consciousness which does not revel in the archetypal personal release of frustration – hopeless resurgence of the Id which will sooner or later succumb to the omnipresent rationality of the administered world – but which recognizes the horror of the whole in the most private frustration and actualizes itself in this recognition.

I have tried to show how the changes in advanced democratic societies, which have undermined the basis of economic and political liberalism, have also altered the liberal function of tolerance. The tolerance which was the great achievement of the liberal era is still professed and (with strong qualifications) practised, while the economic and political process is subjected to an ubiquitous and effective administration in accordance with the predominant interests. The result is an objective contradiction between the economic and political structure on the one side, and the theory and practice of toleration on the other. The altered social structure tends to weaken the effectiveness of tolerance toward dissenting and oppositional movements and to strengthen conservative and reactionary forces. Equality of tolerance becomes abstract, spurious. With the actual decline of dissenting forces in the society, the opposition is insulated in small and frequently antagonistic groups who, even where tolerated within the narrow limits set by the hierarchical structure of society, are powerless while they keep within these limits. But the tolerance shown to them is deceptive and promotes co-ordination. And on the firm foundations of a co-ordinated society all but closed against qualitative change, tolerance itself serves to contain such change rather than to promote it.

These same conditions render the critique of such tolerance abstract and academic, and the proposition that the balance between tolerance towards the Right and towards the Left would have to be radically redressed in order to restore the liberating function of tolerance becomes only an unrealistic speculation. Indeed, such a redressing seems to be tantamount to the establishment of a 'right of resistance' to the point of subversion. There is not, there cannot be any such right for any group or individual against a constitutional government sustained by a majority of the population. But I believe that there is a 'natural right' of resistance for oppressed and overpowered minorities to use extra-legal means if the legal ones have proved to be inadequate. Law and order are always and everywhere the law and order which protect the established hierarchy; it is nonsensical to invoke the absolute authority of this law and this order against those who suffer from it and struggle against it – not for personal advantage and revenge, but for their share of humanity. There is no other judge over them than the constituted authorities, the police, and their own conscience. If they use violence, they do not start a new chain of violence but try to break an established one. Since they will be punished, they know the risk, and when they are willing to take it, no third person, and least of all the educator and intellectual, has the right to preach them abstention.

Postscript 1968

Under the conditions prevailing in this country, tolerance does not, and cannot, fulfil the civilizing function attributed to it by the liberal protagonists of democracy, namely, protection of dissent. The progressive historical force of tolerance lies in its extension to those modes and forms of dissent which are not committed to the *status quo* of society, and not confined to the institutional framework of the established society. Consequently, the idea of tolerance implies the necessity, for the dissenting group or individuals, to become illegitimate if and when the established legitimacy prevents and counteracts the development of dissent. This would be the case not only in a totalitarian society, under a dictatorship, in one-party states, but also in a democracy (representative, parliamentary, or 'direct') where the majority does not result from the development of independent thought and opinion but rather from the monopolistic or oligopolistic administration of public opinion, without terror and (normally) without censorship. In such cases, the majority is self-perpetuating while perpetuating the vested interests which *made* it a majority. In its very structure this majority is 'closed', petrified; it repels *a priori* any change other than changes within the system. But this means that the majority is no longer justified in claiming the democratic title of the best guardian of the common interest. And such a majority is all but the opposite of Rousseau's 'general will': it is composed, not of individuals who, in their political functions, have made effective 'abstraction' from their private interests, but, on the contrary, of individuals who have effectively identified their private interests with their political functions. And the representatives of this majority, in ascertaining and executing its will ascertain and execute the will of the vested interests which have formed the majority. The ideology of democracy hides its lack of substance.

In the United States, this tendency goes hand in hand with the monopolistic or oligopolistic concentration of capital in the formation of public opinion, i.e. of the majority. The chance of influencing, in any effective way, this majority is at a price, in dollars, totally out of reach of the radical opposition. Here too, free competition and exchange of ideas have become a farce. The Left has no equal voice, no equal access to the mass media and their public facilities – not because a conspiracy excludes it, but because, in good old capitalist fashion, it does not have the required purchasing power. And the Left does not have the purchasing power because it is the Left. These conditions impose upon the radical minorities a strategy which is in essence a refusal to allow the continuous functioning of allegedly indiscriminate but in fact discriminate tolerance, for example, a strategy of protesting against the alternate matching of a spokesman for the Right (or Centre) with one for the Left. Not 'equal' but *more* representation of the Left would be equalization of the prevailing inequality.

Within the solid framework of pre-established inequality and power, tolerance is practised indeed. Even outrageous opinions are expressed, outrageous incidents are televised; and the critics of established policies are interrupted by the same number of commercials as the conservative advocates. Are these interludes supposed to counteract the sheer weight, magnitude, and continuity of system-publicity, indoctrination which operates playfully through the endless commercials as well as through the entertainment?

Given this situation, I suggested in *Repressive Tolerance* the practice of discriminating tolerance in an inverse direction, as a means of shifting the balance between Right and Left by restraining the liberty of the Right, thus counteracting the pervasive inequality of freedom (unequal opportunity of access to the means of democratic persuasion) and strengthening the oppressed against the oppressor. Tolerance would be restricted with respect to movements of a demonstrably aggressive or destructive character (destructive of the prospects for peace, justice, and freedom for all). Such discrimination would also be applied to movements opposing the extension of social legislation to the poor, weak, disabled. As against the virulent denunciations that such a policy would do away with the sacred liberalistic principle of equality for 'the other side', I maintain that there are issues where either there is no 'other side' in any more than a formalistic sense, or where 'the other side' is demonstrably 'regressive' and impedes possible improvement of the human condition. To tolerate propaganda for inhumanity vitiates the goals not only of liberalism but of every progressive political philosophy.

I presupposed the existence of demonstrable criteria for aggressive, regressive, destructive forces. If the final democratic criterion of the declared opinion of the majority no longer (or rather not yet) prevails, if vital ideas, values, and ends of human progress no longer (or rather not yet) enter, as competing equals, the formation of public opinion, if the people are no longer (or rather not yet) sovereign but 'made' by the real sovereign powers – is there any alternative other than the dictatorship of an 'élite' over the people? For the opinion of people (usually designated as The People), who are unfree in the very faculties in which liberalism saw the roots of freedom: independent thought and independent speech, can carry no overriding validity and authority – even if The People constitute the overwhelming majority.

If the choice were between genuine democracy and dictatorship, democracy would certainly be preferable. But democracy does not prevail. The radical critics of the existing political process are thus readily denounced as advocating an 'élitism', a dictatorship of intellectuals as an alternative. What we have in fact is government, representative government by a non-intellectual minority of politicians, generals, and businessmen. The record of this 'élite' is not very promising, and political prerogatives for the intelligentsia may not necessarily be worse for the society as a whole.

In any case, John Stuart Mill, not exactly an enemy of liberal and representative government, was not so allergic to the political leadership of the intelligentsia as the contemporary guardians of semi-democracy are. Mill believed that 'individual mental superiority' justifies 'reckoning one person's opinion as equivalent to more than one':

> Until there shall have been devised, and until opinion is willing to accept, some mode of plural voting which may assign to education as such the degree of superior influence due to it, and sufficient as a counterpoise to the numerical weight of the least educated class, for so

long the benefits of completely universal suffrage cannot be obtained without bringing with them, as it appears to me, more than equivalent evils.[5]

'Distinction in favour of education, right in itself', was also supposed to preserve 'the educated from the class legislation of the uneducated', without enabling the former to practise a class legislation of their own.[6]

Today, these words have understandably an anti-democratic, 'élitist' sound – understandably because of their dangerously radical implications. For if 'education' is more and other than training, learning, preparing for the existing society, it means not only enabling man to know and understand the facts which make up reality but also to know and understand the factors that establish the facts so that he can change their inhuman reality. And such humanistic education would involve the 'hard' sciences ('hard' as in the 'hardware' bought by the Pentagon?), would free them from their destructive direction. In other words, such education would indeed badly serve the Establishment, and to give political prerogatives to the men and women thus educated would indeed be anti-democratic in the terms of the Establishment. But these are not the only terms.

However, the alternative to the established semi-democratic process is *not* a dictatorship or élite, no matter how intellectual and intelligent, but the struggle for a real democracy. Part of this struggle is the fight against an ideology of tolerance which, in reality, favours and fortifies the conservation of the *status quo* of inequality and discrimination. For this struggle, I proposed the practice of discriminating tolerance. To be sure, this practice already presupposes the radical goal which it seeks to achieve. I committed this *petitio principii* in order to combat the pernicious ideology that tolerance is already institutionalized in this society. The tolerance which is the life element, the token of a free society, will never be the gift of the powers that be; it can, under the prevailing conditions of tyranny by the majority, only be won in the sustained effort of radical minorities, willing to break this

5 *Considerations on Representative Government*, Gateway Editions, Chicago, 1962, p. 183.

6. ibid., p. 181.

tyranny and to work for the emergence of a free and sovereign majority – minorities intolerant, militantly intolerant and disobedient to the rules of behaviour which tolerate destruction and suppression.

References

BARRINGTON MOORE JR (1963), *The Social Origins of Dictatorship and Democracy*, Allen Lane.
MILL, J. S. (1861), *Considerations on Representative Government*. This edition published by Gateway Editions, Chicago, 1962.
SARTRE, J.-P. (1961), preface to Frantz Fanon, *The Wretched of the Earth*, Penguin, 1970.
WIND, E. (1963), *Art and Anarchy*, Faber & Faber.

16 Jürgen Habermas

Theory and Practice in a Scientific Civilization

Excerpt from Jürgen Habermas, *Theory and Practice*, Heinemann, 1974, pp. 253–6, 263–76. First published in 1963. English translation

In the major tradition of philosophy, the relation of theory and practice always referred to the good and the righteous – as well as the 'true' – and to the life, both private and collective, of individuals as well as of citizens. In the eighteenth century this dimension of a theoretically guided praxis of life was extended by the philosophy of history. Since then, theory, directed toward praxis and at the same time dependent on it, no longer embraces the natural, authentic, or essential actions and institutions of a human race constant in its essential nature; instead, theory now deals with the objective, overall complex of development of a human species which produces itself, which is as yet only destined to attain its essence: humanity. What has remained is theory's claim of providing orientation in right action, but the realization of the good, happy, and rational life has been stretched out along the vertical axis of world-history; praxis has been extended to cover stages of emancipation. For this rational praxis is now interpreted as liberation from an externally imposed compulsion, just as the theory which is guided by this interest of liberation is interpreted as enlightenment. The cognitive interest of this enlightenment theory is declaredly critical; it presupposes a specific experience, which is set down in Hegel's *Phenomenology of Mind*, just as it is in Freud's psychoanalysis – the experience of an emancipation by means of critical insight into relationships of power, the objectivity of which has as its source solely that the relationships have not been seen through. Critical reason gains power analytically over dogmatic inhibition.[1]

1. I have treated this since in *Knowledge and Human Interests*, Heinemann Educational, 1972.

Reason takes up a partisan position in the controversy between critique and dogmatism, and with each new stage of emancipation it wins a further victory. In this kind of practical reason, insight and the explicit interest in liberation by means of reflection converge. The higher level of reflection coincides with a step forward in the progress toward the autonomy of the individual, with the elimination of suffering and the furthering of concrete happiness. Reason involved in the argument against dogmatism has definitely taken up this interest as its own – it does not define the moment of decision as external to its sphere. Rather, the decisions of the subjects are measured rationally against that one objective decision, which is required by the interest of reason itself. Reason has not as yet renounced the will to the rational.

Now this constellation of dogmatism, reason, and decision has changed profoundly since the eighteenth century, and exactly to the degree to which the positive sciences have become productive forces in social development. For as our civilization has become increasingly scientific, the dimension within which theory was once directed towards praxis has become correspondingly constructed. The laws of self-reproduction demand of an industrially advanced society that it look after its survival on the escalating scale of a continually expanded technical control over nature and a continually refined administration of human beings and their relations to each other by means of social organization. In this system, science, technology, industry, and administration interlock in a circular process. In this process the relationship of theory to praxis can now only assert itself as the purposive-rational application of techniques assured by empirical science. The social potential of science is reduced to the powers of technical control – its potential for enlightened action is no longer considered. The empirical, analytical sciences produce technical recommendations, but they furnish no answer to practical questions. The claim by which theory was once related to praxis has become dubious. Emancipation by means of enlightenment is replaced by instruction in control over objective or objectified processes. Socially effective theory is no longer directed towards the consciousness of human beings who live together and discuss matters with each other, but to the behaviour of human beings who manipulate. As a productive force of industrial development, it changes the basis of human life, but it no longer reaches out critically beyond this basis to raise life itself, for the sake of life, to another level.

But, of course, the real difficulty in the relation of theory to praxis does not arise from this new function of science as a technological force, but rather from the fact that we are no longer able to distinguish between practical and technical power.[2] Yet even a civilization that has been rendered scientific is not granted dispensation from practical questions; therefore a peculiar danger arises when the process of scientification transgresses the limit of technical questions, without, however, departing from the level of reflection of a rationality confined to the technological horizon. For then no attempt at all is made to attain a rational consensus on the part of citizens concerning the practical control of their destiny. Its place is taken by the attempt to attain technical control over history by perfecting the administration of society, an attempt that is just as impractical as it is unhistorical. When theory was still related to praxis in a genuine sense, it conceived of society as a system of action by human beings, who communicate through speech and thus must realize social intercourse within the context of conscious communication. Through this communication they must form themselves into a collective subject of the whole, that is capable of action – otherwise, the fortunes of a society ever more rigidly rationalized in its particular parts must slip away as a whole from that rational cultivation, which they require all the more urgently. On the other hand, a theory which confuses control with action is no longer capable of such a perspective. It understands society as a nexus of behavioural modes, for which rationality is mediated solely by the understanding of socio-technical controls, but not by a coherent total consciousness – not by precisely that interested reason which can only attain practical power through the minds of politically enlightened citizens.

In industrially advanced society, research, technology, production, and administration have coalesced into a system which

2. See my investigation 'Technology and Science as Ideology', *Toward a Rational Society*, Heinemann Educational, 1971.

cannot be surveyed as a whole, but in which they are functionally interdependent. This has literally become the basis of our life. We are related to it in a peculiar manner, at the same time intimate and yet estranged. On the one hand, we are bound externally to this basis by a network of organizations and a chain of consumer goods; on the other hand, this basis is shut off from our knowledge, and even more from our reflection. The paradox of this state of affairs will, of course, only be recognized by a theory oriented toward practice, even though this paradox is so evident: the more the growth and change of society are determined by the most extreme rationality of processes of research, subject to a division of labour, the less rooted is this civilization, now rendered scientific, in the knowledge and conscience of its citizens. In this discrepancy, scientifically guided techniques and those of decision theory – and ultimately even cybernetically controlled techniques – encounter a limitation which they cannot overcome; this can only be altered by a change in the state of consciousness itself, by the practical effect of a theory which does not improve the manipulation of things and of reifications, but which instead advances the interest of reason in human adulthood, in the autonomy of action and in the liberation from dogmatism. This it achieves by means of the penetrating ideas of a persistent critique . . .

The positivistic isolation of reason and decision [Enscheidung]

Prior to positivism, critical knowledge referred to a scientific orientation in action. Even the knowledge of nature (physics in the classical sense) had its role to play with respect to praxis (to ethics and politics). However, after the empirical sciences of the new type, so successful since the time of Galileo, had attained a consciousness of themselves in positivism, and after analytic philosophy, inspired by the Vienna circle as well as by Peirce and Dewey, had explicated this self-understanding in terms of the philosophy of science, especially in the work of Carnap, Popper, and Morris,[3] the two cognitive functions were distinctly separated – and both deprived of their power of orientation for action.

The *affirmative* achievement of the modern sciences consists in

3. On the semiotics of Charles Morris see Apel (1959), pp. 161 ff., and Bubner *et al.* (1970), pp. 105–44.

statements about empirical uniformities. The hypothetical laws, gained from a deductive connection among statements and tested by controlled experiments, refer to regular co-variances of empirical variables in all the domains accessible inter-subjectively to experience. Under given individual initial conditions, universal laws of this kind serve as explanations. The theoretical statements which permit the causal explanation of effects, in the same way make possible the prediction of effects, given the causes. This predictive application of the theories of experimental science reveals the interest of knowledge which guides these generalizing sciences. As artisans were formerly guided, in working on their materials, by rules of experience which had been proven in the tradition of their trade, so in the same way engineers in all sectors can rely on such scientifically tested predictions in the choice of the means they employ, of their instruments and operations. To be sure, the reliability of the rules distinguished the exercise of technique [*techne*] in the old sense from what we call technique [technology] today. The function of the knowledge of modern science must therefore be understood in connection with the system of social labour: it extends and rationalizes our power of technical control over the objects or – which comes to the same thing – objectified processes of nature and society.

From this affirmative achievement of knowledge reduced to empirical science derives also its other function, its *critical achievement*. For when this type of science attains a monopoly in the guidance of rational action, then all competing claims to a scientific orientation for action must be rejected. This activity is now reserved for a positivistically circumscribed critique of ideology. It is directed against dogmatism in a new guise. Any theory that relates to praxis in any way other than by strengthening and perfecting the possibilities for purposive-rational action must now appear dogmatic. The methodology of the empirical sciences is tacitly but effectively rooted in a technical cognitive interest that excludes all other interests; consequently, all other relations to life praxis can be blocked out under the slogan of ethical neutrality or value-freedom. The economy in the selection of purposive-rational means which is guaranteed by conditional predictions in the form of technical recommendations is the sole admissible 'value',[4] and it too is not seen explicitly as a value, because it simply seems to coincide with rationality as such. In fact, we have here the formalization of one sole relevance to life, namely, the experience of success as feedback control, built into the systems of social labour and already realized in every successful elementary performance of labour.

According to the principles of an analytic philosophy of science, empirical questions which cannot be posed and solved in the form of technical tasks cannot therefore expect to receive a cogent theoretical answer. From the outset, all practical questions, which cannot be answered adequately by technical prescriptions, but which instead also require a self-understanding within their concrete situation, go beyond the cognitive interest invested in empirical science. The only type of science admitted by the positivistic approach is one that is not capable of investigating such questions rationally. And theories which in spite of that offer such solutions can be convicted of dogmatism by these criteria. The goal of a critique of ideology abbreviated in this manner is to respond to every dogmatic assertion with the decisionistic [*dezisionistisch*] thesis that practical questions (in our sense) cannot be discussed cogently and in the final instance must be simply decided upon, one way or another. The magic word for release from the spell of dogmatism is 'decision', decision that has been painfully isolated from reason: practical questions are not 'capable of truth' [*wahrheitsfähig*].

At this point in the positivistic confrontation with the new lineaments of dogmatism,[5] the inverse side of such a critique of ideology is revealed. It is correct in removing the veil of a false rationalization of what has been derationalized in value ethics [*Wertethik*] such as Scheler's and Hartmann's philosophy and in referring ideal objects back to the subjectivity of needs and inclinations, value judgements and commitments. But the result of

4. With the exception of the values immanent to science which are specified by the logical and methodological rules.

5. Ontological doctrines fall under this as well as dialectical ones, classical Natural Law as well as modern philosophies of history. It is not accidental that Popper places Plato in the ranks of the great dogmatists next to Hegel and Marx – as so-called Historicists.

its labours is monstrous enough: from the mainstream of rationality the pollutants, the sewage of emotionality, are filtered off and locked away hygienically in a storage basin – an imposing mass of subjective value qualities. Every single value appears as a meaningless agglomeration of meaning, stamped solely with the stigma of irrationality, so that the priority of one value over the other – thus the persuasiveness which a value claims with respect to action – simply cannot be rationally justified. Thus on this level the critique of ideology involuntarily furnishes the proof that progress of a rationalization limited in terms of empirical science to technical control is paid for with the corresponding growth of a mass of irrationality in the domain of praxis itself. For action still demands an orientation, as it did before. But now it is dissected into a rational implementation of techniques and strategies and an irrational choice of so-called value systems. The price paid for economy in the selection of means is a decisionism set wholly free in the selection of the highest-level goals.

The positivistically cleansed demarcation set between knowing and evaluating of course represents less a result than a problem. For the detached domain of values, norms, and decisions is now seized upon anew by philosophic interpretations, precisely on the basis of that division of labour shared with a reduced science.

The *subjective philosophy of value* is no longer as assured of the reference to meaning split off from the context of life, and hypostatized, as the objective value ethics was, which had immediately made of this a domain of ideal Being, transcending sense experience. It too sought to reclaim the existence of orders of value (Max Weber) and of forces of faith [*Glaubensmächte*] (Jaspers) in a sphere elevated above history. But scientifically controlled knowledge cannot simply be complemented by intuitive knowledge. The philosophic belief that remains midway between pure commitment and rational comprehension must pledge itself to one of the competing orders, without, however, revoking the pluralism of these orders, and without being able wholly to resolve the dogmatic core which is the source of its own life. Polemic, responsible although in principle undecidable, between philosophers, as the intellectually honest and existentially committed representatives of spiritual forces, appears as the only permissible form of discussion in this domain of practical questions. *Decisionism* as a world-view today no longer is ashamed to reduce norms to decisions. In non-cognitive Ethics, in the form of linguistic analysis, the decisionistic complement to a positivistically limited science is itself still conceived positivistically (R. M. Hare). As soon as certain fundamental value judgements are posited as axioms, a deductive chain of statements can be analysed cogently for each; at the same time, such principles themselves are not accessible to rational comprehension: their acceptance is based solely on a decision, a commitment. Such decisions can then be interpreted either in an existential-personal sense (Sartre) or in a public, political sense (Carl Schmitt) or institutionally from anthropological presuppositions (Gehlen), but the thesis remains the same: that decisions relevant to the praxis of life, whether they consist in the acceptance of values, in the selection of biographical [*lebensgeschichtlich*] design, or in the choice of an enemy, are not accessible to rational consideration and cannot form a rationally substantiated consensus. But if practical questions, eliminated from knowledge that has been reduced to empirical science, are dismissed in this way entirely from the controlling powers of rational investigation, if decisions on questions touching on the praxis of life must be pronounced as beyond any and every authority committed to rationality, then we cannot be astonished by the ultimate desperate attempt to secure socially binding pre-commitments on practical questions institutionally by a return to the closed world of mythical images and powers (Walter Bröcker). As Adorno and Horkheimer have shown, this complementing of positivism by *mythology* is not devoid of its logically compelling character, whose abysmal irony can be turned to laughter only by dialectics.

Sincere positivists, in whom such perspectives choke off laughter – thus, positivists who recoil before the half-concealed metaphysics of an objective value ethics and a subjective philosophy of value, as they do before the proclaimed irrationality of decisionism and the resurrection of mythology – seek their foothold in a reified critique of ideology with self-understanding, which, however, in the primitive form of nullifying projections, as developed from the time of Feuerbach down to Pareto, has itself congealed into the programme of a *Weltanschauung*. For the one thing that remains unclarified in all this radicalism is the root: the motive of the critique of ideology itself. If the goal of the latter consists only in differentiating in principle the scientifically rationalized shaping of reality from the 'value-laden forms of a world-view seeking interpretation of the world and self-interpretation of man'[6] – where such attempts at 'enlightening consciousness' cannot make a claim to demonstrable rationality – then the critique of ideology closes off for itself the possibility of justifying its own endeavours theoretically. For as critique, it too is making an attempt to enlighten consciousness, and certainly not to shape reality; it does not produce new techniques; at best it could prevent given techniques from being misapplied in the name of a merely alleged theory. But from what source does this critique draw its power, if reason divorced from commitment must be wholly devoid of any interest in an emancipation of consciousness from dogmatic constraint?

Certainly science must be allowed to exercise its affirmative function as knowledge – it is, so to speak, itself recognized as a value. This is served by the separation, performed by the critique of ideology, of knowing from commitment, and such a separation, once carried out, would have abolished dogmatism. But even so, science in its critical function of knowledge, the combating of dogmatism on a positivistic level, is possible only in the form of a science which reflects on itself and wills itself as an end – thus again a kind of committed reason, the *justified* possibility of which is precisely what the critique of ideology denies. If, on the other hand, it renounces a rational justification, then the dispute of reason with dogmatism itself remains a matter of dogmatic opinion: the impossibility of resolving dogmatism would be admitted at the outset. Behind this dilemma there lies, it seems to me, the problem that the critique of ideology must tacitly presuppose as its own motivation just what it attacks as dogmatic, namely, the convergence of reason and commitment – thus precisely an encompassing concept of rationality. To be sure, this hidden concept of a substantial rationality is conceived differently depending on whether the motivating reflection is persuaded

6. Topitsch (1961).

solely of the value of scientific techniques, or also of the significance of a scientific emancipation for adult autonomy; thus whether the critique of ideology is motivated on the level of understanding by an interest in the empirical sciences' increase in technical knowledge, or is motivated on the level of reason by an interest in enlightenment as such. Positivism is as little capable of distinguishing between these two concepts of rationality as it is capable, altogether, of being conscious that it itself implies just what it seeks to oppose externally – committed reason. But on this, or the proper distinction between these two forms, depends the relation of theory and praxis in a scientific civilization.

The partisanship of the critique of ideology in favour of technological rationality

No matter how much it insists on a separation of theory and commitment in its opposition to dogmatism, positivism's critique of ideology itself remains a form of committed reason: *nolens volens* it takes a partisan position in favour of progressive rationalization. In the case which we will analyse to begin with, its concern, without reservation, is for the extension and dissemination of technical knowledge. In its conflict with dogmatism, as understood by positivism, this critique removes traditionalistic barriers, and ideological barriers of any sort, which can inhibit the progress of the analytic-empirical sciences and the unlimited process of their utilization. This critique is not a value-neutral analysis; its underlying premise is the value of empirical science theories, and this not simply hypothetically, but normatively. For with its first analytic step it already presupposes, normatively, that behaving in accordance with technical recommendations is not only desirable, but also 'rational'. This implicit concept of reason can, of course, not be clarified by means of the conceptual resources of positivism itself, even though this concept expresses its intention. By positivistic criteria, rationality of conduct is a value which we simply decide to accept or reject. At the same time, according to these criteria, it can be demonstrated quite compellingly that rationality is a means for the realization of values, and therefore cannot itself be placed on the *same* level with all the other values. Indeed, the critique of ideology's preparation for rational conduct recommends rationality as the preferred – if not exclusive – means for the realization of values, because it guarantees the 'efficiency' or 'economy' of procedures. Both of these terms betray the interest of knowledge guiding the empirical sciences to be a technical one. They reveal that from the outset rationalization is confined within the limits posed by the system of social labour, that what it refers to is exactly the making available of objective and objectified processes. And in this the power of technical control remains wholly indifferent with respect to the possible value systems, in the service of which it is to be exercised. Efficiency and economy, which are the definition of this rationality, cannot, in turn, be themselves conceived as values, and yet, within the framework of positivism's understanding of itself, they can only be justified as though they were values. A critique of ideology whose sole goal is to make technological rationality prevail, cannot escape from this dilemma: it desires rationality as a value, because it has the advantage over all the other values of being implicit in the rational modes of procedure themselves. Because this value can be legitimized by pointing to the process of scientific investigation and its technical application, and does not have to be justified in terms of pure commitment alone, it has a preferential status as against all other values. The experience of the controlled success enjoyed by rational conduct exercises a rationally demonstrated compulsion toward the acceptance of such norms of conduct; thus even this limited rationality implies a decision in favour of rationality. In the critique of ideology, which at least tacitly realizes this, a particle of committed reason therefore remains active – in contradiction to the criteria by which it criticizes dogmatism. Because, no matter how perverted, it still remains of a piece with committed reason, it also entails consequences which violate its alleged neutrality towards any value systems whatsoever. On the contrary, the concept of rationality which it seeks to make prevail in its commitment ultimately implies an entire organization of society: one in which a technology become autonomous dictates a value system – namely, its own – to the domains of praxis it has usurped – and all in the name of value freedom.

I wish to distinguish four levels of rationalization, on which we extend our technical powers of control qualitatively. On the first two levels, technologies demand an exclusion of normative elements from the process of scientific argumentation; on the two subsequent levels, however, this elimination changes into its opposite in the subordination of values, which have first been pronounced irrational, to technological procedures, which then establish themselves as values.

The *first* level of rationalization depends on the methodological state of the empirical sciences. The mass of corroborated law-like hypotheses determines the extent of possible rational conduct. In this is involved technological rationality in the strict sense: we employ techniques placed at our disposal by science for the realization of goals. If, however, there is a choice between actions of equal technical appropriateness, a rationalization on the *second* level is required. The translation of technical recommendations into practice – thus the technical utilization of theories of the empirical sciences – is also to be subject to the conditions of technological rationality. But the information furnished by empirical science is not sufficient for a rational choice between means which are functionally equivalent, given concrete goals, and which are to be realized within the framework of a value system. Thus instead, this relation between alternative techniques and given goals, on the one hand, and value systems and maxims for reaching decisions, on the other, is clarified by decision theory.[7] It analyses the possible decisions normatively in accordance with a rationality of choice defined as 'economical' or 'efficient'. But in so doing, rationality refers solely to the form of the decisions, and not to objective situations and actual results.[8]

On the first two levels, the rationality of conduct enforces an isolation of values, which are removed from any and every cogent discussion, and can only be related to given techniques and concrete goals in the form of hypothetically entertained impera-

7. Gäfgen (1963).

8. 'The result of the decision must by no means appear as "reasonable" in the ordinary sense, as the actor may have a value system, which though it is coherent in itself, may appear absurd in comparison to that of other actors. Such absurdity can only be defined by comparison to a standard of normality of values and goals . . . this kind of irrationality refers to the content and not to the form of the decisions.' ibid., pp. 26 ff.

tives; these relations are accessible to rational calculation, because they remain external to the values rendered irrational as such. 'What is designated as a value system here is thus a system of rules which prescribe how the consequences described by the information system are to be evaluated *on the basis of the value perceptions* [*Wertempfindungen*] of the actor.'[9] The subjectivistic reduction of the interests which are decisive in the orientation for action to 'sentiments' or 'perceptions', which cannot be rationalized beyond that, is a precise expression for the fact that the value freedom central to the technological concept of rationality functions within the system of social labour, and that all the other interests of the practice of life are subordinated for the benefit of the sole interest in efficiency and economy in the utilization of means. The competing perspectives of interest, hypostatized to values, are excluded from discussion. Revealingly enough, according to the criteria of technological rationality, agreement on a collective value system can never be achieved by means of enlightened discussion carried on in public politics, thus by way of a consensus rationally arrived at, but only by summation or compromise – values are in principle beyond discussion.[10] Naturally, the decision-theoretical assumption of 'autonomous' value systems is not tenable in practice. The institution of formal rationality of choice, thus an extension of technological thinking to the selection of scientific techniques, changes the previously given value systems themselves. By this I mean not only the systematization of value conceptions required by this decision-theoretical analysis; I mean above all the re-formulation or even total devaluation of traditional norms, which fail to function as principles of orientation for a technical realization of concrete goals. The dialectical relation between values which originate in specific configurations of interest and techniques for the satisfaction of value-oriented needs is evident: just as values become depreciated as ideological and then become extinct, when they have lost their connection with a technically adequate satisfaction of real needs over a longer period, so inversely new techniques can form new value systems within changed configurations of interest. As is well known, Dewey was able to derive from the

9. ibid., p. 99.   10. ibid. pp. 176 ff.

interconnection of values with technical knowledge the expectation that the deployment of continually multiplied and improved techniques would not remain bound solely to the [existing] orientation of values, but also would subject the values themselves indirectly to a pragmatic test of their viability. Only because this interrelationship between traditional values and scientific techniques, which decision theory neglects, exists, can Dewey ask: 'How shall we employ what we know to direct our practical behaviour so as to test these beliefs and make possible better ones? The question is seen as it has always been empirically: What shall we do to make objects having value more secure in existence?'[11] This question can be answered in the sense of a reason which is interested in enlightenment; in any case, that is the sense in which Dewey posed it. Meanwhile, we first have to deal with the alternative answer, which subjects even the formation of value systems to technological rationality. With that we reach the *third* level of rationalization.

The latter extends to strategic situations, in which rational conduct in the face of an opponent who also acts rationally is to be calculated. Both adversaries pursue competing interests; in the case of a strictly competitive situation, they evaluate the same consequences according to inverse series of preferences, no matter whether the value systems correspond or not. Such a situation demands a far-reaching rationalization. Those acting do not only wish to gain control technically over a specific field of events by means of scientific prediction, but also to gain the same control over situations of rational indeterminacy; they cannot inform themselves about the conduct of the opponent empirically in the same manner as about processes of nature, by means of law-like hypotheses; their information remains incomplete, not merely to a degree but in principle, because the opponent also has a choice of alternative strategies and thus is not confined to unambiguously determined reactions. What interests us, however, is not the game-theoretical solution of the problem posed, but the peculiar technical compulsion which, in addition, such strategic situations exercise on value systems. A basic value also enters into the technical task itself, namely, successful self-assertion against an

11. Dewey (1960), p. 43.

opponent, the securing of survival. The originally invested values, that is, those value systems with which decision theory initially is solely occupied, are then relativized in terms of this strategic value, by which the game or the conflict is given its orientation.

As soon as the game theory's assumption concerning strategic situations is generalized to cover all decision-making situations, decision-making processes can be analysed under political conditions on all occasions – here I use 'political' in the sense of the tradition from Hobbes to Carl Schmitt, in the sense of existential self-assertion. Then ultimately it is sufficient to reduce all value systems to an, as it were, biological basic value, and to pose the problem of decision-making generally, in the following form: how must the systems by which decisions are made – whether by individuals or groups, specific institutions or entire societies – be organized in order to meet the basic value of survival in a given situation and to avoid risks. The goal functions, which together with the initially invested values furnished the programme, here disappear in favour of formalized goal variables, such as stability or adaptability, which are bound solely to a quasi-biological basic requirement of the system, that of reproducing life. To be sure, this self-programming of feedback systems only becomes possible on the *fourth* level of rationalization, as soon as it becomes possible to turn over the decision-making effort to a machine. Even if today there is a large class of problems for which machines can be utilized successfully in order to simulate the real case, still this last stage of rationalization as yet remains largely a fiction. However, it does reveal for the first time in its entirety the intention of a technological rationality extended over all the domains of praxis, and thereby the substantial concept of rationality, which the positivistic critique presupposes as its premise, and yet at the same time suppresses. Learning machines as cybernetic mechanisms for social organization can in principle take over such decision-making processes under political conditions. As soon as this threshold had been passed, the value systems excluded from the process of rationalization at a lower level would themselves also be rendered interchangeable in accordance with the criteria of rational behaviour; indeed, these values could only enter, as a liquid mass, into the adaptive procedures of a machine which stabilizes its own equilibrium and programmes itself because the values had previously been rendered irrational *qua* values.[12]

In a manuscript on the scientific and political significance of decision theory, Horst Rittel has drawn unmistakable conclusions for the fourth level of rationalization:

Value systems can no longer be regarded as stable over a longer period. What can be desired depends on what can be made possible, and what can be made possible depends on what one desires. Goals and utility functions are not independent variables. They are in reciprocal interaction with the scope of decision-making. Within broad limits conceptions of value can be directed. In the face of the uncertainty which marks the alternatives of future development, there is no prospect for seeking to set up rigid models of decision-making and to offer strategies for longer time periods . . . It proves more meaningful to view the problem of decision-making in a more general way and to look into the suitability of decision-making systems. How must an organization be constituted so that it will be equal to the uncertainty introduced by innovation and political vicissitudes? . . . Instead of assuming a specific decision-making system and a value system as definitely given, the suitability of this system for fulfilling its tasks must be investigated. What feedback mechanisms to its object system are necessary? What data about the object system are needed and to what degree of precision? What devices are necessary for the preparation of this data? Which value systems are at all consistent and guarantee chances for adaptation, and therefore for 'survival'?[13]

The negative Utopia of technical control over history would be fulfilled if one were to set up a learning automaton as a central system of societal control which would answer these questions cybernetically, thus by 'itself'.

The critique of ideology, which for the sake of resolving dogmatism and asserting technologically rational behaviour insistently separates reason from decisions of commitment, in the end automates the decisions according to the laws of the rationality thus made dominant. Critique, however, cannot maintain this separation and only finds its own rationality in its partisanship

12. Rittel (1966), pp. 183–209. 13. See Luhmann (1968).

for rationality, no matter how restricted. That is why even the type of rationalization developed on these four levels is not tolerant, to say nothing of indifferent, toward values. For from this concept of rationality the ultimate decisions concerning the acceptance or rejection of norms are not excluded after all. Even these decisions ultimately are incorporated into the self-regulating process of adaptation of a learning automaton according to the laws of rational behaviour – connected to a process of knowledge oriented toward technical control. The substantive rationality suppressed in the innocent partisanship for formal rationality reveals, in the anticipated concept of a cybernetically self-regulated organization of society, a tacit philosophy of history. This is based on the questionable thesis that human beings control their destinies rationally to the degree to which social techniques are applied, and that human destiny is capable of being rationally guided in proportion to the extent of cybernetic control and the application of these techniques. But such a rational administration of the world is not simply identical with the solution of the practical problems posed by history. There is no reason for assuming that a continuum of rationality exists extending from the capacity of technical control over objectified processes to the practical mastery of historical processes. The root of the irrationality of history is that we 'make' it, without, however, having been able until now to make it consciously. A rationalization of history cannot therefore be furthered by an extended power of control on the part of manipulative human beings, but only by a higher stage of reflection, a consciousness of acting human beings moving forward in the direction of emancipation.

References

APEL, K. O. (1959), 'Sprache und Wahrheit', *Philosophische Rundschau*, no. 7, pp. 161 ff.
BUBNER, R., *et al.* (1970), 'Szientismus oder transzendentale Hermeneutik?', *Hermeneutik und Dialektik*, vol. 1, Tübingen, pp. 105–44.
DEWEY, J. (1960), *The Quest for Certainty*, New York, p. 43.
GÄFGEN, G. (1963), *Theorie der wissenschaftlichen Entscheidung*, Tübingen.
HABERMAS, J. (1968), *Knowledge and Human Interests*, Heinemann Educational, 1972. (Translation of *Erkenntnis und Interesse*.)

HABERMAS, J. (1970), 'Technology and Science as Ideology', *Toward a Rational Society*, Heinemann Educational, 1971.
LUHMANN, N. (1968), *Zweckbegriff und Systemrationalität*, Tübingen.
RITTEL, H. (1966), 'Überlegungen zur wissenschaftlichen und politischen Bedeutung der Entscheidungstheorien', *Studiengruppe für Systemforschung*, Heidelberg, pp. 29 ff.
RITTEL, H. (1966), 'Instrumentelles Wissen in der Politik', in H. Krauch, ed., *Wissenschaft ohne Politik*, Heidelberg, pp. 183–209.
TOPITSCH, E. (1961), *Die Sozialphilosophie zwischen Ideologie und Wissenschaft*, Neuwied, p. 279.

17 Jürgen Habermas

Systematically Distorted Communication

Excerpt from Jürgen Habermas, 'On Systematically Distorted Communication', *Inquiry*, vol. 13, 1970, pp. 205–18.

Where difficulties of comprehension are the result of cultural, temporal, or social distance, we can say in principle what further information we would need in order to achieve understanding: we know that we must decipher the alphabet, become acquainted with lexicon and grammar, or uncover context-specific rules of application. In attempting to explain unclear or incomprehensible meaning-associations we are able to recognize, within the limits of normal communication, what it is that we do not – yet – know. However, this 'hermeneutic' consciousness of translation difficulties proves to be inadequate when applied to systematically distorted communication. For in this case incomprehensibility results from a faulty organization of speech itself. Obvious examples are those clearly pathological speech disturbances to be observed, for example, among psychotics. But the more important occurrences of the pattern of systematically distorted communication are those which appear in speech which is not conspicuously pathological. This is what we encounter in the case of pseudo-communication, where the participants do not recognize any communication disturbances. Pseudo-communication produces a system of reciprocal misunderstandings which, due to the false assumption of consensus, are not recognized as such. Only a neutral observer notices that the participants do not understand one another. However, as long as we communicate in a natural language there is a sense in which we can never be neutral observers, simply because we are always participants. That is, and as I have argued elsewhere,[1] any attempt to locate misunderstanding

1. See Habermas (1967), pp. 101 ff. The problem is discussed at length in Cicourel (1964), pp. 21 ff.

in communication is itself part of a further (or possibly the same) process of reciprocal communication, and therefore not the result of 'observing' such processes. The critical vantage-point can never be better than that of a partner in the communication. Consequently we have no valid criterion at our disposal for determining in general whether we are labouring under the mistaken conviction of normal understanding, and thus wrongly considering difficulties to be hermeneutically explicable when they actually require systematic analysis.

Freud dealt with the occurrence of systematically deformed communication in order to define the scope of specifically incomprehensible acts and utterances. He always envisaged the dream as the standard example of such phenomena, the latter including everything from harmless, everyday pseudo-communications and Freudian slips to pathological manifestations of neurosis, psychosis, and psychosomatic disturbance. In his essays on cultural theory, Freud broadened the range of phenomena which could be conceived as being part of systematically distorted communication. He employed the insights gained from clinical phenomena as the key to the pseudo-normality, that is to the hidden pathology, of collective behaviour and entire social systems. In our discussion of psychoanalysis as a kind of linguistic analysis pertaining to systematically distorted communication, we shall first consider the example of neurotic symptoms.

Three criteria are available for defining the scope of specific incomprehensible acts and utterances. (a) On the level of language, distorted communication becomes noticeable because of the use of rules which deviate from the recognized system of linguistic rules. Particularly semantical contents or complete semantical fields – in extreme cases the syntax, too – may be affected thereby. Using dream texts, Freud examined, in particular, condensation, displacement, absence of proper use of grammar and the use of words with opposite meaning. (b) On the behaviour level, the deformed language-game appears in the form of rigidity and compulsory repetition. Stereotyped behaviour patterns recur in situations involving stimuli which cause emotionally loaded reactions. This inflexibility is symptomatic of the fact that the semantical content has lost its specific linguistic independence of the situational context. (c) If, finally, we consider the system of distorted communication as a whole, we are struck by the discrepancy between the levels of communication; the usual congruency between linguistic symbols, actions, and accompanying gestures has disintegrated. The symptoms, in a clinical sense, offer nothing but the most recalcitrant and tangible proof of this dissonance. No matter on which level of communication the symptoms appear, whether in linguistic expression, in behavioural compulsion, or in the realm of gestures, one always finds an isolated content therein which has been excommunicated from the public language-performance. This content expresses an intention which is incomprehensible according to the rules of public communication, and which as such has become private, although in such a way that it remains inaccessible even to the author to whom it must, nevertheless, be ascribed. There is a communication obstruction in the self between the ego, which is capable of speech and participates in intersubjectively established language-games, and that 'inner foreign territory' (Freud), which is represented by a private or a primary linguistic symbolism.

Alfred Lorenzer has examined the analytical conversation between physician and patient from the standpoint of psychoanalysis as analysis of language.[2] He considers the process by which the meanings of specific incomprehensible manifestations are decoded as an understanding of scenes linked by analogy to those in which the symptoms occur. The purpose of analytical interpretation is to explain the incomprehensible meaning of the symptomatic manifestations. Where neuroses are involved, these manifestations are part of a deformed language-game in which the patient 'acts': that is, he plays an incomprehensible scene by violating role-expectations in a strikingly stereotyped manner. The analyst tries to make the symptomatic scene understandable by associating it with analogous scenes in the situation of transference. The latter holds the key to the coded relation between the symptomatic scene, which the adult patient plays outside the doctor's office, and an original scene experienced in early childhood. In the transference situation the patient forces the doctor into the role of the

2. Lorenzer (1970).

conflict-defined primary reference person. The doctor, in the role of the reflective or critical participant, can interpret the transference situation as a repetition of early childhood experiences; he can thus construct a dictionary for the hidden idiosyncratic meanings of the symptoms. 'Scenic understanding' is therefore based on the discovery that the patient behaves in the same way in his symptomatic scenes as he does in certain transference situations; such understanding aims at the reconstruction, confirmed by the patient in an act of self-reflection, of the original scene.

The re-established original scene is typically a situation in which the child has once suffered and repulsed an unbearable conflict. This repulse is coupled with a process of desymbolization and the formation of a symptom. The child excludes the experience of the conflict-filled object from public communication (and at the same time makes it inaccessible to its own ego as well); it separates the conflict-laden portion of its memory of the object and, so to speak, desymbolizes the meaning of the relevant reference person. The gap which arises in the semantic field is then closed by employing an unquestionable symbol in place of the isolated symbolic content. This symbol, of course, strikes us as being a symptom, because it has gained private linguistic significance and can no longer be used according to the rules of public language. The analyst's scenic understanding establishes meaning equivalences between the elements of three patterns – the everyday scene, the transference scene, and the original scene – and solves the specific incomprehensibility of the symptom; thus it assists in achieving resymbolization, that is, the re-entry of isolated symbolic contents into public communication. The latent meaning of the present situation becomes accessible when it is related to the unimpaired meaning of the original infantile scene. Scenic understanding makes it possible to 'translate' the meaning of the pathologically frozen communication pattern which had been hitherto unconscious and inaccessible to public communication.

If we consider everyday interpretation within the range of ordinary language or translation from one language into another, or trained linguistic analysis in general, all of them leading to hermeneutic understanding of initially incomprehensible utterances, then scenic understanding differs from that hermeneutic understanding because of its explanatory power. That is, the disclosure of the meaning of specific incomprehensible acts or utterances develops to the same extent as, in the course of reconstruction of the original scene, a clarification of the genesis of the faulty meaning is achieved. The What, the semantic content of a systematically distorted manifestation, cannot be 'understood' if it is not possible at the same time to 'explain' the Why, the origin of the symptomatic scene with reference to the initial circumstances which led to the systematic distortion itself. However, understanding can only assume an explanatory function, in the strict meaning of the word, if the semantic analysis does not depend solely on the trained application of the communicative competence of a native speaker, as is the case with simple semantic analysis, but is instead guided by theoretical propositions.

Two considerations indicate that scenic understanding is based on hypotheses which are in no way to be derived from the natural competence of a native speaker. In the first place, scenic understanding is linked to a special design of communication. The fundamental analytic rule introduced by Freud ensures a standard relationship between the physician and his patient, a relationship which meets quasi-experimental conditions. Suspension of the usual restraints of social reality and free association on the part of the patient, along with purposively restrained reactions and reflective participation on the part of the doctor, assure the achievement of a transference situation, which can then serve as a framework for translation. Secondly, the analyst's pre-understanding is directed at a small sampling of possible meanings, at the conflict-disturbed early object-relationships. The linguistic material which results from conversations with the patient is classified according to a narrowly circumscribed context of possible double meanings. This context comprises a general interpretation of early-childhood patterns of interaction. Both considerations make it obvious that scenic understanding – in contrast to hermeneutic understanding, or ordinary semantic analysis – cannot be conceived as being a mere application of communicative competence, free from theoretical guidance.

The theoretical propositions on which this special kind of language analysis is implicitly based can be elicited from three points of view. (1) The psychoanalyst has a preconception of the structure of non-distorted ordinary communication; (2) he attributes the systematic distortion of communication to the confusion of two developmentally following phases of pre-linguistic and linguistic symbol-organization; and (3) to explain the origin of deformation he employs a theory of deviant socialization which includes the connection between patterns of interaction in early childhood and the formation of personality structures. I would like to consider these three aspects briefly.

The first set of theoretical propositions concerns the structural conditions which must be met if normal communication is to obtain.

(a) In the case of a non-deformed language-game there is a congruency on all three levels of communication. Linguistic expressions, expressions represented in actions, and those embodied in gestures do not contradict one another, but rather supplement one another by meta-communication. Intended contradictions which have some informational content, are normal in this sense. Furthermore, ordinary communication implies that a particular portion of extra-verbal meanings must be convertible into verbal communication.

(b) Normal communication conforms to inter-subjectively recognized rules; it is public. The communicated meanings are identical for all members of the language-community. Verbal utterances are constructed according to the valid system of grammatical rules and are conventionally applied to specific situations. For extra-verbal expressions, which are not grammatically organized, there is likewise a lexicon which varies socio-culturally within certain limits.

(c) In the case of normal speech the speakers are aware of the categorical difference between subject and object. They differentiate between outer and inner speech and separate the private from the public world. The differentiation between being and appearance depends, moreover, on the distinction between the language-sign, its significative content (*significatum*), and the object which the symbol denotes (referent, *denotatum*). Only on this basis is it possible to apply situationally non-dependent language symbols (decontextualization). The speaking subject will master the distinction between reality and appearance to the same extent as speech attains a distinct reality for him, distinct, that is, from the denoted objects and their meanings as well as from private experiences.

(d) In normal communication an inter-subjectivity of mutual understanding, guaranteeing ego-identity, develops and is maintained in the relation between individuals who acknowledge one another. On the one hand, the analytic use of language allows the identification of objects (thus the categorization of particular items, the subordination of elements under classes, and the inclusion of sets). On the other hand, the reflexive use of language assures a relationship between the speaking subject and the language community which cannot be sufficiently presented by the analytic operations mentioned. For a world on the level of which subjects maintain mutual existence and understanding solely by virtue of their ordinary communication, inter-subjectivity is not a universal according to which the individuals could be classified in the same way as elements are subordinated to their classes. On the contrary, the relation between I (ego), you (alter-ego), and we (ego and alter-ego) is established only by an analytically paradoxical achievement: the speaking persons identify themselves at the same time with two incompatible dialogue-roles and thereby ensure the identity of the I (ego) as well as of the group. The one being (ego) asserts his absolute non-identity in relation to the other being (alter-ego); at the same time, however, both recognize their identity inasmuch as each acknowledges the other as being an ego, that is, a non-replaceable individual who can refer to himself as 'I'. Moreover, that which links them both is a mutual factor (we), a collectivity, which in turn asserts its individuality in relation to other groups. This means that the same paradoxical relationship is established on the level of inter-subjectively linked collectives as holds between the individuals.

The specific feature of linguistic inter-subjectivity exists in the fact that individuated persons communicate on the basis of it. In the reflexive use of language we present inalienably individual aspects in unavoidably general categories in such a way that we meta-communicatively comment upon and sometimes even revoke direct information (and confirm it only with reservations). We do this for the purpose of an indirect representation of the non-identical aspects of the ego, aspects which are not sufficiently covered by the general determinations and yet cannot be manifestly represented other than by just these determinations. The analytical use of language is necessarily embedded in the reflexive use, because the inter-subjectivity of mutual understanding cannot be maintained without reciprocal self-representation on the part of the speaking subjects. Inasmuch as the speaker masters this indirect information on the meta-communicative level, he differentiates between essence and appearance. The understanding we come to about objects can be direct, but the subjectivity we encounter when we speak with one another remains, in direct information, only at the level of appearance. The categorial meaning of this kind of indirect communication, in which the indefinable individualized aspect of a person is expressed, and his claim upon individuality is maintained, is something we merely reify in the ontological concept of essence. In fact this essence exists only in its appearances.

(e) Finally, normal speech is distinguished by the fact that the sense of substance and causality, of space and time, is differentiated according to whether these categories are applied to the objects within a world or to the linguistically constituted world itself, which allows for the mutuality of speaking subjects. The interpretational schema, 'substance', has a different meaning for the identity of items which can be clearly categorized analytically from that which it has for speaking and interacting subjects themselves, whose ego-identity, as has been shown, just cannot be grasped by analytically clear-cut operations. The interpretational schema of causality, when applied to observable events, leads to the concept of 'cause'; when it is applied to an association of intentional actions it leads to the concept of 'motive'. In the same way 'space' and 'time' undergo a different schematism when viewed in regard to physically measurable properties of observable events from that which they undergo when viewed according to experienced interactions. In the first case the categories serve as a system of co-ordinates for observation controlled by the success of instrumental action: in the latter case the categories serve as a frame of reference for the experience of social space and historical time from a subjective point of view.

The second set of postulates concerns the connection between two genetically successive phases of human symbol-organization.

(a) The archaic symbol-organization, which resists the transformation of its contents into grammatically regulated communication, can only be disclosed on the basis of the data of speech pathology and by means of the analysis of dream material. Here we mean symbols which control interactions, and not just signs, for these symbols already represent interactional experiences. Otherwise, however, the level of palaeo-symbols lacks all the characteristics of normal speech.[3] Palaeo-symbols do not fit into a system of grammatical rules. They are not classified elements and do not appear in sentences which could be transformed grammatically. For this reason, the way in which these symbols function has been compared to the functional manner of analogue computers in contrast to that of digital computers. Freud had already noticed the lack of logical connections in his dream analyses. He draws attention particularly to the use of words with opposite meaning, a remnant on the linguistic level of the genetically earlier peculiarity of combining logically incompatible meanings. Pre-linguistic symbols are emotionally loaded and remain fixed to particular scenes. There is no dissociation of linguistic symbol and bodily gesture. The connection to a particular context is so strong that the symbol cannot vary independently of actions. Although the palaeo-symbols represent a pre-linguistic basis for the inter-subjectivity of mutual existence and shared action, they do not allow public communication in the strict sense of the word. For the identity of meaning is not yet granted and the private meaning-associations still prevail. The privacy of pre-linguistic symbol-organization, so striking in all forms of speech pathology, originates in the fact that the usual distance between sender and addressee, as well as the differentiation between symbolic signs,

3. Arieti (1967); also Werner and Kaplan (1967); Watzlawick, Beavin and Jackson (1967).

semantic content, and items of reference, has not yet been developed. The distinction between reality and appearance, between the public and the private sphere cannot yet be clearly differentiated with the help of palaeo-symbols (adualism).

Finally, pre-linguistic symbol-organization does not allow an analytically satisfying categorization of the objects experienced. Two types of deficiencies are found in the communication and thought disturbances of psychotics: namely, 'amorphous' and 'fragmented' speech disorders.[4] In both cases the analytic operations of classification are disturbed. In the first, a fragmentation of structure is apparent which does not allow disintegrated single elements to be compiled into classes according to general criteria. In the second, an amorphous structure appears which does not allow aggregates of superficially similar and vaguely compiled things to be analysed. Symbol usage is not altogether destroyed, but the inability to form class hierarchies and to identify elements of classes offers, in both cases, proof of the breakdown of the analytical use of language. However, the second variation allows the possibility of achieving an archaic class-formation with the aid of pre-linguistic symbols. And in any case we find so-called primary classes on early ontogenetic and historical levels, as well as in pathological cases; that is, classes that are not formed on the abstract basis of the identity of properties, but where the aggregates contain concrete items which, irrespective of their identifiable properties, are co-ordinated within an all-embracing association of motives, interpreted on the basis of subjective plausibility. Animistic *Weltanschauungen*, for example, are formed in accordance with such primary classes.

(b) The symbol-organization described here, which precedes language genetically, is a theoretical construct. We cannot observe it anywhere. But the psychoanalytical decoding of systematically distorted communication presupposes such a construction, because that special type of semantic analysis introduced here as 'scenic understanding' resolves confusions of ordinary speech by interpreting them either as forced regression back to an earlier level of communication, or as the breakthrough of the earlier form of communication into language. On the basis of the analyst's

4. Wynne (1965), pp. 82 ff.

experience with neurotic patients, we can, as has been shown, recognize the function of psychoanalysis as language analysis, insofar as it allows separated symbolic contents, which lead to a private narrowing of public communication, to be re-integrated into common linguistic usage. The performance of the analyst in putting an end to the process of inhibition serves the purpose of resymbolization; inhibition itself can therefore be understood as a process linked to desymbolization. The defence mechanism of inhibition, which is analogous to flight, is revealed by the patient in his resistance to plausible interpretations made by the analyst. This mechanism is an operation carried on with and by language; otherwise it would not be possible to reverse the process of repulsion hermeneutically, i.e. precisely by means of a special type of semantic analysis. The fleeing ego, which has to submit to the demands of outer reality in a conflict situation, hides itself from itself by eliminating the symbolic representation of unwanted demands of instinct from the text of its everyday consciousness. By means of this censorship the representation of the prohibited object is excommunicated from public communication and banished to the archaic level of palaeo-symbols. Moreover, the assumption that neurotic behaviour is controlled by palaeo-symbols, and only subsequently rationalized by a substitutive interpretation, offers an explanation for the characteristics of this behaviour pattern: for its pseudo-communicative function, for its stereotyped and compulsive form, for its emotional load and expressive content, and, finally, for its rigid fixation upon particular situations.

If inhibition can be understood as desymbolization, then it follows that there must be a correspondingly linguistic interpretation for the complementary defence mechanism, which does not turn against the self but rather against outer reality, i.e. for projection and denial. While in the case of inhibition the language-game is deformed by the symptoms formed in place of the excommunicated symbols, the distortion in the case of this defence mechanism results directly from the uncontrolled penetration of palaeo-symbolic derivatives into language. In this case the therapeutic type of language analysis doesn't aim at re-transforming the desymbolized content into linguistically articulated meaning, but aims rather at a consciously achieved excommunication of the intermingled pre-linguistic elements.

In both cases the systematic distortion can be explained by the fact that palaeo-symbolically fixed semantic contents have encysted themselves, like foreign bodies, into the grammatically regulated use of symbols. Language analysis has the duty of dissolving this syndrome, i.e. of isolating the two language levels. There is, however, a third case: the processes of the creative extension of language. In this case a genuine integration is accomplished. The palaeo-symbolically fixed meaning-potential is then brought into the open and is thus made available for public communication. This transfer of semantic contents from the pre-linguistic into the common stock of language widens the scope of communicative action as it diminishes that of unconsciously motivated action. The moment of success in the use of creative language is a moment of emancipation.

The joke, although a different case, sheds light upon this process of creative language-extension. The laugh with which we react almost compulsively to what is comic in the joke contains the liberating experience which results when one moves from the level of palaeo-symbolic thought to the level of linguistic thought. It is the revealed ambiguity of a text which is funny, an ambiguity which exists because it tempts us to regress to the level of pre-linguistic symbolism, i.e. to confuse identity and similarity, and at the same time convinces us of the mistake of this regression. The laugh is one of relief. The joke lets us repeat virtually and experimentally the dangerous passage across the archaic border between pre-linguistic and linguistic communication. In our reaction to it we assure ourselves of the control which we have attained over the dangers of a developmental stage of consciousness which we have overcome.

Psychoanalysis, which interprets the specific incomprehensibility of systematically distorted communication, can no longer strictly speaking be conceived according to the translation model which applies to simple hermeneutic understanding or ordinary semantic analysis. For the obscurities which controlled 'translation' from pre-linguistic symbolism to language does away with are ones which arise not within the scope defined by a given language-system, but rather within language itself. Here it is the very structure of communication, hence the basis of all translation, that we are concerned with. Semantic analysis of this special type therefore needs a systematic pre-understanding which pertains to language and linguistic communication as such, while on the other hand our ordinary semantic analysis proceeds *ad hoc* from a traditionally determined pre-understanding which is tested and revised within the process of interpretation. The theoretical propositions deal, as described, with the pre-conditions of normal communication, with two levels of symbol organization, and with the mechanism of speech disorder. These theoretical assumptions can be organized in the structural model.

The constructions of 'ego' and 'id' interpret the analyst's experiences in his encountering the resistance of his patients. 'Ego' is the instance which fulfils the function of reality-testing and of censorship. 'Id' is the name given to those parts of the self that are isolated from the ego and whose representations become accessible in connection with the processes of repression and projection. The 'id' is expressed indirectly by the symptoms which close the gap which develops in everyday language when desymbolization takes place; direct representation of the 'id' is found in the illusory palaeo-symbolic elements dragged into the language by projection and denial. Now, the same clinical experience which leads to the construction of an ego- and id-instance, shows also that the defence mechanisms usually work unconsciously. For this reason Freud introduced the category of 'superego': an ego-foreign instance which is formed out of detached identifications with the expectations of primary reference persons. All three categories – ego, id, and superego – reflect fundamental experiences typical of a systematically distorted communication. The dimensions established by id and superego for the personality structure correspond to the dimensions of deformation of the inter-subjectivity of mutual understanding in informal communication. So the structural model which Freud introduced as the categorial frame of meta-psychology can be reduced to a theory of deviant communicative competence.[5]

5. For further elaboration see Habermas (1968).

I have chosen psychoanalysis as my example in order to differentiate between two types of interpretation and two forms of communication.

From the viewpoint of a logic of explanation, this example of the semantic analysis of specific incomprehensible manifestations is of interest because, in a unique way, it affords simultaneous hermeneutic understanding and causal explanation. The analyst's understanding owes its explanatory power – as we have seen – to the fact that the clarification of a systematically inaccessible meaning succeeds only to the extent to which the origin of the faulty or misleading meaning is explained. The reconstruction of the original scene makes both possible at the same time: the reconstruction leads to an understanding of the meaning of a deformed language-game and simultaneously explains the origin of the deformation itself. Of course, the connection between semantic analysis and causal explanation doesn't become evident until one shows that the categorial framework of the theory used – in our case the Freudian meta-psychology – is based on an at least implicitly underlying language theory. I have outlined only some of the assumptions which extend to the structure of normal communication and to the mechanisms of systematic distortion of communication. These assumptions would have to be developed within the framework of a theory of communicative competence, which is lacking as of now.

I can sum up my thesis as follows. The common semantic analysis of incomprehensible utterances, which leads to hermeneutic understanding, makes use of the non-analysed communicative competence of a native speaker. On the other hand, the special type of semantic analysis which deals with manifestations of a systematically distorted communication and affords an explanatory understanding, presupposes a theory of communicative competence. It is only in virtue of an at least implicit hypothesis concerning the nature and the acquisition of communicative competence that explanatory power can be accorded to this (particular) semantic analysis.

References

ARIETI, S. (1967), *The Intrapsychic Self*, Basic Books, New York.
CICOUREL, A. V. (1964), *Method and Measurement in Sociology*, Free Press, Glencoe, U.S.A., pp. 21 ff.
HABERMAS, J. (1967), 'Zur Logik der Sozialwissenschaften', *Philosophische Rundschau*, Beiheft 5, J. C. B. Mohr, Tübingen, pp. 101 ff.
HABERMAS, J. (1968), *Erkenntnis und Interesse*, Suhrkamp Verlag, Frankfurt, chapters 10 and 11. Translated as *Knowledge and Human Interests*, Heinemann Educational, 1972.
LORENZER, A. (1970), *Symbol und Verstehen im psychoanalytischen Prozess, Vorarbeiten zu einer Metatheorie der Psychoanalyse*, Suhrkamp Verlag, Frankfurt.
WATZLAWICK, P., BEAVIN, J. H., and JACKSON, D. D. (1967), *Pragmatics in Human Communication*, W. W. Norton, New York, especially chapters 6 and 7.
WERNER, H., and KAPLAN, B. (1967), *Symbol Formation*, John Wiley, New York.
WYNNE, L. C. (1965), 'Denkstörung und Familienbeziehung bei Schizophrenen', *Psyche*, May 1965, pp. 82 ff.

18 Jürgen Habermas

Problems of Legitimation in Late Capitalism

Excerpt from Jürgen Habermas, 'Was heisst heute Krise?', *Merkur*, vol. 4/5, April/Mai, 1973, pp. 644–67. Translated by Thomas Hall.

What does crisis mean nowadays? Problems of legitimation in late capitalism

Anyone who uses the expression 'late capitalism' is implicitly asserting that even in state-controlled capitalism social developments follow a 'contradictory' or crisis-laden course. I should therefore like to start by clarifying the concept of crisis.

The concept of crisis is known to us from a pre-scientific period as a medical term. Here it refers to the phase in the development of an illness in which it is decided whether the organism's own powers of healing are sufficient to cure it. The critical process, the illness, appears to be an objective matter. An infectious illness, for example, is caused by outside influences on the organism, and the ways in which the affected organism differs from its proper condition, the normal condition of the healthy organism, can be observed and if necessary measured. The patient's self-awareness is not involved in any way; *how* the patient feels and *how* he experiences his illness is at most a symptom of an event over which he himself has hardly any influence. And yet, in a medical case which is a matter of life and death, we would not talk of a crisis if the patient were not caught up in it with his subjective personality in its entirety. A crisis cannot be dissociated from the interior viewpoint of the person undergoing it: the patient discovers his impotence in the face of the objective force of the illness only because he is a subject condemned to a passive role, temporarily deprived of the possibility of being a subject in full possession of his powers.

We associated with crises the idea of an objective force which deprives a subject of some portion of the sovereign independence he normally possesses. In conceiving of a process as a crisis we tacitly give it a normative significance: the solution of the crisis brings liberation for the subject caught up in it.

This becomes clearer when we pass from the medical to the dramaturgical concept of crisis. In classical aesthetics from Aristotle to Hegel, the crisis was the turning-point of a fateful process, which for all its objectivity does not simply burst in upon people from outside. The contradiction which is expressed at the catastrophic point of the dramatic conflict is present in the structure of the dramatic action and in the personalities of the heroes. Destiny is fulfilled in the uncovering of conflicting values, in the course of which the identities of the participants are shattered, if they do not summon up the strength to regain their freedom by shattering the mythical power of destiny.

The concept of the crisis attained in classical tragedy finds its counterpart in that of the gospels. From the eighteenth-century philosophy of history this pattern of thought enters into the evolutionary theories of society of the nineteenth century. Thus Marx is the first thinker to develop a sociological concept of system crisis. It is against this background that we nowadays refer to social or economic crises. When we speak of the great economic crisis at the beginning of the thirties, for example, the Marxist connotations are unmistakable.

Since capitalist societies have the ability to develop the technical forces of production at a relatively steady rate, Marx means by an economic crisis the pattern of *a course of economic growth punctuated by crises.* Capital accumulation is tied to the appropriation of surplus value, which means that economic growth is regulated by a mechanism which simultaneously establishes and conceals a relationship of force. Thus the pattern of increasing complexity is a contradictory one, in the sense that the economic system creates new and greater problems at every stage in the solution of previous ones. The accumulation of total capital is achieved by way of periodic devaluations of certain parts of it: this course of events is the crisis-cycle which Marx observed in his own time. He attempted to explain the classic type of crisis in terms of a theory of value, with the aid of the law of the tendential fall in the rate of profit. But I would prefer not to go into this here. My question, rather, is whether late capitalism is also following the same, or a similar, self-destructive developmental pattern as classical competitive capitalism; or whether the principle on which late capitalism is organized has changed so much that the process of accumulation no longer produces problems which threaten its existence.

I should like to begin with a model of the most important structural characteristics of late capitalist societies (section 1). Then I should like to mention three critical tendencies which, although not specific to any one system, stand in the forefront of debate (section 2). Finally I shall discuss some arguments which are supposed to account for the critical tendencies of late capitalism.

1

The expression organized or state-regulated capitalism refers to two classes of phenomena, which may be traced back to the advanced state of the accumulation process. On the one hand, there is the process in which economic enterprises are concentrated (the rise of national and subsequently also of multinational corporations) and the organization of markets in goods, capital and labour. On the other hand, there is the process whereby the interventionist state steps in to fill the growing gaps in the functioning of the market. The expansion of oligopolistic market structures means the end of competitive capitalism; but no matter how business enterprises widen their perspectives with regard to time and extend their control over their environment, the steering-mechanism of the market is not annulled so long as decisions on investment are taken in accordance with criteria of practical income potential. Equally, the supplementing and potential substitution of the mechanism of the market by state intervention marks the end of liberal capitalism; but to whatever extent the area of private autonomous dealings between the possessors of goods is subjected to administrative limitation, political planning of the allocation of scarce resources will not come into effect so long as the priorities of society as a whole develop as the indirect result of the strategies of private business enterprises. In advanced capitalist societies the economic, administrative and legitimatory systems may be characterized roughly as follows:

The economic system

In the sixties various writers, taking America as the paradigm, developed a tripartite model which is based on the distinction between the private and public sectors. Private economic production is market-oriented, such that one sector of it now as before is regulated by competition, whereas the other is determined by the market strategies of oligopolies, who tolerate a *competitive fringe*. On the other hand, large enterprises have developed in the public sector, especially in the wake of arms manufacture and the space industry, and these can implement their conditions on investment independently of market considerations. The businesses involved here are either under direct state control or private firms that exist on government contracts. In the monopolistic and public sectors it is high-capital industries which predominate, while in the competitive sector it is high-labour industries. In the monopolistic and public sectors the enterprises are opposed by strong trade unions, while in the competitive sector the working class is less well organized; the variation in wage levels correspond to this distinction. In the monopolistic sector we may observe relatively rapid progress in production techniques. In the public sector enterprises do not *need* to rationalize to the same extent, while in the competitive sector they *cannot* do so.

The administrative system

On the one hand the state apparatus regulates the entire economic cycle by means of global planning; on the other it improves the conditions under which capital is exploited.

Global planning is determined negatively by the limits of private control over the means of production (the freedom of investment of private enterprise may not be limited), and positively by avoiding instabilities. To that extent, the measures of fiscal politics which are designed to regulate the cycle, and also the individual measures intended to regulate investment and total demand (price guarantees, subventions, loans, secondary redistribution of income, government contracts arranged in the light of trade-cycle fluctuations) have the reactive character of defensive strategies within the framework of a system which is determined by the doctrinally required balance between the competing imperatives of steady growth, a stable currency, full employment and a balanced set of foreign trade figures.

While global planning manipulates the marginal conditions of private enterprise decisions, so as to *correct* the market mechanism with regard to dysfunctional side-effects, the state *replaces* the market mechanism everywhere where it creates and improves conditions for the exploitation of surplus accumulated capital:

- by 'increasing national competitive capacity' through the organization of supra-national economic blocks, imperialistic protection of international stratification, etc.;
- by unproductive state consumption (armaments and space industry);
- by political channelling of capital into sectors neglected by market autonomy;
- by improving the material substructure (traffic, school and public health systems, recreation centres, town and regional planning, housing construction, occupational training system, further training and retraining programmes, etc.);
- by improving the immaterial substructure (promotion of science, investment in research and development);
- by intensifying the system of social work (educational system);
- by meeting the social and material costs attendant on private production (unemployment benefit, the welfare state, etc.).

The legitimatory system

The functional weaknesses of the market and the dysfunctional side-effects of the market mechanism entail the collapse of the basic bourgeois ideology of just exchange. On the other hand, there arises a stronger need for legitimation. The state apparatus which is now not only used to guarantee the conditions necessary for the production process, but also plays an initiating role in it, must be legitimized in the expanding areas of state intervention; yet it is no longer possible to fall back on the stability of those traditions which competitive capitalism has undermined and exhausted. Moreover, the universalistic value-systems of bourgeois ideology have been brought under the jurisdiction of civil rights, including the right to participate in political elections. For this reason legitimation can only be made to depend on the mechanism of general elections temporarily and in extraordinary circumstances. The problem that this creates is solved by formal democracy.

The style of the formal arrangements and procedures of democracy is such that administrative decisions may be taken relatively independently of the aims and motives of the citizens. Concrete participation by the citizens in the process of forming political aims – in other words, real democracy – would bring into the open the contradiction between administratively socialized production, and a form of acquiring the values produced which remains now as before a private one. In order to eliminate this contradiction as a theme of discussion the administrative system must be sufficiently autonomous in relation to the system of legitimation. This is brought about by a process of legitimation which secures the loyalty of the masses but avoids participation. In the midst of a society which is political in itself the citizens enjoy the status of passive participants, with the right to withhold their approval. Private liberty to decide on investments is complemented by the people's position as merely private citizens.

Class structure

The structures of late capitalism may be seen as a kind of reactive formation. To ward off crises in the system, late capitalist societies direct all their socially integrative forces towards the point of most likely conflict so as to keep it in abeyance all the more effectively.

In this context the quasi-political wage structure which depends on negotiations between business enterprises and trade unions plays an important part. 'Compulsory price fixing', which replaces price competition in oligopolist markets, has a consequence on the labour market: just as the large concerns control the movement of prices on their markets in a quasi-administrative fashion, so on the other hand they aim at quasi-political compromises with their trade union contractors in wage negotiations. In those branches of industry which are central to economic development, in both monopolistic and public sectors, labour power is a commodity with a 'political' price. 'Tariff partners' find a wide region of compromise as increases in production costs can be recouped by price rises and the demands of both sides on the state converge towards a mean. The results of this immunization of the basic sources of conflict are: (a) disparate wage increases; (b) long-term inflation with its corresponding temporary redistribution of income to the disadvantage of unorganized wage-earners and other marginal groups; (c) a long-term crisis in state finances with public poverty (the impoverishment of public transport, school, housing, and health systems); (d) inadequate compensation for disproportionate economic developments in both sectors of the economy (agriculture) and regions of the economy (fringe areas).

In the most advanced capitalist countries it has been possible to keep class conflict latent in its germinal areas during the decades since the Second World War; to flatten out the trade-cycle over a period of time, and to turn the periodic waves in capital devaluation into an inflationary long-term crisis with milder variations in the trade-cycle; and finally to spread out the dysfunctional side-effects of these smoothed-out economic crises and to distribute them among quasi-groups (such as consumers, schoolchildren and their parents, transport users, invalids, old people, etc.) or among minority groups who have only a low degree of organization. In this way the social identity of the classes is reduced and class consciousness is fragmented. The class compromise built into the structure of late capitalism makes (almost) everyone at once both a participant and an affected party. In view of the obvious and growing inequality in the distribution of wealth and power, it is nonetheless a good thing to distinguish who belongs more to the one category or to the other.

2

The rapid process of growth in late capitalist societies has posed problems for the system of world society which cannot be understood as critical phenomena *peculiar to one system*, although the possibilities of dealing with crises are limited by the characteristics of specific systems. I am thinking here of the ecological balance, the change of the personality (alienation) and the explosive strain on international relations.

The ecological balance

If abstract economic growth can be traced back to the technologically informed application of more energy to increase the productivity of human labour, then the capitalist form of society is distinguished by the fact that it has found an impressive solution to the problem of economic growth. Economic growth has become spontaneously institutionalized with the accumulation of capital, so that there is no option for the self-conscious control of this process. The growth imperatives which capitalism has directly pursued have in the meantime attained global importance, through the competition between systems and through diffusion right across the world (despite stagnation or even retrogressive tendencies in some countries of the Third World).

The established growth mechanisms compel population growth and increase in production on a world-wide scale. The economic needs of a growing population and increasing productive exploitation of nature are faced by the following material limitations: on the one hand, finite resources (i.e. the area of land suitable for building and habitation, fresh water, food, as well as irreplaceable raw materials – minerals, fuel, etc.), and on the other hand, irreplaceable ecological systems, which absorb harmful matter such as radioactive waste, carbon dioxide, or waste heat. It is true that the estimates made by Forrester and others of the limits to exponential growth in population, industrial production, exploitation of natural resources, and environmental pollution, still have little empirical foundation. The mechanisms of population growth are as little known as the maximal limit of the earth's absorption capacity for even the most important harmful matter. Moreover, we cannot predict technological development sufficiently to know which raw materials it will be possible to replace or restore by technological means in the future.

Nevertheless, even on the most optimistic estimates, *one* absolute limit to growth can be specified, even though this cannot be determined precisely at the outset: namely, the limit of thermal load imposed on the environment by the consumption of energy. If economic growth is necessarily linked to increasing energy consumption, and if all natural energy which can be used in economic production is eventually released as heat – then growing energy consumption must lead in the long run to an increase in global temperature. Again, it is not easy to ascertain empirically the critical time-spans involved. Nevertheless, these considerations show that an exponential growth in population and production – in other words, the extension of control over external nature – must one day come up against the limits imposed by the biological capacity of the environment.

This is true generally for all complex social systems. The possibilities of averting ecological damage are *specific to individual systems*. Late capitalist societies have difficulty in obeying the imperatives of limiting growth without giving up their basic principle of organization, because the transformation of spontaneous capitalist growth into qualitative growth demands planned production which is oriented towards use-values.

The anthropological balance

While the disturbance of ecological balance indicates the exploitation of natural resources, there are no clear signals to mark the limits of the capacity of personality systems. I doubt whether it is possible at all to identify such things as psychological constants of human nature which mark the inner limits of the socialization process. Nonetheless, I see a limitation in the type of socialization by which social systems have in the past generated motives for action. Our behaviour is oriented according to norms which stand in need of justification, and according to systems of interpretation which guarantee identity. This communicative organization of behaviour can become a hindrance for complex societies. For in organizations the capacity for control increases to the extent that decisions are taken independently of the motivation of the members. In systems with a high degree of inner complexity, the selection and realization of the aims of an organization must be made independently of the supply of narrow, localized motives: this is served by the creation of a generalized willingness to consent, which in political systems takes the form of legitimation. But as long as we are concerned with a form of socialization which brings internal nature into a communicative organization of behaviour, no legitimation of norms of action is conceivable which ensures an unmotivated acceptance of decisions. The motive for the readiness to conform in face of decisions the content of which is still uncertain is the conviction that these decisions are based on a legitimate norm of action. Only if motives for action did not involve norms which needed justification, and personality structures did not have to find their unity by systems of interpretation which guaranteed identity, could the unmotivated acceptance of decisions be made a matter of irreproachable routine; only in such circumstances could readiness to conform be established to any extent required.

The international balance

On another plane there are the dangers of the self-destruction of the world system through thermonuclear weapons. The destructive potential which has been assembled is a result of the high level of development of productive forces which on account of their technically neutral foundations can also assume the form of destructive forces – and indeed have done so, as a result of the spontaneous operation of international relations. Today, the danger to the natural substratum of world society has reached suicidal proportions. For some time now international relations have been subject to a historically new imperative of self-limitation. Once again, this applies generally to all highly militarized social systems; but once again the possibilities of dealing with the problem are limited according to the characteristics of particular systems. Effective disarmament is certainly not likely, in view of the driving forces of capitalist and post-capitalist class societies; but control of the arms race is not *a limine* irreconcilable with the structure of late capitalist societies, insofar as it may be possible to balance out the capacity effect of state demand for unproductive consumer goods by an increase in the use-value of capital.

3

I should now like to leave these three world-wide problems, which result from late capitalist growth, and proceed to examine *the disturbances specific to particular systems*. I shall begin from the thesis, widespread among Marxists, that the basic capitalist structures continue unchanged, while producing economic crises whose form has changed. In late capitalism the state pursues the politics of capital by other means. This thesis appears in two versions.

The orthodox theory of the state asserts that the activities of the interventionist state spontaneously obey economic laws which are no less effective than were the processes of exchange under liberal capitalism. The different forms in which they appear (state financial crises and long-term inflation, growing disparity between public poverty and private wealth, etc.) are to be explained by the fact that the self-regulation of the exploitation process comes about through the control medium of power rather than that of exchange. But since the tendency towards crisis is determined now as before by the law of value – and that means by the structurally enforced asymmetry in the exchange of wage labour for capital – the activity of the state cannot in the long run compensate for the tendency of the falling rate of profit, but can at best create it, i.e. bring it about by its own political means. The replacement of the functions of the market by those of the state does not alter the unconscious nature of the whole economic process. This is shown by the narrow limits within which state manipulation has to operate. The state cannot make substantial attacks on the property structure without sparking off a strike in investments; nor is it able in the long run to avoid cyclic currents in the accumulation process, i.e. endogenically-created tendencies towards stagnation.

A revisionist version of the Marxist theory of the state is held by leading GDR economists. According to this second version, the state apparatus no longer spontaneously obeys the logic of the law of value, but consciously takes notice of the interest of united monopolistic capitalists. This agency-theory, which is designed to fit late capitalism, sees the state not as a blind organ of the exploitation process but as a potent collective capitalist agency which makes the accumulation of capital the aim of its political planning. The high level attained by the socialization of production brings about a convergence between the individual interests of the big corporations and the interest in the preservation of the system, and this all the more in that the stability of the system is threatened from within by forces which transcend the system.

Thus a joint capitalist interest develops, which united monopolists consciously pursue with the aid of the state apparatus.

I consider both versions of the economic theory of crisis to be inadequate. One version puts too little trust in the state; the other ascribes too much importance to it.

1. Against the *orthodox theory* doubts arise in view of the fact that state organization of scientific-technical progress and the wage system negotiated by tariff (which brings about a class compromise, particularly in the intensive-capital and intensive-growth economic sectors) have modified the mode of production. The state which has been drawn into the reproduction process has changed the determinants of the process of exploitation itself. On the basis of a partial class compromise, the administrative system acquires a limited planning capacity, which can be used within the framework of the formal democratic provision of legitimation for the purpose of avoiding crises. Spread out over a period of time and with the edge taken off its social consequences, the crisis cycle is replaced by inflation and a lasting crisis of public finance. Whether these replacements indicate a successful control of economic crises or only a temporary displacement of them into the political system, is an empirical question. In the last instance it depends on whether the *indirectly productive* capital invested in research, development and education succeeds in producing an increase in the productivity of labour, a rise in the rate of surplus value and a reduction in value of the fixed components of capital, which will be sufficient to keep the accumulation process going.

2. Against the *revisionist thesis* the following objections have been raised. Firstly, the hypothesis that the state apparatus, in whoever's interest it may operate, can *actively plan* and carry through a central economic strategy, cannot be empirically verified. The theory of state-monopolistic capitalism ignores (in the same way as do Western theories of technocracy) the limits of administrative planning in late capitalism. The way in which planning bureaucracies operate is to avoid crises by reaction. The various bureaucracies are imperfectly co-ordinated, and on account of their deficient capacity for perception and planning they are dependent on the influence of their clients. Precisely this lack of rationality on the part of the state administration ensures the

success of organized private interests. Nor can any better empirical support be provided for the other hypothesis, that the state is active as the agent of united monopolists. The theory of state monopolistic capitalism overestimates (in the same way as do Western élitist theories) the significance of personal contacts. Studies of the recruiting, composition and interaction of various power élites cannot adequately explain the fundamental connections between the economic and administrative systems.

In my opinion the way in which the late capitalist state functions can be adequately understood, neither by the model which sees the continued existence of unconsciously operating economic laws, nor by the model which sees the united monopolistic capitalists as an agent following a set plan of action. Instead, I would support the thesis advanced by Claus Offe, according to which late capitalist societies are confronted by two difficulties, both of which derive from the fact that the state must step in to fill the growing gaps in the functioning of the market. We may think of the state as a system which employs legitimate force. Its *output* consists of autocratically-executed administrative decisions; for these it requires an *input* of mass loyalty, as little attached to specific objects as possible. Both directions may lead to critical disturbances. Output crises take the form of *crises in rationality*: the administrative system does not succeed in fulfilling the imperatives of control which it has taken over from the economic system. This results in the disorganization of various areas of social life. Input crises take the form of *crises in legitimation*: the legitimation system does not succeed in maintaining the necessary level of mass loyalty. Let us clarify this by taking the example of the acute difficulties in public finance with which all late capitalist societies are having to struggle today.

The treasury is burdened, as we have already mentioned, with the overhead expenses of production which is becoming more and more socialized. It bears the cost of international competition and the cost of the demand for unproductive commodities (armaments and space research); it bears the cost of infra-structural activities directly related to production (transport systems, scientific and technical progress, occupational training); it bears the cost of social consumption which is only indirectly related to production (housing construction, health, leisure, education, social insurance); it bears the cost of social security for the unemployed; and finally it bears the cost of burdens on the environment created by private production. In the last instance, this expenditure must be financed by means of taxation. Thus the state apparatus is confronted with two tasks at once. On the one hand, it must collect the necessary sum in taxes by skimming off profits and income, and put it to such *rational* use that critical disturbances in growth can be avoided. And on the other hand, the selective raising of taxes, the recognizable scale of priorities according to which they are employed, and the administrative procedure, must be such that the need for *legitimation* which here arises may be satisfied. If the state fails in the fulfilment of the first of these tasks there arises a deficit in administrative rationality; if it fails with regard to the second task there arises a deficit in legitimation.

Theorems of legitimation crisis

Let me confine my attention to the problem of legitimation. There is nothing mysterious about the way in which this problem arises: in order for there to be administrative planning there must be legitimate power available. The functions required of the state apparatus in late capitalism and the extension of administratively-processed social life increase the need for legitimation. Now liberal capitalism was organized in the forms of bourgeois democracy, a fact easily explained by the context of the bourgeois revolutions. Therefore the growing need for legitimation must be met today with the methods of political democracy on the basis of a universal suffrage. But formal democratic methods are expensive. The state, in fact, does not only see itself in the role of the total capitalist with regard to the conflicting interests of the various capital factions; beyond this, it must also take into account the generalizable interests of the population to the extent that is necessary to keep the surface of mass loyalty from sinking below the level at which the withdrawal of legitimation would issue in conflict. The state must feel its way to the boundaries of these three areas of interest (individual capitalist, total capitalist, and generalizable interests) in order to pave a way of compromise through the competing claims. A theorem of crisis must establish why the state apparatus is bound to run up against not only *difficulties*, but long-term *insoluble problems*.

First, an obvious objection. The state can avoid problems of legitimation to the extent that it manages to make the administrative system independent of the legitimizing will. This goal is served, for instance, by the separation of expressive symbols, which create a general readiness to follow, from the instrumental functions of the administration. Well-known strategies of this kind are the personalizing of objective problems, the symbolic use of witnesses' testimony, expert opinions, legal oaths and so on. But the advertising techniques borrowed from oligarchic competition, which simultaneously confirm and exploit existing prejudices, and by appealing to the customer, by stimulating unconscious motives and so on, give to some subjects a positive charge and to others a negative one, are also examples of the same thing. The public opinion which is established to effect legitimation has as its chief function the structuring of attention by directing it to certain thematic areas and by playing down uncomfortable themes, problems and arguments. In Niklaus Luhmann's phrase: the political system assumes the task of *planning ideologies*.

This, however, sets narrow limits to the freedom of manipulation, for the cultural system has a peculiarly resistant attitude to administrative control. There can be no *administrative creation of meaning*, only ideological retailing of cultural values. The creation of legitimation is self-destructive as soon as the mode of 'creation' is seen through. A systematic limit to efforts to make up for deficits in legitimation by attempted manipulation thus consists in the structural dissimilarity between the areas of administrative action and cultural tradition.

The proposition that a critical situation exists may, it is true, be construed from this only in connection with a further aspect of the matter: the fact, that is, that the expansion of state activity has the side-effect of a disproportionate increase in the need for legitimation. I consider a disproportionate increase to be likely because those taken-for-granted cultural factors which previously were fringe conditions of the political system are now drawn into the administrative field of planning. Thus traditions which previously had not been involved in public programming and in practical discussion become themes for discussion. One example of the direct administrative revision of cultural tradition is the planning of education, in particular the planning of the curriculum. Whereas in the past the school authorities had only to codify a canon which had developed spontaneously, the planning of the curriculum is based on the premise that the patterns provided by tradition could be otherwise constituted. Administrative planning creates a universal need for justification with regard to a sphere which was distinguished precisely by its power of self-legitimation.

Further examples of the indirect disturbance of taken-for-granted cultural factors are provided by regional and town planning (private property in land and earth), the planning of the health service (the 'classless hospital'), and finally by family planning and marriage laws (breaking down of sexual taboos and lowering the threshold of emancipation). In the end a sense of uncertainty is generated not only for the substance but also for the techniques of tradition, i.e. of socialization. Formal school education begins to compete with the family way of upbringing even in the pre-school years. The fact that the routines of child-rearing become problematic may be observed in the tasks of national popular education which the schools perceive in the institution of parental rights, as well as in pedagogic-psychological scientific publicity.

On all these levels administrative planning has the unintended effect of creating disturbances and publicity, and this weakens the justification potential of the traditions which it has startled out of their spontaneous development. Once the unquestionableness of tradition has been destroyed, the stabilizing effect offered by claims to validity can be achieved only through discussions. The disturbance of taken-for-granted cultural factors therefore promotes the politicization of areas of life which could previously be assigned to the private sphere. But this spells danger for the private status of the citizen which was previously guaranteed informally by the structures of the public sphere. I see signs of this in the quest for participation and alternative models, as they have been developed particularly in schools and colleges, the press, the church, theatres, publishing enterprises, and so on.

The arguments presented above support the assertion that late capitalist societies find themselves in need of legitimation. But do they also suffice to establish the insolubility of the problems of legitimation? Do they suffice to predict a crisis in legitimation? Even if the state apparatus were to succeed in increasing the productivity of labour and in dividing the profits of productivity in such a way that economic growth free from crisis if not from disturbance were assured, this growth would come about in accordance with priorities whose development is not dependent on the generalizable interests of the population. The pattern of priorities which Galbraith has analysed under the heading of 'private wealth v. public poverty' results from a class structure, however much that class structure may be rendered latent. *This*, in the last resort, is the cause of the deficit in legitimation.

We have seen that the state cannot simply take the cultural system under its jurisdiction; rather it is the case that the expansion of the areas of state planning makes problematic previously accepted elements of the cultural tradition. For that reason, the expectations which are arising in the public at large are those oriented towards utility values, i.e. those which can be controlled in their success. The rising level of demand is proportionally related to the growing need for legitimation. The fiscally-exhausted resource 'value' must substitute for the scarce resource 'meaning'. A deficiency in legitimation must be balanced out by compensations which are in harmony with the system. A crisis of legitimation arises the moment claims to compensation in accordance with the system increase faster than the available quantity of values, or when expectations arise which cannot be met with such compensations.

In the meantime, why should the level of claims not be kept within operable bounds? As long as the programme of the welfare state preserves a sufficient amount of privacy for the citizen in conjunction with a widespread technocratic ideology which makes unmodifiable compulsions of the system responsible for bottle-necks, the need for legitimation *must not* come to the point of crisis. Indeed, the formal democratic type of legitimation might involve expenses which cannot be covered if it compels the competing parties to outbid one another in their programmes, thus winding popular expectations to a higher and higher pitch. Even if we presume that this argument is capable of sufficient empirical proof, it remains to be explained why in late capitalist societies formal democracy is still preserved at all. From the point of view of the administrative system alone it could equally well be replaced by that variety of the fascist-authoritarian state which keeps the people at a relatively high level of permanent mobilization. Apparently both varieties are in the long run less accommodating than the constitution of a mass democracy organized along party lines, because the socio-cultural system creates demands which cannot be met in systems run along authoritarian lines.

This consideration leads me to the thesis that only a rigid socio-cultural system which cannot be functionalized at will to serve the needs of the administrative system could explain the way in which the need for legitimation becomes acute and constitutes a crisis in legitimation. Hence this must have at its root a *crisis of motivation*, i.e. a discrepancy between the need for motives which the state and the occupational system announce, on the one hand, and the offer of motivation on the part of the socio-cultural system, on the other.

Theorems of the crisis in motivation

The most important contribution to motivation made by the socio-cultural system in late capitalist societies consists in syndromes of a civic and a family-occupational privatism. Civic privatism means that it is possible to develop interests in the taxation and social welfare procedures of the administrative system, with only slight participation in the process of forming political opinions (a high output/low input orientation). Thus civic privatism corresponds to the structures of a depoliticized public world. Family-occupational privatism has a complementary relationship to the civic one. It consists in an orientation towards the family with cultivated consumer and leisure interests on the one hand, and on the other an orientation towards a career appropriate to the competition for status. This privatism also corresponds to the structures of an educational and occupational system regulated according to competitive performance.

Both patterns of motivation are of fundamental importance for the stability of the political and economic system. But those parts of bourgeois ideologies which are directly relevant to private orientation are now losing their basis as a result of social change.

The ideology of achievement. According to bourgeois ideas, which have remained constant from the beginnings of modern natural law theory right up to present-day election speeches, social compensations should be distributed according to individual achievement. The distribution of gratifications is supposed to represent isomorphically the pattern of achievement differential of every individual. The condition for this is participation with equal chances in a competition which is so regulated as to make it possible to neutralize external influences. The market was an allocation mechanism of this kind. However, since it has become recognizable even among the population at large that social force is exercised even in the form of exchange, the market is losing its credibility as a mechanism for the allocation of chances in life which are in accordance with the system and which justly reflect achievement. In the newer versions of the ideology of achievement, therefore, market success is being replaced by professional success resulting from formal education. However, *this* version of the ideology can claim credibility only if the following conditions are fulfilled:

- equal opportunities of access to schools leading to higher attainment;
- non-discriminatory standards for evaluating educational achievement;
- simultaneous development of the cultural and occupational systems;
- work processes whose essential structure allows evaluation according to the individual's attainments.

While 'school justice' may have increased since the Second World War in all advanced capitalist societies, in terms of opportunity of access and standards of evaluation, a contrary trend may be observed in the other two dimensions. The expansion of the educational system is becoming increasingly independent of changes in the occupational system, so that in the long run the connection between formal education and professional success may weaken. And at the same time the areas are growing in which production structures and work patterns make evaluation according to the individual's personal achievements harder and harder, while instead the extra-functional role-elements of a profession become increasingly important for the allocation of professional status.

For the rest, fragmented and monotonous work processes are making increasing inroads even into sectors in which previously a personal identity could be formed by way of the occupational role. An 'inner-directed' motivation for achievement is less and less supported by the structure of the work process in areas of work which are dependent on market considerations; an instrumental attitude to work is spreading in the traditionally middle-class occupations (civil servants of upper and middle grades, professional men). An achievement motivation thrust upon them from the outside, however, can be adequately stimulated by how well the job pays only:
- if the reserve army in the labour market exercises an effective competitive pressure;
- if an adequate income differential exists between the lowest paid groups and the professionally inactive population.

Neither condition is automatically fulfilled nowadays. Even in capitalist countries with chronic unemployment (e.g. in the U.S.A.), the division of the labour market (into organized and competitive sectors) interrupts the functioning of the spontaneous competition mechanism. With a rising poverty line (as it is recognized by the welfare state) on the sub-proletarian level, the standards of living of the lowest income groups and those who are temporarily released from the labour process are becoming equal.

Possessive individualism. Bourgeois society sees itself as an instrumental group which accumulates social wealth only by way of private wealth; that is to say, it guarantees economic growth and general welfare by way of competition between private individuals acting strategically. Under these conditions collective aims can be realized only by way of the actions of individuals which are oriented towards utility. This system of preferences presupposes:

- that the private economic subjects themselves have a clear recognition of a need which remains constant over a long period, and can calculate it;
- that this need can be met by goods which can be obtained individually (by means of compensations in accordance with the system, normally monetary ones).

Neither presupposition is automatically fulfilled any longer in advanced capitalist societies. Here a level of social wealth has been attained where it is no longer a matter of protection against a few fundamental life hazards and the satisfaction of basic needs; hence the individualistic system of preferences is becoming ill-defined. The constant interpretation and re-interpretation of needs becomes a matter of the collective will, in which free communication can be replaced only by massive manipulation, i.e. by heavy indirect taxation. The greater the degree of freedom enjoyed by the customer in his system of preferences, the more urgent become the problems of market policy for the suppliers – at least when the appearance that the customer has the ability to choose freely for himself must be maintained. An opportunistic adaptation by consumers to market strategies is the ironical form of that autonomy of the consumer which must be preserved as the façade of possessive individualism. For the rest, the share of collective utility goods among consumer goods as a whole grows with the increasing socialization of production. Urban conditions of life in complex societies are becoming increasingly dependent on an infra-structure (transport, leisure, health, education etc.) which is withdrawing further and further from the forms of differential demand and private acquisition.

Orientation towards exchange values. Here we must mention those tendencies which weaken the socialization effects of the market: above all the growth of that section of the population which does not gain its living from labour (schoolchildren and students, people living on the welfare state, people living on dividend from invested capital, invalids, criminals, soldiers, etc.) on the one hand; and on the other the spread of areas of activity in which, as in the civil service or teaching, abstract labour is replaced by tangible labour. Even the relevance which leisure time is gaining with regard to occupational themes, in connection with decreasing hours of work (and increased real income), does not automatically put needs which can be met by financial rewards in a privileged position.

The erosion of bourgeois traditions allows normative structures to emerge which are unsuited to the reproduction of civic and family-occupational privatism. The currently dominant elements of cultural tradition crystallize around a faith in science, a 'post-auratic' art, and universalistic moral ideas. In each of these fields irreversible developments have taken place. From this, cultural barriers have arisen which could be broken through only at the psychological cost of regressions, i.e. with extraordinary burdens on motivation. German Fascism was an example of a wasteful attempt at a collectively organized regression of consciousness below the threshold of basic scientific convictions, modern art and universalistic notions of justice and morality.

Scientism. The political consequences of the authority which the scientific system enjoys in advanced societies are ambivalent. On the one hand, traditional attitudes of belief cannot resist the claim to justification in debate which the development of modern science has established; on the other hand, short-lived popular syntheses of individual pieces of information, which have taken the place of universal interpretations, ensure the authority of science *in abstracto*. Thus the term science can cover both things: both wide-ranging criticism of arbitrary prejudices, and the new esotericism of specialist knowledge and expert opinion. A self-affirmation of science can promote a positivistic ideology which is supported by the depoliticized public. On the other hand, scientism sets standards according to which it may itself be criticized and convicted of vestiges of dogma. Technocracy and élite theories which insist on the necessity for the institutionalization of civic privatism, because they have to present themselves with the claims of theories, are not immune from objections.

Post-auratic art. The consequences of modern art are somewhat less ambivalent. The modern age has made radical the autonomy of bourgeois art. This has been the first sign by which a counter-culture, arising from within bourgeois society itself, has stood out against the possessive-individualist achievement and utility-oriented life-style of the bourgeoisie. In the Bohemian life style, which was first established in Paris as the capital of the nineteenth century, there is embodied a critical claim which had previously taken an unpolemical form in the aura of the bourgeois work of art. There, the *alter ego* of the possessor of commodities, the 'human being', whom the bourgeois could once encounter in solitary contemplation of the work of art, has all at once split off from him and confronted him in the form of the artistic avant-garde as a hostile, or at best as a seductive, power. Whereas the bourgeois could once experience directly in artistic beauty its own ideals and a fulfilment, however fictitious, of the promise of happiness which is merely suspended in everyday experience, it has now had to recognize in radical art the negation of social practice, rather than its complement.

Modern art is the cocoon in which the transformation of bourgeois art into a counter-culture is bred. Surrealism marks the moment in history at which modern art programmatically destroyed the shell of a no longer beautiful appearance in order to take its place, desublimated, in real life. The levelling-out of the stages of reality between art and life is not, indeed, first brought about, as Walter Benjamin held, by the new techniques of mass production and mass reception; but they certainly speeded it up. Modern art itself had stripped off the aura of classic bourgeois art, in that the work made the production process obvious and presented itself as an artifact; but only by yielding up its autonomous status does art penetrate the ensemble of utility. This process is certainly an ambivalent one. It can signify equally the degeneration of art to propagandistic mass art or commercialized mass culture, or on the other hand its transformation into a subversive counter-culture.

Universalistic morality. The stop-go effect which bourgeois ideologies shorn of their functional elements create for the development of the political and economic systems is seen even more clearly in the moral system than in the authority of science and in the self-disintegration of modern art. As soon as traditional societies enter a process of modernization, growing complexity produces problems of control which make it necessary to speed up the transformation of social norms. The tempo characteristic of spontaneous cultural tradition must be increased. Thus there arises the bourgeois formal law which permits the release of values from the dogma of mere tradition and their reshaping along purposively determined lines. On the one hand, legal norms are dissociated from the corpus of privatized moral norms; but on the other hand they need to be created (and justified) according to principles. Whereas justice in the abstract is valid only for areas pacified by the force of the state, the morality of private citizens, likewise elevated to the plane of general principles, finds no hindrance in the continuing condition of nature in the relationship between states. Since morality as a set of principles is sanctioned only by the purely internal authority of the conscience, its claim to universality contains the seed of a conflict with a public morality which is still bound to a concrete state: the conflict between the cosmopolitanism of the 'human being' and the loyalties of the citizen of a state.

If one follows the developmental logic of totally socialized systems of norms (thus leaving the realm of historical instances), a solution of this conflict is conceivable only with the disappearance of the dichotomy between internal and external morality, the realization of the opposition between morally and legally governed areas, and the attachment of the validity of *all* norms to the will of those potentially affected, through discussion.

Competitive capitalism has for the first time given binding force to strictly universal value systems, because exchange itself had to be controlled universally and because, moreover, the exchange of goods of equal value offered a basic ideology effective in bourgeois society. Nowadays, in organized capitalism, the basis of this model of legitimation is breaking down, while at the same time new and increased demands for legitimation are arising. However, just as the system of science cannot intentionally fall behind a particular state of cumulative knowledge once that has been attained, so also the moral system, when once practical discussion is allowed, cannot simply consign to oblivion a state of moral consciousness that has been collectively achieved.

I should like to close with one last thought.

If there exists no adequate harmony between the normative structures, which still possess a certain power, and the politico-economic system, crises in motivation could still be avoided by neutralizing the cultural system – culture would then become a non-committal leisure activity or the object of professional knowledge. But just this way out would be blocked if the basic convictions of a communicative ethic and the characteristic experience of counter-cultures, in which post-auratic art is embodied, were to attain decisive force for determining typical socialization processes, i.e. power to form motives. This supposition is supported by a few characteristic behaviour-patterns which are spreading increasingly among young people: *either* withdrawal as a reaction against excessive demands on the resources of the personality; *or* protest resulting from an autonomous ego-organization which in certain circumstances cannot be stabilized without conflict. On the *activistic* side there are: the student movement, revolts by pupils and apprentices, pacifists, women's lib; the *retreatist* side is represented by Hippies, the Jesus People, the drug subculture, phenomena of under-motivation in schools, etc. It is above all in these areas that our hypothesis, according to which late capitalist societies are threatened by breakdown in legitimation, would have to be tested.

19 Claus Offe

Political Authority and Class Structures

Excerpt from Claus Offe, 'Political Authority and Class Structures – An Analysis of Late Capitalist Societies', *International Journal of Sociology* vol. II, no. 1, 1972, pp. 73–105.

I Rule by Power Groups or by Institutions?

For political systems regarded as democratic, the question of ruling social groups or strata is not as self-evident as it may seem at first glance. *Democratic* rule should, after all, mean that within the social system as a whole *no* group is granted *a priori* particular power privileges. The historical importance of democratically constituted systems has been to render the politically dominant classes, strata, or groups functionally inoperative in a *ruling* capacity. Hence, the question from which an analysis of political authority must proceed should not, without qualification, imply the existence of a 'seat' or 'locus' of political authority within the social structure. Before proceeding in this manner, we must ascertain whether the question, so formulated, is indeed at all meaningful for democratic political systems. The first question, then, to which any systematic treatment of authority within democratic political systems should address itself is not 'Who are the rulers and who are the ruled?' but 'Are we justified at all in applying *the category of ruling groups to democratic socio-political systems, and in so doing contesting their own postulate* that in these systems authority is vested in the constitution rather than in privileged power groups – an authority, moreover, that is beyond partisan politics and legitimated to like extent by all its citizens?'

Many theoretical writings on political sociology contain an implicit answer to this question and may be classified accordingly. The advocates of a *conflict theory* hold the view that even (and especially) late capitalist democratic political systems can be analysed properly only if they are viewed in light of an antagonism between ruler and ruled, between powerful oligarchies, classes, strata, and groups, on the one hand, and relatively powerless groups and classes whose interests are repressed in their expression and thwarted in their prosecution, on the other. This view, which is also shared by Marxist-oriented sociologists and political scientists, is directly countered by the other view, that of the *integration theorists*. They proceed in their analysis of political power from the postulate that society is integrated by a legitimate system of political institutions, which thereby neutralizes any structurally derived power advantages of particular groups, or at the very least ensures the maintenance of an unstable (pluralistic) equilibrium between competing power groups. In this view, a political system of democratic institutions carries out a series of functions which cannot be accounted for by the dominance of one group or the structural subordination of another. Political authority is not directly reducible to power derived from social structure. 'It is not, then, the state of the productive forces, but the state of the political forces which is the main cause of the varying characteristics of each type of society.' The one specific trait of highly differentiated industrial societies is 'the separation of social power and political authority, the differentiation of functions'.[1]

The neutrality of democratic structures of authority vis-à-vis social power, in this integrative view, is expressed in S. M. Lipset's definition at the beginning of his inquiry into 'Economic Development and Democracy':

> Democracy in a complex society may be defined as a political system which supplies regular constitutional opportunities for changing the governing officials, and a social mechanism which permits the largest possible part of the population to influence major decisions by choosing among contenders for political office.[2]

Characteristic of such a democratic system, Lipset states, is the institutionalized competition between political power groups, which confronts the party in power at any given time with the permanent possibility of a legitimate change of power. With this mechanism, political authority is accordingly only the authority

1. Aron (1966), pp. 208–9. 2. Lipset (1965), p. 33.

of institutions, whose specific content of power groups (parties) remains transitory.

The conflict theory is typified by C. W. Mills' concept of the 'power élite', which he derives from an analysis of American society.

> The major institutions of modern society, the state and corporation and army, constitute the means of power today . . . and at their summits there are now those command posts of modern society which offer us the sociological key to an understanding of the role of the higher circles in America.[3]
>
> The conception of the power élite and of its unity rests upon the corresponding developments and the coincidence of interests among economic, political, and military organizations. It also rests upon similarity of origin and outlook, and the social and personal intermingling of the top circles from each of these dominant hierarchies.[4]

Thus, according to this conception, we must deal with consistent social power groups which are *not* controlled and neutralized by democratic institutions, as the integrative view would have it, but which in fact make use of these institutions as a means of power, and furthermore are able because of this to fortify their positions against other competing power groups and to stabilize their dominant roles.

In political sociology, the controversy between the conflict and integration theories sets the tone for the problems that arise in attempting to establish a theoretical framework for the analysis of political authority. The spokesmen for the various perspectives on which such a framework might be based may be classified as conflict theorists insofar as their primary interest is in the social *basis* of power and the *distribution* of the prospects for influence within the social structure, or they may be classed as integration theorists if they are concerned principally with the *role played by a power potential*, regardless of its source or origin, in maintaining the stability of the total social system, i.e., to the extent that they place primary emphasis on the *employment* or *use* of institutions.

The question 'Which groups acquire power on the basis of

3. Mills (1956), p. 5. 4. ibid., p. 292.

what political conditions?' and 'What societal functions are served by the political sub-system as an agency for the use and application of power?' have up to now been treated separately, and to that extent inadequately, by political sociology.[5] Neither position is able to provide solutions that would satisfy the dominant theoretical interest of its opponent. If one examines the answers of the 'distribution theorists' to the question of the political functions of the political exercise of authority, one usually encounters the circular argument that the functions consist essentially in maintaining particular power privileges.[6] The distributive structure of prospects for political influence generate political functions which, in turn, serve mainly to perpetuate the existing pattern of power distribution. The functions generated by a structure are identical with it to the extent that they affect nothing but its continuity; the political system mediates the identity of the dominant class *as* dominant.

Even aside from the fact that this restrictive interpretation of the functions of political authority has never been empirically plausible, it immediately raises the theoretical problem at the basis of any explanation of total social change, i.e., of evolutionary and revolutionary *processes*. For any dynamic analysis to be effective, it must be able to deal with *unanticipated consequences* as something more than residual phenomena, that is, as a category of events of central importance to the system. In other words, structure and function must not exhibit perfect congruence.

A systems analysis of political authority from the integrative viewpoint runs up against a similar dilemma. In this view, the political system generates and distributes a certain type of functionally required facilities for the counter-system.

Within this framework, the question of the concrete political distribution of prospects for political influence has meaning only with reference to the criterion of effective integrative perform-

5. A typical illustration of this separation is found in Talcott Parsons' review of Mills' book. See 'The Distribution of Power in American Society', in *World Politics*, 1957–8, vol. 10, pp. 123–43. Parsons elaborates his controversial view in 'Voting and the Equilibrium of the American Political System', in Burdick and Brodbeck (eds.), *American Voting Behavior*, New York, 1959, pp. 80 ff.

6. This view is characteristic of analyses such as *Imperialism Today*.

ance. The ruling group is always the one which demonstrates the greatest actual or prospective capacity for getting things done in the collective interest of society. Thus, power is manifested no longer merely as the privilege of this group, but as a functionally efficient and arbitrarily expandable product (like money) of total social systems, which the latter generate and apply for the regulation and control of their equilibrium conditions.[7] In this view, then, the conflict theorists' problem of the structural distribution of prospects for political influence among structurally determined social groups becomes meaningless. Privileges falling to particular social groups can never be regarded as anything more than side effects of a regulatory process bearing on the whole of society. The integration theorists are as inclined to deny the relevance of the structural dimensions of the distribution of power as the conflict theorists are to see a political system with self-sufficient, i.e. structurally independent, functions at an analytical level.

Moreover, the ideological implications of the integration approach are quite obvious: by viewing political action and decision as a process that generates regulatory facilities and promotes so-called social goals, assumed to be independent of particular interests, it renders the relationships existing between social privileges and political authority inaccessible to analysis. The repressive factor inherent in any organization of political power evaporates, and accordingly the critical perspective necessary for emancipation from this repression becomes irrelevant.

Nonetheless, this perspective has a certain cogency. The comprehensive state regulation of all the processes vital to society – a feature which distinguishes late capitalist societies from their original bourgeois forms – is certainly brought into better focus and given more explicit treatment by the integration approach than by the competing conflict model. If one approaches the empirical power relations obtaining between societal interest groups as an unstable equilibrium kept in balance by the state apparatus, rather than as a pre-political, natural phenomenon, then the domain of 'civil society', with its semblance of autonomy, must be described in terms that bring out its politically mediated nature. In an era of comprehensive state intervention, one can no

7. Cf. Parsons, op. cit., and Easton (1965).

longer reasonably speak of 'spheres free of state interference' that constitute the 'material base' of the 'political superstructure'; an all-pervasive state regulation of social and economic processes is certainly a better description of today's order. Under these conditions, the official mechanisms sustaining the relationship between the state and society, such as subsidies, co-option, delegation, licensing, etc., reflect but subtle gradations of political control; as such, they help to maintain the fiction of a clear separation between state and society that has in fact become almost irrelevant.

This perspective, which any description of late capitalist welfare and intervention states must take into account, is more compatible with the integration approach, inasmuch as it sees political authority in the light of system-stabilizing performances rather than as an unmediated phenomenon representing particular interests, as in the opposing conflict theory.

The opposite perspective is spelled out by the theoretical conceptions of the conflict theory. Political authority appears merely as the specific form in which contradictory social interests are articulated, it being immaterial whether these interests are the expression of class structure, interest groups, political parties, power élites, or voters' behaviour. To the proponents of this view, the institutions of the political system are important mainly in their *instrumental* function – that is, as a means of power with whose help the pre-political socio-economic structure underlying these interests can be fortified and perpetuated.

Thus, our attempt to provide a theoretical framework for the analysis of the structures of authority in state-regulated capitalist systems has given rise to a dilemma. As we can no longer regard the system of political authority as a mere reflex or subsidiary organization for securing social interests, we are forced to abandon the traditional approach, which sought to reconstruct the political system and its functions from the elements of political economy. On the other hand, by so doing, we run the risk of losing sight of the fundamental authoritarian nature inherent in the organization of political power in late capitalist societies; we would then end up with a political system detached from its autonomous substrata, and as such absolved of any imputed repressed functions. This would amount to the conception that authority is tantamount to the mere temporary constitutional exercise of power and, moreover, is neutralized within a formal democratic system of institutions that conceal the shifting, pluralistic exercise of power. We can resolve this dilemma only by charting out the concrete mechanisms mediating between economics and politics – mechanisms which, on the one hand have 'politicized' social commodity-exchange down to the last detail, but which, on the other hand, have in no sense neutralized the *politicized* economy as the ultimate regulator in the functioning of political institutions.

The political constitution of liberal capitalist societies ensures the dominance of the pre-political interests of a ruling class in two ways which allow the political institutions themselves to be analysed in class terms. First, by means of the processes of political recruitment and consensus formation in a liberal constitutional system of a 'voluntary' party type, the bourgeoisie was able to utilize its ideology, political maxims, and value systems to create the preponderance that enabled it to bring the state's foreign policy, financial policy, and social policy confidently into line with its own interests. The second and most important means of co-ordinating the state apparatus with dominant capitalist interests was through mechanisms that *strictly delimited spheres of activity beyond state authority* and permitted their undisturbed use by economic persons. The restriction of state action to the functions of maintaining public order (military, the courts, police), which were carried out under a strictly neutral financial policy, created the conditions for private capital accumulation. Indeed, the bourgeois state confirmed its class nature precisely through the material limits it imposed on its authority. Any attempts to extend it would have been met with overwhelming resistance from legal institutions within the private sphere, e.g., property, the family, and contractual law.

Today we must face the fact that the defensive function of these legal institutions is no longer able in any serious way to limit the sphere of activities of the political system. Within the total system of late capitalist societies, social processes will almost without exception no longer take place beyond politics; on the contrary, they are regulated and sustained by permanent political intervention.

Thus, if we must assume that such a sphere of commodity exchange exempt from state power is no longer institutionally guaranteed in late capitalist welfare and social states, but that, on the contrary, an all-pervasive system of mechanisms for state intervention has been established, then the question of the concrete channels mediating social interests and political authority must be posed in a new way, namely: *What mechanisms ensure the dominant influence of social interests on the functioning of the political system even though these interests are no longer able to assert their former independence of the system within a free sphere beyond state power?*

In general, the repressive character of a political system – that is, those of its aspects serving to strengthen authority – is measurable in terms of whether it exempts *de facto* certain *spheres of action*, corresponding to the interests of particular groups, from the use of public force, so that these areas become sanctioned as natural and inviolable. The authoritarian character of a system of political institutions, on the other hand, is reflected in whether it accords equal *prospects for political consideration* to all the various classes of mutually incompatible social *interests, needs, and claims*, or whether these prospects are distorted or biased in some specific direction. Such a general concept of dominance or authority enables us to see beyond the momentary prospects of particular power groups and to evaluate the repressive factor intrinsic to the *institutions* distributing these prospects.

In contrast to late capitalist society, in the political structures of the liberal capitalist society the economic system was institutionalized as a domain beyond the authority of the state, and the economically dominant class possessed a *de facto* monopoly in the control of political decisions. Authority, then, was so structured that both *the limits defining the range of action of the political system, as well as those defining the prospects for the political articulation of needs, were commensurate with economically drawn class lines*. Only under such conditions can *political economy* provide the key to an analysis of the overall structures of dominance. Under the conditions of late capitalism, any attempt to explain the political organization of power through the categories of political economy becomes implausible. That is to say, *both* sides of the politically represented class relationship become problematic under the institutional conditions of late capitalist, democratically constituted societies. On the one hand, the boundaries of the exclusive domain of private interests (i.e., not merely in the sense of licensed autonomy or decentralized administration of tasks) are no longer delimitable in view of the state's universal right to intervene. On the other hand, it becomes difficult to discover, within the consensus formation of pluralistically organized interests and of universal suffrage, the institutional barriers that prevent specific interest groups within the society from participation in consensus formation. The late capitalist welfare state bases its legitimacy on the postulate of a universal participation in consensus formation and on the unbiased opportunity for all classes to utilize the state's services and to benefit from its regulatory acts of intervention.

The following reflections are offered as an attempt to describe the *ideological* features of this model of legitimation, whose continued maintenance is nonetheless of extreme importance for the stability of late capitalist socio-political systems. We shall make a point of systematically referring to the restrictions at work in both the 'input' and 'output' aspects of the political process, i.e., in consensus formation (Part II) and in regulatory executive acts (Part III). We call special attention in this attempt to the necessary deviations made from the traditional structural framework, which approached the question of dominance from the vantage point of a disjunction between economically defined classes. Whether this structural framework must be completely replaced, or only amended by the proposed alternative – an alternative based on disjunctions between categories of deprivation or between *vital areas* – is an open question which must be decided empirically.

II Mechanisms of Authority in the System of Political Consensus Formation[8]

If we regard articulated political needs – to the extent that they are processed and controlled as 'external data' by the institutions of a political system[9] – as the 'raw material' of the political process, the repressive character of that system can be evaluated on the basis of the degree of selectivity practised by institutions whose function is to transmit those needs. Or, stated as a question: What qualitatively discrete interpretations of needs are permitted access to the political system and resolution through executive action? And, conversely, what other needs are denied institutional expression and forced to seek non-political or ideological channels for processing?

One relatively crude way to regiment opportunities for political influence is to define political rights in terms of the social status of individuals. In consummate bourgeois constitutional systems such mechanisms – of which class-defined *right to vote* and inheritance or purchasing of public offices are the most obvious examples – are excluded from the list of official instrumentalities for the control of consensus formation. In advanced systems of state-regulated capitalism, political stability can be more reliably ensured through the systematic exclusion and suppression of needs which if articulated would endanger the system, than through the granting of a politically privileged status to a minority that already enjoys economic dominance (for example, through *de facto* or *de jure* restriction of suffrage to the bourgeoisie in the nineteenth century). Consequently, consensus formation is no longer filtered and controlled primarily through positive rights granted to determinate categories of *persons*, but rather through disciplined mechanisms built into the *institutions* charged with the articulation of political needs. With a remarkable consistency, these mechanisms see to the failure or collapse of such political institutions as parties, associations, trade unions, or the parliament as soon as they exceed the limits laid down in a pluralistic

8. Cf., on this section, Massing (1971).

9. Cf. the system-theory model of the political process proposed by D. Easton, op. cit., especially pp. 29 ff.

system for the articulation of needs. The exclusion, then, of deviant motives from the political process does not so much rest with the crude, unreliable techniques of differential distribution of *subjective rights*, which would in any case be difficult to legitimize; instead, all control functions are left to the conditions for success built into the structures of political organization, with, of course, their accompanying strict sanctions and safeguards.[10]

(a) The most important of these structures is the *political party*. The *de facto* or *de jure* (e.g., in the Federal Republic) elevation of the party to an organ of state has often been described.[11] The founding of new *parties*, their *financing*, and their *legal status*, as well as the right to vote, are subject to restrictive conditions whose further tightening is often demanded on the basis of the abstract and technocratic argument of 'maintaining stability'.[12] A party system subject to such sanctions bears unmistakable monopolistic features in that 'access to the market' is certainly rendered more difficult for competing groups, and the jointly administered area of influence extends (especially in the Federal Republic) beyond the narrower confines of the political system (to which, one might add, the publicly chartered communications media – radio and television – do not belong). Besides these formal similarities derived from their privileged legal status, political parties exhibit certain similarities in content as well, and justify our speaking not only of a monopoly, but even of a cartel of parties. It is no coincidence that analogies from the world of organized markets come so readily to mind. Schumpeter called attention a good while ago to the 'war of competition' for the popular vote,[13] for which a vast bureaucratic apparatus is required if it is to be waged permanently (that is, in financing of contributions, publicity, polling, etc.).[14] Because of this competition, the ability to permanently sustain a broad appeal beyond

10. This mechanism has been documented for the organizational forms of party and parliament by J. Agnoli (1968).

11. Article 21, paragraph 1, of the Basic Law.

12. This viewpoint dominates, for example, the discussion on the electoral reform, the permission and prohibition of parties, and party financing.

13. Schumpeter (1950).

14. Cf. even Max Weber (1968).

class, strata, or particular interests has become a *sine qua non* for the success of a party as such. This mechanism forces the parties to expel from the consciousness of their members as voters those opposing social interests which it had been the original purpose of parties to articulate and present to the public at large. Thus, even differences between parties lie not so much with divergent overall political conceptions as with *ad hoc*, played-up timely issues of high press value, which of course must never compromise any actual or potential coalition truce. The smallest common denominator for an election strategy, on the basis of which a party's 'image' (and often that of its top candidates) is constructed, is necessarily in a lower key than the rationally acknowledged contrast of interests between the most important group of voters, such as the rural population, small industry and crafts, and industrial labourers. It lies at the demoscopically perceivable level of privately held values, claims of particular groups for subsidies and compensations, and traditional resentments. Thus it is precisely this area of needs – an area about which there is the least political enlightenment – which turns out to be the most important as a criterion for successful party strategy.

To balance the parties' privileged position, which verges on being a state monopoly, the constitutional text of the Basic Law requires a democratic party structure and the co-operation and active participation of the parties in the shaping of the political will. They must serve as more than the mere vehicle for the transmission of empirical interests and needs; they must also help to generate and articulate the informed political wills of their members within a party atmosphere of rational internal debate and discussion.[15] But the clash of this conception with the most rudimentary precepts of election strategy is obvious. If equal opportunities for representation were granted to minority opinions, if the establishment of an organized opposition within the party were openly condoned, or if the party 'management' were to renounce the prerogative of restrictively influencing the staffing of the party apparatus and the parliamentary faction, any party

15. The judicial and philosophical problems that stand in the way of carrying out this precept are analysed in, for example, Leibholz (1957); Abendroth and Habermas (1968).

would find itself substantially obstructed in its efforts to present a coherent image of itself to a depoliticized public, a consideration which is all the more serious as this image is of paramount importance in ensuring electoral success. Furthermore, these restrictions, if imposed, would diminish the flexibility which for any party is tactically indispensable for effective non-public extra-parliamentary negotiations with organized interests. Given this dilemma, efforts, for strategical reasons, to play down the constitutional precept calling for *intra-party* democracy are only logical.[16]

(b) These restrictions also apply at the level of those interests organized in *associations and trade unions*. We can obtain a more concrete idea of the restrictions that constitute, as it were, the elementary structures within which needs are given political articulation in a pluralistic system of associations if we investigate *the conditions which must be fulfilled* if a social interest is to be at all capable of representation through an association. Accordingly, a social need must be (a) *organizable*, and (b) *capable of conflict*.

Social needs and interests may be considered *organizable* if and only if they are able to mobilize sufficient motivational and material resources for establishing an association or similar instrument for the representation of interests. The organizability of an interest is contingent on whether there exist definite, clearly definable groups of natural or legal persons who, because of their special social position, are interested in the political representation of *specific* needs. Only those interests are organizable which may be interpreted as the special needs of a social group. A further qualification is that this special interest must be sufficiently clear-cut and important to the actual and potential members of the group for them to be prepared to contribute the necessary resources. Accordingly, the *primary* needs (opportunities for consumption or investment, coverage of social risks, allocation of leisure time) of large and relatively homogeneous status groups (farmers, workers, salaried employees, officials, small- and medium-sized businessmen and craftsmen, entrepreneurs, etc.)

16. U. Lohmar makes such an attempt in his book on inter-party democracy (Stuttgart, 1964).

are the easiest to organize. In contrast, vital necessities that are not particular to any clearly delimitable status or functional group but are shared by the totality of individuals are more difficult to organize, if indeed they are amenable to immediate organization at all. Indeed, those general needs (i.e., those bearing on housing, health, transportation, education, civil law, leisure-time activities) concerning the physical, moral, and aesthetic conditions of life in society are for structural reasons refractory to organization in the form of association or interest group.[17] In these cases where this category of needs does find representation within the political system, this representation is achieved not through an association of natural persons, that is, those individuals in whom these needs directly reside, but in either of two ways: (a) through alliances of multi-functional, juridical persons, in other words, organizations whose particular functions predetermine and superintend the specific forms through which these needs are to be satisfied (i.e., municipal assemblies, conferences of school principles, conferences of cultural ministers, health insurance associations); or (b) through such organizations which, because of the nature of their particular economic and professional interests, are directly involved within some sector of such general social needs (e.g., organizations of physicians, transport employees' associations, teachers' unions).

In a pluralistic system of associations, only those interests which derive their definition and legitimation from the functions and counter-functions of subscribing groups of economic persons are able to find the means for organized and politically effective expression. The institutional frame of reference of the system charged with consensus formation defines the citizen as a bearer of needs only within the sphere in which he is also a performing agent. At this point, the institutionalized principle of exchange appears at the political level.

This brings us directly to the second condition for the organiza-

17. This is even stressed by, for example, conservative theoreticians of the state, such as E. Forsthoff: 'There are interests which are so general that they are unable to find a patron in society . . . The chance of realizing an interest that is so general that it lies beyond the limits of societal patronage is slighter than the chance of social interests' (1964), pp. 203 ff.

tion of social interests: they must be *capable of conflict*, and the degree to which they are so determines their prospects for exerting a political influence. The capacity for conflict refers to the capacity of an organization, or the corresponding functional group, to collectively refuse to perform, or to present a plausible threat of such a refusal to the system in a relevant way. A collection of status groups and functional groups is indeed organizable, but not capable of conflict (at any event, not within the institutionally prescribed modes for the expression of conflict). Groups consisting of housewives, secondary school pupils, college students, the unemployed, retired persons, criminals, the mentally ill, and ethnic minorities may be cited as examples. The capacity of these groups to bring their influence successfully to bear is small inasmuch as their functional utility is minimal. Consequently, their refusal to perform does not possess the power of sanction. Interest organizations are available to these groups also. However, as a rule, the existence of such groups, and their admittance to the 'stock exchange' of pluralistic interests, depends on mass moral support or material *subsidies*, which in turn produce a peculiar shift of direction in the activities of these associations. The actual goal of association is not the political representation of members' interests, but the disciplining of members, and the creation of integrative symbols. Within the political system of the Federal Republic there are two typical examples of this mechanism of politically subsidized group interests with no capacity for conflict: the associations of expelled persons, and the German Sports Federation.[18] Both represent sets of needs which must be regarded as totally peripheral to the centralized processes of social utility. Both, therefore, possess a low level of autonomous conflict potential, even though as vehicles for the promotion of national and other integrative sentiments they enjoy considerable opportunity for exercising influence. Other less obvious examples of this sort of 'colonial status' of associations can be seen in the relationships between political parties and youth and student associations, and between the churches and church-affiliated welfare and humanitarian institutions.

18. Until just a few years ago, the U.D.S. (Association of German Students) could certainly have been ranked in this class.

The adverse side of the capacity to give politically pointed expression to claims and demands specific to particular groups is the tendency, inherent in association politics, to blunt the weapon of sanction through too-frequent use. Demands articulated through associations must be negotiable, that is, they must offer concrete prospects for pragmatic success. This means that collective means of struggle (e.g., strikes) retain political cogency only so long as their use is perceived by all those implicated as the exceptional case that must not grow into a permanent confrontation, for just that could deprive the conflicting parties of those motivational and material resources accorded them by their members in the anticipation of a short-term victory. The adage that a protracted conflict is a loss for all is more than merely the rhetoric of pacification – it is part and parcel of the way in which pluralistic interest organizations function. This fact has two consequences for the internal structure of associations and trade unions. In the first place, it means that the formulation of negotiable bargaining positions can decidedly not take place within the association's internal forum. A bargaining strategy would deprive itself of all prospects of success if it were tied to the exhaustively debated directives and binding decisions of the membership. Diplomatic manoeuvring and the flexible exploitation of unforeseen situations would then be made impossible. If, however, the *exclusion* of bargaining strategy from the open forum is made a functional prerequisite of success, internal democracy is lost. Steering committees, negotiating committees, and lobbyists must be shielded against the 'irrelevant', unrealistic demands of the ordinary, uninitiated association member if their own bargaining positions are not to be placed in jeopardy. This requires, in turn, a methodical and ongoing disciplining of members by the association's leaders, at least in organizations such as trade unions, to give the classic example, which must deeply impress on their members the risks involved in 'utopian' statements of their needs.

For an analysis of these contingencies,[19] which we have been able to present only summarily, political sociology need no longer

19. Cf. also the concept, developed by Werner Weber of the 'mediation of the people through associations and parties', in Weber (1958).

be bound by the concept of a 'dominant interest' (that is, intentional aims specific to a ruling class). In the early, less organized period of bourgeois society, mechanisms of suppression and repression still required an explicit act of will on the part of the dominant groups of individuals. Today, this is no longer the case. The very manner in which political institutions function and the immanent conditions for their continuing stability have made these mechanisms automatic. To be sure, the functions are still equivalent: *the pluralistic system of organized interests excludes from the processes concerned with consensus formation all articulations of demands that are general in nature and not associated with any status group; that are incapable of conflict because they have no functional significance for the utilization of capital and labour power; and that represent utopian projections beyond the historically specific* system insofar as they do not unconditionally abide by the pragmatic rules of judicious bargaining.

(c) *Parliaments* comprise the third principal group of institutions sustaining the processes concerned with consensus formation. To be sure, it is nowadays questionable whether parliament's function – to represent and carry out the political will – is still real, or has become merely an ideological postulate. It is an evident fact that the majority of legislative proposals and fundamental political decisions now fall under the responsibility of the executive branch with its vast bureaucratic information and regulatory facilities. It can more reliably decide issues because it has access to more information and greater chances for enlisting co-operation; and it can operate smoothly, without friction, because its non-public decision-making processes are shielded from the pressure of legitimation.

A further indication that the classical *separation* of powers has in fact been transformed into a flexible *distribution of functions* between the executive and legislative branches is the objective necessity for co-operation that is quite evident in the relationship between government and government fraction. If it is, indeed, still meaningful to speak of an institutionalized line of conflict within the political system, it is certainly not drawn between the parliament and the government, but between the government and the government fraction on the one hand, and the parliamentary opposition on the other.

In the institutionalized permanent electoral struggle, the government and parliamentary fraction of the government party are dependent on one another in a way which prohibits the participation of the latter in the public regulatory functions of the parliament. Through this overlapping strategy of its party apparatus, the government and the government fraction are able to exercise complementary functions in maintaining or expanding their share of power. In this interplay the *executive* has the power to meet the demands of important voter groups through social and economic measures at least to the extent that serious loyalty crises may be avoided. The *majority fractions in parliament* assume, then, the responsibility of shaping the parties' public image by giving due evaluation to the government's performances, explaining its good intentions, and providing adequate press coverage of its achievements.

This shift of decision-making to the executive branch, and the agitational competition of the parties within parliament, has come about at the expense of both the initiating and regulatory functions of parliament, and gives much of parliamentary work its tributary character. Even the most enterprising plenary sessions create the impression more of a joint meeting of the public relations departments of the various parties than of a rational struggle over interests for the purpose of working out binding guidelines for political action. In all fairness, however, the ideological postulate that parliament is the *generator* of a representative will must still be credited with some degree of cogency as long as such a mechanism is relevant to the legitimacy of the political system as a whole. *The tensions inherent in parliamentarianism stem directly from this contradictory dual function – namely, first, the fiction that parliament is the permanent generative body of the public will and, second, the processes within the executive sphere that now function largely independently to shield and defend it against publicly articulated demands.*

In view of the institutionalized barriers that surround processes concerned with consensus formation, it is questionable whether the actual functions of parliament still have any bearing at all on this process. The full import of these restrictions is of course first brought out where an effective parliamentary opposition is lacking.[20] But even when this is the case, there are structural reasons for it that lie at least in part in the nature of the party system. I have attempted to show that the privileged organizational form of the political party is in itself an obstacle to the development of special political institutions that transcend the system – institutions which can only exist on the basis of the collective self-enlightenment of the citizens to their social needs. For this reason alone, only a very limited portion of the possible points constituting a political programme can be raised for discussion in parliament as long as the composition and political behaviour of the parliamentary fractions are controlled by the party apparatuses. Another mechanism is also operative: the important function of the parliamentary fractions, especially their political prominence in sustaining the permanent electoral struggle of their respective parties, exposes them to the pressures of conformity in their attitudes towards each other (especially the opposition fraction in relation to the government fraction). Since the voting constituency of the parties does not have a clearly delimited socio-structural composition, but in fact displays extensive overlappings, the large parties ('national parties') at any rate are compelled to defer to almost identical sets of expectations and demands in shaping their public image. Under the structural conditions of the advanced welfare state, it is the government and the parties participating in it that decide and determine the political allocation of means to satisfy these demands.[21] Given this situation, a party in opposition, and its parliamentary fraction, has no other alternative in its electoral tactics than to demand – with a few subtle distinctions – essentially *the same things* that the government has already set out to do. Indeed, only

20. Cf., on the following, O. Kirchheimer's essay 'Wandlungen der politischen Opposition', in *Politik und Verfassung*, Frankfurt, 1964, pp. 123 ff.

21. Cf. Forsthoff, op. cit., p. 203: 'Equivalence of opportunity between government and opposition is eliminated ... to the same extent as the political system is characterized by the structures of a welfare state.'

in this way can it hope to retain its election prospects among the voter groups on whom the government has already bestowed benefits. Such a mechanism produces, on the one hand, a situation of constrained agreement among the parties and fractions over *questions of principle*, while, on the other, it gives rise to ritualistic attempts to create a credible party image through belaboured *hair-splitting, superficial distinctions, and specious polemics.* Controversies over programme are likely to occur only on secondary questions: for example, (a) on questions in which one party assumes the role of advocate for the demands of marginal groupings that other parties regard as too inconsequential to be worth winning over; or (b) in subtle distinctions whose accentuation is meant to suggest an independence in viewpoint that in fact none of the participants in the party 'cartel' could seriously hope to achieve. The depoliticizing implications of this situation of constrained harmony, which in turn serve to reinforce this very situation, are obvious.

The very conditions that are alone able to guarantee the efficient operation and self-perpetuation of institutions charged with consensus formation oblige them – and this is a characteristic shared by all such institutions – to stray from the principle of unrestricted transmission of political motives. In this way they come to function as filter systems that bar certain types of needs from any chance of political articulation. Formally viewed, all such suppressed motives pertain to interests whose sole outlet for discussion is within institutions charged with *consensus formation and serving as vehicles for collective reflection.* The purely instrumental concept of organization, which rests at the basis of the structures of all modern associations and parties, makes no provisions for that other dimension of organized consensus formation, namely, the rational self-enlightenment of individual members on matters concerning their own collective interests.[22] By virtue of just this defect, the prevailing forms of political organization, e.g., the party, trade union, interest group, parlia-

22. On the interconnection between organizational forms and the structures of articulated needs, see G. Lukács' essay 'On the Question of Organization', in *History and Class Consciousness*, Merlin Press, 1971; Abendroth and Habermas, op. cit.

ment, etc., approach the nature of *service enterprises*[23] in that they offer gratification to the specific interests of particular groups through the symbolic affirmation of prevailing values achieved by representing these interests. In return they obtain a formal declaration of organizational loyalty in practice and the acceptance of membership responsibilities. In this type of organization, motives come to constitute a kind of substrate of needs deprived of any prospect of self-realization because they have been eliminated from the community of political interchange that is no longer within the capacities of the party apparatuses to maintain. To the same extent, these needs become private (here, in the quite general categories of private needs, is to be found the structural analogy of the privileged influence which the bourgeois class state accorded to capitalist interests).

Substantively seen, these suppressed needs correspond, then, to the *practical norms*[24] whose formulation can give rise to new forms of social interaction and new forms for the satisfaction of needs – in short, historical progress – because such norms would not be bound to the customary dimensions of equity in performance and exchange, or to the traditional rights claimed by virtue of status.

III The Authority Functions of the State Apparatus[25]

By the new dimension he gave to the concept of class, which he defined as the community of equal opportunities for exploitation of vital services on the market,[26] Max Weber established a theoretical orientation which has today become an almost uni-

23. Although it is not employed critically, this insight also determines the flow diagrams of the political process customary to systems theory, structured on the analogy of processes of exchange in a market economy. Cf. Parsons, op. cit.; Easton, op. cit.; and H. Tingstom, 'Stability and Vitality in Swedish Democracy', in *Political Quarterly*, 1955, 26, pp. 146–58.

24. J. Habermas has developed and demonstrated the distinction between practical and technical or strategical rules in *Theorie und Praxis*, Neuwied, 1963, and especially in *Technik und Wissenschaft als Ideologie*, Frankfurt, 1968, pp. 69 ff.

25. The following arguments are partially derived from the corresponding sections of a paper that G. Brandt *et al.* prepared for the Sociologists' Meeting in Frankfurt, 1968 (Bergmann, 1969).

26. M. Weber (1964), vol. 2, pp. 679 ff.

versal frame of reference for inquiries into social inequality. This general model, compatible with critical[27] and Marxist-inspired[28] analyses alike, derives its justification from a few implicit postulates that may be formulated roughly as follows: (a) the supply of production units – individually provided labour power or units of capital – enter unit markets whose equilibrium conditions at any given moment generate a determinable *unit income*; (b) this *unit income* as it is expended in consumption determines the sum total of life chances available to individuals; (c) variations in the conditions of origin and in the magnitude of income create different types of life chances, which in turn determine the different class positions; (d) the individuals constituting a social system can be ascribed definite class positions within a vertical hierarchy. To these class positions correspond *levels of consciousness*, the conflict between which provides a vehicle for dynamic historical processes.

Various trends suggest that this venerable analytic schema is ripe for re-examination and force us to question the range of its explanatory value. Under the conditions of state-regulated capitalism, the threads holding the individual elements of this conceptual framework together have become timeworn to such an extent that cogent arguments may be put forth against its continued use. We base this view on the following considerations.

(a) The relationship between individual *labour productivity* and the *labour income* accruing from it has become more casual. Under advanced industrial conditions, in which labour has largely become an integrated facet of an overall organized framework with a specialized horizontal and vertical breakdown of functions, this relationship is determined by political and quasi-political mechanisms of appraisal and no longer directly by a market valuation. The market relationship has become virtual rather than real to the owner of labour power. In its place has appeared a traditional kind of consensus on 'appropriate' compensation, to which economic categories of value are no longer pertinent. Moreover, the tendency to subject the level of disposable individual income directly to *political regulation* (incomes policy, legislated social

27. E.g., Kolko (1962).

28. E.g., Institut für Gesellschaftswissenschaften beim Zk der SED (Hrzg.).

services, minimal wage guarantees, etc.) has become a common phenomenon.

(b) For the broad middle group, living above the minimum for a civilized existence but below the top income percentile, the concrete living conditions still within the individual's power to alter through personal allocation of *income* are becoming fewer and fewer in number. The relationship between income and life chances has thus become more tenuous. Beyond the sphere of individual consumption extends a range of vital needs for whose satisfaction the means are not individually purchasable, but are institutionally and politically determined and distributed, for example, education, social security, physical safety, health, transportation, housing, and the use of leisure time, to mention a few.[29] Not only does the consumer find a radically diminished number of categories of life chances in which his income is still sovereign, the sphere of immediate consumption has also been severely curtailed in this respect. Because of the rapid innovations in consumer goods, the market output includes not only use values but also the motives for possessing them *and* their obsolescence; the very concept of 'supply' takes on ideological import. Choice becomes merely the consumer's *reaction* to a pre-established supply that brooks little resistance.

(c) As politically manipulable variables now intervene extensively between labour and income, and between the latter and the concrete structures of life chances, the new forms of *social inequality* are no longer directly reducible to economically defined *class relationships* which they are assumed to reflect. A new approach is necessary. We must discover at the political level those mechanisms that have replaced the 'vertical' system of class inequality with a '*horizontal*' *system of disparities between vital areas*, and that preserve the minor inequalities still directly due to economic causes by foregoing intervention.

(d) The coincidence of these conditions of disparity (which must still be traced functionally) with the remaining instances of

29. Kolko overlooks the loosening of the relationship between income and life chances in just these areas when he explains the poverty to be found in them by inequality of income; cf. Kolko, op. cit., pp. 117 ff.; cf. Galbraith's thesis of 'poverty admits affluence' in *The Affluent Society*.

market-mediated inequality thoroughly vitiates the connections between *class status*, *level of consciousness*, and *historically relevant potential for conflict*. If it is realistic to assume that in the planned capitalist welfare state domination of man over man (or of one class over another) has largely given way to the dominance of a few spheres of social function over others, we cannot expect that this situation will still be manifested in the confrontation of *collectivities*, as was assumed in theories of class struggle. The gap that ran *between* the great position groups in the early stages of capitalist development has shifted, as it were, to within individuals themselves. Some of the vital activities of the individual take place within 'privileged' functional spheres, while other areas of activity remain under-privileged.[30] The remaining lines of inequality are, moreover, so multi-dimensional and intangible[31] that the social conflicts they contain are in part suppressed by flexible adjustments within the political distribution system, and in part softened by subjective perceptions of relative deprivation.[32]

What structural mechanisms are the functional determinants of the political system under conditions that lay the political groundwork for the above-described possibilities of intervention in the social process, and at the same time set the stage for comprehensive social coverage of basic vital needs? In the late capitalist welfare state, how are the top-level political and administrative decision-making processes determined? The organizations that should fulfil these functions – at least according to the democratic constitutional state's own postulates – have in our view degenerated to no more than 'representative' filter systems. It is, accordingly, hardly conceivable that any political administrative action would be directly forthcoming in response to the immediate

30. In these areas are to be found the structural premises for the phenomenon of status inconsistency which has recently come under intense scrutiny by American sociologists; cf. Lenski (1954) and Jackson (1962).

31. The system of multiple cleavages required by disparity relationships is regarded by Lipset as a contribution to the freedom from conflict and stability of democratic systems; cf. op. cit., pp. 88 ff.

32. The concept of relative deprivation takes into account the sub-cultural aspirations and communication structures situated between the 'objective situation' and the effective consequences of social inequality. See Runciman (1966).

claims and interests of the population. However, even in the case of claims that are organizable, capable of conflict, and, consequently, appropriate material for the formation of organized interest groups, it is not easy to perceive to what extent the range of interests, which at this level is already quite limited, can be expected to provide adequate cause for political administrative action. The pluralistic system of countervailing powers owes much of its existence to the multiplicity of divergent claims publicly represented by organized interests; and it is difficult to conceive how any particular interests could attain a position of permanent dominance within such a system. Political parties of the 'national' [*Volks*] or 'representative' [*Vertretung*] types, which unite a plurality of competing claims within their ranks, show as little evidence as the system of organized interest groups of a *structurally guaranteed* supremacy of a particular political strategy, or of a focal point of power that could only be accounted for by the particular structures of the institutionalized consensus formation processes. The social sciences have attempted to find structurally definable social power groups within the political systems of the United States and Western Europe, power groups which would be independently capable of competently managing the executive and administrative functions of the state in their own interests, and which thus could fill the theoretical lacuna of a 'ruling' class.[33] To my knowledge, none of these attempts have produced very enlightening results.

Consequently, we must, as I see it, abandon those perspectives that, along the lines of orthodox Marxism as well as the Weberian tradition of the sociology of authority, analyse the organization of social power on the basis of an *intentional* model of *self-interested use of the means of power*. This shift in perspective requires the replacement of the old frame of reference of structurally privileged *interests of a ruling class* (or its 'executive board') with a new set of criteria for the analysis of systems of political administrative action, namely, a schema consisting of *three fundamental system problems*. The management of these problems has become an *objective imperative*, transcending particular interests, for the political system. The following three sets of problems,

33. See especially Mills, op. cit.; and Domhoff (1967).

which have taken on something of the status of *questions of survival* for the system as a whole, must represent our point of departure in any analysis.

(a) *Problems bearing on economic stability.* These include the problems of guaranteed full employment and balanced economic growth. The crucial problem is to provide those agencies possessed of the institutional competence to make decisions concerning the realization of capital with sufficiently strong incentives and opportunities for investment, and, moreover, to give compensation for lack of opportunity to invest. In such problems – typical of those with which political administrative management centres are confronted – is manifested the continued basic capitalist structure of the economic system. Moreover – and this justifies the qualification of *late* capitalist – there can be no question that the realization of *private* capital is politically mediated down to the last detail precisely because of its key position in maintaining the continued stability of the system as a whole. Subsidies for research and development, tax incentives to the entrepreneurial will to invest, regulation of sales through trade policy, and the regulation of demand volume through market policy[34] – these are only a few indications that in advanced interventionist states the economic system is no longer a *pre-political* substrate but is, in fact, one of the most important areas of state action. From its former status as a realm 'beyond' the domain of commodity exchange, it has become the medium of the latter, and its active regulation ensures the governability of the society as a whole. Autonomous entrepreneurial initiative is not a natural right; it is a functionally implementable motive force, whose agents become the 'executors of an enlightened economic policy'.[35]

(b) *Problems of foreign policy, foreign trade, and military policy.* This area concerns the equilibrium problems generated at the supranational level of organization of the economy and military apparatus. In the face of external threats to the system, which alone issue from neo-colonialist and imperialist claims to geo-

34. Detailed presentations of the multi-faceted economic regulatory methods of late capitalist systems are given in Neumark (1961); and Schonfield (1968).

35. K. Schiller in his introduction to Schonfield, op. cit.

graphic spheres of influence, this set of problems becomes as relevant to the continued stability of the system as economic problems. Its criteria for political and administrative action pertain to the areas of armament, alliances, developmental policy, and monetary policy.

(c) *Problems concerned with ensuring mass loyalty.* These problems pertain to the internal integration of the population. The conditions for mass loyalty are satisfied when the thresholds of conflict between individual interest groups remain unviolated over long periods, and the functionally required level of *apathetic conformity* to the agencies of the political system exists. The concept of mass loyalty marks a point of departure from the traditional concept of *legitimacy* insofar as it consists not in the steadfast acceptance of a given order, but, on the contrary, in the total renunciation of any claim for legitimation. Conflict potentials that would imperil the system are disciplined by modes of political action such as the handing down of decisions, the proclamation of integrative symbols and ideologies, and the forcible suppression of uncontrolled propagation of motives [*Motivbildung*] and of deviant political interpretations of needs.

These three categories of problems are of absolutely paramount importance for the continued stability of the system; moreover, the *political* system of late capitalist society is alone competent and qualified to deal with them. From these three sets of problems two relationships emerge.

First, an imbalance in *one* problem area threatens always to extend to the other two. As an illustration we may recall France in 1968, which experienced a crisis in political loyalty, an economic crisis, and a monetary crisis in rapid succession, all within a period of six months. Second, the high measure of interdependence of the problem areas entails that a dependable clearing up of the crisis in one area is generally accompanied by the risk of actualizing others. An example of this is the British stop-and-go economic policy: through its continual vacillation between foreign trade, military, and market measures in attempting to solve the country's economic problems, it was driven into perpetuating a dilemma that is finally showing signs of growing into a crisis of domestic loyalty (strikes, the racial question).

With these three basic problem areas, and the two interdependence axioms as a frame of reference, the state apparatuses of all late capitalist societies devise the most intricate techniques and methods of technocratic administration. They alone are responsible for the picture of relative stability and adaptability we see. *The principal function of a political system of the type investigated may be described as cautious crisis management and long-term avoidance strategy.*[36] In pursuance of these functions, the share of political demands channelled from institutional sectors to any given functional group within the society will vary, the greatest share always being directed to those groups which are able to make the most effective contribution towards the reduction of risk under the circumstances.

Two important features of this new type of structure for political action are its *institutionalized pattern of priorities* and the new concept of *politics* it represents.

Preventive crisis management as a type of political action is only fully functionable when it is in a position to react to continually changing hazards to the total system with a certain flexibility, and to give priority treatment at any time to that problem area where the gravest danger seems to lie. (In line with this flexible responsiveness, even the effective emancipation of the state apparatus from any possible privileged influence on the part of certain power groups may be an indispensable condition.) But this also means that certain vital areas of society will have slight prospects of state intervention or state subvention when they find themselves in a crisis, simply because the consequences of such a crisis would have no important relevance for the stability of the system as a whole. As an 'overdose' of state interventions generally tends to give rise to problems in other areas, the minimum of permanent regulation necessary for stability will usually not be

36. An authoritative view of preventive coverage of the total socio-political system against factors jeopardizing its stability can be obtained from the list of the most important legislative proposals (stabilization laws, electoral amendment, financial reform, emergency constitution, preventive detention) and socio-political reform projects ('the planned society') that have been produced by the political system of the Federal Republic in recent years.

found wanting, but it will also not be essentially exceeded – in the sense of ambitious structural reforms in the absence of crisis.

From these simple guidelines of rational administration we may construct *a concentric system of priorities* with respect to social needs and problem areas. In this system, the more gravely the violation of any claim or principle of intervention compromises the basic prerequisites for stability, the higher the level of priority that will be assigned to the corresponding problem area. Conversely, social needs that cannot present a credible case for the dangerous consequences that would ensue (or that they could precipitate) if their claim were ignored lie on the periphery of the sphere of state action. The disparity created by this structural mechanism between the various problem areas and spheres of needs increases the more urgently the state's available resources are needed for the central problems of guaranteeing continual prospects for capital realization, sufficient effective demand, maintenance of foreign trade relations, military crisis avoidance, or the prevention or quelling of domestic conflicts. An empirical characteristic of the disparity between vital areas is the various lags in development between the *actually institutionalized level* and the *possible level* of technical and social progress. The discrepancy between the most advanced production and military apparatus and the stagnating organization of transportation, health, and education is likewise a notorious example of the contradiction between rational planning and regulation of fiscal and financial policy, and the anarchic, ungoverned development of cities and regions.

If such contradictions can no longer be plausibly interpreted as *class antagonisms*, they must at least be regarded as *necessary by-products of an integral political system of control* – a system which utilizes the 'driving forces' of capital realization processes and the non-public agreements made between oligarchic political power groups while at the same time subordinating itself to them. A consequence of this control model is that *structurally determined privileges* in functional areas accrue to certain interest groups, which, because of their functional indispensability, if not on the basis of commonly proclaimed and commonly prosecuted interests, are favoured in the enjoyment of political subventions.

A second consequence of the model is that structural curbs are placed on vital areas, social groups, and categories of needs that are incapable of generating dangers to the system as a whole and that therefore can present a less weighty claim to political intervention.

The repressive factor of political authority extends into this functional poising of areas of state action. Specifically, certain groups and vital areas are excluded from enjoying the services of public authority. This seems to be symptomatic of a phase in capitalist development in which areas of crisis peripheral to the central group of problems, however segregated and insignificant they may be within the institutional system, are hindered from generating further disturbances to the system, but are otherwise left to themselves without the privileges of class or stratum playing any further significant role for the overwhelming majority of those concerned. This would mean that the pauperism of the early capitalist proletariat has given way to the modern pauperism of depressed areas: the areas of education, transportation, housing, and health, which affect the *entire population*, are obvious cases in point. Institutions that are marginal to the mainstream of life, such as the pre-school socializing phase, unemployment, old age after retirement, the mentally ill, and criminals, are further examples, as are the exceptional situations of ethnic minorities, branches of the economy with no future, slums, and structural poverty areas. A concept that traces a certain parallel to the strata and class conflicts accentuated by the vertical pattern of social inequality would perhaps be the notion of different '*situational groupings*' – a notion that emphasizes the disparity between vital areas. These would be groups that were exposed to situationally dependent deprivations and frustrations without the individuals' status on the income scale being able to do much to alleviate problems and crises. The examples alluded to tend to confirm the view that *under state-regulated capitalism, all-out class conflict is no longer the driving force of social change. A horizontal pattern of inequality, that is, disparities between vital areas, is emerging increasingly into the foreground.*

Nevertheless, it is still probable that the groups and strata that were under-privileged in the classic phase of capitalism will also be the ones most likely to suffer from the systemic flaws obstructing the harmonious development of productive forces and the emergence of increased prospects for freedom in all areas of social life. The effects of discriminatory distribution and horizontal disparity accumulate, as it were, on the lower levels of the income scale. For this reason, we by no means wish to create the impression that the traditional pattern of vertical inequality has lost its significance for the general trend of things. We wish merely to emphasize that the eclipsing of traditional relationships of class inequality by the new situation of politically determined disparity has brought about a structural transformation of momentous implications for political strategy as well as for mere analytical purposes. Because the lines of conflict are no longer drawn between classes but between vital areas affecting the same individuals, disjunctions in living standards are no longer a fit basis for the organization of conflicts of broad social relevance. But where manifest conflict potentials nevertheless do still accumulate, they are dealt with straight away under the relatively unerring management of a pacifying political administration. How *overtly* the fascistic basic structure linked with this situation is manifested depends on *contingent* factors.

The actual range of action manifested by the political administrative centre of late capitalist societies displays a concentration of regulative performances on actual or conceivable danger zones, with the accompanying disparity that creates between vital areas. But in addition, it is also characteristic that the rules guiding the administrative operations in this area belong to the category of technical preventive rules, i.e., rules that are in principle 'non-practical'.[37] A new *technocratic concept of politics* becomes relevant, a concept whose intention is no longer the seeing through of correct and just vital reforms, but the conservation of social relations which claim mere functionability as their justification. The second analytic criterion for the repressiveness of authority may be applied to this situation, namely, the criterion of the range of particular articulations of needs that are denied access to the political decision-making process. To the extent that the functions of the state apparatus are restricted to inter-

37. Cf. note 24.

ventionist services aimed at maintaining stability, intentions having genuinely democratic origins must rebound without effect from the administrative system, because these services presuppose no more than the ideologically neutral consideration of an objective order;[38] at the most, the intentional surplus the democratic process produces beyond the strictly objectively necessary would be recorded as one disturbance factor among others, while the *status quo* as such is permanently barred from becoming the focus of political motivation.

But when the decision-making processes within the public bureaucracies are no longer predominantly determined by *guidelines for action* based on a consensus, but come to be governed by technically interpreted *avoidance imperatives*, we must once again approach the question of the functional connection between institutions charged, however restrictively, with shaping the political process and those offices entrusted with the executive tasks of ensuring stability. It would be easy to assume that political institutions such as parties, interest groups, trade unions, parliaments, and even elections have largely lost their functions. Why, then, do they not simply wither away? Their seismographic function, that is, to warn of latent conflict potentials, can with little effort be replaced by demoscopic techniques. But such a view would, of course, overlook the *complementary* functions that organizations which still compose their propagandistic image in the categories of practical intentions exercise vis-à-vis sectors oriented predominantly towards avoidance imperatives. Avoidance imperatives are, after all, distinguished by their disruptive social consequences in cases where they evolve into the dominant incentives for action. They immediately pose the question whether they *themselves* were not avoidable. The flood-tide of an infinite regression of this sort, during the course of which all structural constants of the social system would have to be challenged, can only be sustained by institutions which transform the value-free *imperatives of the technocrats into political maxims still subject to a consensus.*

Unconditional technocratic rationality can only flourish in the

38. This correlation has been laid out in detail by Schelsky (1961); Lübbe (1962); and Forsthoff.

shadow of ideological postulates. According to Luhmann,[39] it is the task of the 'ideology planners' to produce this rationality. It is a reasonable assumption, in any event, that an important task of parties and parliaments is the prevention of the disintegrative implications of an explicit technocratic model of decision-making by explaining what would happen anyway to be the result of popular intentions. If one were to pursue this proposed interpretation[40] a step further, one would probably find that political parties, the parliament, and the institution of universal suffrage are the most important state instruments for maintaining the mass loyalty necessary for stability.

References

ABENDROTH, W. (1967), *Antagonistische Gesellschaft und soziale Demokratie*, Neuwied.
AGNOLI, J. (1968), *Die Transformation der Demokratie*, Berlin.
ARON, R. (1966), 'Social Class, Political Class, Ruling Class', in Bendix and Lipset (eds.), *Class, Status and Power*, New York, pp. 208–9.
BERGMANN, J., *et al.* (1969), 'Herrschaft, Klassenverhaltnis und Schichtung', in T. W. Adorno (ed.), *Spätkapitalismus oder Industriegesellschaft?*, Stuttgart, pp. 67–87.
DOMHOFF, G. W. (1967), *Who Rules America*, Englewood Cliffs, New Jersey.
EASTON, D. (1965), *A Systems Analysis of Political Life*, New York.
FORSTHOFF, E. (1964), *Rechtsstaat im Wandel*, Stuttgart.
GALBRAITH, J. K. (1958), *The Affluent Society*, Hamish Hamilton.
HABERMAS, J. (1963), *Theorie und Praxis*, Neuwied/Berlin. Translated as *Theory and Practice*, tr. J. Viertel, London/Boston, 1973.
HABERMAS, J. (1968), *Technik und Wissenschaft als Ideologie*, Frankfurt, pp. 69 ff.
JACKSON, E. (1962), 'Status Consistency and Symptoms of Stress', *American Sociological Review*, vol. 27, pp. 469–86.
KIRCHHEIMER, O. (1964), 'Wandlungen der politischen Opposition', *Politik und Verfassung*, Frankfurt, pp. 123 ff.
KOLKO, G. (1962), *Wealth and Power in America: An Analysis of Social Class and Income Distribution*, New York.
LEIBHOLZ, G. (1957), *Strukturprobleme der modernen Demokratie*, Karlsruhe.
LENSKI, C. (1954), 'Status Crystallization, a Non-Vertical Dimension of Social Status', *American Sociological Review*, vol. 19, pp. 405–13.
LIPSET, S. M. (1965), *Sociology of Democracy*, Neuwied, p. 33.
LOHMAR, U. (1964), *Innerparteiliche Demokratie*, Stuttgart.

39. Luhmann (1962), pp. 431 ff.
40. Agnoli, op. cit., also argues along these lines.

LÜBBE, H. (1962), 'Zur politischen Theorie der Technokratie', *Der Staat*, no. 1, pp. 19 ff.
LUHMANN, N. (1962), *Wahrheit und Ideologie*, *Der Staat*, no. 1, pp. 431 ff.
LUKÁCS, G. (1923), *Geschichte und Klassenbewusstsein*, Berlin. Published in Britain as *History and Class Consciousness*, Merlin Press, 1971.
MASSING, O. (1971), 'Parteien und Verbande als Faktoren des politischen Prozesses – Aspekte politischer Soziologie', in G. Kress and D. Senghaas (eds.), *Politikenwissenschaft*, Frankfurt, pp. 324–67.
MILLS, C. W. (1956), *The Power Elite*, New York, p. 5.
NEUMARK, F. (1961), *Wirtschafts- und Finanzpolitik des Interventionsstaates*, Tübingen.
PARSONS, T. (1957–8), 'The Distribution of Power in American Society', *World Politics*, vol. 10, pp. 123–43.
PARSONS, T. (1959), 'Voting and the Equilibrium of the American Political System', in Eugene Burdick and Arthur Brodbeck (eds.), *American Voting Behavior*, New York, pp. 80 ff.
RUNCIMAN, W. G. (1966), *Relative Deprivation and Social Justice*, Routledge and Kegan Paul, pp. 9 ff.
SCHELSKY, H. (1961), *Der Mensch in der wissenschaftlichen Zivilization*, Cologne-Opladen.
SCHONFIELD, A. (1968), *Geplanter Kapitalismus*, Cologne.
SCHUMPETER, J. (1950), *Socialism and Democracy*, Berne, pp. 427 ff.
TINGSTOM, H. (1955), 'Stability and Vitality in Swedish Democracy', *Political Quarterly*, no. 26, pp. 146–58.
WEBER, M. (1968), *Parlament und Regierung in neugeordneten Deutschland*, in *Gesammelte Politische Schriften*, ed. J. Winckelmann, Tübingen, pp. 294–431.
WEBER, W. (1958), *Spannungen und Kräfte im deutschen Verfassungssystem*, Stuttgart.

Part Four
Critical Theory: Commentaries and Criticisms

In common with other German exiles, the members of the Frankfurt School had initially come under the influence of German Idealism, Marxism and Historicism in their own country; bred in the veneration of theory and history, and a contempt for empiricism and pragmatism, they entered a diametrically opposed intellectual climate in the United States, empirically oriented and ahistorical. Neumann's paper (Reading 20) is included partly because, by implication, it brings out the exilic experience of the School; but also because it analyses the different fates suffered by the intellectual in different political systems. It thus highlights a historical development which lies behind the '*Methodenstreit*' of the sixties: the fact that as the process of bureaucratization extends to the intelligentsia – a trend which culminates in the totalitarian state – the intelligentsia tend to be transformed into functionaries of society. The Readings from Pilot and McCarthy, by contrast, are methodological. Pilot's paper (Reading 21) is one of the most penetrating critiques of Habermas' work, arguing that his 'philosophy of history with a practical intention' depends on the results of empirical research and hence is refutable by them; McCarthy (Reading 22) pulls together the main lines of the theory of communicative competence, concluding with some critical remarks on its strengths and weaknesses.

20 Franz L. Neumann

The Intelligentsia in Exile

Excerpt from Franz L. Neumann, 'The Social Sciences', in *The Cultural Migration: The European Scholar in America*, introduced by W. Rex Crawford, University of Pennsylvania Press, Philadelphia, 1953, pp. 4–25.

'If my country can do without me, I can do without her. The world is large enough.' Thus wrote Hugo Grotius, the great 'natural' and international lawyer after he had succeeded, in 1621, in escaping imprisonment by Maurice of Orange. For ten years he had to live in Paris, and it was there, in exile, that he wrote his most famous book, *De jure belli ac pacis*.

Yet the sentiment expressed by Grotius and his personal fate must not lead us to believe that this is and can be either the sentiment or the fate of the modern exile. Two facts have changed radically: the role of the intellectual and the social environment within which he lives.

The intellectual is, or ought to be, the critical conscience of society in each of its historical periods. His role is to deal critically with society, to show how far a society does or rather does not realize freedom. Why this has to be so, I cannot demonstrate here. It follows from the central conception of social and political theory: the conception of freedom. This should be preserved by the intelligentsia. But no society, past or present, being able to realize fully man's freedom, the critical role of the intellectual in each and every society necessarily follows. He is the conscience of society. In a certain sense, therefore, he is always ostracized, for conscience is always inconvenient, particularly in politics. Thus Socrates, in whom the critical role of the intellectual is most impressively represented, refers to the philosopher as a 'perennial metic', a permanent alien, who questions every form of government, every society as to its philosophic nature.'[1] This is Socrates' belief:

1. Plato, *Republic* (Cornford transl.), Bk VI (Cornford, Ch. XXII).

For I am and always have been one of those natures who must be guided by reason, whatever the reason may be which upon reflection appears to me the best; and now that this fate has befallen me, I cannot repudiate my own words.[2]

These meagre generalizations of the intellectual's role may suffice here. They merely serve to prepare the analysis of the different fates suffered by the intellectual in different political systems.

Clearly, in the Greek city states, the role of the intellectual is the most difficult and the most endangered. Politics and culture are one or, at least, are presented as one. The civilization of the known world is concentrated in one spot so that the remaining world is, or appears to be, barbarian. Already, in view of the identity of culture and politics, exile means death.

In the Hellenistic-imperial period, however, the situation changes. A certain latitude is permitted to the intellectual, for he is tolerated if he is not political. Politics and culture are no longer identical. The Epicurean political philosophy aims precisely at legitimizing the political withdrawal of the intellectual who no longer expects from the state justice but mere maintenance of order and security, while Stoicism with its demand upon political morality leads to severe conflicts. Exile in this situation, although less damaging morally, is equally catastrophic intellectually. The lamentation of Ovid about his expulsion by Augustus to the shore of the Black Sea is a dramatic illustration of the frustrations of a poet so deeply part and parcel of Roman civilization which he had done so much to raise to new levels.

The third situation is that of a universal culture, Christian in content, Latin in form and language, where exile often meant little more than a change of residence, where courts and universities often competed for exiled scholars, where national differences meant nothing; and widespread religious indifference, consequence of the dominant and unchallenged role of the Church in the cultural field, left to the exiled intellectual, no matter where, a

2. Plato, *Crito* (Jowett transl.). I have substituted for 'chance' in the Jowett translation, the word 'fate', which to the English reader seems to express the meaning better.

fruitful field of activity. Indeed, the itinerant scholar – itinerant by choice or compulsion – is a quite normal phenomenon.

Yet there are exceptions. Here are two situations for which this general statement is not fully valid: namely, for the political scholar, and for heretics. I shall not deal with heresy here. Dante and Marsilius of Padua are symbols of the first. 'How salty tastes the bread abroad and how difficult to mount and descend foreign staircases' – these words express Dante's feelings when he had to leave Florence. Yet he was a politician, poet, and scholar, and while exile destroyed, so to speak, the *homo politicus*, it brought to perfection the poet and scholar. Exile, in Dante's case, even changed, and changed fundamentally, his political conceptions. Verona, Bologna, Paris, Oxford, London, Cologne – to name but a few stations of his travels – led to his emancipation from narrow political provincialism to a political conception which, although without much influence in the fourteenth century, was to remain a challenge to provincialism and nationalism.

Another political scholar, Marsilius of Padua, exiled from Paris, simply entered the services of another political system – that of Louis of Bavaria – and through him attempted to put into practice his grandiose scheme of a wholly secular state which he had theoretically developed in his *Defensor Pacis*.

Yet it is important to realize – and important particularly for the full understanding of nationalism – that the period of the expansion of Christianity leads us back to the very first type: the total identification of culture and politics. A linguistic development will make clear what I mean.

Rome, as Greece earlier, often condemned the oppositional intellectual or artist to exile. The general term for this punishment is *exterminatio*, literally meaning expulsion beyond the frontiers. But the meaning of the term changed from about the third century A.D. and then assumed the meaning it now has – that of physical destruction.[3] The reason for this change is the spread of Christianity and the permeation of politics by religion. The sociology of this semantic change is, of course, quite easy to understand: it is the imposition of a new value system, the total permeation of secular society with this new value system, which

3. Coulton (1974).

transforms the oppositional into the heretical; the enemy could not be tolerated since he not only polluted the faith but also could act as the focal point of opposition. Similar situations arise whenever the integrating element of a society is not primarily a rational agreement among its members, but a new religious or semi-religious faith. The very last chapter of Rousseau's *Social Contract* entitled 'Civic Religion' is the modern variant. There Rousseau insists that his society needs a new civic religion so that a true community spirit may be active. Those who violate the moral principles of the community shall be expelled from it; those who pretend to practise them, but violate them, shall be executed. Robespierre, indeed, under the Reign of Terror practised the last chapter of Rousseau. We shall return to this situation.

But once Christianity had become firmly established, the medieval intellectual enjoyed an enviable position between church and state, benefiting from the advantages derived from this perpetual conflict, being free to pursue his calling within certain limits of heresy and political dissent, and being a member of privileged, self-governing corporations, able to shift his residence, to carry, so to speak, his social base with him.

A new situation arises with the formation of the nation-state. In this process, two stages may well be distinguished: the establishment of the state machine; and the emergence of a national consciousness. The unifying concept of these two stages is that of sovereignty. It creates a fundamentally ambiguous relationship between politics and culture and thus between the intellectual and the state. State sovereignty implies a radical separation of state and society, of politics and culture. The state appears and is constructed as an institution separate from society, and thus implies the toleration of all opinions not forbidden by law, that is, not directly detrimental to the operation of the Leviathan. But, simultaneously, the Leviathan cannot accept limits on its power. I have elsewhere formulated the basic dilemma of modern political theory:

> The problem of political philosophy, and its dilemma, is the reconciliation of freedom and coercion. With the emergence of a money economy we encounter the modern state as the institution which claims

the monopoly of coercive power in order to provide a secure basis upon which trade and commerce may flourish and the citizens may enjoy the benefits of their labour. But by creating this institution, by acknowledging its sovereign power, the citizen created an instrument that could and frequently did deprive him of protection and of the boon of his work. Consequently, while justifying the sovereign power of the state, he sought at the same time to justify limits upon the coercive power. The history of modern political thought since Machiavelli is the history of this attempt to justify right *and* might, law *and* power. There is no political theory which does not do both things. The most absolutistic theories (Hobbes and Spinoza) which, at first sight, reject individual rights, admit them, however, through a back door: Hobbes, by transforming the sovereign into a kind of business agent of society with all the power he wants if he conducts his business well, but with none if he fails to secure order and security; Spinoza, by his formula that right equals might, permits any social group that is powerful enough to transform its social power into right, to change from an *alterius iuris* into a *sui iuris*. Locke, the protagonist of right and law, felt compelled to admit the prerogative power authorizing the monarch to act without law, and sometimes even against it, if and when right and law tend to jeopardize the state.[4]

This fundamental ambiguity of modern political theory is manifested in the ambiguous position of the intellectual.

In the first stage – prior to the growth of nationalism – no great difficulties arise for exiles, particularly for those possessing skills (military, administrative, judicial, fiscal) which are badly needed by the absolute monarchs in the organizations of their bureaucratic machines. The early period (fifteenth and sixteenth centuries) and the period of enlightened absolutism are excellent examples for the study of the supra-national character of the intellectual who frequently changes allegiances and residences and, if exiled by one political power, is gladly received by the other.

Nationalism, as the legitimizing base of state sovereignty, however, produces the really modern problem. It is this period that has most relevance for us. For the claims of the nation upon its citizens – no matter what theories are advanced to limit its power

4. My introduction to Montesquieu, *The Spirit of the Laws*, New York, 1949, pp. xxxi-xxxii.

– are basically boundless. The sole limit is – this Luther saw quite clearly – man's conscience.

It was precisely in this period when Grotius lived that the modern problem arose. It is quite fascinating to study the growth of the claims of the nation upon its citizens. This was seventeenth-century France, where the French national state was formed during the struggle between Catholics and Huguenots. The sixteenth-century religious wars – ending with the ascent of Henry IV of Navarre – demonstrated that religious affinity and confessional identification superseded national identification. But under Richelieu the situation changed. Almost imperceptibly the claims of the nation-state superseded all other allegiances. This is most strikingly revealed during the famous siege of La Rochelle. The Calvinist citizens of La Rochelle, while entering into a treaty with Charles I of England and thus unquestionably committing an act of treason to the country, declared simultaneously that nothing in this treaty should be so interpreted. Here, in the midst of a religious war – and in contrast to the eight preceding religious wars of the sixteenth century – the claims of the nation were felt to be as strong as those of religion.

The conflict between sovereignty and man's conscience leads in modern society to a new phenomenon which has recently been called 'inner emancipation'. Four instances may make this clear: Spinoza, the Abbé Meslier, Kant, and Theodor Mommsen. All four shared the rejection of the political order within which they lived and the inability or unwillingness to attack it. Thus Spinoza emancipated himself from all dependence upon the political system in order to lead the life of a philosopher. The Abbé Meslier in the eighteenth century practised throughout his life his profession as a Catholic priest, and only his three-volume testament revealed his atheistic communism. Kant appeared to lead outwardly the life of a Prussian university professor, proud of never having missed a lecture and never having interrupted his routine. Yet in his letters he revealed that he thought thoughts that were revolutionary, but did not dare publish them, adding, however, that he never published anything that was untrue. Theodor Mommsen's testament,[5] released only a few years ago,

5. English translation in *Past and Present*, vol. 1, no. 1, 1952, p. 71.

reveals the conflict of a genuine liberal with a political system which he loathed; his longing for political activity outweighed his desire for scholarly work. Yet all four cases have one thing in common: all four produced and made substantial and, in Spinoza's and Kant's cases, revolutionary contributions to our knowledge.

In the period of liberalism – to which we all tend to look back as the golden age of the intellectual.– the intellectual is a free producer. The free university, the independent newspaper, the system of competing political parties are congenial to the intellectual who lives by the sale of his products in a free market.

In the whole period from the sixteenth to the nineteenth centuries there is for the rebel the possibility of an 'inner exile', an 'inner emigration'. But even if he leaves his country or is expelled from it, he can with relative ease find a new home. There is the court emigration (as we may call it) of the sixteenth and seventeenth centuries; there is the emigration of the eighteenth and nineteenth centuries when the free (or 'uprooted') intellectuals – Herzen, Bakunin, Marx, Byron – roamed freely.

Yet a new phenomenon occurs within the modern nation-state: the bureaucratization of modern society and, with it, the trend to transform the intellectual into a functionary of society. The role of the intellectual encounters ever-growing difficulties. Julien Benda has indicted the intellectuals for treason to their destiny, has accused them of betraying the very moral principles which made their existence possible. If we forget his moral indictment and concentrate on the sociological analysis, we shall find indeed that the intellectuals become increasingly functionaries of society. The process of bureaucratization extends unquestionably to the intelligentsia. Their Socratic function becomes endangered. The intelligentsia thus become the defenders of the *status quo*. It is this change in the status of the intellectual and the change in the social environment which makes the transfer from one to another national culture so difficult a process.

This trend culminates in the totalitarian state. The totalitarian state – and herein lies the difference between it and absolutism – is not and cannot be satisfied with the control of the traditional means of coercion. It must, if it wants to exist as a dictatorial system, completely control man's thoughts, and it must thus transform culture into propaganda. The systematic degradation of thought is something that few people can withstand. Inner emancipation under such conditions means total renunciation of intellectual activity. Indeed, if we ask: What are the intellectual products of the inner emigrants of Germany and Italy? the answer must be: None. The desks of the inner emigrants were empty. There were no manuscripts written during the dictatorship, hidden in desks and waiting to be published after the overthrow of the totalitarian régimes. This is not said to attack anti-Nazi intellectuals, but rather to explain why there was no intellectual production; why the sole remedy for those intellectuals opposed to a totalitarian régime could be but physical emigration.

From what I said before, it is clear that emigration in the period of nationalism is infinitely more painful than ever before. If the intellectual has to give up his country, he does more than change his residence. He has to cut himself off from an historical tradition, a common experience; has to learn a new language; has to think and experience within and through it; has, in short, to create a totally new life. It is not the loss of a profession, of property, of status – that alone and by itself is painful – but rather the weight of another national culture to which he has to adjust himself.

This adjustment is by no means easier if – as in the case of Nazi Germany – emigration is a relief from an intolerable situation. The hatred for National Socialism did by no means ease the psychological difficulties. Not even, or rather, particularly not of those whom I might call 'political scholars', that is, those intellectuals dealing with problems of state and society – historians, sociologists, psychologists, political scientists – who were – or should have been – compelled to deal with the brutal facts of politics. I deliberately say: Specifically the political scholars faced the psychological difficulty; for being political, they fought – or should have fought – actively for a better, more decent political system. Being compelled to leave their homeland, they thus suffered the triple fate of a displaced *human being* with property and family; a displaced *scholar*; and a displaced *homo politicus*.

If we attempt to generalize sociologically, we may perhaps say:

Emigration is eased if the intellectual emigrant can transfer his social base; that is, if the social environment to which he moves has similarities basic to that he has to leave.

Emigration is eased if his old audience is replaced by a new one, similarly constituted so that he can talk and be talked to. (This twin conception has been developed by Hans Speier.)[6]

If we apply these two categories to the five situations, we come to the following results:

If, as in classical Greece, civilization is concentrated in one spot, and if politics and culture are one, emigration by the intellectual will normally lead to an atrophy of his intellectual abilities. He may die an intellectual death.

In the universalist civilization of the Middle Ages the social base as well as the audience were, within limits, identical everywhere. Students and teachers of medieval universities came from virtually all countries speaking and writing one language, sharing the same basic values.

During the period of the emergence of the modern state machine those having special, particularly military and administrative, skills could actually demand a premium. Their social base as well as their audience were essentially identical at every court.

The emerging national state makes emancipation of the intellectual difficult for reasons indicated, but permits inner emigration as well as, in the eighteenth and nineteenth centuries, quite free emigration.

For obvious reasons it is with German totalitarianism that we have to deal more concretely. This can be done only through an analysis of the actual situation of Germany and of the position of the German intellectual.

The German intellectual's state of mind was, long before 1933, one of scepticism and despair, bordering on cynicism. The so-called Revolution of 1918 produced two new contending political theories: Wilsonianism and Bolshevism. The impact of the contending intellectual forces on Europe, and specifically on Germany, can hardly be overestimated. Wilson's grand theory of self-determination, within and without, a League of Nations to end war, expressed the aspirations of German liberalism and the

6. In 'The Social Conditions of the Intellectual Exile', reprinted in *Social Order and the Risk of War*, New York, 1952, pp. 86–94.

German democratic labour movement. Lenin's revolution appeared to workers and some intellectuals as a chiliastic deed, a revolution ending oppression, emancipating the individual, abolishing political power.

Both theories lost out. Democracy had already lost because it was so closely tied to defeat. It never acquired that self-reliant buoyancy that it had in Anglo-Saxon countries. German liberalism had been corrupted by Bismarck and had traded freedom for imperialist expansion; German Social Democracy had become transformed into a vast bureaucratic machine, trading social freedom for higher wages. Bolshevism, in turn, had rapidly transformed itself into a terroristic machine which, misusing the philosophy of Marx, was solely concerned with increasing the power of the U.S.S.R. without, and the stranglehold of the ruling clique within.

In this vacuum, the traditional theories of nationalism, restoration theories, began to dominate again German intellectual and, particularly, university life. The universities became the very centres of anti-democratic thought. Let there be no misunderstanding. I do not consider it the task of universities to preach democracy. In this, I fully stand with the ideas of Max Weber expressed in his famous lecture *Wissenschaft als Beruf* (*Scholarship as a Profession*). But it is most certainly not the function of the universities to ridicule democracy, to arouse nationalist passions, to sing the praise of past systems – and to cover this up by asserting that one is 'non-political'.

Let me give you my personal experience. When I came in the spring of 1918 to the University of Breslau, its celebrated economist – in his very first lecture – denounced the Peace Resolution of 1917 (peace without annexation and indemnities) and demanded the incorporation of Longwy and Brie, the transformation of Belgium into a German protectorate, the German colonization of large stretches of Eastern Europe and overseas colonies. The still more celebrated professor of literature, after having paid homage to Kantian idealism, derived from that philosophy the categorical imperative of a German victory, a German monarchy, and substantially the same peace terms. When I came to Leipzig in the fall of 1918, the economics professor thought it necessary – in October 1918 – to endorse the peace terms of the Pan German Union and of the General Staff, while the historian proved conclusively that democracy was an essentially non-German form of political organization, suitable for the materialistic Anglo-Saxons, but incompatible with the idealism of the Germanic race. When I transferred to Rostock in the summer of 1919 I had to organize students to combat anti-Semitism openly preached by university professors. When I finally landed in Frankfurt, the very first task with which I was faced was to help protect a newly appointed Socialist university professor from attack – political as well as physical – by students secretly supported by a considerable number of professors.

It is well to realize that these doctrines and practices were by no means preached and engaged in by second-rate professors, but by so-called luminaries of the respective universities. The great tradition of Wilhelm von Humboldt no longer existed. Frederic Lilge, in his little book *The Abuse of Learning*, sketches with accuracy and sensitivity the transformation of German learning.

True, there was an Indian Summer from 1924 to 1930. The Republic appeared to be solid. Revolution, Kapp Putsch, Ruhr occupation, inflation, Hitler's Beer Hall Putsch, Communist uprisings – all this seemed to be past. Wilsonianism appeared to make headway. American prosperity made a tremendous impression upon Germany. 'Fordism', as it was called in Germany, seemed to be the solution of all problems. Then came 1930, the Great Depression, unemployment, and the gradual disintegration of the political structure. With this, the restoration tendencies within German university life made themselves more strongly felt, and the seemingly great achievements of the Indian Summer came to nothing; or, rather, produced Nazism.

The intellectual emigration caused by Nazism differed fundamentally from previous ones. One may distinguish four different causes (if one is aware that all four may, and often did, actually coincide within one person). They were political, racial, religious, and moral. Political motivation actually comprised the whole range of German political attitudes from conservative-nationalist to communist. There thus did not and could not exist a political unity among the exiles. It was secondly a racial persecution, and thus hit a group of Jews, half- and even quarter-Jews who may or may not have opposed the régime. It was religious since Nazism was clearly anti-Christian, although the fight against religion could for tactical reasons never be fully carried out. And finally it was simply moral revulsion against the régime, coupled with the conviction that the immorality of the régime made even an 'inner emigration' an impossibility.

Thus there was no similarity to the 1848 emigration, which was entirely political and, being so, was conceived by the exiles to be a mere temporary phenomenon.

But Nazism did not simply change the political system of Germany; it changed Germany. Thus for many, exile either from the very beginning, or shortly thereafter the definitive cutting of the ties with Germany, was a conscious transplantation of one's existence.

I may again refer to my own experience: I spent the first three years in England (1933–6) in order to be close to Germany and not to lose contact with her. I actively participated in refugee politics, besides pursuing post-graduate studies in political science at the London School of Economics. It was precisely in England that I became fully aware that one had to bury the expectation of an overthrow of the régime from within. The appeasement policy of the official ruling groups in Britain, combined with the pacifism of the Labour Party, then in opposition, convinced me and many others that the Nazi régime, far from becoming weaker, would grow stronger, and this with the support of the major European powers. Thus a clean break – psychological, social, and economic – had to be made, and a new life started.

But England was not the country in which to do it. Much as I (and all the others) loved England, her society was too homogeneous and too solid, her opportunities (particularly under conditions of unemployment) too narrow, her politics not too agreeable. One could, so I felt, never quite become an Englishman. Thus the United States appeared as the sole country where, perhaps, an attempt would be successful to carry out the threefold transition: as a human being, an intellectual, and a political scholar.

That this transition has been successful, not only in my case, but in hundreds of others, is primarily due to the United States, her people, and her universities. This is demonstrated by the astounding fact that only a few exiles chose to return to Germany, in spite of the fact that the material and non-material rewards of German universities are, on the whole, greater than they are here.

What were the decisive impressions that an intellectual exile coming to the United States in 1936 received here? There are, I believe, three lasting impressions: the Roosevelt experiment; the character of the people; the role of the universities.

I cannot here analyse in detail what the Roosevelt experiment and the character of the American people meant for us. To the sceptical German, the Roosevelt system meant that the Wilsonianism which had been preached since 1917 was not a mere piece of propaganda, but a reality. It was a demonstration that a militant democracy could solve the very same problems on which the German Republic collapsed.

As impressive, and perhaps more so, was the character of the American people, its essential friendliness, the neighbourly, almost comradely spirit. Many have analysed these traits and sung their praises, and I need not repeat all this. The openness of American society made the process of re-integration exceedingly simple, once one had really made a clean break with Europe, and particularly with Germany.

Yet for a scholar it is university life that counts most heavily. I said before that the transition from one to another culture seems to be eased if the scholar meets a similar social situation. But are the situations in Germany and the United States similar in university matters? Or are the differences greater than the similarities?

The German scholar generally came under three intellectual influences: German idealism, Marxism, and historicism. All three have in common that they are comprehensive systems of thought claiming to fit every phenomenon into its system. All three express the extraordinary weight of an historical tradition. Thus the thought of German scholars was primarily theoretical and historical – rarely empirical and pragmatic. It makes for scepticism. To the historically thinking scholar, the historical process is frequently the repetition of a previous pattern. Innovations are thus belittled at the expense of the 'great historical trend'. It may make for radicalism if – as in the Marxian theory – history is believed to operate in a specific direction; and it always makes for a certain rigidity bordering on dogmatism.

The whole theoretical-historical approach is (or rather was) accompanied by contempt for Anglo-American philosophy. I still hear the sneers of my philosophy professor about Locke, Condillac, and Dewey, while Whitehead was treated with silence then as now.

Thus, on the whole, the German exile, bred in the veneration of theory and history, and contempt for empiricism and pragmatism, entered a diametrically opposed intellectual climate: optimistic, empirically oriented, a-historical, but also self-righteous.

The radical difference was apparent not only in the intellectual tradition, but in the actual position of the universities. The German universities considered themselves to be training grounds for an élite – although that élite was constituted solely by a socio-economic criterion and not by intellectual achievements; the American universities were organs of a democratic educational principle – that is, the participation of the largest possible number of its citizens in the benefits of education, the élite training being a mere fraction of the total educational effort.

The German university alleged to be a *universitas*, to teach humanistic principles, but had long become a mere agglomeration of professional schools for the acquisition of professional skills as lawyers, doctors, or high-school teachers; while the American colleges had, as a matter of fact, resurrected Humboldt's principle in their general education courses.

The German university teacher was part of a privileged caste with fairly high pay and extraordinarily high social prestige. The American college and university teacher enjoyed virtually none of these privileges. The German university teacher very frequently considered students as disturbing elements, preventing him from his true calling of *Forscher*, or research scholar. The American college professor is primarily a teacher and frequently even a father confessor of his students.

Thus intellectually and institutionally the differences are and were indeed great, greater possibly than the similarities. The impact of this new experience may go (and has gone) in three different directions:

The exiled scholar may (and sometimes did) abandon his previous intellectual position and accept without qualification the new orientation.

He may (and sometimes did) retain completely his old thought structure and may either believe himself to have the mission of totally revamping the American pattern, or may withdraw (with disdain and contempt) into an island of his own.

He may, finally, attempt an integration of his new experience with old tradition. This, I believe, is the most difficult, but also the most rewarding, solution.

The study of the last attitude can, perhaps, best be clarified through an analysis of the role of the social and political sciences and the function of the social and political scientist, with which I am most familiar.

As I mentioned, German scholarship is characterized by the evolution of great philosophical systems during the nineteenth century and, simultaneously, the critique of these systems: Kant, Hegel, and Marx, on the one hand, and Nietzsche and Freud on the other. Kant and Hegel, however, became rapidly transformed into stereotypes, and their direct influence on social and political thought was ultimately disastrous. The academic influence of Hegel was conservative – the extra-academic (through Marx) revolutionary. Kantianism provided frequently the idealistic cloak for very materialistic aspirations. This seems to be inherent both in his theory of knowledge and in his ethics. In his epistemology, the gap between reason and reality has never been bridged. In his ethics, the stress upon the form and character of his categorical imperative made it possible to raise every concrete desire, no matter how arbitrary, to the rank of a universal law. Thus Hegelianism as well as Kantianism did not feed any progressive stream of thought. Marx and Freud were ostracized by German universities, and Nietzsche's critique of German bourgeois virtues (or vices) was transformed into its very opposite.

Thus the great achievements were in the fields of history and law. Yet neither history nor law can possibly come to grips with the social and political reality – the study of which thus found virtually no place in German university life. Scholarship meant essentially two things: speculation and book learning. Thus what we call social and political science was largely carried on outside the universities.

There was one exception: Max Weber, whose name is known and honoured wherever social and political science is taught. Weber's greatness consists in a unique combination of a theoretical frame (although for me of doubtful validity), a mastery of a tremendous number of data, and a full awareness of the political responsibility of the scholar. Yet Weber's influence in Germany was very limited. It is characteristic of German social science that it virtually destroyed Weber by an almost exclusive concentration upon the discussion of his methodology. Neither his demand for empirical studies nor his insistence upon the responsibility of the scholar to society were heeded. It is here, in the United States, that Weber really came to life.

This was not always so in Germany. Once, before 1870, Germany and German universities had and practised political science, and it is interesting to know that the Political Science Faculty at Columbia was founded by Burgess after the model of the German *Staatswissenschaft*. Rotteck and Welcker, Robert von Mohl, Bluntschli, Dahlmann, and particularly Lorenz von Stein, were political and social scientists of rank. Public administration, analysis of political parties, comparative political institutions, the structure of society – all this was taught and investigated by them.

This came to an end with the establishment and consolidation of the German Empire, and merely reflects the abdication of liberalism's political role. German liberals concentrated on the *Rechtsstaat* theory (the state based upon law), meaning that the origin, the creation, of law was no longer a concern of theory which confined itself solely to the definition of the right of the citizens, particularly of his property rights, *against* the state. Political and social science was thus replaced by jurisprudence, where the achievement was indeed great.

Thus, from about 1875 on, the *Obrigkeitsstaat* – the authoritarian element – and the *Rechtsstaat* – the legal element – concerned with mere defence of private rights, rapidly destroyed political and social science. The universities train lawyers to administer the state and to defend private rights; teachers to preach the superior virtues of Germandom; technicians; and the theorist and the historian. The social and political scientist, concerned with the reform of society and of politics, is no longer trained. This radically different role of the social and political scientist is perhaps the great difference which the political scholar encountered.

It is quite impossible to assess the contribution of the German exile to the social and political sciences. The character of the Nazi régime caused – as I stressed – the emigration of scholars of radically different orientation, political and theoretical. Thus there is no comparison possible with the flight of Greek scholars from the Byzantine Empire in the fifteenth century. The extraordinary diversity of European refugee scholars makes it virtually impossible to determine their contribution with precision, particularly the contributions made to social and political science – in contrast to those in the natural sciences and, perhaps, in contrast to certain specialized historical and philosophical contributions such as art history, literary history, etc. The influences are too subtle, too diffused, to be easily identified or measured.

Besides, even before 1933 the intellectual interconnections were close between Europe and the United States in the field of social sciences. The importation of Robert Michels, Vilfredo Pareto, and Gaetano Mosca is not due to the post-1933 immigration. The ascent in the United States of the Viennese school of logical positivism seems also to have occurred independently of the political changes in Germany and Austria. Neither of these trends appears to me quite beneficial, both strengthening the a- (or even anti-) historical and anti-theoretical trends in American social sciences.

Those, however, who like myself have been brought up in the tradition of the great philosophical and historical systems of Europe, believe that we may have added two considerations to American social science:

First and foremost, a note of scepticism. To me, and to many others, the extraordinary optimism about the potentialities of social science to change the world cannot be shared. Our expectations are far more modest; the limits to social science presented by the historical process are far narrower.

There is secondly an attempt to put social science research into a theoretical framework. To many of us it appeared and still appears that the significance of the collection of empirical data is overstressed – as against the theoretical frame; that the predominance of empirical research makes it difficult to see problems in their historical significance; that the insistence upon mastery of a tremendous amount of data tends to transform the scholar into a functionary; that the need for large sums to finance such enterprises tends to create a situation of dependence which may ultimately jeopardize the role of the intellectual as I see it.

These four dangers may perhaps be overstated. But they do exist: The refugee scholar, coming from a different tradition, ought to attempt to minimize their dangers by bringing to bear his theoretical knowledge and his awareness of historical connections.

But perhaps more important is that we have received from this concern of American political and social science the demand that scholarship must not be purely theoretical and historical, that the role of the social scientist is the reconciliation of theory and practice, and that such reconciliation demands concern with and analysis of the brutal facts of life. This deepened understanding of the role of social and political scientists, this the United States has given me.

The German scholar returning to Germany for a visit is invariably drawn into the great debate on German university reform. Little has been done to reform the spirit and institutional structure of the German universities, little to change the curriculum. There still exists the deep gulf separating students and teachers; there still is lacking a truly general humanistic education; there still is no evening university; and political and social science is still a very tender plant. But the little that has been done is in large measure due to the example (not the carpet-bagging) of returning refugees and other American visitors: their informality, their concern with students, their much greater concern with the political and social reality.

Invariably the returning scholar finds himself in a strange position. While here at home he frequently has to fight the over-enthusiasm for empirical research, and to stress the need for theory and history, in Germany he becomes, by compulsion, an advocate of empirical research. It is this dual role in which I see today the true significance of the once exiled German political scholar.

References

COULTON, G. G. (1924), 'The Death Penalty for Heresy from 1184 to 1921 A.D.', *Mediaeval Studies*, No. XVIII, pp. 1–18.

MOMMSEN, T. (1952), *Past and Present*, vol. 1, no. 1, p. 71.

NEUMANN, F. (1949), Introduction to the New York edition of Montesquieu's *The Spirit of the Laws*, pp. xxxi-xxxii.

PLATO (*c.* 380 B.C.), *Republic*. Translated by F. M. Cornford, Oxford University Press, 1941.

PLATO (*c.* 400 B.C.), *Crito*. Translated by B. Jowett, Oxford University Press, 1940.

SPEIER, H. (1952), 'The Social Conditions of the Intellectual Exile', *Social Order and the Risk of War*, New York, pp. 86–94.

21 Harald Pilot

Habermas' Philosophy of History

From Harald Pilot, *Habermas' Philosophy of History*, Heinemann Educational, 1968.

Every thorough critique of the objectifying procedures in the social sciences is liable to be suspected of intrigues involving the philosophy of history. Jürgen Habermas abruptly terminates mere suspicion: the declared goal of his writings is a 'philosophy of history with practical intent'.[1] He does not intend, however, that this philosophy of history should formulate necessary historical laws for even a metaphysical meaning, but instead that it should formulate programmes for social action.[2] Such goals for the future of a society must be possible, however, in real terms even in the present time. Consequently, the projections of a philosophy of history are dependent upon the results of empirical research and can, in fact, be refuted by the latter.

Habermas believes that the Marxist philosophy of history, if properly understood, is able to dispense with metaphysical transcendency, since it derives the guiding aims of future action from the 'factual contradictions' of contemporary society. The 'meaning of history' is simply its possible future which is realized through action. 'The experimental philosophy of history no longer searches for a hidden meaning; it rescues the latter by establishing it.'[3]

1. Cf. especially Habermas (1963). Translator's note: The essay referred to here does not appear in the English translation of this volume, and his 'Zur Logik der Sozialwissenschaften', in *Philosophische Rundschau*, Beiheft 5, February 1967, p. 180.

2. Popper has convincingly criticized the possibility of laws which permit prognoses concerning the historical future. Cf. Popper, *The Poverty of Historicism*, Routledge and Kegan Paul, 1961; and his *The Open Society and its Enemies*, 2 vols, Routledge and Kegan Paul, 1962.

3. Habermas (1963), op. cit., p. 303.

Since meaning refers to something which will be real in the future, its pre-conditions can be empirically tested in the present. The philosophy of history with practical intent

> aims both at an historical-sociological analysis of the pre-conditions for the possibility of revolutionary praxis and at an historical-philosophical derivation out of the contradiction within existing society of the concept of society itself, the concept which is the standard of its own critique and the idea of critical-practical activity.[4]

In this way, the projections of a philosophy of history are subjected to a double check before their realization. Both the guiding aims themselves and the means for their realization must be gained from the empirical knowledge of the present. A given projection is impossible if it contradicts empirical analyses. It is, however, only possible in real terms if it is not only compatible with the latter but also expedient for resolving the existing contradictions of a society. It has to prove itself to be society's 'determinate negation'.

But even if a projection meets both conditions, its guiding aims are not theoretically but merely practically necessary. The philosophy of history does not formulate prognoses about the historical future but simply guidelines for action, 'which do not prevail "objectively", but through the will and consciousness of human beings; consequently, they can be calculated and forecast only in their objective pre-conditions of possibility but not however as such'.[5] '. . . its correctness, namely the correctness of all verifiable pre-conditions of a possible revolution is secured empirically, whilst its truth is only certain in the practical establishment of the very meaning which it expresses.'[6] In this way, the revolutionary philosophy of history eludes decisionistic and deterministic pitfalls.

But this programme can only be realized if the 'determinate negation' of existing contradictions can be gained from the results of empirical research. For it is only then that the hope of checking empirically the guiding aims of future action exists. But the self-interpretation of empirical research presents several obstacles to such an attempt. According to the methodological

4. ibid., p. 299. 5. ibid., p. 289. 6. ibid., p. 310.

rules of the 'analytical theory of science'[7] it is, in fact, possible to 'transform technologically'[8] nomological hypotheses, to utilize them as means for pre-given ends – but these rules in no way permit the derivation of the ends themselves from empirical analyses. For this reason, Habermas has 'to criticize the analytical-empirical modes of procedure immanently in the light of their own claim'.[9]

Nevertheless, a crucial limitation is imposed upon this criticism if the empirical control over the philosophy of history is not to dissolve into scepticism. It cannot destroy the criteria of empirical testability but rather its goal can simply be a margin of interpretation within which a hermeneutic procedure can be applied to a domain previously secured. Although Habermas' starting point does not in principle exclude such a 'determination of boundaries', his writings up to now have extended across this boundary in the direction of a 'dialectics of utopian reason'.[10] I wish to discuss this thesis in four steps:

1. Contingent dialectics and empirical analysis: the formal conditions of 'determinate negation'.
2. Value implications of social scientific theories – Habermas' critique of the 'analytical theory of science' and its meta-critique.
3. 'Domination-free communication' as the regulative principle of the philosophy of history.
4. Sceptical consequences of a 'dialectics of utopian reason'.

7. Cf. for terminology, Habermas, 'The Analytical Theory of Science and Dialectics', 1963.

8. Cf. Hans Albert, 'Wissenschaft als Politik', in Ernst Topitsch (ed.), *Probleme der Wissenschaftstheorie*, Vienna, 1960, p. 213: 'By means of tautological transformation, a theory is . . . converted into its technological form. From a set of nomological hypotheses emerges a set of propositions concerning the possibilities of human action with reference to certain goals. This transformation merely presupposes that certain desiderata are hypothetically imputed and does not therefore require the introduction of explicit value-premises.'

9. Habermas, 'The Analytical Theory of Science and Dialectics', p. 169.

10. The latter results when a dialectics of the present situation is extrapolated into the future, when the 'ideological distortion' also embraces the principles of critical practice. Then it is to be feared that the 'dialectical process of mediation' will become infinite.

1

The 'determinate negation' of a contradiction-laden society is supposed to permit the 'dialectical derivation' of situationally-related projections for future action out of a contradiction-laden society. This is disputed by the 'analytical theory of science' for the following reasons: (a) Dialectical thought is devoid of content since it operates through contradictions from which everything follows:[11] (b) Facts cannot contradict one another; (c) Empirical hypotheses are descriptive statements from which guidelines for action cannot follow.

Habermas seeks to evade these objections by means of a 'contingent dialectics'. This is not an *a priori* principle of thought, it does not take place 'prior to and underlying all history, at the stroke of metaphysical necessity . . .',[12] but rather it results from the structures of domination in a society which has not yet been able to liberate itself from natural constraints. 'As a whole it [contingent dialectics] is as contingent as the dominating conditions of labour whose inner contradiction and outer movement it expresses.'[13]

In an ideologically distorted society, thought becomes dialectical since it cannot realize itself as a free dialogue. 'If things can be grasped in a categorical manner whilst human beings can only be conceived adequately through dialogue in their relations with things and with one another, then dialectics may be understood from within the dialogue; certainly not itself as a dialogue but as a consequence of its repression.'[14] Since constraint is its necessary condition, the dissolution of constraint is also the dissolution of dialectics. By opposing constraint through 'critical praxis', dialectics simultaneously turns upon itself. 'Dialectics fulfilled in practice is simultaneously transcended dialectics . . .'[15] It changes into what it always was in terms of its own intention: a 'domina-

11. Cf. Popper, 'What is Dialectic?', *Conjectures and Refutations*, Routledge and Kegan Paul, 1962, pp. 312 f.

12. Habermas, *Theorie und Praxis*, op. cit., p. 321.

13. ibid., p. 319. 14. ibid., p. 318. 15. ibid., p. 319.

tion-free dialogue which could be universally practised'.[16] In the latter, dialectics realizes its second pre-condition: the interest in emancipation [*Mündigkeit*], in 'domination-free communication'. Only if both conditions can be fulfilled is a check on dialectical movement possible. Two things, then, are necessary: 1. To demonstrate empirically the constraint in 'actual contradictions' and, 2. to legitimate the 'interest in emancipation [*Mündigkeit*]'. Only with the aid of these two pre-conditions is it possible to 'derive dialectically' projections into the future as the 'determinate negation' of a contradiction-laden society.

'Actual contradictions' are given in the antagonistic intentions of social groups which, in the form of 'interests', 'attitudes' and 'norms', belong to the object-domain of social scientific hypotheses. Intentions contradict one another if their illusorily real goals are mutually exclusive. From such contrary intentions, however, there does not result directly a further intention which resolves the 'contradiction'; but rather, in order to maintain the 'determinate negation', another 'objective intention' is required: the 'interest in emancipation'. The latter restricts contrary intentions and 'unifies' them in a new intention which negates the first two. Only insofar as the 'determinate negation' resolves the 'contradiction' of contrary intentions does it negate this contradiction. It implies the logical negation[17] of the latter, but distinguishes itself from it, however, through its determinate content.

16. Cf. Habermas (1972), p. 314 (amended translation).

17. This is, of course, a trivial implication, for the formal logical negation of a contradiction is always a tautology and follows from every conceivable statement. Formal logic in propositional calculus permits no difference between contrary and contradictory statements. Both are the negation of a tautology. Nevertheless, contrary and contradictory statements can be distinguished by means of formal logic. According to the statement concerning the excluded third (which is valid in a two-value logic), when there are two contradictory statements one is necessarily true, whilst in the case of two contrary statements *both* can be false (although they need not be false). Consequently, at least without contradiction, one can conceive of a resolution of contrary intention by means of a third, 'objective' intention. But if, on the other hand, the intentions (i.e. statements about them) were opposed to one another in a contradictory manner then one of the two would have to be selected.

In it, the guiding aim is given whose realization would transcend the actual contradiction 'through critical praxis'.[18]

If this procedure could be carried out, the objections mentioned would no longer hold. For the 'determinate negation' is not deduced from a contradiction but instead it resolves the latter. It relates to intentions not to facts; ultimately it derives normative conclusions, not from descriptive but rather from normative premises.

But the empirical confirmation of 'actual contradictions' between intentions encounters considerable difficulties. For since intentions are not contained directly in observable behaviour they can only be extracted from empirical hypotheses if their content is subjected to an interpretation. In its turn, this interpretation can be tested in an 'empirical-analytic' manner. If the methodological rules of the analytic theory of science are valid for *all* empirical statements but, according to these rules, interpretations cannot be tested empirically, then an empirical control of statements concerning intentions and consequently a control of the 'determinate negation' is impossible. The philosophy of history with practical intent would have failed.

Yet could there not exist an intention in the hypotheses themselves, a certain 'value-reference' of the methodological rules which contradicted other 'value-references'? Then the 'universal objectivity' of empirical-analytic rules would open up only one of several domains of possible experience – and in other domains other methodological rules would be conceivable. If, moreover, the 'value-reference' of another domain could claim priority over that of the analytic-empirical rules, the latter could, with its aid, be restricted. This is precisely what Habermas attempts to demonstrate.

18. This interpretation of 'determinate negation' cannot rest upon statements by Habermas since the exact meaning of this principle has not so far been sufficiently explicated. Consequently, it is little more than a suggestion – but there is one reservation: I do indeed consider the two given moments of 'dialectical mediation' to be its necessary conditions, so that my critical reflections are valid even independently of the 'dialectical theory' which has been expounded.

Underlying the empirical-analytic procedures is a 'technical cognitive interest' which is partially opposed to the 'interest in emancipation' yet, nevertheless, subordinated to it. It follows from this that the methodological rules of the 'analytical theory of science' can – and even must – be restricted to the conditions for the 'interest in emancipation', for the 'emancipatory cognitive interest'.

The 'technical cognitive interest' contradicts the 'emancipatory' insofar as it demands general theories of social action which impede progress towards emancipation – or even make it impossible, since they are not able to apprehend the specific character of 'social facts', the intentional component of action. For 'actions cannot be construed without reference to the guiding intentions, that is, they cannot be examined independently of something approximating to ideas'.[19] Intentions can, however, only be determined for a certain domain of culturally and historically specific norms. For this reason, every hypothesis concerning social action implies an understanding of the 'referential norms' (*Bezugsnormen*), which constitute the 'meaning' of the action. For behaviour can 'express' very diverse forms of action, according to the norms which guide it. Since the rules of action are 'not guaranteed objectively through a natural law but rather intersubjectively through the act of recognition of the interpreters involved . . .',[20] they can merely be understood but not explained in a hypothetico-deductive manner. Understanding, however, is realized in the normative context of a tradition and cannot be extended to random contexts. Consequently, hypotheses relating to social action are, of necessity, valid within the same limitations as the relevant norms – and are not generally valid.

Since the 'interest in emancipation . . . can be apprehended *a priori*'[21] whilst the norms are historically fortuitous, one can initially only postulate, with the aid of this interest, that the validity of social scientific hypotheses must be restricted, but that the norms do not lay down the given domain of the latter. Since it

19. Habermas, 'Zur Logik der Sozialwissenschaften', op. cit., p. 76.
20. ibid., p. 75.
21. Habermas (1972), p. 314 (amended translation).

is claimed that statements about norms cannot be tested empirically and analytically yet nevertheless must be open to checks (for they contain assertions about 'historical states of affairs'), the rules for testing understanding, 'the methodological rules of hermeneutics', must be developed. Otherwise, social scientific hypotheses could arbitrarily be restricted in their validity. If, however, the rules of hermeneutics, in their turn, had to be limited by empirical-analytical procedures, as would seem to follow from Habermas' critique of Gadamer's hermeneutics,[22] then Habermas would be caught in a circle. I shall attempt to demonstrate that Habermas' dual critique of empirical-analytical and hermeneutic procedures can only be compelling at the price of sceptical consequences. How, then, can a 'value-reference' of the empirical social sciences be demonstrated and does Habermas' critical programme follow from this?

2

Empirical theories in the social sciences possess value-relevance in three respects:

(a) The selection of research areas (the 'relevance standpoints') depends upon value decisions.

(b) 'Basic statements', by means of which theories refer to reality, are accepted through a 'resolution' on the part of the researchers involved in discussion.

(c) The operationalization of 'theoretical concepts' presupposes a pre-understanding which attributes observable behaviour to the intentional structures of such terms as 'role', 'institution' and 'expectation'.

This threefold reference to meaning postulates is combined in the 'technical cognitive interest' and it is this reference which, in turn, establishes the 'objectivity' and 'value freedom' of empirical research. Now for the social sciences, a value reference on the 'meta-level' is supposed to prove itself incapable of clear delineation from the intentional references of the object domain. 'In opposition to positivism', Habermas [would] 'like to justify

22. Cf. Gadamer (1965).

the view that the research process, which is carried out by human subjects, belongs to the objective context, which itself has to be recognized by virtue of cognitive acts.'[23]

The 'analytical theory of science' does not dispute that the selection of research areas is dependent upon value decisions.[24] Since this value-reference does not affect the validity of the hypotheses so formed, I shall restrict myself to a discussion of the other two points.

Using Popper's explication of the 'basis problem', Habermas demonstrates that empirical theses can only be related to reality by means of an interest. From empirical theories (together with the initial conditions) one can derive the most elementary statements which refer to observable facts. In this relationship, however, there also lies the decisive problem: how can observable facts and statements about such facts be unambiguously co-ordinated? According to Popper, this problem of co-ordination leads to the 'Friesian trilemma' of dogmatism, infinite regress and psychologism.[25] Popper solves this trilemma by applying his criterion of testability even to basic statements. This criterion is to replace the principle of induction.[26] It establishes the empirical content of theories and statements in 'degrees of testability'. The better a statement can be tested (without being falsified) the greater its empirical content. 'Potential falsifiers' are statements whose confirmation would refute a theory. The empirical content grows with the number of potential falsifiers: the best theory is the most prohibitive. For this reason, theories must be as improbable as possible – up to the borderline case of contradiction, which naturally remains excluded.

23 Habermas, 'A Positivistically Bisected Rationalism'. 1964, p. 260.

24. Cf. Hans Albert, 'The Myth of Total Reason', pp. 217 f.; and his 'Wertfreiheit als methodisches Prinzip. Zur Frage der Notwendigkeit einer normativen Sozialwissenschaft', in Topitsch, op. cit., p. 190: 'Scientific activity demands ... *standpoints* which make an evaluation of *relevance* possible. Every approach to a problem, every conceptual apparatus and every theory contains such selective standpoints, in which the direction of our interest finds expression.'

25. Cf. Popper, *The Logic of Scientific Discovery*, Routledge and Kegan Paul, 1959, p. 94.

26. ibid., ch. 1.

If the 'testability' of a theory determines its empirical content, then all its statements must permit the derivation of consequences. The statements of a theory can only be universal statements, from which – together with the marginal limiting conditions – basic statements can also be deduced. 'Every test of a theory . . . must stop at some basic statement or other which we *decide to accept*.'[27] Although we must break off the testing process at a given statement, this too can still be tested further.[28] 'This . . . makes the chain of deduction in principle infinite.'[29] Even basic statements are in no way 'immediate' empirical statements. 'Experiences can motivate a decision, and hence an acceptance or a rejection of a statement, but a basic statement cannot be justified by them – no more than by thumping the table.'[30]

Since even basic statements must be testable whilst theories can only be refuted by means of basic statements, even the refutation of theories is only possible 'for the time being',[31] and can be revised. The corroboration and refutation of theories is reached through a decision on the part of the community of researchers, who discuss whether a theory has been sufficiently tested according to the current knowledge of possible test procedures (or, alternatively, a basic statement which refutes a theory). This decision, for its part, cannot be secured through observation since then the problem would again arise as to how these observations, in their turn, are to be tested. Consequently, this decision must be taken according to teleological standpoints (*Zweckgesichtspunkte*) which are determined by a given interest. This means, however, that although empirical theories do not contain any value judgements, they are, nevertheless, related to an interest with regard to

27. ibid., p. 104.

28. For possible testing procedures (as well as for the whole problem) see Wellmer (1967), especially pp. 158 ff.

29. Popper, *The Logic of Scientific Discovery*, op. cit., p. 105.

30. ibid., p. 105.

31. ibid., p. 111, and also the discussion in Wellmer, op. cit., pp. 164 ff. Wellmer concludes that 'doubting the verifiability of empirical statements would mean doubting the possibility of experience; even if experience can err, it can be corrected by new experience' (p. 170). He disputes the possibility of an infinite testability of basic statements, since he considers that the decision in favour of a given statement would thus be a blind one.

their validity – even if it is only a 'suspended' validity. The 'objectivity' of empirical research therefore implies a normative component, which first makes inter-subjective validity and 'value freedom' possible; normative and descriptive structural determinations are inseparably linked with one another in their validity.[32]

But if even the empirical basis is affected by decisions, does not empirical science then have to become a function of social connections, so that, in an extreme case, every political system and every 'cultural circle' would have its own social science? This consequence only arises if the scientists' interest involved in discussion cannot be apprehended in rules which can be secured through institutions; even if the scientists' decisions are determined through the life-context. Nevertheless, even Popper writes: '. . . what is usually called *scientific objectivity* is based, to some extent, on social institutions.'[33]

But even if the motivations, through which the scientists' 'objective' decisions are reached, are dependent upon a given organization of the research institutions, they nonetheless *also* remain related to experience. The scientists are motivated through experiments, by their perceptions and by reports on the perceptions of others. As long as it is a question of objects and of their relations, the latitude for possible decisions is thus narrowly defined. It is not so easy to break through the manifest evidence of judgements of perception.

The object domain, to which hypotheses in the social sciences refer, is composed primarily of intentional structures. Social action is structured by means of the 'subjective meaning' of action, which is present in the intentions of those acting and is determined by norms. The 'immediate experience' of the social scientist itself already contains normative components, upon which there can be no judgements of perception. Consequently, one might think there can only be a culturally and historically specific social science, in which the rules of socialization at the

32. This in no way implies that 'value-judgements' must be incorporated into empirical theories; instead, it can only be asserted that methodological rules do not permit such a separation.

33. Popper, *The Poverty of Historicism*, op. cit., p. 155.

same time largely determine the rules of research. General theories of social action would be impossible, since the methodological rules would have to alter with the social system. Social science would then have to orientate itself in an essentially historical manner in order to explicate the meaning of the very traditions to which it belonged, even in its rules for testing.

This consequence is, however, only compelling if intentional structures cannot be adequately expressed by means of behavioural variables. But up till now it has not been possible to translate statements about intentions *synonymously* into statements about behaviour.[34] Certainly, too, in the social sciences, 'the law-like hypotheses (must) be formulated with regard to the co-variance of intelligible quantities . . .'[35] But a restriction of the *generality*

34. Cf. Carnap (1960), paras. 13 ff. and the Appendix. Carnap's explication of 'belief sentences' is convincing if the rules of an artificial language, in the form in which he introduces them, can be conceded. Nevertheless, even for such an artificial language one must presuppose the existence of an ordinary language, since the correspondence rules for translation into the artificial language must be established with the aid of ordinary language. The intentional structure of statements can only be expressed by means of dispositions. In this manner, of course, hypotheses can be formulated concerning the meaning content of statements *for* one person, but it is not evident how, in the absence of a homogeneous understanding of the question 'Do you believe that "p"?' the exact intentional content can be ascertained. The homogeneous understanding of the symbols must either be taken for granted or the translation can only achieve an approximate success. In my view, however, a 'behaviouristic' research strategy is still possible even if it were not possible to apprehend the intentional structures completely. For prognoses concerning future behaviour merely presuppose an if–then relation between 'verbal behaviour' and the 'results of the action' prognosticated.

35. Habermas, *Zur Logik der Sozialwissenschaften*, op. cit., p. 65. In my opinion, Habermas' argumentation on the function of understanding in the research process contains an apparent contradiction. Against Theodor Abel's 'The Operation Called *Verstehen*' (in H. Feigl and M. Brodbeck (eds.), *Readings in the Philosophy of Science* (New York 1953)), Habermas rightly raises the objection that understanding should not refer to the relations between social facts but only to the latter themselves: 'Interpretative sociology . . . draws upon understanding for analytical purposes only insofar as the law-like hypotheses must be formulated with regard to the co-variance of intelligible quantities – but the operation of *Verstehen* is immaterial for the logical form of the analysis of law-like regularities of social

of social scientific hypotheses only follows from this if 'a deception with language as such'[36] is possible, if symbolic understanding can be ideologically channelled. It is precisely then, however, that sceptical consequences are inevitable. But to what extent does the specific character of the object domain bind the social sciences to methodological rules, which make even the process of testing itself dependent upon social context?

Social action is rule-governed. Rules, however, can only be determined with the aid of behavioural expectations which are given in a reference group. These expectations refer to *future* behaviour which cannot yet be observed. For this reason, they cannot be apprehended through future behaviour. Instead, the members of a reference group must be *questioned* about their expectations. Their replies are then, however, statements about *future* behaviour. They signify a state of affairs and are thus statements about facts but are not facts in themselves. Nevertheless, a theory of social action must link up the domain of the interview with the domain of manifest behaviour if it is to prognosticate actions. Now this linkage can either be realized by interpreting even the inquiry into behavioural expectations as a behavioural relation, or by projecting both the interview and the prognosticated 'behaviour' onto an intelligible level. In the first case, language is 'behaviouristically' reduced to verbal behaviour; in the second case, on the other hand, even the results of the action must be intelligible and 'hermeneutically' explicable. The logical type rule drives us to this alternative. According to this rule, propositions about future behaviour should not be combined hypothetically with this behaviour itself. For this relation would

---

action' (ibid., p. 65). On the other hand, in his confrontation with functionalism, he advocates the strong thesis that even the relations between social facts must be understandable: 'The meaning intended in action, and objectivated both in language and in actions, is transferred from social facts to the relations between facts. In the domain of social action, there is no empirical uniformity which, though not intended, would not be intelligible. But if the co-variances asserted in law-like hypotheses are to be meaningful in this mode of understanding (*Verstand*) then they themselves must be conceptualised as part of an intentional context' (ibid., p. 81).

36. ibid., p. 178.

have to be formulated in hypotheses whose object domain would consist of statements and facts.[37]

If social scientific hypotheses refer 'behaviouristically' to an object domain of behaviour, then behavioural expectations appear as relations of 'verbal behaviour'. The communicative experience of the interview is apprehended through linguistic hypotheses, by means of which the norms of action are expressed in probabilities of verbal behaviour and can be linked through social-scientific hypotheses to the observed results of actions. Social-scientific hypotheses thus combine 'verbal behaviour' with the actual results of the action of a reference group. This leads to a unified object domain within which all hypothetical relations can be tested by means of observations. All that remains problematical is the co-ordination of behaviour with the intentional structures which are expressed in it. This is particularly valid for linguistic hypotheses. They require correspondence rules in order to translate meanings into probabilities of verbal behaviour. Such rules, however, remain tied to everyday language, since even the rules of an artificial language, in accordance with which expressions of everyday language could be apprehended through verbal behaviour, in their turn already presuppose translation from everyday language. An infinite regress of meta-languages can only be avoided if everyday language is the ultimate meta-language. But then the processes of understanding in everyday language determine even the operationalization of behavioural dispositions, which are contained in the form of 'theoretical concepts' in linguistic hypotheses. In statements such as 'X believes (or: expects, thinks, hopes) that p', we must always understand 'believe' if we seek the verbal behaviour in which 'believe' is expressed with sufficient precision.[38]

37. Cf. ibid., p. 67. It is certainly questionable whether the problems of reflexive statement structures (which would reveal themselves in logical antinomies) can simply be transferred to constitutive problems of the social scientific object domain. For reflexive phrases cannot always be avoided, for which reason the necessity of a strict separation between object domain and meta-domain has to be specifically demonstrated (cf. Popper's essay 'Self-Reference and Meaning in Ordinary Language', in *Conjectures and Refutations*, op. cit., pp. 304–11).

38. Cf. Carnap, op. cit., 'On Belief Sentences', p. 230. 'It seems best to

On account of these translation difficulties, the operationalization of 'theoretical concepts' implies a 'pre-understanding' of the intentional structures which are to be apprehended in behaviour. But this 'pre-understanding' cannot restrict the validity of hypotheses concerning the *relations* between social facts without simultaneously expressing itself in their logical structure. If the 'pre-understanding' defines the *validity* of hypotheses then, even according to the methodological rules of the analytical theory of science, a hypothesis can be rejected. For, either the 'pre-understanding' is identical for the antecedent and the consequent of the hypothesis, in which case the relationship of the two can be subjected to a test, or, the 'pre-understanding' of the two terms is inconsistent, in which case they can be rejected. Then, only the following evaluations of the relational members are possible:

(a) False-True; then the initial conditions can be unrealizable or the antecedent is itself a contradictory concept, both of which can be avoided with a certain amount of care.
(b) True-False; then the hypothesis can always be falsified. (The possibly complicated epistemological structure of this refutation need not be examined.)
(c) False-False; in this case, what has been said concerning (a) holds for the antecedent.

Consequently, the diversity of the 'pre-understanding' can never decide *unnoticed* upon the truth or falsity of hypotheses. Even if a 'pre-understanding' is necessary for operationalization, it follows that *general* social scientific theories are possible which do not contain any ideological fundament.

This only applies, however, so long as the relations between social facts do not need to be determined similarly by a 'pre-understanding'. If, on the other hand, it should emerge that even

---

reconstruct the language of science in such a way that terms like ... "belief" in psychology are introduced as theoretical constructs rather than as intervening variables of the observation language. This means that a sentence containing a term of this kind can neither be translated into a sentence of the language of observables nor deduced from such sentences, but at best inferred with high probability.' In the social sciences, this state of affairs compels one to make heuristic use of 'pre-understanding'.

the relations must be *intelligible*, then the character of hypotheses would have to alter according to the 'pre-understanding'. In which case, an ideological distortion, even of the operationalization of hypotheses, could no longer be excluded with any certainty – unless it proves possible to examine the particular 'pre-understanding' for its ideological implications.

Now Habermas claims both 'that the meaningful structuring of the facts which concern interpretive sociology only permits a general theory of social action if the relations between facts are also intelligible',[39] and that this consequence necessarily results from the structure of the object domain in the social sciences. For the reciprocal interaction between language and praxis requires an intelligible, universal context within which each rule is laid down. Rules change their meaning if they are transferred to a different context and cannot, therefore, be sufficiently determined from mere behaviour as the latter is ambiguous when confronted with the meanings which it acquires through contextual variations.

If, however, rules are, in this sense, contextually determined, they remain dependent upon the various practical contexts in which they appear – and thus upon the ideological distortions, too, which are imposed upon action by structures of domination. But how can such a thesis be grounded? Why should the rules of language be dependent 'upon praxis, *by virtue of their immanent meaning* ...'?[40]

Habermas assumes that the programme of an artificial language cannot be realized because the translation rules, for their part, would have to be formulated in terms of everyday language. Consequently, everyday language is the ultimate meta-language and only through itself can it be handed down, learned and understood. However, this means that 'since everyday language is the ultimate meta-language it contains within itself the dimension in which it can be learned; for this reason, however, it is not merely language but, at the same time, praxis. This connection is logically necessary, otherwise everyday languages would be hermetically sealed-off; they could not be handed down'.[41]

Habermas argues from a *reductio ad absurdum*. If it is granted

39. ibid., p. 87. 40. ibid., p. 139. 41. ibid., p. 142.

that language is not bound to praxis, then rules cannot be explained at all, since language would remain caught up within the circle of its own rules. But language is explicable. It does not, however, necessarily follow from this that it is related to *praxis*, for the circle of linguistic rules resolves itself if the rules are 'present' in another 'external dimension' of language: in behaviour. Both possibilities are at least logically equivalent. The decision in favour of reference to praxis cannot be motivated logically even if it cannot be refuted logically either.[42]

For Habermas, at any rate, language is necessarily related to action and not merely to behaviour. This leads to considerable difficulties but it can explain why even the relations between social facts must be intelligible. Language and action form a unified system of rules whose individual elements must be determined by the total context. The meaning of the rules does not, then, depend solely upon the immediate context of action and communication but, at the same time, upon previous processes of the internalization of norms and upon previous socialization processes. Correspondingly, this is true for nomological hypotheses. Understanding itself is a fictive learning process which virtually carries out a process of socialization. But as the latter, in turn, is determined by the internalized norms, understanding can only be realized as the progressive integration of the system of norms to be understood into the system of norms which has been internalized through previous socialization. The internalized norms of previous socialization processes determine the understanding of new norms, and are determined anew by the latter. For this reason, all understanding remains committed to a 'prejudice', which results from earlier socialization processes. These, however, are dependent upon the specific traditions in which the interpreter (*der Verstehende*) has grown up – and are, of course, dependent upon their ideological distortions.

Since, however, understanding remains bound to earlier social-

42. For the resolution of a circle (or of an infinite regress of metalanguages) does not follow from the latter itself. Nevertheless, in our case, there remains the possibility of resolving the circle through reference to behaviour. This possibility cannot be excluded simply by referring to another possibility.

ization processes, to a prejudice which is given by the tradition in question, 'prejudice' must be apprehended reflexively and rendered harmless. This takes place with the aid of hermeneutic procedures. Yet pure hermeneutics 'converts insight into the prejudice-structure of understanding into a rehabilitation of prejudice as such'.[43] In the rules of language, however, a constraint is also articulated whose ideological consequences cannot be penetrated by pure hermeneutics. 'Language as tradition is . . . in its turn dependent upon societal processes, which cannot be reduced to normative connections. Language is *also* a medium of domination and of social power.'[44] Hermeneutics is incapable of apprehending this ideological moment of language, because it can, at most, integrate one linguistic norm into another, but does not recognize their being bound to natural constraints.

A pure hermeneutics has, therefore, an ideological character. This only appears, of course, when the 'pre-understanding' (prejudice) is related to the objective constraints upon which it occasionally depends. These constraints themselves can, however, be taken up by the objectifying procedures of the analytical theory of science. In the hermeneutic approach, they would have to dissolve into phenomena of consciousness. If, then, the methodological rules of an ideology-free hermeneutics are also to take up natural constraints, then the rules of the analytical theory of science must be added to these hermeneutic rules. The complete set of methodological rules of hermeneutics would have to be compatible with *all* the rules of the analytical theory of science. This is particularly valid for the generality postulate. A hermeneutics which could not accept the general theories of social action would be suspected of ideology. For only at the price of having to accept every 'pre-understanding' – even one determined by constraint – can the objections to the analytical empirical procedures in the social sciences be maintained.

Habermas' critique of hermeneutics is compelling if he can demonstrate at least one pre-understanding which possesses an ideological structure. But this is only possible if the constraint can also be objectivated from which the pre-understanding is derived. For this reason, the critique of hermeneutics presupposes the

43. ibid., p. 174. 44. ibid., p. 178.

rules of the analytical theory of science and, in particular, the postulate of generality. On the other hand, the critique of general theories of social action presupposes that a 'pre-understanding' must also be assumed for relations between facts, a pre-understanding that reveals ideological traits. Habermas' critique of the analytical theory of science presupposes the ideology-free structure of hermeneutics, whilst his critique of hermeneutics presupposes the ideology-free validity of *general* hypotheses (generality is the precondition for their testability) and, to this extent, the ideology-free validity of the analytical theory of science. Both critiques, therefore, were mutually exclusive.

This contradiction in the critiques rests upon an incomplete disjunction, for the presuppositions of both critiques could differ from both procedures criticized. It would then be necessary to demonstrate ideological structures, independently of both, with the help of the emancipatory cognitive interest. But this presupposes its independent legitimation. Since the complex of rules in a society determines every structure, each realization of this interest must also be subject to the distortions which are claimed to be true for the rules criticized. Thus, Habermas' critique presupposes an 'ideology-free' interest in emancipation, yet asserts, on the other hand, that this interest is in no way real so long as the ideological distortions of the society criticized are not removed or at least penetrated: '. . . on the one hand, it is only possible to see through the dogmatism of a congealed society to the degree to which knowledge has committed itself to being guided by the anticipation of an emancipated society and by the actualized emancipation of all people; but, at the same time, this interest demands successful insight into the processes of societal development, since in them alone it constitutes itself as an objective interest'.[45]

Even if the emancipatory cognitive interest can legitimize itself, one must ask in what manner the analytical theory of science can be criticized with its aid. For here proof is still required that the emancipatory cognitive interest has priority over the technical interest. This priority must make it possible to restrict the generality postulate of the analytical theory of science. This

45. Cf. Habermas (1963), p. 262.

strong demand can only be implemented, however, if the technical cognitive interest not only presupposes the emancipatory interest but also implies it. For only then does a logical constraint exist which restricts all the results achieved with the methodological rules of the technical cognitive interest to the conditions of the emancipatory interest. Only then could one infer from an ideological distortion of the necessary pre-condition (for the emancipatory interest) an ideological distortion of the sufficient pre-condition (for the technical interest) according to the *modus tollens.* If hypotheses were to contradict the emancipatory interest they could be rejected, since their validity would depend upon the 'possibility' of the latter.

(If, on the other hand, we wished to reverse the logical relation and treat the technical interest as the necessary condition for the emancipatory interest, then, together with the technical interest, the objectivity of the empirical social sciences would also become logically independent of the emancipatory interest. Then Habermas' critique would no longer be logically compelling.[46])

Habermas' critique of empirical-analytical procedures therefore presupposes that the emancipatory cognitive interest is at least a necessary condition for empirical objectivity and, consequently, that it must always be actually achieved in successful empirical knowledge. Now since the interest in emancipation requires that undistorted (ideology-free) knowledge be gained in a 'domination-free dialogue',[47] it must be possible to conceive at least of such a dialogue and thus of an 'emancipatory objectivity' of empirical analyses, even for an ideologically deformed society. But then the methodological rules themselves cannot be distorted. Rather this can only be true of their *usage.*[48]

If the usage is to be criticized, then the 'domination-free

46. Habermas has not specifically classified the logical relations between the cognitive interests. In my view, however, it follows from his comments in *Knowledge and Human Interests* (Appendix) that the emancipatory interest precedes the technical interest. In any case, a compelling critique must assert the given logical relations. Nevertheless, logical relations between interests would have to be examined in 'deontic logic'.

47. Cf. Habermas, *Knowledge and Human Interests*, op. cit., p. 314.

48. Habermas is naturally correct in insisting that the free dialogue of scientists is only, in part, a reality in contemporary institutions. For a free

dialogue' must be real in the critique – otherwise the critique, in its turn, would be subject reflexively to a suspicion of ideology. Its standards could express an ideological distortion. Since the critique, however, cannot relate to the methodological rules themselves, but only to their usage, then the condition for its realization is nothing less than the existence of the 'domination-free dialogue of *scientists*'. For only in this way could ideological research results be distinguished from other research results.

This is not only a condition for a possible critique of empirical theories but also one for the philosophy of history with practical intent. 'For the interest in emancipation only posits a standpoint and not a domain'.[49] The concrete guiding aims of action, the means for their realization, and the possible subsidiary consequences only result with the aid of this standpoint from the store of tested hypotheses. If the *validity* of these hypotheses (which depends upon the decision of the community of scientists) could, for its part, be ideologically distorted, and if the relations between social facts could be represented 'ideologically' in the theory, then either the means and the subsidiary consequences could no longer be examined for their ideological content, or the standpoint itself would become the condition for 'validity'. The 'interest in emancipation' would then, in fact, have to permit a distinction between 'ideologically' determined validity and 'emancipatory validity'. Then the utopian standpoint and not the empirical sciences would decide upon the structure of the facts and their relations.

If, on the other hand, the discussion amongst scientists is a *real* anticipation of the 'domination-free dialogue', then firstly, general theories of social action can be permitted and secondly, even their 'ideologically' deformed initial conditions can be isolated in critical reflection and possibly removed through praxis. Must Habermas not, therefore, forgo a *universal rehistorization* of sociology? After all, he does not take his bearings from a 'domination-free

---

usage of the methodological rules, democratically organized research institutions are also necessary and these are not generally to be found in contemporary universities.

49. Habermas (1963), p. 289.

dialogue' even in an ideologically deformed society. How, then, can the 'interest in emancipation' be conceptualized?

3

The interest in emancipation is not mere fancy for it can be apprehended *a priori*. What raises us out of nature is the only thing whose nature we can know: language. Through its structure, emancipation is posited for us. Our first sentence expresses unequivocally the intention of universal and unconstrained consensus. Emancipation constitutes the only idea that we possess in the sense of the philosophical tradition.[50]

The interest in emancipation can be apprehended as a mere intention. The idea of domination-free consensus justifies itself in the anticipation of this intention: in linguistic communication. The understanding of a statement cannot be enforced. Linguistic communication is only possible if domination is at least partially eliminated.

But since language is also determined by the context of action, it remains constantly exposed to ideological deformations in a society distorted by constraints. Despite its intention to secure freedom from constraint, linguistic communication is marked by traces of violence in an unemancipated society. Consequently, 'only in an emancipated society, whose members' emancipation had been realized, would communication have developed into the domination-free dialogue which could be universally practised, from which both our model of reciprocally constituted ego-identity and our idea of true consensus are always implicitly derived'.[51]

This formulation permits two different interpretations corresponding to two positions of a critique of ideology which threaten to destroy Habermas' starting point. First of all, it can mean that in an unemancipated society the 'domination-free dialogue' cannot, of course, be 'universally' practised but nevertheless is possible, within narrowly defined conditions, and then does not reveal any ideological distortions. Secondly, it means that in an unemancipated society ideological distortion is universal and in-

50. Habermas (1972), p. 314 (amended translation).
51. ibid., p. 314 (amended translation).

cludes even the idea of emancipation itself. In the first case, the idea of emancipation can be the principle of the philosophy of history with practical intent. In the second case, on the other hand, sceptical consequences are inevitable.

Given the first interpretation, the following conditions result for the philosophy of history with practical intent:

1. In the 'domination-free' discussion of the community of scientists, hypotheses must be formed and empirically tested which both describe the social facts and determine their relations by means of explanations. But the *empirical* content of such hypotheses then contains facts and relations whose structure 'contradicts' the 'interest in emancipation'. For this reason, the contents of social scientific theories 'contradict' the necessary conditions for their validity. This class of 'contradictions' is, at the same time, actually given, since the institutions of research must guarantee a free dialogue, whilst the tendencies within society 'contradict' this free dialogue. But since the institutions are also a condition for validity, the 'objectivity' of the theoretical approach (upon which validity depends) implies an interest in the changing of ideological structures in society. This interest on the part of the scientist is primarily aimed, however, at the preservation and maximization of an already existing 'domination-free' dialogue of the sciences and is not aimed, for instance, at its gradual abolition in favour of certain social-political goals. Consequently, a free science is able to attack reactionary tendencies in society – and in fact it must do so – without abandoning its 'value freedom' which guarantees its 'objectivity'.
2. The store of tested hypotheses existing at any particular time is to be examined with the aid of critical reflection,

> to determine when theoretical statements grasp invariant regularities of social action as such and when they express ideologically frozen relations of dependence that can in principle be transformed . . . Of course, to this end a critically mediated knowledge of laws cannot through reflection alone render a law itself inoperative, but it can render it inapplicable.[52]

52. ibid., p. 110.

For occasionally 'false consciousness' belongs to the initial conditions of hypotheses. (Thus, election results can express an apparent consensus, which rests upon psychologically controlled manipulation. A consensus reached in this manner does not result from objective constellations of interests but from 'fortuitous' response to a stimulus. This apparent consensus is dissolved if the human subjects are enlightened concerning the mechanism which brought it about.) If interpretations of the acting human subjects belong to the initial conditions of a hypothesis – interpretations resting upon ideological distortion – then reflection can eliminate these interpretations, and then the actions, which according to the hypotheses are hypothetically necessary, must also disappear.

But since not every external constraint reflected in subjective interpretations of a situation can be transcended by means of reflection, the possibility of such a reflectively conditioned transcendence must be confirmed by means of a test. Since the influence of external constraints upon subjective interpretations will be secured, in many cases, through institutions, the identity of each particular institution perpetuating the constraint must also be ascertained. To this end, a test situation in which it is merely possible to establish the abstract possibility *that* a subjective interpretation rests upon constraint and not upon anthropological invariants, is in no way sufficient. Knowledge of the given institutions which stabilize ideologically distorted socialization processes is also necessary. For only when the institutions are recognized can they possibly be abolished by means of emancipatory praxis.

Such an investigation of the interpretations would permit both an investigation of law-like hypotheses in terms of a critique of ideology (without a restriction of the validity of such hypotheses), and a check on the 'pre-understanding' which is determined by tradition – that is, on the hermeneutic procedures as well. A procedure involving random samples is conceivable which, with the aid of psychoanalytic techniques, tests 'emancipatory' hypotheses, according to which certain initial conditions of sociological laws can disappear if a general educational process is introduced and implemented in society.

In this way, the chances of a revolutionary praxis can be estimated, but, above all, the possibly dangerous subsidiary effects can be better calculated.

3. The 'structural freedom from constraint' of linguistic communication must be shown to be the 'intention focused on an emancipated society'.

This last condition leads us to the second – in my view, untenable – interpretation of the 'intention focused on emancipation'. For it is, above all, this interpretation which may have compelled Habermas to corroborate the regulative principle of his philosophy of history in a dialectic 'that takes the historical traces of suppressed dialogue and reconstructs what has been suppressed'.[53] For the attempt to infer the idea of emancipation from the structural conditions of language but, nevertheless, to relate it necessarily to praxis, leads to the dilemma of only being able to assume a necessary reference of linguistic communication to praxis when not only 'deceptions in a language, but rather . . . deception with language as such'[54] is possible – or of having to forgo the necessary connection between the two. Only if language is simultaneously a life-form can the linguistic intention be focused on a future emancipated society.[55] But it is precisely at this point that language participates in the ideological distortion of the society in which it is spoken. Then, however, the idea of emancipation itself would be distorted. In an unemancipated society, the idea of emancipation itself would still contain

53. ibid., p. 315.

54. Habermas (1967), p. 178.

55. A connection between language and praxis can certainly also be asserted if language is not ideologically deformed in a *structural* manner. But then one presumably cannot avoid the consequence that, since the rules of language are inseparable from the rules of life-praxis, they stabilize the conditions of domination. This consideration underlies the criticism of Ludwig Wittgenstein whose statement 'philosophy can in no way tamper with the actual usage of language . . . It leaves everything as it is' (*Philosophical Investigations*, Oxford, 1958, p. 51), has become a matter of scandal for Marxist theory (cf. Herbert Marcuse, *One-Dimensional Man*, London/Boston, 1964, pp. 148 ff.). Nevertheless, Wittgenstein is able to evade the aporia in which a 'dynamic' critique of ideology becomes entangled when it determines linguistic rules as life-forms, yet suspects them of being ideological distortions.

ideological distortions which could only be eliminated through a critical praxis. Together with the ideological distortions of the unemancipated society, the distorted utopia of an emancipated society would also disappear. It would be the actual 'domination-free dialogue which could be practised universally' which would make it possible to conceive of the 'true' idea of emancipation. From this it follows, of course, that the idea of emancipation cannot directly initiate a critical praxis since it is itself exposed to the suspicion of ideology. Not only would the interpretation of the present have to proceed 'dialectically', but also the anticipation of future emancipation. A philosophy of history whose regulative principle would have to be identified as dialectical in this manner would require a 'dialectic of utopian reason'. Is this possible?

4

If the regulative principle of the philosophy of history is, for its part, structured 'dialectically', then the following dilemma results:

1. Either, its dialectic is not contingent but rather the universal structure of thought – this would contradict Habermas' presupposition and would presumably lead to an *a priori* metaphysics of history;
2. Or, its dialectic is contingent and rests upon ideological distortion – then one can neither see how the standards of self-reflection can still be certain *a priori*, nor how knowledge is supposed to be possible at all.

The universal dialectic of thought is suggested since the 'interest in emancipation' can be apprehended *a priori*. But if this interest itself is structured dialectically, yet nevertheless can be apprehended *a priori*, then its dialectic too must be posited *a priori*. Accordingly, on the other hand, a contingent dialectics of the 'interest in emancipation' would also have to imply a contingent *a priori*. We shall let the matter rest at this point and merely ask what consequences result for the philosophy of history with practical intent from a contingent dialectic of this sort.

The contingent 'dialectic' corresponds to the ideological distortions through societal constraints. The 'accident' which evokes them lies in the organization of the labour process. Thought becomes 'dialectical' when it is ideologically distorted. If this is also true of the 'interest in emancipation', then 'critical theory' begins to oscillate between its principle and the societal conditions analysed with its aid. The suspicion of ideology becomes reflexive, turns back upon its presuppositions and from these back to the conditions in society. This oscillation leads to a sceptical regress which can never be assuaged by any knowledge. Such a sceptical theory is no longer capable of initiating an emancipatory praxis. It persists in its scruples and ought to be left to them.

In my view, the motion of sceptical regress can only be brought to a halt if the regulative principle of the philosophy of history is determined as both '*objective*' interest and interest in objectivity, as an actual anticipation of the domination-free dialogue in the discussion between scientists. This means, of course, in a double function: on the one hand, as an interest in the stabilization, reproduction and maximization of scientific objectivity, but, on the other hand, as an interest in the practical negation of all the rules of social action which contradict this 'objectivity'.

The 'scientific approach' of the scientists requires institutional securities. These imply a *practically* orientated interest, a political interest of science. Such a 'contradiction' between the domination-free dialogue of the scientists and societal conditions may, of course, no longer be 'dialectical' – but what then constitutes dialectics?

References

ABEL, T. (1953), 'The Operation Called *Verstehen*', in H. Feigl and M. Brodbeck (eds.), *Readings in the Philosophy of Science*, New York.

ALBERT, H. (1960), 'Wissenschaft als Politik', in Ernst Topitsch (ed.), *Probleme der Wissenschaftstheorie*, Vienna, p. 213.

CARNAP, R. (1960), *Meaning and Necessity*, 3rd edition, Chicago.

GADAMER, H.-G. (1965), *Wahrheit und Methode*, 2nd edition, Tübingen.

HABERMAS, J. (1963), *Theorie und Praxis*, Neuwied/Berlin. Translated as *Theory and Practice*, tr. J. Viertel, London/Boston, 1973.

HABERMAS, J. (1967), 'Zur Logik der Sozialwissenschaften', *Philosophische Rundschau*, Beiheft 5, February 1967, J. C. B. Mohr, Tübingen, p. 180.

HABERMAS, J. (1968), *Knowledge and Human Interests*, Heinemann Educational. (Translation of *Erkenntnis und Interesse*.)

Habermas, J. (1963), 'The Analytical Theory of Science and Dialectics'.
Habermas, J. (1964), 'A Positivistically Bisected Rationalism'.
Marcuse, H. (1964), *One-Dimensional Man*, Routledge and Kegan Paul, pp. 148 ff.
Popper, K. R. (1959), *The Logic of Scientific Discovery*, Routledge and Kegan Paul, p. 94.
Popper, K. R. (1961), *The Poverty of Historicism*, Routledge and Kegan Paul.
Popper, K. R. (1962), *The Open Society and its Enemies*, Routledge and Kegan Paul.
Popper, K. R. (1962), *Conjectures and Refutations*, Routledge and Kegan Paul.
Wellmer, A. (1967), *Methodologie als Erkenntnistheorie*, Frankfurt.
Wittgenstein, L. (1958), *Philosophical Investigations*, Oxford University Press.

22 T. A. McCarthy

A Theory of Communicative Competence

Excerpt from T. A. McCarthy, 'A Theory of Communicative Competence', *Philosophy of the Social Sciences*, vol. 3, 1973, pp. 135–56.

Looking at the intellectual scene in Germany today one is reminded of the *Methodenstreit* which preoccupied German thinkers around the turn of the century and of the later methodological disputes characteristic of the Weimar times. Once again a debate about the epistemological and methodological foundations of the social sciences is at the focus of intellectual activity. The contemporary protagonists are, on the one hand, representatives of a neo-positivist approach (re-) imported from Anglo-American philosophy and social theory and, on the other hand, representatives of the Frankfurt School of social thought, that is, of a type of approach steeped in the indigenous traditions of Idealism and Marxism.

A recent issue of this journal was devoted to a critical appraisal of the presently most influential member of this latter school of thought, Jürgen Habermas.[1] Since this discussion, occasioned as it was by the recent publication of an English translation of his *Erkenntnis und Interesse*, dealt primarily with Habermas' position as it is there presented, it would be worthwhile to consider his more recent attempts to develop systematically the philosophical underpinnings of his critical theory of society. These recent publications are especially deserving of attention since they extend his 'systematic investigation of the relationship between theory and practice in the social sciences' in a new direction – the theory of communicative competence – which is much closer to Anglo-American thought. It is clear, moreover, that Habermas makes this 'linguistic turn', at least in part, as an attempt to

1. See the symposium on Habermas in *Philosophy of the Social Sciences*, vol. 2, 1972, pp. 193–270.

provide answers to the critics of his earlier work. In what follows I will attempt to pull together the main lines of his theory of communicative competence and will conclude with some critical remarks on its strengths and weaknesses.

Communicative competence

A thoughtful reading of his earlier works will show that Habermas' recent turn to the theory of language and communication constitutes a shift in attention rather than a radically new departure. In his discussion of Hegel's *Philosophy of Mind*, in his critique of science and technology as the modern ideology, as well as in *Knowledge and Human Interests*, language (along with work and domination) was characterized as a universal medium in which the social life of the human species unfolds. The sociocultural form of life was perceived as essentially bound to systems of symbolically mediated interaction. In his discussion of Wittgenstein and Winch, Habermas left little doubt as to his own views on the direction which a search for philosophical foundations would have to take: 'Today the problem of language has replaced the traditional problem of consciousness; the transcendental critique of language supersedes that of consciousness.'[2] While thus clearly anticipated, the recent preoccupation with communication theory just as clearly constitutes a shift of theoretical attention with far-reaching consequences for the formulation of the fundamental ideas of critical theory.[3] Perhaps the best way to introduce this new perspective is through Habermas' treatment of several authors whose work in the theory of language is widely known in English-speaking philosophical circles: Chomsky, Austin and Searle.

In his *Aspects of the Theory of Syntax*, Chomsky introduced the distinction between linguistic competence and linguistic performance. The concern of his linguistic theory is with the former –

2. 'Zur Logik der Sozialwissenschaften', Beiheft 5, *Philosophische Rundschau*, Tübingen, 1967.

3. These consequences become clear if one compares the formulation of the idea of a critical theory and the working out of the philosophical foundations in the *Zeitschrift für Sozialforschung* during the 1930s and in the later writings of the Frankfurt School (Horkheimer, Adorno, Marcuse *et al.*) with Habermas' most recent efforts.

that is, with the capacity of the ideal speaker to master an abstract system of rules based on an innate language apparatus – in abstraction from the latter – that is, from the actual use of the system under the limiting conditions (memory, attention, error, etc.) of concrete speech situations. Based on this model for syntax, the Chomsky school of linguistics has developed a programme of general semantics which assumes that the ultimate meaning components are part of the innate equipment of the individual speaking subject, that they are prior to all experience, and that the semantic content of all possible natural languages consists of combinations of these components.[4] In his critique of this programme, Habermas argues that 'semantic universals can also be part of an inter-subjectively produced cultural system', that they can 'reflect the universality of specific scopes of experience', and that 'semantic fields can be formed and shifted in structural associations with global views of nature and society'. From this critique he concludes that the Chomskian conception of communication as an application, limited by empirical conditions, of a monological linguistic competence is inadequate, that a general theory of communication could be developed only in terms of a universal pragmatics.

In contrast to empirical pragmatics (psycho- and sociolinguistics) which investigates the *extra-linguistic*, *empirical* and *contingent* limiting conditions of actual communication, universal pragmatics, or the theory of communicative competence, undertakes the systematic investigation of *general structures* which appear in *every possible* speech situation, which are *themselves produced through* the performance of specific types of *linguistic expressions*, and which serve to situate pragmatically the expressions generated by the linguistically competent speaker.

The notion of communicative – as opposed to linguistic – competence can be further explicated in the context of the Austin–Searle tradition of linguistic philosophy. Following Searle, Habermas designates the speech act as the elementary unit of linguistic communication. A speech act is not a symbol, word or

4. See for example Katz and Postal (1965). Habermas takes his interpretation of this programme from M. Bierwisch, 'Strukturalismus' in *Kursbuch*, No. 5, Frankfurt-am-Main, 1966, p. 96 ff.

sentence, or even the token of a symbol, word or sentence, but rather the 'production or issuance of a sentence token under certain conditions', the transformation of a sentence into an utterance. Utterances can in general be analysed into a propositional content *and* an illocutionary force. For example, in the utterances: 'I assert that *p*', 'I promise that *p*', 'I command that *p*', '*p*', the same propositional content appears with varying illocutionary force. Put another way, each speech act consists (in the deep, not necessarily in the surface, structure) of two sentences: a dominating sentence (e.g. 'I promise', 'I assert', etc.) and a sentence of propositional content. The dominating sentence establishes the illocutionary force of the utterance, the mode of communication between speaker and hearer, and thus the pragmatic situation of the dependent sentence. The dependent sentence, consisting in general of an identifying phrase and a predicate phrase, establishes the connection of the communication with the world of objects, events, etc. The competence of the ideal speaker, Habermas argues, must be regarded as including the ability to structure modes of communication, situations of intersubjectivity in which ordinary language communication is possible.

In as much as it abstracts from the varying pragmatic features of concrete speech situations and attends only to the universal pragmatic structures of utterances the theory of communicative competence is concerned with an ideal speech situation.

> Above all communicative competence relates to an ideal speech situation in the same way that linguistic competence relates to the abstract system of linguistic rules. The dialogue-constitutive universals at the same time generate and describe the form of inter-subjectivity which makes mutuality of understanding possible. Communicative competence is defined by the ideal speaker's mastery of the dialogue-constitutive universals, irrespective of actual restrictions under empirical conditions.

Although the pragmatic features inherent in speech situations *need not* be expressly verbalized (for example, in a given situation the utterance of '*p*' may amount to 'I assert that *p*', 'I promise that *p*', 'I command that *p*', etc.) they *can* be expressed in explicit discourse with the aid of certain classes of linguistic elements, viz. the dialogue-constitutive universals.

If this be the case, however, we should assume that these elements do not serve as a subsequent verbalization of a previously co-ordinated speech situation; on the contrary, they must be the very factors which enable us to generate the structure of potential speech.

Based on the work of D. Wunderlich, Habermas distinguishes five classes of dialogue-constitutive or pragmatic universals: (a) personal pronouns and their derivatives, and (b) forms of address and speech introduction (vocative, greeting, etc.), which are correlated with the general structure of the roles assumed by speakers, hearers and potential participants in communication; (c) deictic expressions (expressions of place and time, articles, demonstratives, etc.), which are correlated with the place and time of the utterance, the perceptual field of the speakers/hearers, as well as with the objects of possible predication; (d) performative verbs (assert, promise, command, etc), which determine the sense of the utterance as such, the speakers' relation to this utterance, and the relation of speaker to hearer; (e) non-performative intentional verbs and some modal verbs, which are correlated with the intentions and attitudes of the speaker. A theory of communicative competence, or universal pragmatics, would have to work out the logic behind the use of all these different classes of expressions. The problems involved vary from case to case.[5] Habermas has concentrated most of his attention on the performatives, for which he has attempted to work out and justify a systematic classification. The result is a fourfold classification into *communicatives* (e.g. say, express, speak, ask, mention), which express the pragmatic meaning of utterances *qua* utterances; *constatives* (e.g. state, assert, describe, explain), which explicate

5. The logic of deictic expressions would, according to Habermas, have to be worked out within the context of a theory of experience. He makes some preliminary suggestions for this logic in 'Theorie der Gesellschaft oder Sozialtechnologie? Eine Auseinandersetzung mit Niklas Luhmann', *Theorie der Gesellschaft oder Sozialtechnologie – Was leistet die Systemforschung?* (1971), pp. 202–20. For some remarks on the logic of personal pronouns in the context of a theory of inter-subjectivity see pp. 186–95 of the same work.

the meaning of statements *qua* statements; *representatives* (e.g. admit, confess, conceal, deny), which are used with propositional contents containing intentional verbs (e.g. like, wish, want) to explicate the meaning of the self-representation of the speaker before the hearer; and *regulatives* (e.g. command, forbid, allow, warn), which explicate the meaning of the speaker/hearer's relation to rules which can be followed or broken.[6]

Since every speech act involves, explicitly or implicitly, a performative, this is at the same time a classification of speech acts in general. It is important to note, says Habermas, that the mastery of these classes of speech acts is fundamental to the ability to mark the distinctions basic to any speech situation. The employment of constatives makes possible the distinction between a public world (being, that which really is) and a private world (appearance). The employment of the representatives makes possible the distinction between the individuated self and the various utterances, expressions and actions in which it appears. The employment of regulatives makes possible the distinction between what is and what ought to be.

With this sketch of Habermas' pragmatics-oriented view of linguistic communication behind us, we are now in a position to examine several of the central tenets of his recent work: the distinction between communicative action (interaction) and discourse, the consensus theory of truth, and the supposition of the ideal speech situation.

Action and discourse

The distinction between the everyday and the theoretic attitudes has in its many different forms (e.g. *doxa-epistémé*, common sense-science, ordinary language-scientific language, the natural standpoint – the phenomenological standpoint) frequently played a central role in western philosophy. Habermas attempts to draw a related distinction between two different forms of communication: communicative action (interaction) and dis-

6. Habermas employs the terms: *Kommunikativa, Konstativa, Repräsentativa, Regulativa.* See 'Vorbereitende Bemerkungen zu einer Theorie der kommunikativen Kompetenz', *Theorie der Gesellschaft oder Sozialtechnologie – Was leistet die Systemforschung?*, op. cit. (1971).

course. A smoothly functioning language game, he argues, rests on a background consensus formed from the mutual recognition of at least four different types of validity claims (*Geltungsansprüche*) which are involved in the exchange of speech acts: the claims that the utterance is understandable and that its propositional content is true, and the claims that the speaker is veracious or sincere (*wahrhaftig*) in uttering it and that it is right or appropriate (*richtig*) for him to be performing the speech act which he performs.

In communicative action these implicitly raised validity claims are naively accepted. But it is possible for situations to arise in which one or more of them become problematical in a fundamental way, that is, in a way which cannot be dealt with by simply requesting information, clearing up misunderstandings and the like, within the accepted framework of opinions and norms. In such cases, that is, when the background consensus is fundamentally called into question, specific forms of problem resolution are called for to remove the disturbance and restore the original, or a new, background consensus. These are different for each type of claim. The claim to understandability must be either factually redeemed in the course of further interaction or some agreement about linguistic usage must be worked out. The claim to veracity can likewise be redeemed in the course of further interaction as it becomes apparent that the 'other side' is really co-operating or that he is merely pretending to communicate while in fact he is acting strategically. The validity of problematic truth claims or of problematic norms, however, can be redeemed discursively and only discursively, that is, by entering into a discourse, which has the sole purpose of judging the truth of the problematic opinion or the correctness of the problematic norm. In the first case we have what Habermas calls a theoretic discourse, in the second a practical discourse.

The speech situation of discourse represents a certain break with the normal action context in that, ideally, it requires a 'virtualization of the constraints of action', a putting out of play of all motives except that of a willingness to come to an understanding, and a 'virtualization of validity claims', a willingness to suspend judgement as to the existence of certain states of affairs (they may or may not be the case) and as to the rightness of certain norms (they may or may not be correct). On the other hand, the normal context of interaction contains an implicit reference to discourse. In as much as interaction involves regarding the other as subject, it involves supposing that he knows what he is doing and why he is doing it, that is, that he intentionally holds the beliefs he does and intentionally follows the norms he does, and that he is capable of discursively justifying them if the question should arise. In other words, the 'model of pure communicative action (interaction)' involves the assumption that the interacting subjects are capable of discursively justifying their beliefs and norms, and thus points implicitly to discourse as a possible form of communication.

Habermas is of the opinion that this supposition of accounability, this expectation that the other could account for his behaviour in the same way that (we are convinced) we could account for ours, is a normal feature of functioning language games. At the same time he is well aware that this assumption is usually contra-factual, that the exception is the rule in human history. 'We know that institutionalized actions do not as a rule fit this *model of pure communicative action*, although we cannot avoid contra-factually proceeding as if the model were really the case – on this unavoidable fiction rests the humanity of intercourse among men who are still men . . .' That this assumption is contra-factual and that it nevertheless persists as an expectation can, according to Habermas, be explained in a theory of systematically distorted communication.

But if this is the case, how can the contra-factual expectations be stabilized? This can only be achieved by means of the legitimation of the ruling systems of norms and through the anchoring of the belief in legitimacy in systematic barriers to will-forming communication. The claim that our norms can be grounded is redeemed through legitimating global views of man and nature. The validity of these global views is in turn secured in a communication structure which excludes discursive will-formation . . . The barriers to communication which make a fiction precisely of the reciprocal imputation of accountability, support at the same time the belief in legitimacy which sustains the fiction and prevents its being found out. That is the paradoxical achievement of ideologies, whose individual prototype is the neurotic disturbance ...

The recognition of the ideality or contra-factual character of the expectation of discursive justifiability for beliefs and norms reflects clearly on the situation of discourse as well. In the light of the possibility of systematic distortion, how can a discursively realized agreement be distinguished from the mere appearance of discursively founded agreement? Which, that is, are the criteria of a 'true' as opposed to a 'false' consensus? If there are no reliable criteria, then Habermas' recourse to the theory of communication will have left him with many of the same problems which the theory of cognitive interests first raised.

The consensus theory of truth

In his inaugural lecture of 28 June 1965 at Frankfurt University, Habermas proclaimed that his theory of knowledge and human interests remained faithful to the core of the classical tradition of philosophy, that is, to the 'insight that the truth of statements is linked in the last analysis to the intention of the good and true life'. His recent work on the consensus theory of truth can be regarded as the attempt to make good on this claimed linkage. In the *Vorbereitende Bemerkungen zu einer Theorie der kommunikativen Kompetenz*, where he first develops his version of the consensus theory, the notion of consensus is introduced rather without preparation as an immediate implication of the notion of discourse. In a soon-to-be-published paper on the topic, Habermas develops his ideas in explicit counterpoint to several theories which are current in analytical circles, thus providing a convenient point of departure for our treatment.[7]

Against the semantic theory of truth Habermas argues with Strawson that not sentences but statements – what I say in an assertion – are properly said to be true or false.[8] He immediately

7. The manuscript is entitled 'Wahrheitstheorien' and provides the most detailed discussion to date of his consensus theory of truth.

8. Habermas' discussion of analytic theories of truth refers primarily to the essays collected in G. Pitcher (ed.), *Truth*, Englewood Cliffs, New Jersey, U.S.A., 1964.

goes on, however, to supplement Strawson's account by incorporating certain features of the Austin–Searle tradition. While Austin was mistaken in holding that truth or falsity is properly predicted of a certain class of speech acts, viz. of assertions, Searle's view, that only in acts of this type does the propositional content appear strictly speaking in the form of a proposition, is correct. Statements derive their assertive force through being embedded in assertions, that is, through being asserted. The conclusion of this line of thought is the thesis that truth is a validity claim that we connect with statements by asserting them – we claim that the asserted statement is true. The meaning of 'truth' then has to be explained in connection with the pragmatics of a certain class of speech acts, viz. the constatives.

Against Ramsey's view that in all statements of the form '*p* is true' the expression 'is true' is redundant, Habermas wants to retain the difference between a first-order assertion about the objects of our experience and a second-order statement to the effect that the truth claim made in such an assertion is justified. He argues that it is precisely in discourse, in which truth claims that have been called into question are thematized and (regarded now as hypothetical) checked, that statements about the truth of statements are not redundant. At the level of communicative action an explicit expression of the truth claim, that is in any case connected with an assertion, would be redundant.

Against the correspondence theory of truth, Habermas holds with Strawson to the difference between 'things or happenings on the face of the globe, witnessed or heard or seen' and facts which 'statements, when true, state'. He goes on to argue with Peirce that if the term 'reality' can have no other meaning than that connected with statements about facts, then the relation of correspondence between facts and reality can only be determined once again through statements. 'The correspondence theory of truth attempts in vain to break out of the sphere of language . . .'

Facts are, it is true, in some sense 'given', although not in the same ways as the objects of our experience. In the context of everyday communicative action our assertions are about the latter. It is only when some question arises, and the need for checking truth claims leads to the discursive attitude, that facts, as facts, become the theme of communication. 'In the context of action the assertion conveys information about experience with objects; in discourse it is a statement with a problematic validity claim.'

As mentioned above, a functioning language game rests, according to Habermas, on a background consensus about the truth of certain beliefs and the correctness of certain norms. Insofar as experience does not clash with expectations it remains the inconspicuous foundation of these opinions and norms, that is, it stabilizes the exchange of validity claims involved in communicative interaction. Once called into question, however, truth claims can be justified only discursively, through argumentation. 'Experiences support the truth claim of assertions . . . But a truth claim can be made good (*einlösen*) only through argumentation. A claim *founded* (*fundiert*) in experience is by no means a *grounded* (*begründet*) claim.' The elucidation of the notion of truth thus necessarily involves an analysis of the discursive justification of validity claims. In Habermas' terms, it calls for a (pragmatic) logic of discourse.

It is important to keep in mind that of the four types of validity claims implicit in communicative interaction not only the truth claims but also the correctness claims – that the norms which guide actions and evaluations are the proper ones – were said to require discursive justification. Thus the logic of discourse and the consensus theory which it develops will have to take into account not only the truth of statements but also the correctness of norms. It will be a logic of 'practical' as well as of 'theoretical-empirical' discourse. Of course the logical conditions for the realization of a rationally-motivated consensus will differ in the two cases.

We have now come to the point at which the question raised at the close of the last section will have to be directly confronted. Discursive justification is a normative concept. Were every contingently achieved agreement to be understood as a 'consensus', then the latter obviously could not serve as the criterion of truth. 'Truth is not the fact that a consensus is realized, but rather that at all times and in any place, if we enter into a discourse a consensus can be realized under conditions which identify this as a founded consensus. Truth means "warranted assertability".' The problem is now: under what conditions is a consensus a founded consensus?

In the *Vorbereitende Bemerkungen zu einer Theorie der kommunikativen Kompetenz* Habermas considers various suggestions for a criterion which might serve to distinguish a true from a false consensus. He comes to the conclusion that there is no such criterion which would not itself require discursive justification. '... the truth of statements cannot be decided without reference to the competence of those who might possibly judge, and this competence cannot be decided without an evaluation of the veracity of their expressions and the correctness of their actions.'[9] On the other hand, it belongs to the very meaning of speech and, in particular, of the discursive examination of hypothetical truth claims that a genuine consensus can be achieved and that it can be distinguished from a merely apparent one. Without this supposition the notion of discourse, and with it the notion of truth, are in danger of losing their sense. Habermas attempts to solve this puzzle by introducing the notion of the 'ideal speech situation'. He argues that the meaning which discourse has for us can only be explained if discourse involves a supposition by the participants that they are in an ideal speech situation, that is, that they are discussing under conditions which guarantee that the consensus they achieve will be genuine.

Before analysing more closely this 'supposition of the ideal speech situation', it might be well to consider the more detailed argumentation through which it is introduced in the manuscript on theories of truth. The consensus theory is, as indicated above, faced with the problem of distinguishing a true from a false consensus. If the relevant criteria themselves require discursive justification we are moving in a circle; if not, we have transcended the consensus framework in establishing it. The only way out of

9. In the course of the argument Habermas allows that 'these are non-conventional ways for testing empirical statements, about which a controversy cannot sensibly arise, so that we can say that anyone who can employ these may count as a competent judge'. He is referring to the methods of the empirical sciences. Their non-conventional character he explains in terms of the interest theory of knowledge.

this dilemma must, according to Habermas, lead through a characterization of the 'force of the better argument' entirely through 'formal properties of discourse'. A principal task, then, of the logic of discourse will consist in providing an analysis of the notion of 'rational motivation' in terms of the formal properties of argumentation.

But this logic is not 'formal' in the usual sense. Since in the pragmatic perspective an argument consists not of sentences but of speech acts, the move from one unit to the next cannot be explained in purely formal logical terms. The fundamental modality is not formal logical necessity or impossibility (contradiction) but the pragmatic modality of cogency or soundness (*Triftigkeit*). The guiding idea is that an argument should rationally motivate us to accept a truth claim or a claim to correctness; it should be cogent or sound.

Borrowing from Toulmin, Habermas analyses the structure of an argument into the *conclusion* that is to be grounded, the *data* that is put forward as relevant, the *warrant* which establishes the connection between the data and the conclusion (e.g. a general law of physics, a universal moral rule) and the *backing* for the warrant, that which establishes it as plausible (e.g. the observational and experimental backing for a hypothesis, the consequences of following a given norm for the satisfaction of accepted needs). On the basis of this analysis, he attempts a very general characterization of the conditions under which argumentation can lead to a 'rationally motivated' or grounded consensus.

His central thesis is that these conditions must permit a progressive radicalization of the argument; there must be the freedom to move from a given level of discourse to increasingly reflected levels. More particularly, there must be the freedom not only to enter into discourse, to seek discursive evaluation of problematic claims, and to offer and evaluate various theoretical explanations for problematic statements or justifications for problematic norms, but also to call into question and modify the originally accepted conceptual framework (meta-theoretical, meta-ethical discourse). That this is required becomes obvious once one recognizes that the cogency of an argument depends on the linguistic system in which it is formulated, on the conceptual schema in terms of which phenomena and data are selected and described. At the most radical level there must be the freedom to reflect on the systematic changes in these conceptual systems in an attempt to reconstruct the progress of knowledge (critique of knowledge) and to reflect on the dependency of our need structures on the stage of our knowledge and our capabilities (cognitive-political will-formation).

At this last level the boundaries between theoretical and practical discourse are no longer sharp. On the one hand, the critique of knowledge requires a thematization of the question: what should count as knowledge? which in turn requires a consideration of the various interests (control of nature, undistorted communication, self-emancipation) which knowledge can serve. On the other hand, the interpretation of our needs must proceed in the light of the available information about what can be made or achieved.

Only to the degree to which there is this freedom to move from level to level of discourse is there a guarantee that the consensus which is realized will be rationally motivated, the result of the force of the better argument, and not of external or internal barriers to communication. Our question now reads: which are the formal properties of discourse which would make this freedom possible? And Habermas' answer is: the properties of the ideal speech situation.

The supposition of the ideal speech situation

The very act of participating in a discourse, of attempting discursively to come to an agreement about the truth of a problematic statement or the correctness of a problematic norm, carries with it the supposition that a genuine agreement is possible. If we did not suppose that a grounded consensus were possible and could in some way be distinguished from a false consensus, then the very meaning of discourse, indeed of speech, would be called into question. In attempting to come to a 'rational' decision about such matters we must suppose that the outcome of our discussion will be the result simply of the force of the better argument and not of accidental or systematic constraints on discussion. This absence of constraint, this exclusion of systematically distorted communication (e.g. ideological or neurotic distortions) can,

Habermas argues, be characterized formally, that is in terms of the pragmatic structure of communication. His thesis is that the structure is free from constraint only when for all participants there is a symmetrical distribution of chances to select and employ speech acts, when there is an effective equality of chances for the assumption of dialogue roles.

From this 'general symmetry requirement' there follow particular requirements for each of the four classes of speech acts. (1) All potential participants must have the same chance to employ *communicative* speech acts so that they can at any time initiate and perpetuate a discourse. (2) All participants must have the same chance to employ *constative* speech acts, that is to put forward or call into question, to ground or refute statements, explanations, interpretations and justifications, so that in the long run no opinion remains exempt from consideration and criticism. The next two requirements refer only indirectly to discourse and directly to the organization of interaction, since the freeing of discourse from the constraints of action is only possible in the context of pure communicative action. The conditions of the ideal speech situation must insure not only unlimited discussion but also discussion which is free from all constraints of domination, whether their source be conscious strategic behaviour or the communication barriers secured through ideology or neurosis. (3) To discourse are admitted only speakers who have, as actors, the same chance to employ *representative* speech acts, to express their attitudes, feelings, intentions, etc., so that the participants are truthful or sincere in their relation to themselves and can make their 'inner nature' transparent to others. (4) To discourse are admitted only speakers who have, as actors, the same chance to employ *regulative* speech acts, to command and to oppose, to permit and to forbid, etc., so that privileges in the sense of one-sidedly binding norms are excluded and the formal equality of chances to initiate discourse can in fact be practised.

There are a number of implications to be drawn from this analysis of the requirements of the ideal speech situation. In the first place, the conditions for ideal discourse are connected with conditions for an ideal form of life. Just as the notion of pure communicative action or interaction implies the possibility of discourse,[10] the notion of pure discourse cannot be conceived apart from the conditions of pure interaction. In Habermas' words, the requirements of the ideal speech situation, in which discourse results in genuine consensus, include linguistic conceptualizations of the traditional ideas of truth, freedom and justice. 'Truth' cannot be analysed independently of 'freedom' and 'justice'.

It is apparent that the conditions of actual speech are rarely, if ever, those of the ideal speech situation. Indeed the space-time limitations, the psychological limitations, and the like, of actual discourse seem to exclude a perfect realization of these conditions. But this does not of itself make illegitimate the ideal, as an ideal which can in actual speech situations be more or less adequately approximated, which can serve as a guide for the institutionalization of discourse or the critique of systematically distorted communication.

Of course this raises the problem of whether it is at all possible to decide empirically if and to what extent the conditions of the ideal speech situation are realized in a particular case. The problem is especially acute if, as Habermas contends, the very intention of participating in discourse involves the supposition that these conditions do obtain, that the outcome of the discussion will be rationally motivated. Although we can frequently determine in retrospect that this supposition was contra-factual, there is not, according to Habermas, a general independent criterion which would permit one to judge with certainty in any given case whether an intended discourse were genuinely free from constraint. There is always the possibility that the implicit supposition of ideal conditions will prove to be illusory. Now if in every discussion we assume that we are really discussing, that we can come to a genuine consensus, and that we are in a position to distinguish a genuine from an illusory consensus; if, furthermore, the ideal speech situation represents those conditions under which a consensus is genuine or rationally motivated; and if, nevertheless, we cannot in any actual discussion empirically determine with certainty whether the conditions of the ideal speech situation do obtain, then

10. See the discussion of 'Action and discourse' above.

the ideal speech situation is neither an empirical phenomenon nor simply a construct, but a reciprocal supposition or imputation (*Unterstellung*) unavoidable in discourse. This supposition can, but need not be, contra-factual; but even when contra-factual it is a fiction which is operatively effective in communication. I would therefore prefer to speak of an anticipation of an ideal speech situation . . . This anticipation alone is the warrant which permits us to join to an actually attained consensus the claim of a rational consensus. At the same time it is a critical standard against which every actually realized consensus can be called into question and checked . . .[11]

The result then of Habermas' analysis of the structure of communication is that it rests on a normative basis. In discussing we assume the reality of the ideal speech situation. It is 'anticipated', but, as anticipated, also 'effective'. Whether this anticipated form of communication, this anticipated form of life is simply a delusion, or whether the empirical conditions for even its approximate attainment can be practically realized is a question which does not admit of an *a priori* answer. 'The fundamental norms of rational speech which are built into universal pragmatics contain from this point of view a practical hypothesis.'

I will conclude this sketch of Habermas' recent work on the theory of communicative competence with some very brief remarks about his theory of deviant communication. Although there can be no certainty as to whether we are deceiving ourselves in judging a particular speech situation to be free from constraint, there are possible forms of communication which can serve to locate and overcome systematic distortions. The model for these is to be found in psychoanalysis, which Habermas interprets as a form of linguistic analysis aiming theoretically at the explanatory understanding of initially incomprehensible acts and utterances and practically at self-emancipation.[12] In this interpretation, Freud's structural model and the categories of his meta-psychology are embedded in a theory of deviant communicative competence, which presupposes of course the theory of communicative com-

11. Cf. 'Wahrheitstheorien', p. 65.

12. For details of this interpretation see sections 10, 11 and 12 of *Knowledge and Human Interests*, as well as 'Der Universalitätsanspruch der Hermeneutik' and 'On Systematically Distorted Communication'.

petence. Therapeutically, the method of psychoanalysis is dialogic self-reflection. The analytical talk between the patient and the analyst has the peculiar form of a communication in which not only truth claims but also veracity claims are made good. In accepting and confirming the interpretation which the analyst proposes and 'works through', the patient at the same time sees through his self-deception. The true interpretation makes possible the truthfulness of the subject in the experiences with which he had previously deceived himself and others.

Transposed to the realm of social analysis and political practice, this model is, Habermas contends, serviceable for conceiving the normative relations of political organizations aiming at human emancipation to the masses which, through them, are to achieve enlightenment concerning their own social situation. Critical social theory can be employed to initiate and guide processes of reflection and to dissolve barriers to communication. Although proposed explanations are subject to the normal scientific procedures for testing hypothetical explanations and interpretations, the ultimate confirmation of the critique of ideology is to be found – as in psychoanalysis – in its unconstrained acceptance by the addressees and the successful formative processes resulting from this.

> The theory serves primarily to enlighten its addressees about the position which they occupy in an antagonistic social system, and about the interests of which they could become conscious as objectively their own in this situation. Only to the extent that organized enlightenment and counsel lead to the target-group's recognizing itself in the proffered interpretations does the analytically proposed interpretation become an actual consciousness, and the objectively attributed interest situation the real interest of a group capable of action.

Concluding remarks

The theory of communicative competence is a sweeping attempt to lay the philosophical foundations for a reconceptualization of the theory-practice problematic. While rejecting a return to the ontological and epistemological views of classical philosophy, Habermas seeks, in opposition to the positivist tradition of thought, to reformulate and defend some of its central theses: the inseparability of truth and goodness, of facts and values, of theory and practice. By situating the problem within the theory of language he attempts to walk the fine line between naturalistic and transcendental philosophy and to provide a language-theoretic re-formulation of the epistemological presuppositions of historical materialism. The point of orientation for this undertaking is the normative foundation of ordinary language communication, for in every act of speaking the *telos* of understanding is inherent . . . Understanding is a normative concept; everyone who speaks a natural language is intuitively familiar with it and trusts himself to distinguish a true from a false consensus.

In the space that remains I would like to consider briefly some of the problems raised by this theory of communicative competence.

(i) The consensus theory of truth does seem to provide a middle ground between classical objectivism and historical or naturalistic relativism. In Habermas' version truth is at once essentially bound to communication processes *and* irreducible to any natural or historical fact of configuration. The normative dimension, and with it a sense of 'objectivity', remains. But the view that 'truth' 'means the promise to reach a rational consensus' has been widely criticized, for example with the observation that 'to be true' has quite another meaning than 'to gain truth'. On this reading the consensus theory rests on a 'category mistake'.

Habermas defends himself against this type of objection by tying 'truth', not to particular methods or strategies for arriving at true statements, but rather to 'universal pragmatic relations between speech acts, to speakers and to speech situations'. Central to his analysis is the notion of a validity claim (*Geltungsanspruch*). Truth is a validity claim that we make apropos of statements that we assert, the claim, namely, that the statements are true. We justify this claim discursively, that is by presenting arguments for it and countering arguments against it. The question is: can we identify the meaning of the claim with the promise of discursive justification? Habermas argues that the meaning of a claim is the mode of its redemption, the way in which it can be made good. This seems to be true in certain cases.

For example, the claim by a boxer that he is the best means that he can better any opponent, and the claim is made good by his doing so. In other cases the identity is questionable. To take one of Habermas' own examples, the claim that one owns a piece of property seems to mean that one has the right to dispose of it as he wishes. In one sense this claim is made good by doing so. In another, in the sense of justification, the claim is made good, when contested, in the law courts. Here the justification of the claim does not seem to fall together with the meaning of the claim.[13] Although it could be argued that truth claims can only be discursively justified, discursive justification does not seem to be what is *meant* when one designates a statement as true.

The formulation most frequently employed by Habermas, however, is that 'the condition for the truth of statements is the potential agreement of all others'. This formulation, while contending that the possibility of a discursively realized rational consensus is necessarily implied in claiming a statement to be true, leaves open the question as to how the meaning of 'true' (apart from this implication) could be further analysed. This weaker thesis does seem to be plausible – there is something strange about claiming a statement to be true while allowing that competent, truthful, etc. subjects might reasonably hold the opposite – and would be sufficient for Habermas' main point, viz. that the notion of truth is essentially bound up with the notion of rational consensus.

Along with the *identity* version and the *necessary condition* version of the consensus theory, Habermas seems often to be defending a third version: rational consensus is the *criterion* of truth. The argument here amounts essentially to a criticism of all other proposed criteria, especially that of a correspondence between thought and reality. The fact that 'rationally motivated consensus' is introduced at such a general level makes this version compatible with any particular standards of argumentation for particular types of statements (e.g. the employment of observation, measurement, experimentation, etc., in physics, the employment of interviewing techniques, statistics, etc., in the social

13. One could perhaps argue that the meaning of the claim itself is ambiguous.

sciences, the employment of need interpretations in discussions about norms, and so on). The claim is simply that, whatever the particular methods of problem resolution employed, a claim to truth is ultimately accepted or rejected in the light of a discursively attained consensus among those competent to judge (and not, e.g., on the basis of experiences of certainty, direct insights, or the like).[14] This version also seems plausible, and it fits well with the second version: if discursively attained consensus is the only possible criterion of truth, then the possibility of such a consensus must be implied in the claim that some statement is true.

(ii) A second objection frequently made against the consensus theory of truth is that 'truth' is a normative concept and thus cannot be made to depend upon the *de facto* attainment of consensus. It will be recalled that Habermas seeks to avoid this difficulty by distinguishing a 'true' from a 'false' consensus. The apparent circularity of this move is overcome by seeking out 'formal' properties of discourse which would guarantee that its outcome be rationally motivated. Departing, on the one hand, from the observation that such a discourse situation would have to be free from internal and external constraints and, on the other hand, from the necessity to guarantee freedom of movement from level to level of discourse, he arrives at the notion of a symmetrical distribution of chances to employ the various types of speech acts. The question arises whether symmetry in this sense is a necessary and sufficient condition for rational discourse.

At first glance one would want to argue that empirical conditions are also required – for example, conditions referring to the intelligence, competence, psychological normality, etc., of the participants. Habermas clearly believes that such factors are taken account of in his model *at the formal level*. Thus, symmetry of chances to employ representatives may be thought of as guaranteeing truthfulness, regulatives as guranteeing freedom from coercion, constatives (perhaps?) as guaranteeing intelligence and competence. From this perspective the empirical conditions of rational dialogue and genuine consensus are absorbed into the

14. Of course, any actual consensus, even among those competent to judge, may prove to be a false consensus.

formal conditions. If this be the case, then 'formal' has a rather peculiar meaning here. We have a fairly clear idea of what it means to speak of formal properties of statements, arguments, etc., in the context of formal logic. What is being abstracted from can be determined rather precisely. What is Habermas abstracting from when he designates his conditions as formal?

On his definition, universal pragmatics deals with speech acts in abstraction 'from the variable components of the speech situation'. It considers only 'the general structures of speech situations in general'. It is obvious that this characterization does not apply to the specification of the ideal speech situation. This specification is 'formal' in the sense that it abstracts from the different methods and strategies proper to the resolution of different types of problems. It is also 'formal' in that it employs the concepts of universal pragmatics. But in requiring symmetry of *chances* to exercise the different speech acts it clearly involves the dimension proper to empirical pragmatics, that is the empirical conditions which vary from speech situation to speech situation. In this sense the anticipation of the ideal speech situation is the anticipation of a form of life.

To return to our question: is symmetry in this sense a necessary and sufficient condition of rational discourse? On the one hand, the argument for its necessity can be made plausible only if 'rational' is taken in the very strong sense of perfect rationality proper to the philosophic tradition. At the level of theoretic explanation – for example, in the natural sciences or in mathematics – what counts as rational discourse does not seem to require this symmetry, does not seem to be incompatible with any number of psychological, moral or political, peculiarities of the participants so long as these do not occasion a departure from the standards accepted within their discipline. It is only if this level of discourse is regarded as resting on presuppositions which themselves must be discussed (foundations of science) and ultimately upon assumptions about the nature and limits of human knowledge that rational discourse as such may plausibly be argued to imply complete freedom from the constraints of ideology, neurosis or any form of domination. But to make this case for even the more reflected forms of knowledge would clearly require a much more detailed analysis than Habermas has yet offered.

On the other hand, it is extremely difficult to see how his notion of 'formal' symmetry is a sufficient condition for what he describes as the structure of rational argumentation. In particular, how does this symmetry requirement insure the freedom to move from level to level of discourse? The freedom, for example, to consider alternative conceptual schemata or to reflect upon the conditions of knowledge seems to require presuppositions about the reflective capacities of the participants and about the cultural traditions to which they belong. It is, to say the least, rather unclear how these are already covered by the symmetry requirement.

(iii) The action-discourse distinction assumes an important function in the preservation of a sense of 'objectivity' within the framework of a theory of cognitive interests.[15] If knowledge is regarded as essentially related to action the danger arises that 'truth' and 'objectivity' will themselves have to be analysed as *directly* action related. In order to avoid being forced into a radical pragmatism such as that of James, or into a system-theoretic approach like that of Luhmann, it is necessary for Habermas to locate a mode of communication which transcends in some way the action framework. For 'only the structure of this peculiarly unreal form of communication guarantees the possibility of a discursively realizable consensus which may count as rational'.

But the description of discourse as a form of communication in which the constraints of action are virtualized – the only operative motive being that of a co-operative willingness to come to an understanding – and the validity claims are virtualized – facts and norms are regarded as hypothetical – is problematic. On the one hand, this description reminds one of Husserl's methodological bracketing of *all* validity claims on the way to a transcendental-

15. For Habermas' theory of cognitive interests see *Knowledge and Human Interests*, op. cit.; for various critical statements to the effect that this linking of knowledge to interest results in a form of reductionism and/or relativism that is incompatible with objectivity, see *Philosophy of the Social Sciences*, Vol. 2, 1972, pp. 193–270.

phenomenological point of view.[16] But this cannot be what Habermas has in mind if the notion of discourse is to cover the usual forms of scientific activity. At the other end of the scale, one is reminded of Peirce's theory of fallibilism, according to which any particular opinion or opinions can be called into question and either further grounded or rejected. In this model we swim, so to speak, in a sea of belief and are able to 'step out' only at one point at a time; and this 'stepping out' is itself necessarily based on unquestioned presuppositions. Translated into Habermas' terminology, discourse would amount to a thematization of specific problematic validity claims and would itself rest on a host of background assumptions. The move from action to discourse would not amount to the total shift of communication structures which Habermas seems to describe it as being.[17]

This piecemeal model is obviously much closer to what actually transpires in scientific discourse. It also fits more neatly with Habermas' model of the levels within discourse. The range of the hypothetical can be thought of as extended at each level – the consideration of possible alternative theoretical frameworks, for example, seems to require a broader 'virtualization' of validity claims than the search for an explanation within an accepted theoretical framework, and the reflection on the foundations of knowledge seems to require an even more extensive suspension of belief.

It does not appear that the acceptance of this piecemeal model for the redemption of validity claims would undermine Habermas' attempt to preserve a sense of the objectivity of knowledge. The distinction between simply accepted claims and discursively grounded claims remains. At the same time, the notion of discursive justification, and with it the notion of objectivity, take on a more restricted meaning – discursive justification always rests

16. Habermas himself suggests this comparison with Husserl's bracketing procedure. He says: 'in discourse, he brackets, to speak with Husserl, the general thesis' ('Einleitung' to the new, revised edition of *Theorie und Praxis*, Frankfurt, 1971, p. 38).

17. In a recent conversation, Habermas indicated that he does have something like Peirce's model in mind. We are, in his words, 'always immersed in a sea of interaction'. In this case it would be necessary to revise and leave the formulation of the action-discourse distinction.

on discursively unjustified background assumptions, objectivity presupposes the subjectivity of not yet founded beliefs.

(iv) Habermas undoubtedly regards the thesis of the normative foundation of linguistic communication as the keystone of his theory of communicative competence. With this thesis stands or falls the attempt to overcome the separation between fact and value, between theory and practice, which has been enshrined in the positivistic theory of knowledge, and with it the attempt to provide philosophic foundations for a *critical* theory of society, for a social theory designed with a *practical* intention: the self-emancipation of men from the constraints of unnecessary domination in all its forms. His argument departs from an analysis of communicative interaction which shows it to be based on the mutual recognition of validity claims which require discursive justification when questioned. It proceeds through an analysis of discourse which shows it to imply the supposition of the ideal speech situation, that is, a situation characterized precisely by the freedom from constraint which is the content of the emancipatory interest guiding critical theory. Thus the emancipated form of life, which is the goal of critical theory, is at the same time inherent in the notions of discourse and truth: it is anticipated in every act of communication.

No matter how the inter-subjectivity of mutual understanding may be deformed, the *design* of an ideal speech situation is necessarily implied in the structure of potential speech, since all speech, even of intentional deception, is oriented toward the idea of truth. This idea can only be analysed with regard to a consensus achieved in unrestrained and universal discourse. Insofar as we master the means for the construction of the ideal speech situation, we can conceive the ideas of truth, freedom, and justice, which interpret each other – although of course only as ideas. On the strength of communicative competence alone, however, and independent of the empirical structures of the social system to which we belong, we are quite unable to realize the ideal speech situation; we can only anticipate it.

It is this connection between truth and the good life which Habermas had in mind when he proclaimed in his inaugural lecture at Frankfurt University in 1965 that 'The human interest in autonomy and responsibility (*Mündigkeit*) is not mere fancy, for it can be apprehended *a priori*. What raises us out of nature is the only thing whose nature we can know: *language*. Through its structure autonomy and responsibility are posited for us. Our first sentence expresses unequivocally the intention of universal and unconstrained consensus.' The argument for the connection is meant to be analytical. The analysis of speech shows it to be oriented toward the idea of truth. The analysis of 'truth' leads to the notion of a discursively achieved consensus. The analysis of 'consensus' shows this concept to involve a normative dimension. The analysis of the notion of a grounded consensus ties it to a speech situation which is free from all external and internal constraints, that is, in which the resulting consensus is due simply to the force of the better argument. Finally, the analysis of the ideal speech situation shows it to involve assumptions about the context of interaction in which speech is located. The end result of this chain of argument is that the very structure of speech involves the anticipation of a form of life in which autonomy and responsibility are possible. 'The critical theory of society takes this as its point of departure.' Its normative foundation is therefore not arbitrary, but inherent in the very structure of social action which it analyses.

Is this connection between 'truth', 'freedom' and 'justice' defensible? That it is not *prima facie* implausible is suggested by a reflection on the paradoxical fate of deterministic accounts of human behaviour. The determinist argues that every human act, in all its dimensions – mental as well as physical – can be explained in the same way as, say, the physicist explains natural phenomena, that is, by means of citing the relevant initial conditions and the relevant laws. In the case of human behaviour, these are variously designated as being biological, physiological, psychological or sociological facts, laws and theories. The paradox arises when one considers that these theories are themselves the products of human action and thus, from the determinist's point of view, causally determined by prior states of affairs. Are they then true? Or were the scientists who proposed them, those who tested them, and those who accepted them, as well as the determinist who employs them, simply determined to do so? There is undoubtedly something paradoxical in maintaining both. The notion of truth seems to involve the possibility of 'freely' considering, testing and accepting or rejecting hypothetical statements. This brief reflection suggests that the commonly accepted notion of truth is connected with the possibility of autonomy and responsibility on the part of judging subjects.[18]

The theory of communicative competence is clearly still in a highly speculative stage of development. There is an undisputed need for much more detailed analysis of all of its central tenets. Habermas has not (nor does he claim to have) finally resolved the epistemological and methodological problems which have confronted the critical theory of society since Marx. His merit consists rather in having re-thought and re-formulated them in the context of contemporary philosophic and scientific research. The presuppositions for the long overdue dialogue between critical and analytical philosophies of social science are hopefully now at hand.

References

ADORNO, T. W., *et al.* (1969), *Der Positivismusstreit in der deutschen Soziologie*, Neuwied/Berlin.

AUSTIN, J. L. (1962), *How to Do Things with Words*, Oxford University Press.

CHOMSKY, N. (1965), *Aspects of the Theory of Syntax*, Cambridge, Massachusetts, sections 1 and 2.

HABERMAS, J. (1967), 'Arbeit und Interaktion. Bemerkungen zu Hegels Jenenser, "Philosophie des Geistes"', in H. Braun and M. Riedel (eds.), *Natur und Geschichte*, Stuttgart, pp. 132–55.

HABERMAS, J. (1968), *Knowledge and Human Interests*, Heinemann Educational, pp. 146–68. (Translation of *Erkenntnis und Interesse*.)

HABERMAS, J. (1971), *Toward a Rational Society*, Heinemann Educational, pp. 9–47.

HABERMAS, J. (1970), 'On Systematically Distorted Communication', 'Towards a Theory of Communicative Competence', *Inquiry*, no. 13, pp. 205–18, 360–75.

HABERMAS, J. (1970), *Zur Logik der Sozialwissenschaften*, Frankfurt, pp. 71–310.

18. One could, of course, seek to revise the everyday notion and attempt to formulate a concept of truth compatible with determinism. The paradox then arises when one goes on to defend the merits of the new version in a discourse with others. What notion of truth is presupposed in this discussion?

HABERMAS, J. (1971), 'Der Universalitätsanspruch der Hermeneutik', *Hermeneutik und Ideologie Kritik*, pp. 120–59.
HABERMAS, J. (1971), 'Vorbereitende Bemerkungen zu einer Theorie der kommunikativen Kompetenz', and (with N. LUHMANN) 'Theorie der Gesellschaft oder Sozialtechnologie? Eine Auseinandersetzung mit Niklas Luhmann', both in *Theorie der Gesellschaft oder Sozialtechnologie – Was leistet die Systemforschung?*, Frankfurt, pp. 101–41, 142–290.
KATZ, J., and POSTAL, P. M. (1965), *An Integrated Theory of Linguistic Description*, Cambridge, Massachusetts.
MARTIN, R. M. (1972), 'Truth and its Illicit Surrogates', *Neue Hefte für Philosophie*, nos. 2 and 3, pp. 95–110.
PITCHER, G. (ed.) (1964), *Truth*, Englewood Cliffs, New Jersey.
SEARLE, J. R. (1969), *Speech Acts*, Cambridge University Press.
WUNDERLICH, D. (1971), *Beiträge zur Literaturwissenschaft und Linguistik*, Bad Homburg.

Further Reading

Part One

The Hegelian–Marxist Tradition

E. Bahr and R. G. Kunzer, *Georg Lukács*, New York, 1973.

P. Berger and S. Pullberg, 'Reification and the Sociological Critique of Consciousness', *History and Theory*, vol. IV, no. 3, S. Dakota, 1965.

E. Bloch, *Geist der Utopie*, Munich/Leipzig, 1918.

E. Bloch, *Erbschaft dieser Zeit*, Zürich, 1935.

E. Bloch, *Das Prinzip Hoffnung*, 3 Bd., Berlin, 1954.

D. Böhler, *Metakritik der Marxschen Ideologiekritik*, Frankfurt, 1971.

P. Chiodi, *Sartre e il marxismo*, Rome, 1965.

H. Fleischer, *Marxism and History*, Allen Lane, 1973.

L. Goldmann, *Recherches dialectiques*, Paris, 1959.

L. Goldmann, *Pour une sociologie du roman*, Paris, 1964.

L. Goldmann, *The Human Sciences and Philosophy*, trans. H. V. White and R. Anchor, Cape, 1969.

L. Goldmann, *Marxisme et sciences humaines*, Paris, 1970.

L. Goldmann, *Structures mentales et création culturelle*, Paris, 1970.

K. Hartmann, *Die Marxsche Theorie, eine philosophische Untersuchung zu den Hauptschriften*, Berlin, 1970.

K. Korsch, *Three Essays on Marxism*, New Left Books, 1971.

K. Korsch, *Marxism and Philosophy*, New Left Books, 1972.

G. Lichtheim, 'Sartre, Marxism and History', *History and Theory*, vol. III, no. 2, S. Dakota, 1963–4.

G. Lichtheim, *Georg Lukács*, Viking, New York, 1970.

G. Lukács, *History and Class Consciousness*, trans. R. Livingstone, Merlin Press, 1971.

M. Merleau-Ponty, *Sens et non sens*, Paris, 1948.

M. Merleau-Ponty, *Adventures of the Dialectic*, trans. N. Bien, Heinemann, 1974.

G. ROHRMOSER, *Emanzipation und Freiheit*, Munich, 1970.
JEAN-PAUL SARTRE, *Critique de la raison dialectique*, Paris, 1962.
JEAN-PAUL SARTRE, *The Problem of Method*, trans. H. F. Barnes, Methuen, 1963.
JEAN-PAUL SARTRE, *L'idiot de la famille*, Paris, 1971.
M. THEUNISSEN, *Die Verwirklichung der Vernunft*, Beiheft 6, *Philosophische Rundschau*, Tübingen, 1970.

Part Two

The Hermeneutic Tradition

K. O. APEL, *Analytical Philosophy of Language and the Geisteswissenschaften*, Dordrecht, 1969.
E. E. BETTI, *Die Hermeneutik als allgemeine Methodik der Geisteswissenschaften*, Tübingen, 1962.
M. VAN ESBROECK, *Herméneutique, structuralisme et exégèse*, Paris, 1968.
H.-G. GADAMER, *Wahrheit und Methode*, Tübingen, 1965.
H.-G. GADAMER, *Kleine Schriften*, 3 Bd., Tübingen, 1967–73.
Hermeneutik und Dialektik, 2 Bd., Tübingen, 1970.
Hermeneutik und Ideologiekritik, Frankfurt, 1971.
A. LORENZER, *Kritik des psychoanalytischen Symbolbegriffs*, Frankfurt, 1970.
A. LORENZER, *Sprachzerstörung und Rekonstruktion*, Frankfurt, 1970.
W. PANNENBERG, 'Hermeneutik und Universalgeschichte', *Zeitschrift für Theologie und Kirche*, no. 60, 1963, pp. 90–121.
P. RICOEUR, *Le conflit des interpretations; essais d'herméneutique*, Paris, 1969.
P. RICOEUR, *Freud and philosophy; an Essay on Interpretation*, New Haven, Connecticut, 1970.
P. RICOEUR, 'The Model of the Text: meaningful action considered as a text', *Social Research*, no. 38, 1971, pp. 529–62.
A. DE WAELHENS, 'Sur une herméneutique de l'herméneutique', *Revue philosophique de Louvain*, no. 60, 1962, pp. 573–91.
J. WOLFF, *The Hermeneutic Philosophy and the Sociology of Art*, Routledge & Kegan Paul, 1975.

Part Three

Critical Theory

A. *Primary Literature*

The following references aim at providing a reasonably good coverage of works by writers associated with the Frankfurt School. For the period 1923–50 a comprehensive bibliography may be found in M. Jay, *The Dialectical Imagination*, Heinemann, 1973. In cases where translations of works originally published in German are available, at the time of compiling this bibliography, reference to the translation only is given.

Zeitschrift für Sozialforschung (*1932–1941*).
New edition, Munich, 1970.
Studies in Philosophy and Social Science.
Vol. VIII, 3–IX, 3 (1939–41), New York.

T. W. ADORNO (with E. Frenkel-Brunswick, D. T. Levinson, R. Newitt Sanford), *The Authoritarian Personality*, New York, 1950.

T. W. ADORNO, 'Freudian Theory and the Pattern of Fascist Propaganda' in *Psychoanalysis and the Social Sciences*, ed. G. Roheim, New York, 1951.

T. W. ADORNO, *Minima Moralia, Reflexionen aus dem beschädigten Leben*, Frankfurt, 1951.

T. W. ADORNO, *Versuch über Wagner*, Frankfurt, 1952.

T. W. ADORNO, *Dissonanzen, Musik in der verwalteten Welt*, Frankfurt, 1956.

T. W. ADORNO, *Zur Metakritik der Erkenntnistheorie*, Kohlhammer, 1956.

T. W. ADORNO, *Aspekte der Hegelschen Philosophie*, Frankfurt, 1957.

T. W. ADORNO, *Philosophie der neuen Musik*, Frankfurt, 1958.

T. W. ADORNO, *Noten zur Literatur*, I–III, Frankfurt, 1958–64.

T. W. ADORNO, 'Contemporary German Sociology', *Transactions of the Fourth World Congress of Sociology*, vol. 1, London, 1959.

T. W. ADORNO, *Einleitung in die Musiksoziologie*, Frankfurt, 1962.

T. W. ADORNO, *Drei Studien zu Hegel*, Frankfurt, 1963, 1969.

T. W. ADORNO, *Moments musicaux*, Frankfurt, 1964.

T. W. ADORNO, *Kierkegaard: Konstruktion des Aesthetischen*, rev. ed. Frankfurt, 1966.

T. W. ADORNO, 'Thesen zur Kunstsoziologie', *Kölner Zeitschrift für Soziologie und Sozialpsychologie*, vol. XIX, no. 1, March 1967.

T. W. ADORNO, *Prisms*, tr. S. and S. Weber, Neville Spearman, 1967.

T. W. ADORNO, 'Sociology and Psychology', *New Left Review*, no. 46, 1967, pp. 67–80.

T. W. ADORNO, *Stichworte*, Frankfurt, 1969.

T. W. ADORNO, *Aufsätze zur Gessellschaftstheorie und Methodologie*, Frankfurt, 1970.

T. W. ADORNO, *Eingriffe*, Frankfurt, 1970.

T. W. ADORNO, *Kritik. Kleine Schriften zur Gesellschaft* (ed. R. Tiedemann), Frankfurt, 1971.

T. W. ADORNO, *Negative Dialectics*, tr. E. B. Ashton, Routledge and Kegan Paul, 1973.

T. W. ADORNO, *Ästhetische Theorie*, ed. R. Tiedemann, Frankfurt, 1973.

T. W. ADORNO, *The Jargon of Authenticity*, tr. K. Tarnowski and F. Will, Routledge and Kegan Paul, 1973.

T. W. ADORNO, *Philosophy of Modern Music*, tr. A. G. Mitchell and W. V. Blomster, New York, 1973.

T. W. ADORNO (with M. Horkheimer), *Dialectic of Enlightenment*, tr. J. Cumming, Allen Lane, 1973.

T. W. ADORNO (with M. Horkheimer), *Aspects of Sociology*, tr. J. Viertel, Heinemann, 1973.

T. W. ADORNO, 'Correspondence with Benjamin', *New Left Review*, no. 81, 1973, pp. 55–80.

W. BENJAMIN, *Schriften*, 2 volumes, ed. T. W. Adorno and G. Adorno, Frankfurt, 1955.

W. BENJAMIN, *Zur Kritik der Gewalt und andere Aufsätze*, Frankfurt, 1965.

W. BENJAMIN, *Illuminations*, tr. H. Zohn, Cape, 1970.

W. BENJAMIN, *Understanding Brecht*, tr. A. Bostock, New Left Books, 1973.
W. BENJAMIN, *Charles Baudelaire: a Lyric Poet in the Era of High Capitalism*, tr. H. Zohn, New Left Books, 1973.
F. S. BURN and K. L. SLELL (eds.), *Politics, Law and Social Change: Selected Essays of Otto Kirchheimer*, Washington, D.C., 1969.
J. HABERMAS (with L. Friedeburg, C. Oehler, F. Weltz), *Student und Politik*, Frankfurt, 1961, 1969.
J. HABERMAS, *Strukturwandel der Öffentlichkeit*, Frankfurt, 1962.
J. HABERMAS, *Protestbewegung und Hochschulreform*, Frankfurt, 1970.
J. HABERMAS, *Zur Logik der Sozialwissenschaften*, Frankfurt, 1970.
J. HABERMAS, 'Towards a Theory of Communicative Competence', *Inquiry*, no. 13, 1970, pp. 360–75.
J. HABERMAS, *Toward a Rational Society*, tr. J. Shapiro, Heinemann Educational, 1971.
J. HABERMAS, *Philosophisch-politische Profile*, Frankfurt, 1971.
J. HABERMAS, N. LUHMANN, *Theorie der Gesellschaft oder Sozialtechnologie*, Frankfurt, 1971.
J. HABERMAS, 'Der Universalitätsanspruch der Hermeneutik', in *Hermeneutik und Ideologiekritik*, Frankfurt, 1971.
J. HABERMAS, *Knowledge and Human Interests*, tr. J. Shapiro, Heinemann Educational, 1972.
J. HABERMAS, *Theory and Practice*, tr. J. Viertel, Boston, 1973.
J. HABERMAS, 'A Postscript to "Knowledge and Human Interests"', *Philosophy of the Social Sciences*, no. 3, 1973, pp. 157–89.
J. HABERMAS, *Legitimationsprobleme im Spätkapitalismus*, Frankfurt, 1973.
J. HABERMAS, *Kultur und Kritik*, Frankfurt, 1973.
M. HORKHEIMER (ed.), *Studien über Autorität und Familie*, Alcan, Paris, 1936.
M. HORKHEIMER, *Eclipse of Reason*, Oxford University Press, 1947.
M. HORKHEIMER (ed.), *Studies in Prejudice*, New York, 1949–50.

M. HORKHEIMER, *Zur Kritik der instrumentellen Vernunft*, Frankfurt, 1967.

M. HORKHEIMER, *Kritische Theorie*, 2nd ed., Frankfurt, 1968.

M. HORKHEIMER, *Critical Theory; Selected Essays*, tr. M. J. O'Connell and others, New York, 1972.

M. HORKHEIMER (with T. W. Adorno), *Dialectic of Enlightenment*, tr. J. Cumming, Allen Lane, 1973.

O. KIRCHHEIMER (with A. R. L. Gurland and F. Neumann), *The Fate of Small Businesses in Nazi Germany*, Washington, D.C., 1943.

O. KIRCHHEIMER (with G. Rusche), *Punishment and Social Structure*, New York, 1939.

A. LORENZER, *Kritik des psychoanalytischen Symbolbegriffs*, Frankfurt, 1970.

A. LORENZER, *Sprachzerstörung and Rekonstruktion*, Frankfurt, 1970.

A. LORENZER *et al.*, *Psychoanalyse als Sozialwissenschaft*, Frankfurt, 1971.

L. LOWENTHAL (with N. Guterman), *Prophets of Deceit*, New York, 1949.

L. LOWENTHAL, *Literature and the Image of Man*, Boston, 1957.

L. LOWENTHAL, *Literature, Popular Culture, and Society*, Englewood Cliffs, New Jersey, 1961.

H. MARCUSE, *Eros and Civilization*, Allen Lane, 1964.

H. MARCUSE, *One-Dimensional Man*, Routledge and Kegan Paul, 1964.

H. MARCUSE, *Kultur und Gesellschaft*, 2 Bd., Frankfurt, 1965.

H. MARCUSE, 'On Science and Phenomenology', *Boston Studies in the Philosophy of Science*, no. 2, 1965, pp. 279–90.

H. MARCUSE (with R. P. Wolff and Barrington Moore), *A Critique of Pure Tolerance*, Boston, 1965.

H. MARCUSE, 'The Obsolescence of Marxism', in *Marx and the Western World*, ed. N. Lobkowicz, Notre Dame, 1967.

H. MARCUSE, *Negations*, Allen Lane, 1968.

H. MARCUSE, *Soviet Marxism*, Routledge and Kegan Paul, 1968.

H. MARCUSE, *Reason and Revolution*, Routledge and Kegan Paul, 1968.

H. MARCUSE, *Hegels Ontologie und die Theorie der Geschichtlichheit*, Klostermann, Frankfurt, 1968.

H. MARCUSE, *Ideen zu einer Kritischen Theorie der Gesellschaft*, Frankfurt, 1969.

H. MARCUSE, *An Essay on Liberation*, Allen Lane, 1969.

H. MARCUSE, *Five Lectures*, Allen Lane, 1970.

H. MARCUSE, *Studies in Critical Philosophy*, tr. J. de Bres, New Left Books, 1972.

H. MARCUSE, *Counter-revolution and Revolt*, Boston, 1973.

O. NEGT, (ed.), *Aktualität und Folgen Hegels*, Frankfurt, 1970.

F. NEUMANN, *Behemoth: The Structure and Practice of National Socialism, 1933–1944*, revised edition, New York, 1944.

F. NEUMANN, *The Democratic and the Authoritarian State: Essays in Political and Legal Theory*, New York, 1957.

F. NEUMANN (with A. R. L. Gurland and O. Kirchheimer), *The Fate of Small Businesses in Nazi Germany*, Washington, D. C. 1943.

C. OFFE, 'Politische Herrschaft und Klassenstrukturen, Zur Analyse spätkapitalistische Gesellschafssysteme', in G. Kress and D. Senghaas, (ed.), *Politikwissenschaft, Eine Einführung in ihre Probleme*, Frankfurt, 1969.

F. POLLOCK, 'State Capitalism: Its Possibilities and Limitations' *Studies in Philosophy and Social Science*, vol. IX, no. 2, 1941.

F. POLLOCK, 'Is National Socialism a New Order?', *Studies in Philosophy and Social Science*, vol. IX, no. 3, 1941.

F. POLLOCK (ed.), *Gruppenexperiment: Ein Studienbericht; Frankfurter Beiträge zur Soziologie*, volume II, Frankfurt, 1955.

F. POLLOCK, *The Economic and Social Consequences of Automation*, tr. W O. Henderson and W. H. Chalmer, Oxford University Press, 1957.

A. SCHMIDT, 'Über Geschichte und Geschichtsschreibung in der materialistischen Dialektik'; in *Folgen einer Theorie, Essays über 'Das Kapital' von Karl Marx*. Frankfurt, 1967.

A. SCHMIDT, 'Zum Erkenntnisbegriff der Kritik der politischen 'Ökonomie', in *Kritik der politischen Ökonomie heute 100 Jahre 'Kapital'*, ed. W. Euchner and A. Schmidt, Frankfurt, 1968.

A. SCHMIDT, 'Der strukturalistische Angriff auf die Geschichte', *Beiträge zur marxistischen Erkenntnistheorie*, ed. A. Schmidt, Frankfurt, 1969.

A. SCHMIDT, *The Concept of Nature in Marx*, New Left Books, 1971.

B. *Secondary Literature*

1. *General Works on Critical Theory*

H. D. BAHR, *Kritik der Politischen Technologie*, Frankfurt, 1970.

W. R. BEYER, *Die Sünden der Frankfurter Schule*, Berlin, 1971.

D. BÖHLER, *Metakritik der Marxschen Ideologiekritik*, Frankfurt, 1971.

R. BUBNER, 'Was ist kritische Theorie?', *Philosophische Rundschau*, nos 3/4, 1969, pp. 213–49.

E. FLEISCHMANN, 'Fin de la sociologie dialectique?', *Archives européennes de sociologie*, no. XIV, 1973, pp. 159–84.

C. GROSSNER, *Verfall der Philosophie, Die Politik deutscher Philosophen*, Hamburg, 1971.

P. HAMILTON, *Knowledge and Social Structure*, Routledge and Kegan Paul, 1974.

J. H. HEISELER, *Die Frankfurter Schule im Lichte des Marxismus*, Frankfurt, 1970.

F. JAMESON, *Marxism and Form; Twentieth-Century Dialectical Theories of Literature*, Princeton, New Jersey, 1971.

M. JAY, *The Dialectical Imagination*, Heinemann, 1973.

A. KÜNZLI, *Aufklärung und Dialektik*, Freiburg, 1971.

G. LICHTHEIM, *From Marx to Hegel*, Orbach and Chambers, 1971.

N. MCINNES, *The Western Marxists*, Alcour Press, 1973.

A. MCINTYRE, *Marcuse*, Fontana, 1970.

J. ORR, 'German Social Theory and the Hidden Face of Technology,' *Archives européennes de sociologie*, no. XV, 1974, pp. 312–36.

A. QUINTON, 'Critical Theory', *Encounter*, October 1974, pp. 43–53.

J. RITSERT and C. ROLSHAUSEN, *Der Konservatismus der kritischen Theorie*, Frankfurt, 1971.

P. A. ROBINSON, *The Freudian Left*, New York, 1969.
G. ROHRMOSER, *Das Elend der kritischen Theorie*, Freiburg, 1970.
G. E. RUSCONI, *La teoria critica della società*, Mulino, 1968.
G. E. RUSCONI, 'Cognoscenza e Interesse in Habermas', *Quaderni di Sociologia*,no. 19, 1970, pp. 436ff.
H. J. SANDKÜHLER, *Praxis und Geschichtsbewusstsein*, Frankfurt, 1972.
S. J. SCHMIDT, 'Zue Grammatik sprachlichen und nichtsprachlichen Handelns', *Soziale Welt*, 1968, pp. 360–72.
A. SCHMIDT, *Die 'Zeitschrift für Sozialforschung', Geschichte und gegenwärtige Bedeutung*, Munich, 1970.
F. W. SCHMIDT, 'Hegel in der kritischen Theorie der "Frankfurter Schule" ', in O. Negt (ed.), *Aktualität und Folgen der Philosophie Hegels*, Frankfurt, 1970.
K. SCHRADER-KLEBERT, 'Der Begriff des Transzendentalen bei J. Habermas', *Soziale Welt*, 1968, pp. 342–59.
T. SCHROYER, *The Critique of Domination*, New York, 1973.
T. SCHROYER, 'Toward a Critical Theory for Advanced Industrial Society' in H. P. Dreitzel (ed.), *Recent Sociology*, New York, 1970.
T. SCHROYER, 'Marx and Habermas', Continuum 8, 1970, pp. 52ff.
T. SCHROYER, 'The Dialectical Foundations of Critical Theory: J. Habermas' Metatheoretical Investigations', *Telos*, no. 12, 1972, pp. 93ff.
P. SEDGWICK, 'Natural Science and Human Theory: A Critique of Herbert Marcuse', *Socialist Register*, Merlin Press, 1966, pp. 163–92.
E. SHILS, 'Daydreams and Nightmares: Reflections on the Criticism of Mass Culture', *Sewanee Review*, no. LXV, 1957.
P. SZONDI, 'Hoffnung im Vergangenen', in *Zeugnisse, Theodor W. Adorno zum sechzigsten Geburtstag*, Frankfurt, 1963.
Theodor W. Adorno zum Gedächtnis, Frankfurt, 1971.
G. THERBORN, 'A Critique of the Frankfurt School', *New Left Review*, no. 63, 1970, pp. 65–96.
M. THEUNISSEN, *Gesellschaft und Geschichte*, Berlin, 1969.
Über Theodor W. Adorno, Frankfurt, 1968.

Über Walter Benjamin, Frankfurt, 1968.

S. UNSELD (ed.), *Zur Aktualität Walter Benjamins*, Frankfurt, 1972.

'Walter Benjamin: Towards a Philosophy of Language', *The Times Literary Supplement*, 8 January 1971.

A. WELLMER, *Critical Theory of Society*, New York, 1971.

B. WILLMS, *Revolution oder Protest*, Frankfurt, 1969.

B. WILLMS, *Kritik und Politik. Habermas oder das politische Defizit der 'Kritischen Theorie'*, Frankfurt, 1973.

2. *Works on Individual Authors*

R. ALTMANN, 'Brüder im Nichts? Zur Auseinandersetzung Jürgen Habermas' mit Arnold Gehlen', *Merkur*, 266, June 1970, pp. 577–82.

K. O. APEL, 'Wissenschaft als Emanzipation? – Eine kritische Würdigung der Wissenschaftskonzeption der "Kritischen Theorie", *Zeitschrift für Allgemeine Wissenschaftstheorie*, no. 1, 1970.

H. ARENDT, 'Walter Benjamin, 1892–1940', in *Men in Dark Times*, Cape, 1970.

J. P. ARNASON, *Von Marcuse zu Marx*, Frankfurt, 1971.

K. BALLESTRAM and A. MCCARTHY, 'Thesen zur Begründung einer Kritischen Theorie der Gesellschaft', *Zeitschrift für Allgemeine Wissenschaftstheorie*, no. 3, 1972.

F. BÖCKELMANN, *Über Marx und Adorno*, Frankfurt, 1972.

P. BREINES (ed.), *Critical Interruptions. New perspectives on Herbert Marcuse*, New York, 1970.

J. COHEN, 'Critical Theory: The Philosophy of Marcuse', *New Left Review*, no. 57, 1969, pp. 35–51.

F. DALLMAYR, 'Reason and Emancipation', *Man and World*, 5, 1972.

F. DALLMAYR, 'Habermas: Knowledge and Human Interests and its Aftermath', *Philosophy of the Social Sciences*, 2, 1972.

Die Linke antwortet Jürgen Habermas, Frankfurt, 1968.

G. FLÖISTADT, 'Social Concepts of Action: notes on Habermas' Proposal for a social theory of action', *Inquiry*, no. 13, 1970, pp. 175–98.

H.-G. GADAMER, 'Replik', in *Hermeneutik und Ideologiekritik*, Suhrkamp, 1971, pp. 283–317.

H. J. GIEGEL, 'Reflexion und Emanzipation', in *Hermeneutik und Ideologiekritik*, Suhrkamp, 1971, pp. 244–82.

G. GÜNTHER, 'Kritische Bemerkungen zur gegenwärtigen Wissenschaftstheorie', *Soziale Welt*, 1968, pp. 328–41.

J. HABERMAS (ed.), *Antworten auf Herbert Marcuse*, Frankfurt, 1968.

H. H. HOLZ, *Utopie und Anarchismus – Zur Kritik der Kritischen Theorie Herbert Marcuses*, Cologne, 1971.

H. JANSON, *Herbert Marcuse*, Bonn, 1971.

G. KAISER, *Benjamin, Adorno. Zwei Studien*, Frankfurt, 1974.

W. KRAFT, 'Walter Benjamin hinter seinen Briefen', *Merkur*, XXI, 1967, pp. 226–32.

C. K. LENHARDT, 'Rise and Fall of Transcendental Anthropology', *Philosophy of the Social Sciences*, no. 2, 1972, pp. 231–46.

W. LEPENIES, 'Anthropology and Social Criticism: A view on the controversy between Arnold Gehlen and Jürgen Habermas', *The Human Context*, no. 3, 1971, pp. 205–25.

H. LEY and TH. MÜLLER, *Kritische Vernunft und Revolution*, Cologne, 1971.

N. LOBKOWICZ, 'Interest and Objectivity', *Philosophy of the Social Sciences*, no. 2, 1972, pp. 193–210.

N. LUHMANN, 'Systemtheoretische Argumentationen. Eine Entgegnung auf Jürgen Habermas', in J. Habermas und N. Luhmann, *Theorie der Gesellschaft oder Sozialtechnologie*, Frankfurt, 1971, pp. 291–405.

The 'Methodenstreit'

T. W. ADORNO *et al.*, *Der Positivismusstreit in der deutschen Soziologie*, Frankfurt, 1969.

H. ALBERT, *Traktat über kritische Vernunft*, Tübingen, 1969.

H. ALBERT, *Plädoyer für kritischen Rationalismus*, Frankfurt, 1971.

H. ALBERT, *Konstruktion und Kritik. Aufsätze zur Philosophie des kritischen Rationalismus*, Hamburg, 1972.

H. BAIER, 'Soziologie und Geschichte', *Archiv für Rechts – und Sozialphilosophie*, no. 52, 1966, pp. 67–91.
H. BAIER, 'Soziale Technologie oder soziale Emanzipation?' in B. Schäfers (ed.), *Thesen zur Kritik der Soziologie*, Frankfurt, 1969.
M. VON BRENTANO, 'Die unbescheidene Philosophie. Der Streit um die Theorie der Sozialwissenschaften', *Das Argument*, no. 9, 1967, pp. 102–16.
D. FRISBY, 'The Popper-Adorno Controversy: the Methodological Dispute in German Sociology', *Philosophy of the Social Sciences*, II, 1972, pp. 105–19.
J. HABERMAS, *Zur Logik der Sozialwissenschaften*, Frankfurt, 1971.
J. HABERMAS, *Knowledge and Human Interests*, trans. J. Shapiro, Heinemann, 1972. (Translation of *Erkenntnis und Interesse*.)
L. KOLAKOWSKI, *Positivist Philosophy*, Penguin, 1972.
G. LICHTHEIM, 'Marx or Weber: Dialectical Methodology', in *From Marx to Hegel*, Orbach and Chambers, 1971.
B. MAGEE, *Popper*, Fontana, 1973.
K. R. POPPER, 'Reason or Revolution?', *Archives européennes de sociologie*, no. XI, 1970, pp. 252–62.
T. SCHROYER, 'The Politics of Epistemology: A Marxist perspective on the current debates in German sociology', *International Journal of Sociology*, vol. I, no. 4, winter 1971/2, pp. 315–35.
E. TOPITSCH, *Die Sozialphilosophie zwischen Ideologie und Wissenschaft*, Neuwied/Berlin, 1961.
E. TOPITSCH, *Die Sozialphilosophie Hegels als Heilslehre und Herrschaftsideologie*, Neuwied/Berlin, 1967.
E. TOPITSCH, *Mythos–Philosophie–Politik, Zur Naturgeschichte der Illusion*, Freiburg, 1969.

Acknowledgements

For Readings reproduced in this volume acknowledgement is made to the following sources:

Reading 1 Humanities Press Inc., New Jersey, and George Allen and Unwin Ltd.
Reading 2 Penguin Books Ltd.
Reading 3 Penguin Books Ltd.
Reading 4 Merlin Press Ltd.
Reading 5 B. G. Teubner, Stuttgart.
Reading 6 The Seabury Press Inc., New York, and Sheed and Ward.
Reading 7 Suhrkamp Verlag, Frankfurt-am-Main.
Reading 8 *Review of Metaphysics*, Washington D.C.
Reading 9 Yale University Press Ltd.
Reading 10 The Seabury Press Inc., New York.
Reading 11 Europäische Verlagsanstalt GmbH, Cologne.
Reading 12 Heinemann Educational Books Ltd, and Harper and Row Inc., New York.
Reading 13 Neville Spearman Ltd.
Reading 14 Harcourt Brace Jovanovich Inc., New York, and Jonathan Cape Ltd.
Reading 15 Beacon Press, Boston, and Jonathan Cape Ltd.
Reading 16 Beacon Press, Boston, and Heinemann Educational Books Ltd.
Reading 17 Universitetsforlaget, Oslo.
Reading 18 *Merkur*, Munich.
Reading 19 International Arts and Sciences Press Inc., New York.
Reading 20 The University of Pennsylvania Press, Philadelphia.
Reading 21 Heinemann Educational Books Ltd.
Reading 22 *Philosophy of the Social Sciences*, Ontario.

Author Index

Subject Index